Florence White, daughter of an old line of Sussex innkeepers, probably knew more than anyone in England of the distinctive dishes, the culinary products and the local resources of every part of the country. She collected, and tested with her own hands, many hundreds of recipes, the best of which are offered here in thoroughly practical, up-to-date form, for use in kitchens where the resources and equipment are those of our own days, and where wise economy in materials and method has to be studied. In arrangement and presentation every care has been taken to make this book thoroughly useful to the practising cook, professional or amateur. And the editor's notes on local and historical characteristics provide a thoroughly enjoyable accompaniment.

Edited by Florence White

Good Things in England

A Practical Cookery Book
For Everyday Use, Containing Traditional
And Regional Recipes Suited to Modern Tastes
Contributed by English Men and Women
Between 1399 and 1932

Futura Publications Limited

A Futura Book

First published in Great Britain in 1932
by Jonathan Cape Limited
First Futura Publications edition 1974

ISBN 0 8600 7102 2
Printed in Great Britain by
Hazell Watson & Viney Ltd
Aylesbury, Bucks

Futura Publications Limited
49 Poland Street,
London W1A 2LG

CONTENTS

'The cookery of a nation is just as much part of its customs and traditions as are its laws and language.'

P. MORTON SHAND, *A Book of Food*, 1929

'Clean, tasty English cooking — the fruits of a thousand years of civilization.'

JOSEPH PULITZER in *The Caterer*, 1929

GENERAL INTRODUCTION

THIS book is an attempt to capture the charm of England's cookery before it is completely crushed out of existence. It is an everyday book. The recipes are simple and practical, and arranged for the convenient use of beginners as well as a speedy reference for 'the accomplisht cook.'

Many collections of English recipes have been made — chiefly from books — and some gastronomic histories have been compiled by careful study of contemporary documents; but these are more or less 'museum pieces.' Men and women still living have come forward and helped to compile the present collection. They have written of good things they remember eating in days gone by, and of things made in their own homes to-day from recipes that have been in their families for over a century. These are so many and so varied that the present volume is merely a small instalment of our kitchen and stillroom riches. England does not know her wealth.

They have written of good things — amusing things too! — they enjoyed in schooldays and have never met since, throughout sixty or seventy years, in spite of frequent enquiries. Famous housekeepers, now grandmothers and great-grandmothers, have told stories of seeing oatcakes baked on the 'bak' ston' ' in the West Riding of Yorkshire by men whose grandsons are making and baking them in much the same way to-day. Old ladies' eyes have brightened at the memory of girlhood days when pies and stews were made of lambs' tails in various ways; these are still used in similar fashion in country places.

A practical cook trained in historical research has travelled from county to county, talking to every one who appeared interested, stirring up their memories, and inspiring them to hunt up written and printed records. Articles have been written to defray the expenses of this direct research; letters have been published in *The Times* and advertisements inserted; some money prizes have been offered. It was delightful to see how everyone was interested when once the veneer of fashion for foreign cookery and modern fads was chipped. At first some simple country folk would be shy or apologetic: 'we must go with the times, those things are out of date.' But always there was found a genuine love of the good old English dishes, when it was realized that these had once more come into their own and were now 'the vogue.'

This is natural. All food is inevitably linked up with home or places visited with our nearest and dearest, whether family, friends, or lovers. We delight to offer the best we have in the way of entertainment and these 'good things' colour our memories.

> 'Stands the church clock at ten to three?
> And is there honey still for tea?'

9

asks Rupert Brooke in his idyll of 'The Old Vicarage, Grantchester.'
'Are there no mutton pies made now in Oxford?' asked one of the
members of the English Folk Cookery Association who, in January 1931,
searched throughout the city for the successor of Ben Tyrrell the noted
Oxford Pieman of 1760. Small raised mutton pies were one of the glories
of the English kitchen. The recipe for this delicacy as served in 1805 in
the Marquess of Buckingham's country house in Essex will be found in
its proper place with something of its story. Yes, a whole book could be
written on 'The Pies of Old England' and many treasured recipes have
been given up to join this small collection, which is but a small selection
from the mass of English traditional recipes.

Melton Mowbray makes its contribution. So do Coventry, Grasmere,
Ambleside, Cheshire, Lancashire, Warwickshire, Devon, Cornwall,
Somersetshire, Kent, Sussex, Yorkshire — almost every county and many
a town has its special pie or other delicacy.

'Where,' asks Mr. Lucas pathetically, 'where are certain simple delicacies of yesteryear? Where is that ancient nocturnal amenity the devilled
bone? — and, indeed, where are the bones fit to devil?'

Only waiting, Mr. Lucas, *for English cooks to cook them, and English
men and women to enjoy them!* The recipes (or receipts as they used to be
called) are here. Not only directions for devilling bones, but also for
serving marrow bones; not to mention marrow served on toast as Queen
Victoria enjoyed it, or made into a pudding as they still serve it on the
Border.

Many of these good things for which we give recipes have been contributed by cooks who love their job. 'Will your book be printed?' asks
one. 'It would be worth while saving up every penny to buy it.' Masters
and mistresses of stately homes that can no longer be maintained have
sent others, amongst them some delectable drinks; but only those have
been chosen that are within the scope of modern economics.

A recipe for making Clotted or Scalded Cream comes from one who as
a girl learnt to make it in the dairy of the Home Farm belonging to
Knightshayes Court, near Tiverton.

The recipe is here also for the White Hunting Stew always provided at
Stoodleigh Rectory in the days when the Devon and Somerset Staghounds
met near by. At that same rectory, with its wonderful gardens, its delightful soldier gardener, John, and above all its much loved 'maister' and
mistress — God rest their souls! — the 'Sunday Pudding' made during
the week and the Stone Cream made on the Saturday (the recipes are
given) — were regular features of the midday dinner or of its unique
Sunday supper, consisting of tea, cold meat, beetroot, potatoes (baked in
their skin) in the winter, or salad in the summer, and boiled new-laid
eggs all the year round. You could have what you liked — but you must

not use more than one plate, because it was Sunday and the servants must not have too much 'washing o' dishes.' Then after supper the Rector — the dear 'Maister' — read out Keble's *Christian Year* for the day, the beloved mistress went to the piano, the servants trooped in and the whole household sang favourite hymns. *This* was Victorian England. . . .

But you must turn over the leaves and find recipes also for the delicacies enjoyed in the reigns of Queen Anne and Queen Elizabeth and even earlier, all suited to modern customs, modern tables and modern appetites. And all characteristic of our own country and our own people. No nation's cookery is so peculiarly its own; and one of our aims should be to preserve its individuality and not allow our proximity to the Continent to destroy its traditional distinction and difference. Its merits are proved by the recipes selected from our greatest writers on food and cookery. I have given them instead of merely giving recipes of my own, because one of my aims has been to prove that England had formerly a complete collection of national food preparations — and none better.

Some people may smile at the simple elementary details and still simpler recipes given. But experience has taught me that it is the little things that matter: 'A little thing is a little thing, but faithfulness in little things is a very great thing.'

Many of the recipes for dishes and cakes, etc., may have been introduced from other lands — we have always been adventurers willing to admire others and learn from them and deprecate our own, but those we liked have become naturalized and suited to our constitutions, and represent — as far as 'receipts' and recipes go — our national taste in food, English cookery at its best.

Our kitchen has more in common with America than with any other country. This is natural, as the foundations of both the English and American kitchens were the same up to 1620; England is proud of the national kitchen American women have developed on their own individual lines, and one of the great interests of this, the *direct* research, collated with the writings of authorities on which the present book is based, has been to come across continual evidence of our common family interests with our cousins across the Atlantic.

In a new and vast country far from Europe they have been able to preserve the integrity of their own kitchen far better than we have, and to develop it on individual lines. If we want to learn how to improve our own cookery — and we should want to do this — it is to America we should turn, not to France. French Cookery is of course very good, but there has always been a great sameness about it; its chief merit lies in its fixed, unchanging system; every French cook is splendidly trained on exactly the same lines, and can therefore serve in any kitchen controlled by a French chef. This also helps France to preserve the individuality of its own cuisine and advertise it as they have done with so much success. But it cannot be allowed to crush out our individual English kitchen or even to take credit for its many merits. The Scots kitchen owes more to France than does our English kitchen.

We can learn from the Commonwealth countries. They have the same advantage as America of developing the cookery of the Homeland in a new setting. We have much in common also with Norway, Sweden, Denmark and Holland. According to a leader in *The Times* (December 12, 1931), 'It is a common saying that a man is what he eats, and equally common that character is destiny, so that it seems logical that if we eat what our forefathers ate, we shall become like them and enjoy some of their good fortune.' And we have Viking blood in our veins.

Anyhow, we must not become a weak inferior imitation of any other country, however great or friendly, or however much we may admire its people and their ways. Personally I love France, have lived in Paris for years, spent months in its provinces and spent all my spare time when in Paris at the School for Chefs. Some of my best and dearest friends have been great Frenchmen and their wives, who have loved England; but I could not love France as much as I do if I did not love England more. There is no reason why the famous French cuisine and our fine traditional English cookery should be bitter rivals. Both are absolutely distinctive, but equally good in their different ways, and there is plenty of scope in the world, even in England, for both.

The English Folk Cookery Association is not a commercial enterprise or associated with any commercial enterprise, but a learned society formed originally for purposes of research, with the firm intention of restoring and maintaining England's former high standard of cookery.

FLORENCE WHITE.

London,
1932
[The English Folk Cookery Association appears to have lapsed on the death of the author in 1940.]

BRITISH AND AMERICAN
WEIGHTS AND MEASURES

In the United States of America only 16 fluid ounces go to the pint, whilst in Great Britain (by the Act of 1878) 20 fluid ounces make up one pint. Canada, Australia, New Zealand, Newfoundland, the Channel Islands, and the Irish Free State, all use the same liquid measures as Great Britain.

In this book in recipes dated after 1878 20 fluid ounces go to the pint unless otherwise stated, but as it has been compiled as much for Americans who love England as for Britons who, along with its Editor, love Americans, when necessary the amount of liquid to be used is stated as so many liquid ounces instead of so many pints or half pints.

It is impossible in this book to include all weights and measures. Those interested will find about nine pages of up-to-date useful information on this subject in the current number of *Whitaker's Almanack*.

WHAT IS 'A CUP'?

This is a question frequently asked. A cup is such a handy measure; everyone does not possess scales; and in America they use the 'cup' measure in nearly all their recipes.

The American 'cup' measure used in American cookery books contains 8 fluid ounces which are marked off into $\frac{1}{4}$, $\frac{1}{2}$, $\frac{3}{4}$ and one cup; and into $\frac{1}{3}$ and $\frac{2}{3}$ of the cup. I have an aluminium one brought from America in 1924 and it is interesting and useful to know that when filled to the brim this cup holds exactly half a pint (or 10 ounces) English measure; the American half pint being marked on the cup two liquid ounces lower down.

An English 'cup' therefore should contain 10 liquid ounces.

An American 'cup' therefore should contain 8 liquid ounces.

But as the *bulk* of dry goods varies considerably, the contents of $\frac{1}{2}$ an American pint or one cupful does not always *weigh* half a pound avoirdupois which is the weight used for many of the ingredients used in cookery.

As a rule the ordinary English weights and measures are used in this book with the necessary explanation, if required, in parentheses.

HOW CAN WE ACQUIRE A MEASURING CUP?

(1) One can be bought easily in America, and now in London.

(2) We can use an ordinary English breakfast cup that holds exactly

WEIGHTS AND MEASURES

half a pint (English measure) and keep it for a measuring cup for cookery.
The following tables will help us to find one that will serve our purpose.
1 fluid pint of 20 oz. = 1 lb. or 16 oz. solid measure.
A pinch of pepper = about ½ saltspoonful.
1 saltspoonful = ⅓ a teaspoonful or ½ a fluid dram or about 30 drops.
1 teaspoonful = 1 fluid dram or about 60 drops.
(A middling-size teaspoon will hold about 1 liquid dram; with this as a guide it should be easy to find how much any cup or glass will hold.)

2 teaspoons = 1 English dessertspoonful.
3 teaspoons = 1 American tablespoonful.
4 teaspoons = 1 English tablespoonful.
2 English dessert spoons = 1 English tablespoonful.
2 English tablespoonfuls = 1 English kitchen cooking spoon or table gravy spoon, and this is frequently the measure used in old English recipes when a spoonful is mentioned.
3 English tablespoonfuls or 12 English teaspoons = 1 sherry wineglass.
1½ sherry wineglass or 18 teaspoons = 1 port wineglass or ½ a teacup.
3 sherry wineglasses or 32 teaspoons = 2 port wineglasses or 1 teacup.
2 teacups = 1 breakfast cup or 1 tumbler, or ½ English pint of 10 ounces.
2 breakfast cups or two tumblers = 1 pint, or 20 fluid ounces or 1 fluid pound.
1 fluid pound of 20 oz. = 1 lb. of 16 solid ounces.

It is not nearly so easy to measure solids, and I advise the use of weights and measures: but the following may be useful:

(1) A spoonful in England means as much above the bowl of the spoon as there is in it. In this book this is the measure used for an ordinary spoonful; it is equal to 2 level spoonfuls whichever size is used. When only a level spoonful is required a level spoonful of the required size is definitely stated.

(2) A level spoonful means a spoonful the contents of which are level with the bowl of whatever spoon is used.

Glass measures can be bought, on which the following English weights of ordinary solid food are marked:
Bread-crumbs 2 oz. Baking powder 2 oz.
4 oz. of flour, sago, currants, ground rice, peel, sugar, tapioca, chopped suet, ground almonds, sultanas, raisins, rice. From these we get the approximate English weights in a marked cup of 8 or 10 fluid ounces. Roughly speaking if we fill it up to the marked liquid measure of 8 oz. with bread-crumbs, we get a weight of 2 oz. or 4 oz. (¼ lb.) of

bread-crumbs; two ounces only if put in lightly, 4 oz. (or ¼ lb.) if pressed down.

If we fill any cup up to the marked liquid measure of: —

7 oz. with flour or ground almonds, the flour or almonds will weigh ¼ lb.
6½ oz. with sago the sago will weigh 4 oz. or ¼ lb.
6 oz. with currants the currants will weigh 4 oz. or ¼ lb.
5 oz. with ground rice, this will weigh 4 oz. or ¼ lb.
4 oz. with chopped peel this will weigh 4 oz. or ¼ lb.
3 oz. with castor or granulated sugar this will weigh 4 oz. or ¼ lb.
8 oz. with tapioca this should weigh 4 oz. avoirdupois or solid weight.

7 oz. with chopped suet	,,	4 oz.	,,	,,
5½ oz. with sultanas	,,	4 oz.	,,	,,
5 oz. with raisins	,,	4 oz.	,,	,,
4½ oz. with rice	,,	4 oz.	,,	,,
2½ oz. with baking powder	,,	2 oz.	,,	,,

In most American Cookery Books equivalents to their 'cups' are given in the solid weights of many things, but the difference in English and American measures given above must be remembered.

For example in that excellent American Cookery Book *The Way to a Man's Heart, The Settlement Cookery Book*, we read on page 3 '4 level tablespoons of flour = 1 oz.,' but these are American not English tablespoons; the equivalent in English tablespoons would be 3 level tablespoons not 4, because 12 teaspoons make 4 American tablespoons, but 12 teaspoons make only 3 ordinary English tablespoons.

The teaspoon in both countries holds the same quantity of liquid. It is therefore the basic measure for both America and England.

The juice of one lemon = about 1 tablespoonful or ½ a fluid ounce; but syrup, oil and cream weigh a little heavier than water, vinegar and milk; and wine and spirits a little less.

A middling sized teaspoon holds about a drachm or 60 drops.

TAKING THE GUESSWORK OUT OF COOKERY

OVEN TEMPERATURES AND THERMOMETERS FOR BOILING AND FRYING

THE PAPER TEST FOR OVEN HEAT

'Moderate' Oven. If a piece of white writing paper put into a heated oven turns golden brown in 5 minutes the heat is said to be 'moderate.'

'Hot' Oven. If the paper becomes dark brown in 5 minutes the oven is said to be 'hot.

'Slow' Oven. The heat is said to be 'slow' if it takes 7 minutes for the 'paper to become a golden brown.

OVEN THERMOMETERS

Ovens differ in size and make, and heat differently. Their habits vary and their whims and fancies have to be studied individually.

Mr. Kirkland, our leading bakery expert, says: 'Even steam-pipe ovens bake cakes at varying temperatures: while 380°F. may be considered a sound hot oven in one case, another oven will not produce the same results until it is about 420°F.'

Therefore buy a set of thermometers and test your own oven, even if it be one with automatic control and a heat regulator.

Put in the oven thermometer when the oven is cold; when it registers 270°F. put in a piece of white note-paper: if it turns a golden brown in 7 minutes, make a note of the degrees registered on the thermometer and state the fact that in your oven these degrees (and the corresponding number on your heat regulator) indicate a 'slow' oven, and so forth as above.

It is quite worth while doing this; baking is a fine art and must be studied.

THE TAYLOR HOME SET

This has now been made in England for some years by Short & Mason, the famous aneroid makers of Walthamstow, Essex.

An oven thermometer, a saccharometer, and a sugar-boiling thermometer are all put up in one box, together with a very clear book of instructions (including recipes) for their use, and for the use of the frying thermometer which is sold separately.

Her Majesty Queen Mary accepted one of these sets in 1924 to show her interest in Home Cooking.

FRUIT AND VEGETABLE BOTTLING

Thermometers for this purpose can be bought or ordered at any furnishing ironmongers in England.

Those who are not accustomed to the use of thermometers should remember that sudden changes of temperature will break the glass, therefore I always teach my pupils to put the thermometers in a saucepan containing cold water and stand it over a corresponding heat, when I put the sugar or fat on to heat. Then when the sugar or fat is liquid, they lift out the thermometer, wipe it and use it; the saucepan with hot water is kept hot, and when the thermometer is finished with it is put back into the hot water for a few minutes and can be easily cleaned and wiped dry.

GOOD THINGS IN ENGLAND

1

ENGLISH BREAKFASTS

ANY type of breakfast can be had in England. All one has to do is to know what one wants, order it in good time, and have the money to pay for it.

(1) We have inherited from India the *chota-hazri* consisting of a large breakfast cup of coffee made with milk and accompanied by two bananas; this is served in our bedrooms at five or six in the morning before we go for our usual morning ride, which is followed by a tub and some luscious mangoes, the proper place for eating which *is* one's tub! After this comes luncheon at 11 o'clock, or *tiffin*, which corresponds to the French *déjeuner*.

(2) There is the normal workers' breakfast at 8 o'clock consisting of tea or coffee, toast, butter and marmalade, eggs and bacon or some similar dish; and porridge during the winter months.

(3) The Country House Breakfast described by Ethel, Lady Raglan in *Memories of Three Reigns* (1928).

'I always remember what a great feature was made of the breakfasts at my grandfather's (the Earl of St. Germans) house parties at Port Eliot (in Cornwall; 1870), and of the numerous courses that succeeded each other.

'There would be a choice of fish, fried eggs, and crisp bacon, a variety of egg dishes, omelets, and sizzling sausages and bacon. During the shooting parties hot game and grilled pheasants always appeared on the breakfast menu but were served of course without any vegetables.

'On a side table was always to be found a choice of cold viands; delicious home-smoked hams, pressed meats, one of the large raised pies for which Mrs. Vaughan (the cook) was justly famous, consisting of cold game and galantine, with aspic jelly.

'The guests drank either tea or coffee, and there were the invariable accompaniments of home-made rolls (piping hot) and stillroom preserves of apple and quince jelly; and always piled bowls of rich Cornish cream.

'The meal usually finished with a fruit course of grapes or hothouse peaches and nectarines.'

(3) We have learnt from Americans to preface all our meals (with the exception of afternoon tea) with grape fruit. The Medical Research Council of Great Britain and Ireland has taught us to eat oranges and drink orange juice on every available occasion; and as oranges, owing to our South African relations, are available now all the year round these can be obtained anywhere at any time; so can hot water.

England, Wales, Scotland and Ireland are therefore particularly well provided with varied fare for breakfast; and Scotland in particular is noted for this meal.

Even the Indian *chota-hazri* is obtainable when required; but those in England who want cream with their coffee must mention it beforehand. Cream with tea is a mistake if the milk be good.

How to Make Tea

There are about 96 level teaspoons in a ½ lb. of tea:
    2 will make 1 breakfast cup of tea.
    3 ,,   2   ,,   cups ,,

DIRECTIONS

1. Warm the teapot.
2. Put in the tea.
3. Pour on ½ pint freshly boiling water for each breakfast cup.
4. Let it infuse 3 minutes.
5. Pour off the tea into another well-warmed pot and cover it with a cosy.

In this way the tea does not stand on the leaves, and consequently is free from tannin. Some people do not even let it stand 3 minutes, but pour it straight off without troubling to put it into a second pot. A cosy should never be placed on a teapot containing hot water and tea-leaves. After the first brew of tea has been poured out, more hot water may be put on the leaves and poured off again as stated in direction 3.

People who really like tea don't as a rule care for cream in it—it is too clogging; top milk may be used, or a slice of lemon in the tea, without milk, makes a refreshing drink.

N.B.—(1) China tea in England is frequently badly made because the above rules are not observed; it should be a golden liquid, not a drabbish brown and should be served without either milk or lemon, but with a saucer of preserved kumquats or litchis. (These can be bought in London at the Army and Navy Stores, at the Civil Service Supply Association Stores and the various Chinese restaurants.)

(2) Tea made and poured off as above, using freshly boiled milk instead of water, is most refreshing. Sir Henry Thompson, a leading authority on food and feeding, says:

'It would be almost as rational to add cream and sugar to wine as to fine and delicately flavoured tea! Occasionally tea is served with lemon in this country, but it is mostly added in excess. A very slight shaving which contains both peel and pulp is ample for an ordinary cup.'

Coffee

There are about 50 level tablespoonfuls in ¼ lb. ground coffee.

1. A mixture of 3 parts Mocha to 1 part Plantation coffee is a good blend. (Kenya coffee is also good).
2. Most English people dislike chicory with coffee; if, however, you must use it, buy the best French ground chicory and allow 1 ordinary teaspoonful to 6 teaspoonfuls of coffee and 1 pint of boiling water.

These directions are given by Mrs. Roundell, Dorfold Hall, Nantwich, Cheshire, 1898.

How to make Good Coffee

Colonel Kenney Herbert ('Wyvern')

1. Having obtained really good berries they should be roasted as required with care to obtain well-flavoured coffee; a burnt berry will spoil the whole brew.
2. The best way is to melt a very little butter in a stewpan, put in a tablespoonful of berries at a time, stir them about over a very low heat 'till they turn a light Havana brown. If a berry takes a darker tint, throw it away at once.'
3. Roast them in relays of a tablespoonful a time, and pass them straight to the hand coffee-mill from the pan.

N.B.—'The butter prevents the escape of much of the fragrance of the berries whilst roasting, and becomes quite dried up before the process is finished;' but only sufficient should be used to lubricate the berries. [Col. Kenney Herbert was a noted epicure and amateur cook, and his advice is always worth consideration. He is one of the 'Good Things in England' and will frequently be quoted in this book. Mrs. Roundell's practical *Cookery Book* (*see* Authorities) is another of our 'good things.' What she doesn't know about country house housekeeping and cooking isn't worth knowing. She also will be frequently quoted.—ED.]

1. Be liberal with the coffee.
2. Allow 1 ordinary tablespoonful for each person — this will make a small cup of black coffee, and a breakfastcupful of coffee with milk.

Drip Coffee

This is made with a percolator coffee-pot.

1. Fill the upper chamber with as much hot ground coffee as you require, and ram it down firmly.

2. Calculate the exact amount of absolutely boiling water required and pour it a little at a time through the upper strainer upon the powder.

3. The slower the water is added, the more thoroughly the coffee will become soaked and, the dripping being retarded, the essence will be as strong as possible. As soon as the coffee has run through, pour it into the cups.

4. Let the coffee pot stand in a shallow vessel containing boiling water during the process — for, in this way, the liquid can be kept hot for some little time without deterioration. It does not do to heat up cold coffee.

5. Heat the cups as well as the coffee pot.

6. If coffee has to wait, keep the coffee pot in a pan of boiling water.

7. If the scalding hot milk is poured into the cups before the coffee, the flavour is better. Do not *boil* the milk.

How to make Coffee in a Jug or Billy-Can

Florence White, 1926

1. Roast and grind the coffee as above or get it ready roasted and ground from the Army and Navy Stores or Civil Service Supply Association.

2. Make a kitchen jug or billy-can hot, put into it one good ordinary tablespoonful of the coffee for each person and a pinch of salt for the whole jug.

3. Pour on this $\frac{1}{2}$ pint of absolutely boiling (freshly boiled) water, allowing $\frac{1}{2}$ pint for each tablespoonful of coffee.

4. Give it a stir round with a tablespoon.

5. Pour out a cupful and pour it back; do this 3 times.

6. Then put in a tablespoonful of cold water.

7. Have ready another hot jug or billy-can and stand it in a pan of boiling water; cover the top of this jug with a clean piece of butter muslin, folded to make 4 thicknesses.

8. Pour your coffee through this muslin into the jug. The muslin will catch up every grain, and the coffee will be deliciously clear and hot *if* the directions have been carefully followed.

This makes the best coffee in the world, and one of its merits is that no special apparatus of any kind is required except a supply of butter muslin, which may be washed in clean water and will serve again if neither soda nor soap be used in the process. It is therefore 'top-hole' for campers, hikers and backwooders.

THE CONA COFFEE POT

This coffee pot makes extremely good coffee, it has been tested in the Experiment Kitchen of the English Folk Cookery Association.

How to make Good Toast

I

1. Cut the bre..d (which must be at least a day old) in level slices, about ¼ inch thick.
2. Dry each side before allowing it to brown.
3. Then brown each side.
4. Put each slice as it is done into a toast rack.

N.B.—It is worth noting that very good toast can be made on a Scotch girdle over a gas ring, or a wood fire, or an oil stove, or any other suitable heat.

II

Dry Toast

Sir Henry Thompson

1. Cut stale bread in slices ⅜ of an inch thick.
2. Toast them patiently at some little distance from a clear fire till slightly coloured on both sides.
3. Pass a sharp knife horizontally through the soft centre part, making two pieces of each slice.
4. Now toast the inner sides as before.

N.B.—'This toast is crisp, not scorched outside and flabby inside, as toast is when put close to the fire according to the general custom. The bread for toast ought to be two days old.'

Oatmeal Porridge—Scotch Method

INGREDIENTS: Medium Oatmeal 2 oz.; water 1 pint, salt 1 teaspoonful.

TIME: 30-45 minutes.

METHOD

1. Boil the water.
2. Add the salt.
3. Sprinkle in the oatmeal whilst the water is bubbling.
4. Stir all the time with a porridge stick or spurtle (failing this use a large fork).
5. Go on stirring till the porridge is quite thick or it will get lumpy.
6. Then let it simmer either at the side of the fire or on an asbestos mat placed over a gas burner with the flame of gas turned down low.
7. Stir occasionally, and if it gets too thick add more water or milk.
8. Pour boiling hot into plates and serve with top milk or cream, whole milk or skim milk.

N.B.—More salt can be added if required, but it is not the same as when put in the water before cooking.

Frumenty

North of England Method

From an ancient manuscript in the British Museum Frumenty appears to have been used formerly as an accompaniment to animal food, as 'venison with frumenty,' and 'porpoise with frumenty' formed part of the second course served at the Royal banquet given to Henry IV at Winchester on his marriage with Joan of Navarre; and again at the Coronation feast of Henry VII and the heiress of the House of York we meet with 'venison and frumenty;' but at the present day it is usually boiled with new milk and sugar, to which some add spices, currants, yolks of eggs, etc., and is occasionally eaten cold as a dinner sweet at various times of the year — as Mid-Lent, Easter, and Christmas; but in the North it is considered to form part of the Christmas fare alone, and is eaten hot without any other addition than new milk, sugar, nutmeg, with a little flour mixed with the milk to thicken it and then prepared (*see* p. 27). If the wheat be sufficiently boiled and prepared as follows it forms a cheap, pleasant and wholesome breakfast food usually much relished by children.

INGREDIENTS: Hulled or pearled wheat 1 quart (that is to say wheat with the first husk removed, it can sometimes be bought at a corn shop, and is stocked by the Army and Navy Stores, 105 Victoria Street, London, S.W.1.), water 5 pints; milk; sugar; nutmeg; and a little flour.

I

TIME: To cree the wheat soak 12 hours; and to boil 2 hours.

METHOD

1. Put the wheat covered with cold water for 12 hours or more in a warm oven; it is wise to put it in after the cooking for the day is done and leave it all night; or it can be put in a pot into a Poore's fireless cooker between heated stones; or it can be boiled up and put into a hay-box cooker.

2. It is then taken out, put on the stove, and boiled up till it is swollen and soft, taking care by stirring it often (as it thickens in boiling) that it does not burn; then pour it into a deep dish to cool and it will turn out a stiff glutinous mass which is called 'cree'd' or stewed wheat, from which frumenty, properly so-called, is made.

II

To Make Frumenty

1. Take as much frumenty wheat, or cree'd wheat, prepared as above, and boil it with double its quantity of milk until thick and creamy.

2. If required take a little flour and mix it with a little milk and stir it in to thicken it.

3. It can then be eaten as a breakfast porridge or cereal. In America this is known as 'cracked wheat.'

N.B.—It is one of the best remedies in the world for intestinal stasis for those who can take it, but the grains of wheat embedded in it might sometimes cause irritation. Another of its merits is that it is rich in vitamins A and B.

For further information and recipes *see* Local and National Specialities, pages 341, 348, 349, 361, 362, 363, 364, 365, and Index.

Bacon for Breakfast

1. Do not fry it in a frying-pan (except when hiking), if you can avoid it For one thing the fat splashes the stove.

2. If by any chance you have a game oven you can hook a rasher on each hook and toast it in front of the fire.

3. You can put it in a double grid that hangs on the bars of a fire if you have bars.

4. You can toast it on a toasting fork.

5. You can grill it under an electric or gas grill. As a matter of fact it cooks extremely well under an electric grill because there are no gas fumes.

6. You can roll up your slices of bacon and put them in a tin in a moderate oven and bake them for about half an hour, turning them at the end of fifteen minutes. The time depends on the heat of the oven.

N.B.—The rind and rusty bits should be cut off the bacon. For this purpose there is nothing better than scissors.

Baked Rashers

Mrs. Roundell, Nantwich, Cheshire

1. Melt a tiny piece of bacon fat in a baking tin.
2. Cut the rashers from the back of the side of bacon, as the fat and lean in that part are more equally divided.
3. When the melted bacon fat is hot but not scorching hot, lay the rashers in the tin, being careful to put the fat half of one rasher over the lean half the other.
4. Bake for about 10 minutes in a hot oven.

Relishing Rashers of Bacon

Dr. Kitchiner's Recipe, 1817

1. If you have any cold cooked bacon, you may make a very nice dish of it by cutting it into slices about $\frac{1}{4}$ inch thick.
2. Grate some crust of bread and powder the rashers well with it on both sides.
3. Toast them in front of the fire (or under a gas or electric grill).
4. They will be browned on one side in about three minutes. Turn them and do the other.

N.B.—These are a delicious accompaniment to poached or fried eggs; the bacon having been boiled first is tender and mellow — they are an excellent garnish round veal cutlets or sweetbreads, or calf's-head hash, or green peas, or beans, etc.

Potatoes and Fried Bacon

An old Devonshire Breakfast Dish
Mrs. Arthur Hillyard, Stoodleigh Rectory, 1890

It is the custom in Devonshire to re-cook the potatoes left over from the day before, in the pan in which the breakfast bacon has been fried and serve the two together. The potato is mashed, seasoned with pepper and salt, turned into the hot bacon fat, stirred about over the fire and finally shaped into a thick flat cake, well browned underneath and turned over brown side uppermost on to a hot dish. The crisp curls of bacon are placed on it and around it, or in a separate dish.

[There was nothing more individual than English housekeeping and cooking in Victorian days; we all had our own little ways until we tried imitating our neighbours. In Devonshire and many other places in England they always fry their breakfast bacon.]

Yorkshire Way of Cooking Bacon

Mr. A. Dupuis Brown writes: 'Recollections of my boyhood in York-shire remind me of the method of cooking the breakfast bacon, which was always roasted in an oblong tin dish suspended by hooks from one of the bars of the open fire range. It was not fried.'

The Double Hanging Grid

Wherever there was an open range with bars, sprats, bloaters, fresh herrings, dried or finnan-haddock, as well as sausages, kidney and bacon, chops, etc., were all beautifully and easily cooked between the wires of a double grid which possessed a tin tray underneath to gather the 'drips,' and hooks on top to attach to the bars. There were hooks on both sides and a handle on top by which the contraption could be easily turned completely round when one side was sufficiently cooked; the double grid was kept together and the food kept in its place by means of a strong, wire band which was fixed on the handle side and slipped over the other.

[This is worth mentioning because it required less attention and gave better results than a frying-pan, and we are apt to think the twentieth century takes the palm for labour-saving! It is also worth noting because a correspondent writes 'my mother used to say "good cooking in England went out when closed kitchen ranges and stoves were introduced and generally adopted".' — Ed.]

The Small Game or Dutch Oven

From William III and Mary's Days

This can be used most successfully for breakfast dishes as well as for small game, chops, etc., for luncheon or supper dishes in any room that possesses an open gas fire. There are small makes of electric grills also, with which it can be used, and it is ideal for a wood fire made on a stone hearth, or in the open air — its height merely requiring adjustment by standing it on bricks or stones (or on a tin turned upside down).

Frying

Good frying is in fact boiling in fat, and the frying-pan should be perfectly flat with a thick bottom, 12 inches long, 9 inches broad, with perpendicular sides and must be half-filled with fat. Before using make sure that the pan is quite clean, rub a little fat over it and then make it warm and wipe it out with a clean cloth.—WILLIAM KITCHINER.

1. Never use any oil, butter, lard, or dripping but what is clean, fresh, and free from salt. Anything dirty spoils the look; anything bad-tasted or stale spoils the flavour, and salt prevents its browning.
2. Dripping, if clean and fresh is almost as good as anything: it may be easily clarified.
   [N.B.—The top fat off the liquor in which bacon or ham has been boiled, if clarified, is good for shallow fat frying.—ED.]
3. The fat must be quite hot: that is to say it must have done hissing; if the fat is not hot enough, you cannot fry fish either a good colour, or firm and crisp. To be quite certain, throw a little bit of bread into the pan; if it fries crisp the fat is ready; if it burns the bread it is too hot.
4. [Remember that each cutlet or piece of fish, etc., you put in the piping-hot fat cools it, and pause a moment between each piece to allow the fat time to recover its proper heat. After the fried food is taken out of the pan it should be well drained on a piece of paper or, better still, soft muslin, and kept crisp in the oven ready for dishing up.—ED.]
5. Oatmeal is a very satisfactory, and an extremely economical, substitute for bread-crumbs.
6. The fat can be used three or four times if it has not burned; but it must be poured through a fine hair sieve into a clean basin; if you do not find it enough, simply add each time a little more to it. Fat in which fish has been fried must not be used for another purpose.

Frying with a Thermometer

The guesswork is taken out of frying if a thermometer made for this purpose be used. These, which came to us from America (in 1924), are now made in England by Short & Mason, the famous makers of aneroids (and other delicate instruments), Walthamstow, Essex, England, or Taylor Instrument Company, Rochester, N.Y., U.S.A. A cookery-book of frying temperatures is supplied with the thermometers.

Different foods require to be fried at different temperatures. These thermometers have been tested in the Experiment Kitchen of the English Folk Cookery Association and found perfectly satisfactory.

Frying in a very little Fat

This is very useful and corresponds to the French *sauter*. Only a very little fat is put in the pan and made hot according to the requirements of the food to be cooked; these should be stated in the recipes.

Broiling and Grilling

1. Keep the gridiron quite clean between the bars, and bright on top; when it is hot wipe it well with a linen cloth; just before you use it, rub the bars with a piece of clean mutton fat to prevent the meat being marked by the gridiron.
2. Let all the bars of the gridiron be hot through, but yet not burning hot upon the surface; this is the perfect condition for the gridiron.
3. Upright gridirons which can be used in front of the fire are best, as they can be used at any fire without fear of smoke; and the gravy is preserved in the trough under them.—WILLIAM KITCHINER.

[Electric grillers, especially electric table grillers are most satisfactory: Tested in the E.F.C.A. Experiment Kitchen.—ED.]

Bacon Olives

The Fanny Calder School of Cookery, Liverpool, 1904

INGREDIENTS: Cold cooked meat minced about ¼ lb.; bread-crumbs 3 ordinary tablespoonfuls; chopped parsley 1 ordinary teaspoonful; chopped onion 1 teaspoonful; dried herbs ½ teaspoonful; pepper and salt; a little egg. Rashers of Bacon about 8 cut thin; square pieces of toast or fried bread 8.

TIME: 15 minutes in a moderate oven.

METHOD

1. Trim the rashers of bacon with a pair of scissors.
2. Cut each rasher across into halves.
3. Mix all the other ingredients, except the toast, together, to make a stuffing or forcemeat.
4. Spread some of this on each piece of bacon.
5. Roll up and put on a baking tin.
6. Bake 15 minutes in a moderate oven.
7. Meantime make square pieces of toast or fried bread large enough to hold two of the bacon olives.
8. Serve up two olives on each piece of toast.

Bacon Rolls

This simple but excellent way of using up cold cooked porridge is exactly the kind that is useful in a collection of English cookery recipes, as it proves English housekeepers and cooks are still economical and clever in spite of the sneers to which they have been subjected recently. It was sent in 1931 by Mrs. Lester of Eastbourne College, Sussex.

INGREDIENTS: Cold cooked porridge; some chopped parsley; some mixed herbs; bread-crumbs; pepper; salt; rashers of bacon.

The quantities of the seasoning, etc., depend on the amount of cold porridge to be used up.

TIME: about 10 to 15 minutes.

METHOD

1. Chop the parsley and powder the herbs.
2. Mix them with the cold porridge.
3. Add enough bread-crumbs to stiffen the porridge.
4. Season with salt and pepper.
5. Spread on a rasher of bacon.
6. Roll them up.
7. Fry till the bacon is cooked.
8. Serve very hot on squares of fried wholemeal bread or toast.

Potato Bread fried with Bacon

A North of Ireland dish
Miss C. Clarke

Potato bread fried with bacon is a favourite dish in the North of Ireland.

Bacon Fraize or Froise

1826

This is a very old English dish. It is made with streaky bacon cut into strips or dice and cooked gently in a frying-pan; a good pancake batter

32

is then poured over the hot bacon and when cooked on one side is turned over and cooked on the other.

It is served, folded over flat or rolled as a pancake according to its thickness.

Sausage meat can be done in the same way; also flaked fish or fruit.

Apple Fraize or Froise
1845

1. Make some batter with 1 egg, 4 oz. flour and ½ pint milk.
2. Pare, core, quarter and slice some apples thinly and fry them for a few minutes in a little butter. Take out and keep hot.
3. Put ¼ oz. butter or lard into a frying-pan — make it hot; it must just well grease the pan all over.
4. Pour in enough batter to cover the pan thinly.
5. On this place some of the slices of apple, sprinkle with sugar.
6. Cover with more batter and cook gently.
7. When brown on one side, turn over and brown on the other.

Delicious English Sausages

Dr. Kitchiner says 'Sausages are best when quite fresh made.' The secret of frying sausages is:

1. To let them get hot very gradually, then they will not burst if they are quite fresh.
2. Do not prick them with a fork because this lets all their gravy out.
3. Dredge them lightly with flour, rubbing it smooth and discarding the loose flour.
4. Put a bit of butter or clarified dripping into a clean frying-pan.
5. As soon as it is melted (and before it gets hot) put in the sausages.
6. Shake the pan for a minute, and keep turning them but be careful not to prick or break them in so doing.
7. Fry them over a very slow fire till they are nicely browned all over.

N.B. 'Some over-economical cooks' Dr. Kitchiner says, 'insist that no butter or lard is required; the fat of the sausages being sufficient to fry them. We have tried it, — the sausages were partially scorched and had that pie-bald appearance that fried things have when sufficient fat is not allowed.'

(Poached eggs, pease-pudding, and mashed potatoes are agreeable accompaniments to sausages, and sausages are as welcome with boiled or roasted poultry or veal or boiled tripe, and are a convenient, easily digested and invigorating food for old folk and those whose teeth are not strong.)

Savoury Balls, Cakes or Sausages
1857

1. Mince any cooked meat or fish very fine; season it.
2. Then reduce (by boiling) some white (or brown) sauce according to whether you are using white meat or fish or otherwise, to a thick consistency. If necessary you may add the yolk of one or more eggs, and heat up the mixture till it thickens.
3. Add the mince to the sauce, let it boil, taste, and if necessary add a little more seasoning.
4. Spread the mixture on a dish; when cold it should be stiff.
5. Make up into balls, or shape as sausages, or small pears (with a bit of baked pastry stuck in for the stalk) or in the case of fish into round flat cakes $\frac{3}{4}$ inch thick.
6. Egg and bread-crumb and leave to dry for one hour. If this is done the frying is more satisfactory.
7. Egg and bread-crumb again; dry again and fry in deep fat till a golden brown.

To Make Very Good Oxford
Sausages

Miss Wettin's manuscript book, 18th century

Lent by Lady Gomme

INGREDIENTS: Pork and veal equal quantities; good beef suet half as much; pepper, salt, nutmeg, sage and thyme; eggs, 1 or more; a little water as required; a little flour.

METHOD

1. Free the pork and veal from all sinews and skin.
2. Chop the meat very small.
3. Chop the suet and add that.
4. And chop all together till very fine.
5. Then season with pepper, salt, nutmeg, and the sage, and thyme minced small.
6. Then work it up with one or more eggs and a little water as you see good.
7. Make it up into the shape of sausages by rolling it with floured hands on a floured board, and fry.

Skinless Sausages

Miss Rogers writes from Marazion, Cornwall, 'I think our skinless sausages are peculiar to this part of the country. They are well-flavoured

34

with herbs. When we were children, we regarded them as proper sausages and the larger skinned form as base imitations.'

And Professor Saintsbury in *A Scrap Book* (1922) asks 'What has come to . . . that admirable variety, the Oxford Sausage (much herbed, skinless and moulded into sausage shape only just before cooking), which was not to be found the last time I ordered it there.'

These skinless sausages are claimed therefore by both Cornwall and Oxford. They can be bought at Oxford (1931). Mr. Charles Clark, The Middle Avenue, Market, still makes them for sale, and claims to be the sole maker of the real thing.

And here is a very old recipe for those who live far away and wish to make them at home. In these days of small hand-mincing machines or mincers, it would be quite easy to do so; putting them into skins is the difficulty.

Recipe for Oxford Sausages

1826

INGREDIENTS: Young pork, fat and lean 1 lb.; lean veal 1 lb.; beef suet 1 lb.; grated bread ½ lb.; half a lemon; a nutmeg; fresh sage leaves 6; pepper 1 teaspoonful; salt, 2 teaspoonfuls, a little thyme, savory and marjoram.

METHOD

1. Remove all skin and gristle from the meat and suet, and
2. Put all through the mincer or chop very finely.
3. Grate the bread and add it to the meat.
4. Shred half the rind of the lemon, and grate the nutmeg.
5. Chop the sage, thyme, savory and marjoram very fine, and add all these with the pepper and salt to the meat and bread.
6. Mix well all together and press down in a pan till you want to use it.
7. Then with floured hands roll portions of the sausage meat the size and shape of ordinary sausages; and fry in clarified fat or grill a fine golden brown (*see* pp. 29 and 33).

Epping Sausages

1826

This also is a recipe for skinless sausage and easy to make. It is quite simple to make any smaller quantity.

INGREDIENTS: Young pork 6 lb.; beef suet 6 lb.; sage leaves, a handful; some thyme, savory and marjoram; lemon 1; nutmegs 2; pepper, a spoonful; salt, a large spoonful; egg as much as will make it smooth.

METHOD

1. Put the pork free from skin, gristle and fat through a mincer, and pound it fine in a mortar.
2. Chop the beef suet very fine.
3. Shred the sage leaves finely.
4. Spread the meat on a clean dresser-[board] and shake the sage over it.
5. Shred the rind of the lemon very fine and throw it with some chopped sweet herbs on the meat.
6. Grate the nutmegs over it, powder with the pepper and salt.
7. Chop the suet finely and throw that over it.
8. Mix all well together, and put down close in a pot ready for use.
9. Then roll it up into sausages with as much egg as will make it smooth, and fry in clarified fat, or grill.

Summer Sausage Rolls

1842

Equal portions of cold roast veal and ham, or cold fowl and tongue minced and seasoned with a teaspoonful of powdered sweet herbs, and a spoonful of salt and cayenne pepper mixed. Mix well together with some thickened delicately-flavoured gravy to make the mixture the consistency of sausage meat. Heat all together, and when cold, with floured hands make up into sausages, egg and bread-crumb, leave for an hour, egg and bread-crumb again and fry; or roll out some puff pastry very thin, cut into squares, put a sausage-shaped piece of the mixture in the centre, roll up in the pastry, pinch together, brush over with egg and milk and bake in a quick oven. May be eaten hot or cold.

Skinless Sausages

Mrs. J. Rowley, Tendring, Suffolk, 1857

INGREDIENTS: Pork, lean and fat, 4 lb.; bread-crumbs, ½ lb.; sage; pepper; salt; and a very little spice.

METHOD

1. Mince the pork finely, there should be about one-third fat to two-thirds lean.
2. Add the bread-crumbs, finely chopped fresh sage or powdered dried sage, salt, pepper and a little powdered allspice.
3. Mix well, and
4. Make up into sausages with a little flour, and fry as required. Will keep two or three days in a cool place in winter if well seasoned; and it is possible to make with half quantities

Skuets

An Eighteenth Century Recipe

1. Take several ordinary modern metal skewers with a small ring at the top of each. Stainless skewers can now be bought.
2. Stew till tender some lambs' sweetbreads, or a calf's sweetbread, cut into inch or inch and a half cubes. Remove all skin and gristle and allow to get cold.
3. Cut some good bacon into thin squares about the same size.
4. Season all well by dipping them in egg and rolling them in seasoned bread-crumbs.
5. Thread them on the skewers alternately — bacon and sweetbread. Then hang on hooks in a Dutch roaster, or grill under gas or electricity, and baste.

[N.B. — It is an improvement to introduce a peeled mushroom cup dipped in oiled butter under each piece of sweetbread, so that it catches the 'drip' from both bacon and 'bread.' Skuets of oysters rolled in bacon are delicious, and crowds of others can be invented by the imaginative mind. — ED.]

Devilled Kidneys

Tendring Hall, Suffolk, 1867

INGREDIENTS: Sheeps' kidneys; mustard; pepper; butter.

TIME: 8 to 10 minutes.

METHOD

1. Split the kidneys open without dividing them.
2. Strip off the skin and fat.
3. Score them and rub in mustard and pepper.
4. Run a fine skewer through the joints and across the back of the kidney to keep it flat while broiling.
5. Lay them on a greased gridiron over a clear fire with the cut sides towards it or in a hanging grid, Dutch oven or electric or gas griller.
6. Turn them in three or four minutes, and, in as many more, dish them up quickly.

Broiled Bones

Tendring Hall, Suffolk, 1863

Pepper and salt the bones well, spread a little butter on them to moisten them. Place on a gridiron over a clear fire (or on a gas or electric grill); turn them over two or three times until they are done.

Pour over them the Broil Sauce.

Broil Sauce

INGREDIENTS: Worcester Sauce; common vinegar; made mustard; butter.

METHOD

1. Measure equal portions of the sauce and vinegar, and half one portion of made mustard.
2. Mix well.
3. Add a little bit of butter.
4. Make all very hot.
5. And pour piping hot over the broiled bones.

Devilled Bones

Boodle's Club, 1923

INGREDIENTS: Bones with a little meat on; butter 4 oz.; dry mustard; ground black pepper; salt; curry powder; a teaspoonful of each; cayenne pepper ½ teaspoonful; Worcester sauce 1 tablespoonful; a sauce-boat of Devil sauce.

METHOD

1. Work the butter, mustard, pepper, salt, curry powder, cayenne pepper, and Worcester sauce all together; keep on ice.
2. First score the meat, then grill the bones.
3. After grilling coat with the devilled butter and put under the grill for two or three minutes and serve, with or without a Devil or grill sauce.

Devil or Grill Sauce

Dr. Kitchiner, 1823

INGREDIENTS: Gravy ½ pint; butter 1 oz.; flour 1 ordinary table-spoonful; mushroom or walnut ketchup, 1 tablespoonful; lemon juice 2 teaspoonfuls; made mustard one teaspoonful; minced capers 1 tea-spoonful; black pepper ½ teaspoonful; lemon, grated rind of one quarter; essence of anchovies; shallot, a very small piece; chilli vinegar a very little, and a few grains of cayenne.

METHOD

1. Heat the gravy.
2. Melt an ounce of fresh butter.
3. Add a tablespoonful of flour, and brown it over a moderate fire but be careful not to burn.
4. Remove from fire and dilute gradually with the hot gravy, beating it in
vigorously to make it quite smooth.
5. Add the rest of the ingredients.
6. Simmer all together for a few minutes.
7. Pour a little on the grill and serve up the rest in a sauce tureen.

N.B.—For other sauces *see* Index, and pages 117 to 125.

English Kedgeree

INGREDIENTS: Patna rice 4 oz.; water 2 quarts; salt 2 teaspoonfuls; cooked finnan-haddock, or other cooked fish, or cold boiled ham 4 oz.; hard-boiled eggs 1 or 2; butter 2 oz.; chopped watercress 2 teaspoonfuls, pepper, salt; a little tomato sauce or ketchup (1 dessertspoonful more or less according to taste).

TIME: to cook about 30 minutes.

METHOD

1. Boil the rice as you would for curry in boiling salted water (*see* p. 182).
2. Remove all skin and bone from the fish and chop it finely.
3. Chop up the white of the hard-boiled egg.
4. Put the butter into a stewpan; when it is melted toss the rice in it with pepper and salt.
5. Add the fish or meat and chopped white of egg.
6. Stir a dessertspoonful of tomato ketchup or sauce into it.
7. Toss all together over the fire till piping hot.
8. Then stir in the chopped watercress,
9. And serve quickly on a dish also piping hot, scattering the chopped or grated hard-boiled yolk of egg over the top.

Fish Cakes

Mrs. Brewitt, Melton Mowbray, 1927

INGREDIENTS: Potato (cooked) 2 lb.; cold fish (cooked) 1 lb.; lemon juice 2 teaspoonfuls; anchovy essence 2 teaspoonfuls; chopped parsley 2 teaspoonfuls; cayenne, a dash; some pepper and salt.

METHOD

1. Mash up all the ingredients and mix together.
2. Make into little round flat cakes ½ inch thick.
3. Egg and bread-crumb.
4. Leave to dry for half an hour.
5. Fry in a very little clarified dripping or bacon fat.
6. Drain on a clean cloth.

N.B. — Fat off the top of boiled bacon, clarified, is one of the best mediums for frying.

Finnan-Haddock

Mrs. Brewitt, Melton Mowbray, 1927

INGREDIENTS: Haddock; water; rashers of bacon not smoked.

TIME: 30 minutes.

METHOD

1. Put a skinned haddock in a frying-pan in cold water, simmer for 5 minutes.
2. Leave it in the same water for 5 minutes.
3. Lift out, drain and put it in an oven dish.
4. Cover with rashers of bacon.
5. Cook it all in the oven till the bacon is done.

[N.B.—Finnan-haddock may be skinned by holding it for a few minutes skin side near the flame over a lighted gas-ring or any other heat of the same strength; the skin will cockle and can be easily pulled off.—ED.]

Creamed Cod Fish

Mrs. Brewitt, Melton Mowbray, 1927

INGREDIENTS: Fish 1 lb.; milk 1 pint; butter 2 oz.; flour 2 oz.; mashed potatoes ½ lb.; salt and cayenne pepper.

TIME: 1 hour.

METHOD

1. Place the fish in cold water and boil or steam over water till tender.
2. Strain, bone, skin and flake with a fork.
3. Make a sauce of the milk, butter and flour in the usual way (see p. 117), season with cayenne pepper and salt
4. Lay in the fish and the mashed potatoes.
5. Whisk all together with a fork or Scotch whisk.
6. Serve as hot as possible.

To Fry Sprats

A good Southwold Recipe, sent by Mrs. Loftus

INGREDIENTS: Fresh sprats; flour or fine oatmeal, coarse salt.

METHOD

1. Wash and dry the sprats well.
2. Dust with flour or fine oatmeal.
3. Sprinkle the bottom of the frying-pan with warm salt.
4. Make it hot.
5. Then put in your sprats, and fry them a nice brown.

N.B.—No fat is needed as the salt draws out the fat of the sprats.

Finnan-Haddock and Tomato

Florence White, Westminster, 1922

1. Butter a piedish.
2. Put a finnan-haddock in cold water, boil it up for a few minutes until the flesh leaves the bones easily.

3. Remove all skin and bones, and flake the fish. If you have any sauce left over mix it with it.

4. Skin some tomatoes by pouring boiling water over them; the skins will then come off easily. Slice the tomatoes.

5. Arrange alternate layers of flaked fish and slices of tomatoes, sprinkle with dabs of butter and a little pepper: no salt.

6. Cover with fine bread-crumbs, sprinkle with oiled butter and bake till nicely browned; about 20 minutes.

N.B.—Any white fish may be cooked in the same way. It is simple to do, and delicious; also economical as left over fish can be thus used up.

Kippers

1. These may be cooked gently in a little hot butter in a frying-pan putting the underneath side downwards at first and then turning it over and doing the other; serve very hot.

2. By this method the flavour of the kippers is too strong for some people who like to put them into a pan, and pour boiling water over them; they are then just boiled up to heat through thoroughly, lifted out, drained, spread with a little butter and put in the oven for a few minutes.

Fresh Herrings

The way in which King Edward VII liked them cooked

1. Cut the heads and tails off the herrings, and clean them.

2. Split them down the back.

3. Take out the backbone and with it as many of the small bones as you can.

4. Dip them in oatmeal and

5. Fry or grill them.

This recipe is interesting in another way: writing in 1817 Dr. Kitchiner recommends oatmeal as a cheap substitute for bread-crumbs, when crumbing is required.

New-Laid Eggs

These are delicious either boiled and served in their shells, or poached, and it is worthy of note that an egg that is not new-laid will not poach without breaking. A man writes that for this reason he always, when he wants an egg in a teashop, asks to have it poached.

To Boil Eggs in the Shell

Miss Acton, 1845

'Even this simple process demands a certain degree of care, for if the eggs be brought from a cold larder, and suddenly plunged into boiling water they will frequently break immediately, and a large portion will often escape from their shells. In winter they should be held over the steam for an instant before they are laid in, and they should be put in gently. They should be put into sufficient boiling water to cover them completely.'

TIME: 1. To boil very lightly (for people who like the whites in a partially liquid state) 3 minutes.

2. To cook the whites to a milky consistency, $3\frac{1}{2}$ minutes.

3. To cook the whites firm but leave the yellow liquid, 4 to $4\frac{1}{2}$ minutes; not a second more.

4. To boil hard, 8 to 10 minutes; for salad dressing, 15 minutes.

To Cook an Egg in the Shell without boiling it

'An admirable receipt for Invalids.'

(Taken by Miss Acton from 'The Cottage Gardener' and tested by her.)

METHOD

1. Put boiling water in a basin and let it remain for a few seconds and turn it out.

2. Put the egg into the basin and roll it over to take the chill off the shell that it may not crack.

3. Pour in on the egg quite boiling water from the kettle until it is completely immersed.

4. Put a hot plate over it instantly, and let it remain on the table for 12 minutes. It will then be found to be perfectly and beautifully cooked so lightly and delicately dressed as to suit people who cannot take eggs at all when boiled in the usual way.

Bantams', Guinea Fowl's, Turkeys' or Swans' Eggs

Miss Acton, 1845

Bantams'. To boil hard for a salad, 6 minutes, 'They make an elegant decoration for a salad.' To poach, $2\frac{1}{2}$ to 3 minutes; delicious with a mince of fowl, or veal and oysters.

Guinea Fowl's Eggs. 'Much esteemed by epicures.' To boil quite hard, 10 minutes. To boil so that the whites are firm, 3½ to 4 minutes.

Turkeys' Eggs. 'Though large they are delicate in flavour.' To boil so that the white is firm, 6 minutes; to poach, 4 minutes.

Swans' Eggs. Only those of young birds should be used. 'They are much more delicate than from their size might be supposed; and when boiled hard and shelled, their appearance is *beautiful*, the white being of remarkable purity and transparency.' They are excellent stuffed and served with salad. To boil them hard: take as much water as will cover the egg well in every part, let it boil quickly, then take it from the fire, and as soon as the water ceases to move put in the egg, and leave it by the side of the fire — without allowing it to boil, for 20 minutes, and turn it gently once or twice in the time; then put on the cover of the stewpan, put it on the fire and boil it gently for a quarter of an hour; take it from the fire, and in five minutes put it into a basin and throw a cloth once or twice folded over it, and let it cool slowly. It will retain the heat for a very long time, and as it should be quite cold before it is cut, it should be boiled early if wanted to serve the same day.

Savoury Baked Eggs

Florence White, 1931

For these use the delightful little slip-ware pipkins made by Michael Cardew at Winchcombe, Gloucestershire.

1. Butter the inside of each pipkin.
2. Put in a spoonful of nicely seasoned minced meat mixed with a little thickened gravy; or skinned tomato and thickened gravy; or shelled shrimps blended with a little white sauce; or some minced ham mixed with a little made tomato sauce; or some flaked cooked finnan-haddock mixed with a little fresh skinned tomato finely chopped; or some green peas and butter; or some asparagus tips and butter or sauce; any odd 'left over' that is delicious and suitable.
3. Break an egg on top of this without breaking the yolk.
4. Put a dab of butter on it and a little chopped parsley.
5. Put on the lid of the pipkin, and bake till the egg is set, about five or seven minutes according to the heat of the oven.

Baked Omelet

Florence White, Chelsea, 1924

1. Butter a small piedish.
2. Beat up one or two new-laid eggs with 1 or 2 dessertspoonfuls of milk, a little pepper, and salt.
3. Pour into the dish, and bake in a moderate oven till set.
4. Time five to ten minutes according to heat of oven.

N.B.—Some minced cooked ham, or parsley, or flaked fish may be mixed with the beaten-up eggs, but will take longer to cook.

To Poach Eggs

Miss Acton, 1845

1. Fill a wide and delicately clean pan about half-filled with the clearest water.
2. Throw in a small saltspoonful of salt.
3. Place over a fire quite free from smoke(!)
4. Break some new-laid eggs into separate cups, and do this with care that the yolks may not be injured.
5. When the water boils, draw back the pan, and glide the eggs gently into it, and let them stand until the whites appear almost set which will be in about a minute.
6. Then without shaking them move the pan over the fire, and just simmer them from two and a half to three minutes. Lift them out separately with a slice, quickly trim off the ragged edges and serve them upon spinach, minced veal, turkey or chicken, or upon delicately toasted bread, sliced thick and freed from crust; it is an improvement to have the bread buttered, but it is then less wholesome(!)

TIME: to poach eggs — Swans' eggs 5 to 6 minutes; Turkeys' eggs 4 minutes; hens' eggs 3 to 3½ minutes; Guinea-fowl's 2 to 3 minutes. Bantams' 2 minutes.

Scrambled Eggs

Florence B. Jack, 1914

INGREDIENTS: Eggs 4; milk, thin white sauce or stock 4 tablespoonfuls; butter 1 oz.; seasoning; buttered toast 2 slices; parsley.

METHOD

1. Prepare the toast, cut off the crust and keep the toast hot.
2. Melt the butter in an aluminium or earthenware saucepan.
3. Beat up the eggs with the liquid chosen and the seasoning.
4. Pour into the saucepan and stir over a moderate fire till the mixture gets thick and creamy.
5. Remove from fire stirring all the time—it will get a little thicker from the heat of the saucepan, and pile on the toast.
6. Garnish with parsley and serve at once; it must not be allowed to stand.

N.B.—If cooked too long the eggs will be hard and tough and watery; if not cooked long enough they will be thin and 'runny.' They require care and if well-made are quite as delicious as an omelet.

Variations of Scrambled Eggs

Florence B. Jack, 1914

Miss Jack gives nine ways of varying scrambled eggs:
1. Mixing in anchovy essence.
2. Adding a little grated cheese to ordinary scrambled eggs.
3. Adding a few green peas to ordinary scrambled eggs.
4. Adding some minced ham to ordinary scrambled eggs.
5. Blending the egg with diced sheeps' kidney (cooked).
6. Blending the egg with diced mushrooms   „
7. Serving them in the midst of a circle of spinach „
8. Serving them with tomatoes   „
To which may be added blending them with flaked finnan-haddock or minced ham and parsley.

Raised Meat and Game Pies

MELTON MOWBRAY PORK PIE

Mr. Fred Wright's Family Recipe, given July, 1927

It was Mrs. Brewitt who suggested that Mr. Fred Wright should be asked to give his mother's recipe for Melton Mowbray Pork Pie which had been in her family for generations. Mr. Wright most generously gave it and thereby saved it for the world, because he has since died and all trace of his mother's cookery book is lost. Mrs. Brewitt said 'There are no pies nearly as good.' When giving the recipe which follows Mr Wright emphasized two important points: *the anchovy used as seasoning,*

BREAKFASTS

and the putting of the hot strong stock made from the gristly bits into the pies *directly they come from the oven.* 'Those are the secrets,' said Mr. Wright.

This recipe has been tested in the Experiment Kitchen of the English Folk Cookery Association and found perfect. It is not difficult to carry out if the directions are carefully followed.

INGREDIENTS: *For the hot water crust:* Flour 1 stone; lard 4 lb., salt a good handful; water 4 pints.

N.B.— 1 pint of water to 1 lb. lard; a quarter of a stone of flour will make from 2½ to 3 lb. pies.

For the meat filling: Pork 9 lb.; salt 3 oz.; white pepper ½ oz.; essence of anchovy 1 dessertspoonful.

N.B.— 9 lb. of meat will make 6 pies. There should be quite one-third fat in proportion of two-thirds of lean meat.

TIME: to bake, about 2 to 5 hours or more in a slow oven according to size.

METHOD

1. Prepare the meat by removing all gristly bits, skin and bone and put them on in cold water to stew well to make a stiff jellied stock when cold. Season and strain before using.
2. Make the hot-water crust, by boiling the lard in water, and immediately after it has boiled use the lard and a portion of the water and knead it half an hour, then place it in a warm earthen pan covered with a warm cloth for half an hour.
3. If you cannot 'raise' the crust, line a cake tin that has a loose bottom, with the pastry; to do this grease the inside of the tin well and take off a piece of the paste for a cover, make the rest into a round cone-shaped ball and press it out from the centre outwards until you have a round large enough to cover the bottom of the cake tin, and come well up the sides. Drop this into the tin which should first be warmed, and with your hands mould it to the tin with your fingers, bringing the crust to about half an inch above the top of the tin.
4. Take a piece off the portion left for the top to make some leaves and a rose for decoration.
5. Press out the top piece till it is large enough to cover the top of the tin — and keep this and the decorations warm but not too warm whilst you pack the pie closely with the prepared meat.
6. Do not put any liquid in the pie, but press the meat, which must be chopped and seasoned, well down.
7. Then cover it with the lid, pinch the edges together, make a hole in the top; put the cut-out leaves of paste in place and the rose into the hole in the middle.
8. Brush all over with yolk of egg mixed with a little milk and bake as above.
9. When the pie is baked, directly it comes from the oven remove the rose and with a funnel pour in as much of the strained hot stock as it will hold, and don't replace the rose until the pie is quite cold. Then the rose may be replaced and if necessary stuck in with a little white of egg.

How They Raise a Piecrust in Warwickshire

Mrs. Loudon, 1851

Mrs. Loudon says: 'In my native Warwickshire half a pound of lard is put into a saucepan containing a quart of water. The saucepan is set on the fire, and stirred till the water boils. The boiling lard and water is slowly poured into as much flour as will suffice to make it into a smooth and very stiff paste, and mixed with a wooden spoon, after which it must be beaten with a rolling-pin. When the ingredients are thoroughly incorporated the paste is put into an earthen pan, covered with a linen cloth, and placed near the fire where it is left for about half an hour. The meat is now prepared by being separated from every particle of bone, skin, and gristle, and cut into pieces about the size of dice. Care is taken to keep the fat and lean separate; but both are well seasoned with pepper and salt.

'A piece of the paste large enough to form one pie is then broken off the mass, and the rest is again covered up, as it cannot be worked if it is too cold, though it will not stand if it is too warm. If it breaks and crumbles, instead of being plastic, it is too cold; and if it is too soft when raised, it is either too warm or too rich.

'When it is just of the right heat to bear being moulded, and yet to retain whatever shape may be given to it, the piece of paste is worked with the hands on a pasteboard, into the form of a high-peaked hat with a broad brim; and then the peak of the hat being turned downwards on the board, one of the hands is put inside the hat, and the other is used to raise and smooth the sides, till the pie is gradually worked into a proper shape. The meat is then put into the crust in layers, two of lean and one of fat, and pressed as closely as possible, in order that the pie may cut firm when cold.'

In Some Parts of Staffordshire

Mrs. Loudon says: 'In Leicestershire, and some parts of Staffordshire, a layer of raisins is often put below the meat, and

In Northamptonshire

Pork-pies or pasties are made with the same kind of crust as I have described, but, instead of being raised, it is rolled out, and then cut into pieces of a proper size for the top and bottom, with a long piece of the

47

necessary width for the sides. The bottom is cemented to the walls with egg, the two parts which are to adhere being pinched together; and the crust is filled with well-seasoned meat, put in layers of fat and lean as before; the lid is then put on, and after it has been made to adhere to the walls, it is washed over with a feather dipped in white of egg.

'These pies,' continues Mrs. Loudon, 'are frequently baked in a tin which is made so as only to support the walls, and is fastened on one side with a kind of skewer, which may be drawn out, so as to allow the tin to be removed without breaking the crust. As, however, the sides sometimes look too pale when the pie is baked in a tin, the pie may be put into the oven again for a few minutes after the tin is removed in order that the walls may be properly browned.'

Pig's Head Brawn

A Somersetshire Recipe, Frome, about 1832

INGREDIENTS: 1 pig's head; brine or 2 handfuls of salt and a small piece of saltpetre; water, carrots, turnips; onion; shallots; 1 bunch of herbs, 4 peppercorns, 2 blades of mace, 4 cloves, 12 allspice.

TIME: to be laid in brine, one night; to be kept boiling about 2 hours.

METHOD

1. Wash and clean the head thoroughly and lay it in brine all night, or sprinkle over with the salt and saltpetre.
2. Rinse it well.
3. Put it in a pan (a boiling pot).
4. Cover it with cold water.
5. Boil 2 hours or until the meat will easily leave the bone.
6. Then cut it up in dice – also the ear and tongue after skinning the latter.
7. Return the bones to the liquor.
8. Boil up.
9. Add vegetables and seasoning.
10. And boil until greatly reduced for about one hour (there should be about 1½ pints liquor).
11. Strain off the liquor into another pot.
12. Lay in the pieces of meat, season with pepper and salt if required and let it come to the boil.
13. Rinse a mould in cold water.
14. And pour in the meat and liquor.
15. When cold and set, it is ready for use.

Norfolk Pork Cheese

Mrs. Hilda Apperley

INGREDIENTS: A hock of pork (pickled), salt, pepper, sage (if liked) water.

TIME: about 3 hours.

48

METHOD

1. Leave the hock of pork in cold water all night to remove some salt.
2. Put it in a pot with enough cold water to cover.
3. Boil it till the meat leaves the bone quite clean.
4. Lift out the pork and take all the bones out.
5. Put the bones back into the liquor and simmer whilst you prepare the meat.
6. Salt and pepper the meat and add a little fresh sage chopped fine if you like it.
7. With a knife and fork cut up the whole of the meat, etc., quite fine.
8. Strain the liquor on to it (there should be only about ½ a pint).
9. Mix well, taste for seasoning and pour into a well wetted basin.
10. Turn out when cold.

[N.B.—At Norwich these hocks can be bought from 1s. to 1s. 6d. each (1930).—ED.]

Pork Cheese

A Frome, Somersetshire, Recipe

INGREDIENTS: 2 or more pig's feet, part of the ears and some bones, pepper; salt; nutmeg; allspice; soy and ketchup; water; slices of hard-boiled egg.

TIME: to boil 3 or 4 hours; and then 10 minutes.

METHOD

1. Boil the feet, etc., 3 or 4 hours (till the meat leaves the bones).
2. Pick the meat off.
3. Spice it with pepper, salt, nutmeg and ground allspice.
4. Add a few drops of ketchup and soy.
5. Mix all together and boil 10 minutes.
6. Put some slices of hard-boiled egg in the bottom of well wetted basins.
7. Pour the meat and liquor mixed together into the shapes and leave till set.

Stuffed Chine

Mr. H. V. Thompson, Stoke-on-Trent, writes (March, 1930):

'With reference to your letter in *The Times Literary Supplement* of February 6th I wonder if you have "stuffed chine" in your list of county recipes. This "dish" is, I believe, peculiar to North Lincolnshire and the East Riding of Yorkshire, though the number of people now able to prepare it is sadly diminishing.

'In former days the repast at Old Clee (Lincolnshire) Feast, Trinity Sunday, used to be stuffed chine and "saucer" curd cheese cakes. I enclose recipe.'

BREAKFASTS

[At Aldsworth, Northleach, Gloucestershire, they had a favourite dish for the sowing feast which was usually held on the last Sunday in April. It consisted of a good big fore-chine, sometimes called the 'christening chine' with large suet puddings. Mrs. Caudle, of Honeybourne, who was the daughter of a Herefordshire farmer, says 'The christening or fore-chine was cut down each side of the backbone or chine of a pig and it was so called because one was generally saved for a christening. Miss Lanchbury of West Kissington, Gloucestershire, says her mother always cooked a christening chine for 'Mothering Sunday.'— ED.]

North Lincolnshire Recipe

INGREDIENTS: A neck chine of bacon; herbs (parsley chiefly) a quantity will be required; thyme and marjoram, a small amount; raspberry and blackcurrant leaves, a few nice young ones; lettuce, a small quantity; spring onions, a few; flour and water to make a stiff paste.

TIME: to soak the chine 24 hours; to bake (according to size) 20 minutes for each lb. and 20 minutes over.

METHOD

1. Soak chine overnight.
2. Pick and well wash all the herbs.
3. Score both sides of the chine.
4. Put all the herbs through the mincing machine, once will be enough.
5. Mix them and stuff them tightly in all the scorings until they are all filled.
6. Make a stiff pastry of flour and water and cover the chine entirely with it.
7. Bake in a moderate oven, length of time according to size.
8. When cooked take off the paste carefully and place the chine on a dish strainer.
9. Eat when quite cold.

To Make Calf's Head Brawn

'Eliza Powell her Book, 23rd January, 1753.' This manuscript book of recipes is just an ordinary school exercise book on the outside cover of which is a wood engraving of the great Earl of Montrose. It was lent by Miss A. H. Carter, of Haywards Heath

INGREDIENTS: A calf's head; sweet herbs; anchovies; lemon peel; salt; spice; water.

TIME: 2 hours; then 15 minutes; then one hour.

METHOD

1. Take a calf's head with the skin on.
2. Scald the hair off with boiling soft water.
3. Boil it sufficiently in enough water to cover it, long enough to take out the bones (about 2 hours).
4. When boned, boil it about ¼ of an hour.
5. Then lay it flat on a board.
6. Then take chopped sweet herbs, boned and chopped anchovies and a little lemon peel shredded small.
7. Mix them to your taste with a little salt and spice.
8. Strew it all over the inside of the head.
9. Then roll it up very close in a cloth like other collared meat.
10. Tie it up securely.
11. Boil it but 1 hour.

N.B.— Must be kept in common pickle which must be renewed upon occasion and it will keep a quarter of a year. [But it can be eaten at once without being put in pickle. In this case the cloth should be taken off whilst hot and the collar rolled up in it again *very tightly*, and left on until the brawn is cold. It may be pressed till cold between 2 dishes.]

Oxtail Mould

One of Miss Heath's delightful recipes, inherited from her grandmother who was married in 1823 (*see* pp. 291 and 306).

INGREDIENTS: Oxtail 1; butter 1 oz.; flour to dredge it; cold water; onion 1; cloves 3; vinegar about ¼ gill; a bunch of herbs; pepper, salt; hard-boiled egg.

TIME: stew till the meat leaves the bones.

METHOD

1. Cut the fat off the oxtail.
2. Cut it into joints.
3. Put the butter into a saucepan and shake till brown.
4. Dredge the oxtail lightly with flour.
5. Put it into the hot butter and brown it.
6. Add enough water to cover it and about a ¼ gill of vinegar.
7. Add the onion sliced, a bunch of herbs, pepper and salt.
8. And stew till the meat leaves the bones.
9. Take the meat from the bones.
10. Butter a plain mould or cake tin.
11. Line it with slices of hard-boiled egg.
12. Put in the meat and as much of the stock as the mould will hold.
13. When cold turn out as you would a jelly, and serve with salad.
14. Cut down in thin slices.

Potted Beef

Leicester, made in 1860 and earlier

This recipe has been very kindly sent by the Misses Hope, Henfryn, Reading, who have a marvellous collection of manuscript cookery books handed down from one generation to another for 300 years. They exhibited cakes etc. at the first English Folk Cookery Exhibition and amongst others sent a delicious cake known as 'Aunt Nelly's cake' and made by Mrs. Spokes, of Tilehurst, Berkshire.

INGREDIENTS: Leg of beef; water; essence of anchovy; pepper; salt; clarified butter or mutton fat to cover.

TIME: to boil the beef 4 hours or more.

METHOD

1. Put the beef in cold water, bring it slowly to boiling point and boil gently till the flesh will separate with a fork.
2. Separate the meat from all gristle and fat.
3. Pound it in a mortar and during this process season it with the anchovy essence, etc. (A little of the liquor may be used to assist the process of pounding, but be careful not to put too much.)

N.B.—Boil the bones and gristle in the soup for an hour or more to improve the quality. Let it stand all night, take off the fat next morning and it will be most strengthening.

Potted Beef

From a Yorkshire woman's scrap-book, 1931

INGREDIENTS: Beef steak ½ lb.; ground mace ½ small teaspoonful; hot water to just cover meat; pepper; salt; butter.

TIME: 1½ to 2 hours according to the tenderness of the steak.

METHOD

1. Cut up steak into very small pieces.
2. Stew gently until tender.
3. Put through mincer twice.
4. Mix to a paste adding some of the gravy left over.
5. Season with mace, pepper, and salt.
6. Put into mould.
7. And when cold cover with oiled butter.

Beef Potted

Worcester Early 18th Century

Bake a tender piece of beef in butter till very tender. Drain it from the gravy, season it with cloves, mace, nutmeg, pepper and salt. Pound it in a stone mortar with a wooden beater adding fresh butter; when smooth and fine put it in your pots, close, clear the oyl'd butter from the gravey and pour over; if not enough oyle some butter and pour over.

A Modern Midland Recipe

Mrs. Jones, Ravenswood, Northampton

INGREDIENTS: Neck of beef 1 lb.; water 1 tablespoonful; a little mixed spice; pepper and salt to taste; anchovy essence a small dessert-spoonful; butter.

TIME: about 4 hours.

METHOD

1. Put the beef, water, and mixed spice into a double saucepan (or into a stoneware jar standing on a piece of wood in an iron saucepan) and cook for 4 hours.

2. When the meat is cold put it two or even three times through the mincer till it is quite fine and smooth.

3. Then add the anchovy sauce, pepper, salt, and gravy from the meat; mix well.

   Put into small dishes, and pour a little butter over them.

N.B.—The meat will cook in a hay-box (or fireless cooker) if it is allowed to get well started on the fire; say after the first half hour.

To Pot Pigeons, Grouse, Woodcock, Partridges, etc.

Worcester, Early 18th Century

Take and clean them very clean and wipe them dry. Season them inside as well as out with cloves, mace, nutmeg, pepper, and salt and put them (breast downwards) into a stean (stoneware) pot and cover them well with butter, cover the pot (so that it is airtight) and bake them in a slow oven for 1 hour or more according to their age, then drain them from the gravy, putt them into pots and take the oil'd butter from the gravey and pour over the birds. If not enough, oil more butter and cover half an inch thick.

A Modern and More Economical Way

1. Prepare and bake them as above.
2. Lift them out and drain well.
3. Leave the butter to get cold, then remove it from the gravy which will be found underneath.
4. Oil the butter again and use it to cover the potted game.

5. Cut all the meat off the bones of the birds whilst warm and pack it as it is in fillets very close together in a well-buttered potting dish (a pie-dish will do) a very little oiled butter may be poured over each layer but no gravy. Press down well; when cold cover with oiled butter as above, and it will keep a month or more in a cold dry place. It can at any time be put into a hot oven for half an hour and reheated; the butter will rise to the top and set again when cold.

6. When required for use take all the butter off the top, stand the dish for a few seconds in hot water but not too long, and the potted meat will turn out whole in the shape of the dish and can be cut across in slices. It will make delicious sandwiches if cut thin.

N.B.—1. The gravy underneath the butter in which the birds are baked can be added to soup or used as gravy for game; and the butter removed from the top can be used for basting so this need not be an extravagant dish.

2. The meat instead of being left in fillets can be minced and pounded in a mortar and made with butter into a paste, but this is a type of 'potting' of quite a different character, for which the recipes for potting beef given on page 52 can be used.

English Hams and Bacon

October, 1838

'There is an immense quantity of both bacon and ham consumed in London; yet none of it ever comes from the counties where the best is produced; because in those counties the whole is consumed at home, none being made for sale.

'In Buckinghamshire where the best bacon in England is made, in Gloucestershire also — especially in the Royal Forest of Dean — the swine feed heartily on beech mast, acorns, and the various productions of the woodlands. This imparts great sweetness and solidity to their flesh, the fattening of which is completed by peas or beans, and potatoes.

'The Buckinghamshire bacon is the very best in England, but the whole of that which is made is consumed in the county. In the farmhouse kitchen, as well as in the common room of the cottar, a couple of flitches of bacon will be seen hanging in the chimney, subject to the action of the smoke arising from the wood fire in use there. Suspended from the ceiling of the room is the bacon rack, containing several flitches more, destined in their turn to occupy the sides of the chimney.

'The Hampshire bacon and hams come next in repute to those of Buckinghamshire.

'In both counties and in most country places the time for slaughtering hogs is Michaelmas; they can then be smoked by the winter fire without additional expense.

'Along the sea-coast the bacon and hams are smoked with dried seawe d which gives them a delicious flavour.

'Suffolk produces the best hams in England, but their excellence depends upon the mode of curing.

'Yorkshire hams are equally famous but cured differently.'

The following is

A Very Special Recipe for Pickling Hams

County unknown

INGREDIENTS: Bay salt 1 lb.; common salt 1 lb.; moist sugar 2 lb.; saltpetre 4 oz.; salt prunella 2 oz.; juniper berries ¼ lb.; bay leaves 3; thyme, sweet basil, marjoram, sweetbrier, tarragon; a sprig of each; a few whole peppercorns and allspice; 1 quart of the strongest old ale.

TIME: to salt and press 24 hours; in pickle a month.

METHOD

1. The moment the hams are cut from the hog they are to be rubbed with common salt.
2. Then placed upon a flat board, with another over them and two half-hundred-weights placed on the upper board over each ham — under this pressure they must remain 24 hours.
3. They are then taken up and wiped ready for the pickle which must be prepared in readiness.
4. The ingredients for the pickle given above must be prepared as follows: Bruise the juniper berries in a mortar and put them in a pot with the ale; add all the other ingredients except the herbs, and boil for 20 minutes.
5. When this pickle is cool enough to bear the hands the herbs are thrown into the pickling-pan.
6. The hams placed immediately upon them, and
7. The whole of the hot pickle poured immediately upon them, and
8. Well rubbed into them.

N.B.—The brine is soon formed, and the hams are to be turned in it and basted with it every day for a month, when they must be taken out, dried, and smoked in the following manner:

To Smoke the Hams

1. Hang them in a large chimney belonging to an open hearth. (It must have no grate.)
2. Put a layer of dry straw on the hearth.
3. Upon this a layer of mixed wood shavings.

4. Next a layer of mixed sawdust.
5. A good handful of juniper berries.
6. And over this a mantle of wet straw or litter, which makes the fir
smoulder and emit much smoke without burning rapidly.

N.B.—This smoking must be repeated several times until the hams ar
quite dry, when they must be placed in the warm kitchen upon shelve
near the fireplace and turned twice a week.

To Cure Bacon

Bacon may be cured by the same process. The only difference is
that another 1 lb. each of common and bay salt should be added, and the
sugar is reduced to 1½ lb. All the rest of the process is the same.

A Cheap and Simple Way of Cooking a Ham

Kensington, 1920

1. Soak the ham for 24 or 48 hours according to its requirements; a
Suffolk sweet-cured ham requires soaking 48 hours; a Bradenham 4 days;
a mild-cured Yorkshire ham 24 hours.
2. Scrape it as usual.
3. Put it into a pot of cold water sufficient to cover it.
4. Bring it slowly to boiling point.
5. Simmer for 30 minutes.
6. Then plunge the still simmering pot quickly into a hay-box cooker;
pack the hay round very tight, cover with hay and a blanket, and leave
for 8 or 10 hours according to size.
7. Take the pot out, lift off the lid, and it will be found to be perfectly
cooked if these directions have been carefully followed.
8. Leave in its liquor till cold as this mellows the ham.

N.B.—The above is not only a saving of gas or electricity, it is also a
saving of trouble. The expenditure for fuel is the cost of cooking it for
at most 2 hours, whilst when it is once in the hay-box cooker it does not
require watching.

Anyone can make a hay-box for cooking purposes: any wooden box
with a lid can be used and newspapers used for stuffing instead of hay.

To Cook a Ham

A 'luxury' recipe

This was found written on a loose piece of paper in an old book, and its date and origin are unknown beyond the fact that it is English.

INGREDIENTS: Water; sherry or Marsala 1 pint; beer 1 pint; brown sugar a large cupful; real black treacle 1 lb. [*not* golden syrup!] any cut up vegetables, onions, carrots, cabbage, etc.

TIME: 4 days to soak in water; about 4 or 5 hours to cook.

METHOD

1. Soak the ham 4 days in water, which must be changed every day.
2. Scrape as usual.
3. Put in pot with fresh cold water, the sherry or Marsala, beer, sugar and treacle.
4. The liquor must cover the ham.
5. A few cut-up vegetables improve the flavour; bring to boiling point, and simmer till done.

Ham Loaf

INGREDIENTS: Cooked ham about 1 lb. ($\frac{1}{4}$ fat); bread 2 oz; milk 1 gill; finely chopped parsley 1 teaspoonful; pepper, a little ground mace; egg 1.

METHOD

1. Put ham through the mincer.
2. Boil up the milk and pour it over the bread to soak it.
3. Mix all up well together.
4. Season with pepper.
5. Mix with one well-beaten egg.
6. Grease a plain mould or basin.
7. Press the mixture firmly down and bake in a moderate oven till nicely browned.
8. Do not turn out until cold. If there should be any difficulty in turning it out loosen it by slipping the blade of a knife round it, and then stand it for a few minutes in hot water, when it should turn out quite easily.

To Salt Hams

(*An Old Devon Recipe*)

The Hon. Mrs. H. Hannen, of Boughton Monchelsea, Kent, writes (in 1931)
'I enclose a recipe for curing hams that may be useful. It is out of an old book bought amongst a lot at a sale about 30 years ago. In those days we used to keep our own pigs and thought we would try to cure our hams by it. We found it so good that since then we have never used any other. It is very full-flavoured and somewhat like a Spanish ham we think. The book is dated 1764.'

INGREDIENTS. Water 3 or 4 gallons; bay salt 4 lb; white salt 8 lb.; saltpetre ¼ lb.; prunella salt 2 oz.; brown sugar 8 lb.

TIME: to pickle 4 or 5 weeks.

METHOD

1. Boil all the ingredients together for 15 minutes.
2. Skim well.
3. When it is cold pour it from the bottom into the vessel you keep it in.
4. Let the hams lie in this pickle four or five weeks.
5. Dry them in a stove or the chimney of a wood fire.

Sweet Pickle for Hams

Mrs. Martin, Frome, Somersetshire, 1850

INGREDIENTS: Juniper berries 1 oz.; allspice 2 oz.; long pepper 1 oz.; black peppercorns 1 oz.; treacle ½ lb.; old strong beer 1 pint.

METHOD

1. Bruise all the berries.
2. Boil in ½ pint of the beer with the spices.
3. Warm the treacle till it liquifies.
4. Mix it with the unboiled beer, and with the boiled beer strained off the spices.
5. Salt the ham slightly for 2 weeks.
6. Pour the pickle over it and keep in it 4 or 5 weeks, turning it over and over and basting it well each day.
7. Dry and smoke as usual.

Ham Pickle

An Oxfordshire Recipe, 1929

The following recipe for pickling hams was kindly given in 1929 by Mr. George Hawkins, at that time owner and landlord of the Langston Arms, Kingham, Oxfordshire. Mrs. Hawkins says, however, that, although Mr. Hawkins always attends to the pickling himself most carefully, much of the excellence of their hams depends on the feeding, housing and care he gives to his pigs. When he has run short of hams and has had to buy from other people, the hams cured in exactly the same manner have not always been so good.

INGREDIENTS: Old beer 1 quart; peppercorns 2 oz.; saltpetre 2 oz. black pepper 2 oz.; bay salt 2 oz.; juniper berries 2 oz.; common brown sugar 4 lb.; salt 1 lb. This is sufficient for 2 large or 3 small hams.

TIME: Salt lightly for a fortnight, then put in pickle for a month or 5 weeks.

METHOD

1. Lightly salt the hams for 2 weeks, rubbing in the salt.
2. Boil the ingredients for the pickle all together for 15 minutes.
3. Let it get cold.
4. Pour it over the hams.
5. Dry and smoke in stove or chimney of wood fire.

To Cure Hams

Mrs. Anger's Receipt, Burnham-on-Crouch

INGREDIENTS: Salt 1 lb.; coarse sugar 1 lb.; bay salt ¼ lb.; salt prunella 1 oz.; saltpetre 1 teaspoonful; vinegar ½ pint.

TIME: let them lie in the pickle a month, if large five weeks.

N.B.— *See* Whip Sillabubs, page 258.

To Pickle Hams

Colonel Wilson's 'excellent' receipt: Tendring Hall, Suffolk, 1857. Suffolk sweet-cured hams are famous.

INGREDIENTS: A leg of pork; salt of prunella 1 oz.; saltpetre 1½ oz.; coarse salt 1 lb.; bay salt 4 oz.; coarse sugar 1½ lb.; treacle ½ lb.

TIME: to remain in pickle one month; then smoke for three weeks.

METHOD

1. Rub the ham hard for an hour with the above ingredients well mixed.
2. Let the ham remain in the pickle one month.
3. Rub it as directed three times a week during the month.
4. Then smoke it for 3 weeks.

Hamburg Pickle for Beef, etc.

'This,' says Miss Anstey, 'is probably a German receipt, as one of my grand-uncles married a wife from Hamburg.'

INGREDIENTS: Water 6 quarts; common salt 9 lb.; coarse sugar ¾ lb.; saltpetre 6 oz.

TIME: The beef or tongues must be kept in this liquor 8 or 9 days.

METHOD

1. Boil all the ingredients together.
2. Skim clear.
3. When cold put in the beef or tongues.
4. Keep them well-covered with the liquor 8 or 9 days; they will then be fit for use but may be kept longer if wished.

N.B.—The liquor can be boiled and skimmed once a month, and used again and again, fresh being added to it when necessary.

Mrs. Barton's Recipe for Potting Char

1807

An Ulverston friend sends this receipt. Mrs. Barton was the wife of the Rector of Windermere at this period. 'Char is a fish chiefly remarkable for its scarceness,' writes Bickerdyke, sometime Angling Editor of *The Field*. 'He is a lake fish — much resembles trout, but is redder on the belly and has smaller scales — and generally more gorgeous in colouring. They are found in many lakes of the United Kingdom — in Loch Doon, Ayrshire; Loch Achilty, Ross-shire; Loch Knockie, Inverness-shire; The Tarff, Kircudbrightshire; Corry Lair; and in Lochs Dochart, Ericht and Fruchie. They are found in a number of lakes, large and small, in Ireland — in Lough Cona (for example); in Wales, and in the Cumberland and Westmorland lakes; in Goats Water, and Hawes Water as well as Windermere, Buttermere and Crummock. The American brook trout is a beautiful char.'

The fish are excellent eating, and potted char is a well-known delicacy. The friend to whom we owe the recipe says it is equally good for trout.

INGREDIENTS: Char or trout $7\frac{1}{2}$ lb. or 1 dozen fish; black pepper and salt; white pepper $1\frac{1}{2}$ oz.; cloves 6 drams; ground mace 2 drams clarified butter 2 lb.; cayenne pepper.

TIME: 12 hours to salt; 4 hours to bake.

METHOD

1. Clean your fish, head and tail them, lay them 12 hours in black pepper and salt, sprinkle inside and out.
2. Then season inside and out with the white pepper, cloves and mace.
3. Lay them in a baking dish one by one and barely cover with clarified butter.
4. Bake 4 hours very slowly.
5. When cooked lay them open one by one.
6. Take out the backbone and scrape with a knife point the thickest of the seasoning from the inside of them, and
7. Dredge a little cayenne pepper in them.
8. Have your pots dry, lay the fish in on their backs, side by side, head and tail.
9. Fill up the ends with small fish, and press all tightly down with your hands.
10. Then barely cover them with clarified butter and when it has well soaked in, quite cover them.

N.B. — $7\frac{1}{2}$ lb. fish is called a dozen, and 2 lb. of butter is required for covering this quantity. Some people clean, and lay in the bottom of the baking dish, the heads and tails as they keep the fish from burning; they are good to eat with the bones, but not to pot.

Watercress

Watercress in England is very good, and is specially cultivated for sale. It is most excellent for breakfast; the Greeks esteem it good for the brain. It contains iodine, iron phosphates, potash and other mineral salts.

One precaution must be observed: do not eat watercress gathered from a stream which runs by a meadow where sheep graze; it is not wholesome.

Fresh Tomatoes

It may not be generally known that one good-sized fresh uncooked tomato or orange a day will give a man as much vitamin C as he requires to keep in good health.

Honey and Marmalade

Serve in Michael Cardew Pottery, Winchcombe, Gloucestershire, as at the Lygon Arms, Broadway, Worcestershire.

Fresh Fruit for Breakfast

Grapefruit, oranges, bananas and apples can now be obtained in England all the year round.

Apricots, peaches, nectarines and plums in January, February and March from South Africa.

Cox's Orange pippins, October, November, December, January and February.

Pears and grapes from South Africa in February and March, and from New Zealand also in April and May.

Strawberries in June and July.

English cherries and raspberries in July and August.

English peaches and nectarines in July and August.

Mulberries in September.

Ripe English green figs in September, near the sea in Kent, Sussex and South Devon.

South African pineapples in August.

English greengages in August.

English melons in June, July, August, September and October.

HOME-MADE BREAD, CURRANT AND SPICE BREAD, TEA-CAKES, HOT AND COLD SCONES, WHIGS, HUFFKINS, MUFFINS, PIKELETS.

MANY of the old recipes require ale yeast, but this has been translated into its equivalent in compressed yeast, or what used to be called German yeast, and those who live in 'out of the way' places of the Empire may be glad to know that 'Royal Yeast Cakes' (a Canadian product) can be sent anywhere, properly packed for tropical and semi-tropical climates, by the Army and Navy Stores, 105 Victoria Street, London, S.W.1. General equivalents of both compressed yeast and yeast cakes will be found on page 63. It must always be remembered when using yeast that the flour and milk and everything employed must be lukewarm but not on any account too warm; both cold and heat kill yeast.

Anyone who wants first-hand up-to-date practical and scientific information on yeast foods and on chemical aerating agents such as soda, pearlash, baking powders, etc., cannot do better than consult Mr. Kirkland's *Modern Baker, Confectioner and Caterer* (1924). Mr. John Kirkland was for years Lecturer and Teacher of Bread-making, National Bakery School, London, and what he does not know on this subject is not worth knowing.

Baking powders are comparatively modern means of aeration. Mr. Kirkland says: 'It is safe to say about 80 years ago no chemicals except pearlash and ammonia were used by the baker as aerating agent.'

Pure cream of tartar and bicarbonate of soda combine better and are more convenient for this purpose than any other chemical, for the simple reason that 'when treated with water cream of tartar does not quickly enter into action with the soda; but when the goods are brought into the oven, the increased temperature facilitates the solution of the acid salt, and causes a rapid evolution of gas just at the time it is most necessary. Tartaric acid acts very quickly, and the bread, scones, etc., made with it must be put in the oven at once.' For this reason I generally use cream of tartar bought at a chemist's and bicarbonate of soda instead of baking powder.

For the same reason self-raising flour in which cream of tartar is an ingredient, is preferable to one in which tartaric acid or any cheaper agent is used. I know the formula employed by the Civil Service Supply Association is quite sound and their self-raising flour can be recommended because it is made with cream of tartar, not tartaric acid. Self-raising flour is simply plain flour to which chemical raising-agents are added. A word of warning is necessary here: unless otherwise stated, plain household flour is meant in all the recipes given, and to this any raising agent can be added; whereas none should be added to self-raising flour unless definitely stated in the recipe.

A complaint is frequently made that so many eggs are required in good English cookery and that these are expensive; but this is quite a wrong idea, the result of ignorance or wilful misrepresentation. There are of course recipes in which much cream, or butter and eggs are used, and some of these are useful for special occasions; but as a rule when we read of cakes requiring a number of eggs and so forth, if we examine the recipe we shall find that the amount of flour is correspondingly great. Families were larger one hundred years ago, and household staffs were more in number; therefore much greater batches of bread, scones, etc., had to be provided, and baking day was a serious business.

There is no reason, however, why we should not make some bread and scones at home for a treat, even if we live in a small town flat, or in the country where we can have only an oil stove with an oven; or merely a girdle over a wood fire made on a hearth or out of doors. Many of the recipes given are suitable for all these methods of baking.

In many houses and hotels in England all the bread and cakes, tea-breads, etc., are made at home; but as in most other cases it is still necessary to ask for what we want. The demand will create the supply.

Brewers' Yeast, Compressed Yeast and Yeast Cakes

2 tablespoonfuls of fresh brewers' yeast = 1 oz. compressed yeast.
1 oz. compressed yeast = 1 cake of Royal yeast.

Cream of Tartar and Bicarbonate of Soda

2 ordinary teaspoonfuls (or 4 level ones) of cream of tartar; half this quantity of bicarbonate of soda, and quarter the amount of salt, is sufficient to raise one pound of white household flour. Rice flour is simply mixed with these ingredients to make them keep well, i.e. prevent them 'caking' or getting lumpy. 3 ordinary teaspoonfuls of ground rice added to 2 ordinary teaspoonfuls of cream of tartar and 1 ordinary teaspoonful of bicarbonate of soda, sifted together three times makes a very good baking powder.

Baking Powder

6 teaspoonfuls of such a baking powder is equivalent to 2 ordinary teaspoonfuls of cream of tartar and 1 of bicarbonate of soda. Half a teaspoonful of salt must be used with it when mixing bread or cake unless otherwise stated.

Delicious Home-made Bread made with Yeast

Miss Veronica Cook, 1931

INGREDIENTS: Plain flour 3½ lb.; salt 2 teaspoonfuls; compressed yeast 1 oz.; sugar and salt 1 teaspoonful each to every lb. flour; warm milk and water, about 1¾ pint (half and half).

TIME: to rise until double its volume; to bake 30 to 45 minutes according to size of loaves in a hot oven.

METHOD

1. Warm all basins.
2. Mix the salt in with the flour in warm basin.
3. Cream the yeast with the sugar.
4. Add it to the milk and water.
5. Make a well in the middle of the flour, pour in the yeast mixture gradually and make into dough.
6. Knead for 15 minutes.
7. Divide and put into greased tins filling them half full.
8. Put to rise covered up in a warm place till the dough comes to the tops of the tins.
9. Then put in hot oven and bake till done.

N.B.—You can make sure when a loaf is cooked by putting a clean cloth on your left hand, turning the loaf out of the tin on to it and rapping it underneath with the knuckles; if it sounds hollow it is done.

Yeast Bread (another Recipe)

Somersetshire, 1892

INGREDIENTS: Plain flour 3 lb.; compressed yeast 1 oz. (or 2 tablespoonfuls of brewers' yeast); salt 2 teaspoonfuls; sugar 1 teaspoonful; tepid water 1½ pints.

TIME: to mix—10 minutes to rise; to knead, 10 minutes; to rise again, 30 minutes in summer and 1 hour in winter; and to bake 1 hour to 1¼ hours according to size of loaves.

METHOD

1. Mix the salt with half the flour.
2. Cream the yeast with the sugar and add it to a gill of tepid water (but be very careful the water is really tepid, neither hotter nor colder or your bread will be heavy).
3. Put the unsalted flour into a warmer (but not hot) mixing bowl.
4. Make a hole in the middle and pour in the yeast mixture.
5. Stir in enough flour to make a rather thick batter, cover with a cloth and stand it for 10 minutes near the fire or gas oven to rise.
6. Then add the remainder of the flour and rest of the water, and mix well until the flour is all mixed in.
7. Knead it well on a floured board for 10 minutes; put the dough back in the basin.
8. Cut it across the top in the form of a cross.
9. Cover it with a cloth and let it rise again for ½ an hour in summer and 1 hour in winter.
10. Divide the dough into as many portions as you need loaves.
11. Mould them into shape, and bake in a moderate oven from 1 hour to 1½ hours according to the size of the loaves.

Quickly-made Bread

1910

INGREDIENTS: Plain white flour ½ lb.; wholemeal ½ lb.; cream of tartar one teaspoonful; bicarbonate of soda 1 teaspoonful; salt ½ teaspoonful; castor sugar 1 teaspoonful; milk and water ½ pint.

TIME: to bake in moderately hot oven 40 to 45 minutes.

METHOD

1. Sift the cream of tartar, bicarbonate of soda, and salt with the white flour.
2. Mix it with the wholemeal flour and sugar.
3. Make into a firm dough with the water.
4. Knead lightly and put it into a greased tin smooth side uppermost.
5. Bake in a moderately hot oven.

Soda Bread

1904

INGREDIENTS: Plain white flour ¼ stone; sugar, salt, cream of tartar and bicarbonate of soda ½ oz. of each; buttermilk about 1 quart.

METHOD

1. Mix all the dry ingredients well together.
2. Make into a firm dough with the buttermilk.
3. Put on to a greased tin, and bake in hot oven.

Soda Bread Baked in a Frying-Pan

Mrs. Fowler, Preston, Lancashire, says when she was a child in Shropshire her grandmother used to make soda bread and bake it in a frying-pan as follows:

INGREDIENTS: Plain white flour 1 lb.; butter 2 oz.; bicarbonate of soda 1 teaspoonful, not too much or it will be bitter; cream of tartar 1 teaspoonful; salt ½ teaspoonful; milk, sour milk, or buttermilk, ½ pint.

METHOD

1. Rub the butter into the flour.
2. Sieve in the soda, cream of tartar and salt.
3. Make into a dough with the milk.
4. Rub a frying-pan over with a piece of mutton fat.
5. Make the dough into a flat loaf to fit the pan and cook it over the fire, cutting the bread into quarters and turning it until it is done.

Variations of Quickly-made Bread

1. The 'Quickly-made Bread' may be made richer by rubbing 1 or 2 or 3 oz. butter into the flour before mixing in the cream of tartar, etc., and by mixing with milk, sour milk or buttermilk, instead of milk and water.

2. This may be made into delicious nut bread by mixing a half cupful of broken nut meats in with the dry ingredients.

3. It may be turned into fruit bread by adding sultanas or currants, or stoned raisins instead of nuts; and (if liked) a little more sugar and a little spice.

N.B.—Nut bread and fruit bread should be made and baked the day before they are required.

Rye Bread

At one time visitors to Penrith were able to buy loaves of appetising rye bread, but of late years they have not been made for sale. They can be made at home from the following recipe:

INGREDIENTS: Rye flour 2½ lb.; wheat flour 2½ lb.; salt 1 oz.; yeast 1½ oz.; sugar 1 teaspoonful; water 1 quart at 104°F.

TIME: to rise 1 hour; then 30 minutes.

METHOD

1. Mix the rye and wheat flour and salt together.
2. Cream the yeast with the sugar.
3. Add the water and use it to make the flour into a dough.
4. Let it stand in front of a fire or heated gas oven for one hour.
5. Then knead well, and at the end of another half hour knead again.

Mr. Kirkland who gives this recipe says 'they are moulded round or oval, or long, and allowed to prove either upside down on cloths or on flour-dusted boards and covered over with cloths.'

They may be baked in a No. 7 Regulo 375°F. Junior New World Cooker.

Mr. Kirkland gives a recipe for another sort of rye bread which he says 'usually contained a small quantity of spice and was common as a kind of cheap gingerbread in Scotland many years ago, and may still be found in isolated places.'

It can be made by the following modern method:

Fruit or Caraway Rye Bread

INGREDIENTS: Rye flour 2½ lb.; wheat flour 2½ lb.; salt 1 oz.; golden syrup 3 oz.; yeast 2 oz.; sugar 1 teaspoonful; caraway ½ oz.; water 3 pints at 104°F.

TIME: 1 hour to rise in warm place; then 1 hour or 1½ hours to prove.

METHOD

1. Mix the two flours, the caraway seeds and the salt together.
2. Mix the syrup with the water.
3. Cream the yeast with the sugar and add that to the syrup and water.
4. Use the mixture to make the flour into a dough.
5. Leave it in a warm place for an hour.
6. Knead well.
7. Put into greased tins.
8. Leave to rise for 1½ hours.
9. Bake in a rather slow oven (No. 4 in the Junior New World cooker) or 335°F.

It should not be eaten new, but, like some gingerbread, keeps moist and soft if left out instead of being kept in a tin.

Sultanas and candied peel may be used instead of caraways.

Bran Brack

An Original Family Receipt, 1825

INGREDIENTS: Flour 3 lb.; castor sugar ½ lb.; eggs 3; caraway seeds 2 oz.; small beer yeast 2 tablespoonfuls; (1 oz. compressed yeast creamed with a little castor sugar and warm water can be substituted for this); butter 4 oz.; milk sufficient to make a light paste, about 1¼ pints, or rather less; but it is impossible to specify the exact quantity as some flour takes up more than others. Half this quantity will make a moderate sized cake.

TIME: three hours to rise; ½ hour to 'prove'; 1 to 2 hours to bake (in quick oven) according to size.

METHOD

1. Mix the flour, sugar and caraway seeds together.
2. Beat up the eggs.
3. Melt the butter in half a pint of hot milk, add it to the beaten-up eggs;
4. Measure it; you will want about 1¼ pints of liquid to make 3 lb. flour into a light dough, in addition to the yeast.
5. Cream the yeast with a little sugar and warm water.
6. Use it with the eggs, butter and milk to make the dry ingredients into a light paste.
7. Let it stand in a warm place for about 3 hours.
8. Then put it in a greased tin ready to bake.
9. Stand it in a warm place to 'prove' for half an hour before putting it in the oven.

Lancashire Bun Loaf

INGREDIENTS: Dough 2 lb.; raisins ½ lb. (currants ½ lb. added by some people); candied peel, preferably citron, 3 oz.; butter 6 oz.; mixed spice a saltspoonful; (some add salt and a little sugar).

TIME: to rise a little longer than bread and bake with the bread about 40 minutes to 1 hour, according to the size of the loaves.

METHOD

1. Melt the butter.
2. Work it in the dough.
3. Then the candied peel very finely chopped.
4. The raisins and spice.
5. Some people add salt and a little sugar.
6. Put the mixture into a buttered or otherwise greased tin.
7. Let it rise for rather longer than one would allow for bread.
8. Bake in the oven with the bread.

Yorkshire Currant Bread

This recipe was kindly sent by a B.B.C. listener, E. S.

INGREDIENTS: Flour, 1¾ lb.; lard 6 oz.; butter (or margarine) 6 oz.; currants 1 lb.; raisins 1 lb.; sugar ½ lb.; mixed peel 6 oz.; bicarbonate of soda 1½ teaspoonfuls; cream of tartar 3 teaspoonfuls; salt 1 teaspoonful; treacle 2 tablespoonfuls; eggs 3, and a little milk.

TIME: to bake about 1 to 1½ hours, according to size of loaves, in moderate oven.

68

METHOD

1. Rub the butter and lard into the flour.
2. Mix in the soda, cream of tartar and salt.
3. Add the currants washed and picked.
4. The raisins stoned and chopped.
5. The sugar.
6. And the peel chopped.
7. Mix well together.
8. Then blend with the treacle melted.
9. And the eggs well beaten with a little milk, say about ½ pint. Some flour takes up more moisture than others, therefore it is not possible to be definite.

N.B.—This quantity makes 3 loaves, and this bread improves by keeping. Never cut until 2 days after it has been baked. If when taken out of the oven it is wrapped in a hot cloth or blanket the crust will be soft.

Fruit Bread

As made at Boston, Lincolnshire, E. Cullen

INGREDIENTS: Flour 1½ lb.; clarified dripping ¼ lb.; moist sugar ¼ lb.; currants ¼ lb.; raisins ¼ lb.; mixed peel cut small 2 oz.; compressed yeast 1 oz.; milk 1 pint.

TIME: ½ hour to rise; 2 hours to bake.

METHOD

1. Rub the fat into the flour.
2. Clean the currants.
3. Stone the raisins.
4. Cut the peel small, and add the sugar, currants, raisins, peel, to the flour.
5. Mix well.
6. Cream the yeast with a little sugar, warm the milk and add that.
7. Use this to make the dry ingredients into a dough.
8. Divide into four.
9. Put into warmed slightly greased tins.
10. Leave to rise by the fire ½ hour.
11. Bake 2 hours in a moderate oven.

Gipsy Bread or Spiced Bread

Given by Miss Chappell, Dipley, Hartley Wintney, Hants, to Mrs. (Dorothy) Allhusen

INGREDIENTS: Flour 1¼ lb.; brown sugar ½ lb.; sultanas ½ lb.; grated peel 2 oz.; mixed spice ½ teaspoonful; ground ginger, a good teaspoonful; black treacle ¾ lb.; eggs 3; milk 1½ gills; ½ teaspoonful bicarbonate of soda. Two good-sized cake tins greased and floured, each large enough to hold 2 lb. of cake.

TIME: about 2 hours to bake.

METHOD

1. Mix dry ingredients — flour, sugar, sultanas (cleaned and dried), peel, spice, ginger – all together.
2. Warm the treacle with 1 gill of the milk.
3. Whisk the eggs well.
4. Whisk in the treacle and milk.
5. Mix this with the dry ingredients.
6. Finally, when the cake is well mixed, dissolve the ½ teaspoonful of bi-carbonate of soda in the remaining ¼ gill of milk and sprinkle it all over the cake batter.
7. Mix quickly and well so that the soda is well incorporated, and put half the quantity into each tin.
8. Bake in a slow oven till done. It will take at least 2 hours.

Yorkshire Spiced Loaf

A very old receipt

This comes by way of Ross-on-Wye.

INGREDIENTS : Flour 1 lb.; butter 4 oz.; currants ½ lb.; raisins 2 oz.; raw sugar 4 oz.; treacle 1 oz.; eggs 1; compressed yeast 1 oz.; lemon peel and candied peel to taste; new milk to mix, about ½ pint.

TIME : bake about 2 hours.

METHOD

1. Rub butter into flour.
2. Add sugar, currants and raisins stoned and well-chopped, also candied lemon and orange peel.
3. Mix well.
4. Warm treacle and milk separately.
5. Dissolve the yeast in half the warm milk.
6. Beat up the rest of the milk with the egg.
7. Now stir the warm treacle into the dry ingredients, then the egg and milk, and finally the milk and yeast. Beat well, put into a greased bread tin and bake in a very moderate oven very slowly and carefully. This need not be put to 'prove' as it will rise in the rather slow oven.

Ripon Recipes

These have been very kindly lent by Mr. Herbert M. Bower who retains the copyright of all the recipes he sends of the good things familiar to him in his old home at Ripon: Christmas Bread, Christmas Spice Bread (like Yule cake); Plum Cake or Christmas Cake; Frumenty for Christmas Eve and New Year's Eve; Parkin for November 5th; Wilfra Tarts for Wilfra or Wilfred week in August, and, for all seasons, Ginger Cake. The other recipes will be found in the sections to which they belong.

Ripon Christmas Bread

INGREDIENTS: Bread dough 2 lb.; lard 6 oz.; raisins 4 oz.; candied peel 2 oz.; sugar 4 oz.; cleaned currants ½ lb.; allspice ½ teaspoonful.
TIME: bake 2 hours in moderate oven.

METHOD

1. Mix the lard into the dough with the hand, then—
2. All the other ingredients.
3. Mix very well.
4. Put in greased bread tins.
5. Put to rise in warm place.
6. Then bake 2 hours in moderate oven.

Ripon Spice Bread

Like Yule Cake

Mr. Herbert M. Bower's recipe for Christmas Eve and New Year's Eve.
INGREDIENTS: Bread dough 2 lb.; lard ½ lb.; raisins ½ lb.; currants ½ lb.; sugar ½ lb.; candied peel 2 oz.; allspice 1 teaspoonful.
TIME: to rise 1 hour; bake in slow oven 1 hour.

METHOD

1. Melt the lard in a stewpan, and then
2. Mix it well into the dough with the hand.
3. Add the other ingredients.
4. When well mixed place it before the fire in a bread tin, and let it rise for 1 hour.
5. Then bake in a slow oven for about 1 hour or longer.

Manchets

Gervase Markham, Nottinghamshire, 1615

'Your best and principal bread is Manchet, which you shall bake in this manner: First, your meal being ground upon the black stones, if it be possible, which makes the whitest flower, and passed through the finest boulting cloth, you shall put it into a clean kimnel, and opening the flower hollow in the midst, put into it of the best ale-brew, the quantity of 3 pints to a bushel of meal, and some salt to season it with; then put in your liquor reasonable warm, and knead it very well together with both your hands, and through the brake, or for want thereof, fold it in a cloth, and with your feet tread it a good space together, then letting it lye an hour or thereabouts to swel, take it forth and mould it into Manchets round and flat, scotch them about the waste to give it leave to rise, and prick it with your knife in the top, and so put it into the oven, and bake it with a gentle heat.'

71

Manchetts for the Queen's Maides

From Ordinances made at Eltham in the 17th year of King Henry VIII
'In the morning one chet lofe, one manchet, one gallon of ale; for afterwards one manchett, one gallon of ale; for after supper one chet lofe, one manchet, two gallons of ale, dim'pitcher of wine.'

Apparently only dukes and duchesses, and such people, the master of the household, clerks of the kitchen and maids of honour, were served with manchets. The date is 1526, and this information is taken from the Harleian M.S., No. 642, British Museum. It is inserted because a correspondent wished to know when manchets were served at Court and in whose reign.

Lady Arundel's Manchet
1676

'Take a bushel of fine wheat flour, twenty eggs, and three pounds fresh butter, salt and balm, as to the ordinary manchet, temper it with new milk pretty hot; then let it lie the space of half an hour to rise so you may work it up into bread, and bake it and let not your oven be too hot.'

1932 RECIPE

INGREDIENTS: Fine wheat flour 2 lb.; salt $\frac{1}{2}$ oz.; butter 2 oz.; egg 1; new milk (warm, not hot) 1 pint; compressed yeast 1 oz.; castor sugar 1 teaspoonful.

TIME: to rise, 30 minutes; to bake about 20 minutes according to size of manchets.

METHOD

1. Mix the salt in the flour, rub in the butter.
2. Cream the yeast with the sugar.
3. Add it to $\frac{3}{4}$ pint of the warm milk.
4. Beat up the egg and mix with the yeast and milk.
5. Make a well in the flour, pour in the yeast mixture, and mix into dough.
6. Shape the dough into small flat round cakes about $\frac{1}{4}$ inch thick and $3\frac{1}{2}$ inches across.
7. Mark them across with lines to form diamonds 1 inch in length.
8. Put to rise for 30 minutes.
9. Then bake in moderate oven as above.

Cornish Manchants
Penzance, 1931

Miss M. W. Rogers (Marazion) writes:
'As to Manchets. In this part of the world, a "manchant" is a loaf of bread shaped by hand, not baked in a tin. The term is still used by Penzance bakers, and the derivative is obvious.'

Manchets Fine

Sent by Miss Ogleby, Washington, Ventnor, Isle of Wight.

For soups, and stews and choice ragouts Nell Cook was famous still;
Her manchets fine were quite divine, her cakes were nicely brown'd;
Her boil'd and roast they were the boast
Of all the 'Precincts' round. From *The Ingoldsby Legends*.

Huffkins

An East Kent Tea-bread

All over England there are to be bought small traditional tea-breads similar in type but differing more or less in varying districts.

There are for example: Surrey Manchets still made at Guildford and Chertsey; Cornish splits; Devonshire Chudleighs; Bath whigs; Hawkshead wiggs; Yorkshire oven cakes; Norfolk rusks; Kentish huffkins to be found at Maidstone and Elham, near Canterbury, and many others. There are almost if not quite as many varieties of whigs or wiggs (as they are spelt in different districts) as there are of Scotch scones — the plain lighter variety of which they much resemble. They are very good indeed eaten either hot or cold; and are quite easily made.

Huffkins are simply thick flat oval cakes of light bread; with a hole in the middle:

INGREDIENTS: Plain flour 1 lb.; lard 1 oz.; sugar 1 teaspoonful; salt ½ teaspoonful; compressed yeast 1 oz.; about 2½ gills of warm milk and water. It is impossible to give the exact quantity of liquid as some flours take up more than others.

TIME: to rise 1 hour; time to 'prove' ½ hour; to bake 15 to 20 minutes according to size in a fairly hot oven (Regulo No. 7 in the Junior New World cooker is a good heat 375° to 385°F.).

METHOD

1. Warm the mixing basin.
2. Sift the flour and salt together into one basin.
3. Rub in the lard.
4. Cream the yeast with the sugar in another basin.
5. Add the lukewarm milk and water to it.
6. And with it make the flour into a light dough.
7. Cut a cross on it and stand it in a warm place for one hour to rise.
8. Knead well.
9. Divide up into flat oval cakes about ¼ inch thick; make a hole in the middle.
10. Flour well.
11. Place on warm tin.
12. Allow to 'prove' in warm place till well risen.
13. Then bake in hot oven from 10 to 20 minutes according to size.
14. Take out and wrap in a warm blanket till cold; this keeps the outside soft and tender as it should be.

[N.B.—'Self-baster' meat tin (*see* p. 146) is ideal for baking huffkins, and indeed bread and cakes of many kinds.—Ed.]

Cornish Splits

Mrs. R. Bennett's Recipe

INGREDIENTS: Flour 3 lb.; butter ½ lb.; lard 2 oz.; yeast 2 oz.; milk 1 gill; salt 1 teaspoonful, sugar 1 teaspoonful, warm water ½ pint.

TIME: sufficient to rise twice. Approximately 1½ hours.

METHOD

1. Put yeast in basin with sugar, then add the warm water and add a tablespoonful of flour.
2. Cover with a cloth and leave to rise in a warm place.
3. Put milk, butter and lard in a saucepan to get warm.
4. Warm the flour and put in a mixing bowl.
5. Make a well in the middle and pour in the milk, etc., and yeast mixture.
6. Mix all into a nice soft dough and put to rise as before.
7. When well risen, knead and place on baking tin in small rounds and let them rise again.
8. Then bake in a moderate oven.
9. Take out and rub over while hot with a slightly buttered paper, to give them a gloss.
10. Place them all on a warm blanket or cloth, and cover lightly with the same. This makes the outside soft instead of crisp.

Devonshire Chudleighs

These are made in the same way but smaller.

Whigs 1826

Some plain rolls known as Hawkshead wigs or whigs and a cake known as Hawkshead cake exactly similar to those eaten by Wordsworth when he was a boy at school are still made and sold at Hawkshead; some were shown at the first English Folk Cookery Exhibition held in London on January 16th, 1931.

The following recipe makes whigs slighty richer than the Hawkshead rolls and more like those made and sold at the Red House Restaurant, Bath.

INGREDIENTS: Flour 2 lb.; 1 teaspoonful salt; butter 4 oz.; cream or milk about ½ pint; warm water ¼ pint; castor sugar 1 oz.; compressed yeast 1 oz.; nutmeg; ground mace and cloves; caraway seeds ¼ oz.; ½ lb. sugar.

METHOD

1. Mix the salt with the flour.
2. Rub in the butter.
3. Cream the yeast with the sugar, add the warm cream (or milk) and water.
4. Use it to make the flour into a light paste.
5. Set it to rise.
6. When it is double its bulk, add the nutmeg, mace, cloves, caraway seeds and sugar.
7. Work all in.
8. Roll out tolerably thin.
9. Make up into any shape you please (they are, says the recipe, usually made into large round cakes, crossed so as to be easily divided into quarters).
10. When made up put them on tin plates.
11. Set them before the fire.
12. Or place them in front of the oven till they rise again.
13. Then bake in a quick oven.

N.B.—Dough will rise quite well on the rack of a gas stove or in front of a gas oven.

Scarborough Muffins

From the manuscript of Miss Wettin, the celebrated London confectioner.
(Lent by Lady Gomme, President of the English Folk Cookery Association.)

I

INGREDIENTS: Eggs 2; skim milk 1 pt. (16 oz.); new yeast 2 tablespoonfuls (compressed yeast 1 oz.) flour ¼ peck (3½ lb.); a little salt.
TIME: about 1 hour to rise and 20 minutes to bake.

METHOD

1. Make milk lukewarm.
2. Beat in the yeast, which must first be creamed with a little sugar in the usual manner if using compressed yeast.
3. Beat up the eggs and blend them with the milk and yeast.
4. Mix the salt with the flour.
5. Lightly blend with the milk, etc.
6. Knead well together.
7. Let it stand half an hour before the fire.
8. Then cut it into cakes.
9. And put them for a short time before the fire to rise.
10. Then put them in a hot oven.

N.B.—Yeast cakes can of course be used instead of either new yeast or compressed yeast (*see* p. 63).

II

To Make Scarborough Muffins

COMMONLY CALLED FRENCH ROLLS
Miss Bludworth's receipt; same MS. book.

INGREDIENTS: Flour 2 quarts; (1¾ lb.); new milk 1 pint (16 oz.); eggs 2 or 3; yeast 2 tablespoonfuls (or compressed yeast 1 oz.); a little salt.
TIME: to rise ½ hour.

METHOD

1. Dry the flour well and mix in the salt.
2. Warm the milk.
3. Stir in the yeast.
4. Beat the eggs and add them to the milk, etc.
5. Blend this with the flour using the hand.
6. Cut it round into cakes.
7. And let it stand half an hour at the fire.
8. Then put them in a hot oven.

N.B.—These are excellent breakfast rolls.

How to Serve Muffins

'A pikelet, I believe,' writes Mr. Dupuis Brown in 1931, 'is only the Yorkshire term for "crumpet." But I should like to draw attention to the old method of toasting the muffin in the North of England, slightly opening its joint all round before toasting it both front and back; then tearing it open and buttering the inside halves liberally. I have seen them served this way in some of the London Clubs, but in all the teashops where I have ordered muffins it was toasted on the inside, thus causing it to be tough, leathery and indigestible.'

(Muffins are served in the correct manner at the National Liberal Club, London.)

Recipe for Muffins, 1826

INGREDIENTS: Flour 2½ lb.; water 1 pint (16 oz.); milk ½ pint and ½ a gill (or 10 liquid ounces altogether); salt ½ oz.; sugar ¼ oz.; compressed yeast 1 oz.

TIME: 2 hours to rise and 'prove.' Time to bake, 8 to 10 minutes.

METHOD

Make into a very soft dough,
1. By mixing the flour and salt together.
2. Creaming the yeast with the sugar.
3. Mixing the water and milk to a lukewarm temperature.
4. Use to mix flour.
5. Knead the dough well.
6. Place in a warm place for 1 hour to rise.
7. Then knead again very well indeed, dipping the hands from time to time in warm water to keep them as free from the dough as possible.
8. Leave to rise again for half an hour.
9. Then fill a wooden baker's tray or lid of wooden box with flour to about one inch deep, warm it, make holes in the flour about 2 inches across.
10. Drop about 2½ oz. of the soft dough into each and leave to prove for another half hour.
11. Then carefully lift off each one on to a moderately warm girdle or iron plate – a strong thick frying-pan will do, putting the side that was on top on the girdle first.
12. When this is cooked, turn the muffin and cook the other side.
13. When properly cooked they should be about 3 inches across and about 2 inches thick.
14. Some people bake these in rings but this is not so satisfactory.

Oatmeal Cakes, 1826

'These are made in the same way as muffins, only substituting fine oat-meal for flour; bake them the same, and observe never to use a knife for either, as that will make them heavy and spoil them; but scotch them round the waist, and when toasted crisp on both sides pull them open with the thumb and finger, and they will appear like a honeycomb; put in as much butter as is requisite; close and set them before the fire; when the butter is melted on one side, turn them that it may spread on the other; only use a knife to cut them across.'

Sally Lunn's Cake

VERY GOOD

From Miss Wettin's manuscript.

INGREDIENTS: The finest flour 1 lb.; eggs 3 yolks and 2 whites; good small beer yeast (or its equivalent 1 oz. in compressed yeast) 3 large tablespoonfuls; good rich cream (or evaporated milk) ½ pint (8oz.); a little salt; warm water sufficient to make into dough; butter half a pound, to spread on the cake.

TIME: to rise about 1½ hours, to bake 15 minutes.

METHOD

1. Beat the eggs and strain them.
2. If using compressed yeast cream it with sugar.
3. Then whisk the eggs up well with the yeast and cream.
4. And as much warm water as will lightly wet the flour and all the above ingredients well together.
5. With a light hand add a little salt.
6. Before you knead it, set it before the fire to rise for about 1½ hours.
7. Make up the dough into a thick flat round cake like a batch loaf.
8. Put it into a hot oven.
9. Bake it for about half an hour, but keep your eye on it as it may be done before.
10. When done scotch yourcake round the waist and tear it open.
11. Butter it to your taste and put it in the oven again to dissolve your butter thoroughly.

N.B.—Half a pound of butter is sufficient to butter this cake. [It is not correct to use butter for Sally Lunn: half a pound of scalded cream should be used instead.—ED.]

Teacakes

Lancashire

INGREDIENTS: Flour 1 lb.; salt 1 teaspoonful; lard 2 oz.; compressed yeast 1 oz.; lukewarm milk ½ pint; sugar to cream the yeast 2 teaspoonfuls.
TIME: 10—20 minutes.

METHOD

1. Warm the flour slightly, but don't make it too hot.
2. Mix in the salt and rub in the lard.
3. Cream the yeast with the sugar.
4. Mix it with the lukewarm milk and beat it smoothly into the flour with a wooden spoon.
5. Then set in a warm place to rise.
6. When well risen turn on to floured board.
7. Knead slightly.
8. Cut into 8 pieces.
9. And make into round pieces.
10. Lay on a greased and floured tin.
11. And set near the fire to rise again for about 15 minutes.
12. Bake in a moderate oven 10—15 minutes.

N.B.—Immediately after taking from the oven, rub over with a buttered paper, and cover with a light clean blanket; this gives them a soft skin.

For a change use currants and a little sugar and an egg and, if liked, a little spice may be added after the first rising. In this case, however, the teacakes must be baked in greased tins.

West Riding Oatcake or Riddle Bread

(Can be bought [1931] from Mr. James Leach, oatcake baker, 24, Hardcastle's Yard, High Street, Skipton, Yorkshire; business established 1858.)

INGREDIENTS: Fine Yorkshire oatmeal, a little yeast, salt and water. This is made into a thick cream and thrown in a narrow strip on to the 'bak' stone' when the steam immediately puffs it up, and this, Mrs. Marshall, of Skelwith Fold, says is why the under part is smooth and the top rough. When baked it is damp and flexible and is hung on the wooden clothes rail before the fire to dry or on lines across the kitchen ceiling. It must be crisped quickly immediately before it is to be eaten.

'It has then,' says a member of an old Yorkshire family, 'a most characteristic slightly bitter and very appetising flavour, and a most agreeable texture all its own.'

'It can be used to soups, fish, fowl, cheese, butter, or any kind of meat in place of any other kind of bread or biscuit.'

Derbyshire Oatcake

As made in 1811 and still made to-day, 1931

INGREDIENTS: Fine oatmeal 2 lb.; water 1 quart (32 oz.); barm, or compressed yeast, ½ oz.

TIME: leave mixture to stand for 2 hours before baking.

METHOD

1. Put barm or yeast into the water which must be warm.
2. Put all into the meal.
3. Mix by hand till smooth.
4. Leave mixture to stand for 2 hours before making.
5. Pour a cupful on to a hot stone (a baking tin or frying-pan, if no stone is available).
6. Turn the cake so that it is done on both sides.
7. When cold cut across into four pieces, cut and butter them.

Wheaten Meal Scones

One of the many good things made at Boston, Lincolnshire, sent by Miss Cullen, of Dundee.

INGREDIENTS: Wheaten meal ¾ lb.; flour ¼ lb.; cream of tartar ¾ teaspoonful; bicarbonate of soda ¾ teaspoonful; ½ teaspoonful of salt; butter 1 to 2 oz.; sour milk sufficient to mix.

TIME: to bake 20 minutes.

METHOD

1. Sieve the dry ingredients into a basin.
2. Rub in butter until free from lumps.
3. Make a well in centre, and pour in enough sour milk to make a softish dough.
4. Turn out lightly on to a floured board and form into a round.
5. Mark it across in four, place on greased baking sheet.
6. And bake in a moderate oven for about 20 minutes. When nearly ready break into 4 pieces, brush them over with milk or beaten egg, dry in the oven for a few more minutes, and serve hot.

Wholemeal Scones

The Fanny Calder School of Cookery, Liverpool, 1904

INGREDIENTS: Wholemeal 1 lb.; white flour 4 oz.; lard 2½ oz.; castor sugar 2 oz.; egg 1; pinch of salt; cream of tartar 1 large teaspoonful; carbonate of soda ¼ teaspoonful; buttermilk ½ pint.

TIME: 20—30 minutes according to size and thickness in a quick oven.

METHOD

1. Rub the lard into the white flour.
2. Blend it with the wholemeal, sugar, salt, cream of tartar and carbonate of soda.
3. Mix well.
4. Beat up the egg.
5. Make into a light dough with one egg and about ½ pint buttermilk.
6. Form into flat rounds, brush with egg.
7. Bake in a quick oven.

Cream Scones

North Country

INGREDIENTS: Flour 1 lb.; salt 1 teaspoonful; cream of tartar 1 teaspoonful; bicarbonate of soda ½ teaspoonful; eggs 2; cream or evaporated milk ¼ pint; milk, a little if needed; butter 2 oz.

TIME: about 15 minutes.

METHOD

1. Rub the butter into the flour.
2. Add salt and cream of tartar and bicarbonate of soda.
3. Beat the eggs and mix with the cream.
4. Mix into the flour to make a light dough using a little milk if necessary (some flours take up more moisture than others).
5. Turn on to a floured board.
6. Knead lightly.
7. Roll out ¾ inch thick.
8. Cut into rounds with a cutter.
9. Place on a greased and floured tin.
10. Prick top to prevent blistering.
11. Bake in a quick oven about 15 minutes and serve cold.

Oatmeal Scones

Boston, Lincolnshire, Miss Cullen

INGREDIENTS: Flour 7 oz.; oatmeal 3½ oz.; sugar 3 oz.; butter 3 oz. lard 1 oz.; baking powder 1 teaspoonful; egg 1; a pinch of salt; ¼ cup cold water.

TIME: to bake 10 to 15 minutes.

METHOD

1. Mix dry ingredients together.
2. Melt the butter with the lard; mix well in.
3. Beat the egg in the cold water.
4. Mix well in.
5. Put dough on floured board.
6. Roll out thin.
7. Cut out rounds about 2 inches across. Bake on a well-greased tin in a moderate oven.

Maize or Indian Meal Scones

1904

INGREDIENTS: Maize or Indian meal ¼ lb.; white flour ¼ lb.; lard 1 oz.; sugar 1 teaspoonful; cream of tartar ½ teaspoonful; bicarbonate of soda ¼ teaspoonful; milk ¼ pint.

TIME: 20—30 minutes.

METHOD

1. Rub the lard into the flour.
2. Mix it with the meal.
3. Add sugar, salt, cream of tartar and bicarbonate of soda.
4. Moisten with milk.
5. Knead well.
6. Cut into 4.
7. Place on a floured tin in a quick oven till nicely browned.

Cornish Potato Cake

1852

INGREDIENTS: Boiled potatoes 6; flour 1½ lb.; dripping ½ lb.; currants ½ lb.; egg 1; milk ¼ pint (4 oz.); cream of tartar 1 teaspoonful; bicarbonate soda ½ teaspoonful.

METHOD

1. Rub the dripping into the flour.
2. Add the rest of the dry ingredients and mix well.
3. Mash the potatoes and mix them in.
4. Make into a dough with the egg and milk.
5. Roll out one inch thick and bake till brown.

Devonshire Potato Cakes

One of Mrs. Seldon's excellent recipes

INGREDIENTS: Boiled and mashed potatoes 1½ lb.; flour ½ lb.; dripping 6 oz.; sugar 2 oz.; currants 2 oz.; egg 1, and a little salt.

TIME: 15 to 20 minutes.

METHOD

1. Rub the dripping into the flour.
2. Add the other ingredients.
3. Roll out, cut into rounds.
4. Bake in a hot oven.
5. Or if preferred fry the cakes.
6. Serve hot for tea.

Dorset Apple Cake

Miss Annette Vipan says: 'I send the recipe of the apple cake as it was given me by a farmer's wife in this village, North Chideock, Bridport. The quantities are my own as she weighed nothing.'

RECIPE

INGREDIENTS: Apple and flour equal quantities; fat half the quantity, sugar half the quantity; salt, a pinch; baking powder 3 teaspoonfuls to the lb. of flour; milk enough to make a firm dough.

TIME: To bake ¾ to 1 hour.

METHOD

1. Rub the fat into the flour.
2. Add the salt and the baking powder.
3. Mix the sugar with the pared and chopped apple.
4. Stir into the flour mixture.

5. Make into a firm dough with the milk.
6. Make into a flat cake about ¾ inch thick.
7. Bake in a round flat tin ½ to 1 hour.
8. Cut open, butter well, and eat hot.

[N.B.—Miss Vipan says: 'Some make it in a cake tin 2—3 inches deep and eat it hot or cold with butter or cream. Also I am told they make it with gooseberries instead of apple, but I have not met with it. Some put in currants, but I think it is nicest as a tea cake, and it heats up well the next day.'—ED.]

Lancashire Potato Cakes

Mrs. A. L. Pollitt's recipe

INGREDIENTS: Cold potatoes, preferably mashed, 6 oz.; flour 3 oz.; butter 2½ oz.; salt, a pinch (about ¼ teaspoonful); baking powder half a teaspoonful.

METHOD

1. Put all together in mixing bowl.
2. And work well together with the hand.
3. Roll out ½ inch thick making round cakes size of small plates.

4 Pinch the edges.
5. Bake in a good oven turning the cakes to brown.

Eat them the same day.

Norfolk Rusks

'Very nice for tea, buttered, and will keep (in closed tin) fresh for a week or two.'

Mrs. K. M. SLAYMAKER, N. Topham, Diss, Norfolk.

INGREDIENTS: Plain flour ½ lb.; butter ¼ lb.; 1 egg; pinch of salt; pinch of baking powder. Milk if needed.

TIME: to bake 20 to 25 minutes all told.

METHOD

1. Rub the butter into the flour.
2. Mix in the salt and baking powder.
3. Make into a stiff paste with the egg well beaten and if required a little milk.
4. Roll out about half inch thick or a little more.

5. Cut into rounds with small cutter.
6. Bake in fairly hot oven on a baking tin until risen.
7. Take out, pull in half and put back, rough side up, to brown. Should be nice and crisp-looking on the uneven side.

Suffolk Cakes

This recipe from Mrs. Anstey's receipt book was obtained by her when staying with relatives in Suffolk before her marriage in 1859.

INGREDIENTS: Eggs 4; fine white sugar ½ lb.; lemon, the grated rind of half; butter ¼ lb.; flour ¼ lb.

TIME: to bake about 15 to 20 minutes in a quick oven.

METHOD

1. Beat the whites and yolks of the eggs separately; the whites to be beaten to a very stiff froth, and
2. the well-beaten yolks added.
3. Sift in the sugar.
4. Add the grated rind of half a lemon.
5. Beat in the butter which must be warmed.
6. Sift in the flour.
7. Bake in nests of small moulds, or small separate tins.

Cumberland Girdle Cakes

This is another of the excellent recipes sent from Ross-on-Wye.

INGREDIENTS: Flour 3 oz.; butter 1 oz.; salt, a pinch; baking powder saltspoonful; milk or cream to make into a dough that will roll out.

METHOD

1. Rub the butter into the flour.
2. Mix in the salt.
3. Make into a dough with milk or cream.
4. Roll out thin.
5. Bake in heavy iron frying-pan or on Scotch girdle, rubbed with a bit of mutton fat.
6. When brown one side turn over on other.
7. Cut into squares.
8. Split and butter.
9. Serve on hot dish for tea.

Singin' Hinnie

Miss Bright, Northern Counties School of Cookery, 1929

INGREDIENTS: Plain flour 1 lb.; lard 4 oz.; butter 4 oz.; salt ¼ teaspoonful; cream of tartar ½ teaspoonful, bicarbonate of soda ¼ teaspoonful, currants 6 oz.; milk, sufficient to make a stiff paste. Butter to spread.

METHOD

1. Rub the butter and lard into the flour.
2. Mix in the salt, cream of tartar and bicarbonate of soda.
3. Add the currants well cleaned.
4. Make into a firm dough with the milk.
5. Shape it into a round.
6. Roll it out ¼ inch thick.
7. Rub a girdle with a bit of mutton fat and make it hot.
8. Place the cake on it.
9. Cook till the under side is brown.
10. Then turn it with a broad-bladed knife (in northern counties they use a wooden spurtle) and cook the other side.
11. Turn it again to heat it well through, cut into convenient pieces, split, butter, and serve piping hot.

Scotch Pancakes

These are the delicious, soft 'flannel' scones that are so good to eat cold spread with butter. Mrs. R. Bennett's recipe is excellent. Girdles in varying sizes can be bought at the Army and Navy Stores, and the Civil Service Supply Association.

INGREDIENTS: Flour plain 2 teacupfuls (½ pint, 7 oz.); bicarbonate of soda ½ a small teaspoonful; cream of tartar 1 small teaspoonful; salt ¼ teaspoonful; eggs 2; milk ¼ pint.

METHOD

1. Sift the flour, soda, cream of tartar and salt all together.
2. Beat up the eggs well.
3. Then beat them up with the milk.
4. And mix them with the flour to make a thick batter; as the size of eggs varies, and some flour takes up more moisture than others it is difficult to give the exact measure of the liquid required, so don't use too much of it as the batter must be thick.
5. Grease the girdle well with butter.
6. Don't have it too hot.
7. Drop the batter on it in rounds.
8. When browned on one side turn over and brown on the other.

Pikelets or Girdle Cakes

North Country

INGREDIENTS: Flour ½ lb.; salt ½ teaspoonful; castor sugar 2 teaspoonfuls; cream of tartar 1 teaspoonful; carbonate of soda ½ teaspoonful; egg 1; milk ¼ pt.; water ¼ pt.

TIME: 8—10 minutes.

METHOD

1. Put all the dry ingredients into a basin and mix well.
2. Separate the yolk from the white of the egg and beat each separately.
3. Beat the yolk in with the milk and water.
4. And use it to make the flour into a batter.
5. Fold in the well-whisked white of egg.
6. Rub the girdle over with a piece of mutton fat.
7. Make it hot.
8. Pour the batter on in tablespoonfuls.
9. When brown on one side turn with a knife and brown the other.
10. Butter and serve very hot.

Girdle Scones

Miss Naismith, Liverpool, 1904

INGREDIENTS: Flour ½ lb.; butter or lard 2 oz.; cream of tartar 1 teaspoonful; bicarbonate of soda ½ teaspoonful; salt ¼ teaspoonful; sugar 1 oz.; milk ¼ pint.

TIME: to bake on girdle 10—15 minutes.

METHOD

1. Rub butter or lard into flour.
2. Mix in the other dry ingredients.
3. Make into a fairly soft dough with the milk, if necessary adding a little more.
4. Roll and cut into small rounds (this quantity should make 12).
5. Rub a hot girdle with a piece of mutton fat.
6. Bake the scones on it, turning frequently for 10—15 minutes.
7. Split and butter – serve hot.

III

LUNCHEON, DINNER AND SUPPER
DISHES

THE variety of food served in England for luncheon, dinner and supper is so great that it is impossible here to give any but a few examples of each class or type.

We are told we have no special soup: we have a great number, both clear and thick, but some of the richer heavier ones such as our famous hare soup should never be served to preface even a small modern dinner of four courses. It is a meal in itself and a very good one; nothing could be better for luncheon on a cold November day; and it will not be found too heavy even in town if followed by nothing more substantial than apple pie or apple fritters, or a salad, or even by an omelet, although this is not such a good gastronomic contrast as a salad, unless we can have one stuffed with mushrooms or tomatoes. It is a mistake to say we can't make omelets in England. The best I ever tasted — a perfect one! — was made at Stoodleigh Rectory in the eighteen-nineties and served for luncheon. It was not what is known as a French *omelette*, nor exactly American, but a cross between the two: light and puffy — but creamy in the middle more like those served in Holland.

Another good English luncheon dish is curry, especially prawn, or fish curry of the Malay type. The pity is we don't always take the trouble to make it properly, or cook its bowl of rice as it should be cooked.

Even if one holds a brief for English cookery at its best this does not mean that its advocates must maintain that English cooks are always right or have nothing to learn.

There is no doubt that English cookery to-day is not what it should be, but this is because we have neglected the preparation of our traditional dishes or allowed them to be cooked by foreigners who, however good they may be in their own particular line cannot be expected to excel in preparing another nation's dishes. Especially when they have not the remotest idea what the dishes should be or how good they can be. As Mr. P. Mortor

Shand justly says, we have lost our own good cookery and have not acquired really good French cookery in its place—merely an international compromise which is deplorable.

Many have never seen good English cookery at all; others know it only in a degenerate form. It is absurd to think we can recover our lost prestige by asking foreign cooks to teach us.

Exhibitions and dinners of correctly cooked and served food are necessary to show us how English dishes should be cooked and served. A foreign cook with the best will to please will turn an Old English trifle into a French *gâteau*, because he has never seen the real thing. We should do the same ourselves with foreign cookery.

One thing is certain when we do find English cookery correctly prepared: it is the best and wholesomest in the world, because it is the most simple and retains the delicious flavour of food noted for its excellence; a failure cannot be camouflaged. A roast or boiled joint must be 'done to a turn' and a small slice of roast beef or boiled leg of mutton so cooked with suitable trimmings can be as delicate fare as any elaborately made dish, provided the portions served are not too large. Indeed nothing can be more delicate if the meat be prime Scottish beef or Southdown or Welsh mutton (that literally melts in one's mouth) and the trimmings be judiciously chosen and daintily served. If, however, we offer a heavy slab of solid batter pudding with about 4 oz. of meat as well as four or five halves of potatoes, baked and browned in the pan and roughly prepared kale, then we disgrace our country and its heritage of good things. A slab of solid batter pudding is *not* Yorkshire Pudding, but merely an insult to Yorkshire.

Our roast meats and grills are notoriously good in the hands of a good cook because our meat is so good, but they are not our only good things.

English hot-pots, stews, 'jugs,' pies and puddings are all excellent. Try any of the recipes given here, and own they are worth while.

'Casserole' cooking is only a fashionable word for our own hot-pots, which were formerly cooked in Staffordshire and Nottinghamshire baking pots and pans; and served in Sheffield plate dishes, because the designs of the brown ware were not suitable for sending to table; the contents had to be dished up and this added to the washin' o' dishes. But there are modern English fireproof glass oven-dishes that are excellent for all purposes, and are particularly suited to Lancashire hot-pots, and similar dishes that require slow cooking in the oven. By following some of the recipes given here the young wife, who is merely a beginner, can prepare a delicious little dinner in the morning and finish it off in the evening without getting flustered, hot and irritable. The great thing is to choose our food judiciously and arrange our dishes harmoniously. It is in this direction we should try to improve our cookery. There are certain food constituents that don't combine to our benefit when taken at one meal, and every nation should study its cookery from this standpoint if progress is to be made.

The discovery of vitamins has revolutionized our ideas of food, but science has in this case, as in others, upheld much of the wisdom of our ancestors. So-called conservative cooking of vegetables, soda in the water in which they are cooked, and prolonged cookery have all been pronounced by the highest authorities to be destructive of accessory food constituents vital to health. Many of our old English ways of cooking vegetables can be adapted quite easily and with advantage to modern tastes and modern wisdom.

Another quotation from Lady Raglan's *Memories of Three Reigns* contains definite instruction:

'On the night of my coming-out ball, supper was served in the dining-room . . . Mrs. Vaughan — my grandfather's cook — had endeavoured to surpass herself that night. She had been many years in the family and was devoted to my mother, so she tried to convey her devotion as usual by the skill of her culinary achievements.

'I think I have said before that she was famed for her meat and game pies. On this occasion the delicacy proved to be "Charter pie," the ingredients of which consisted of boned chicken covered in cream sauce and chopped parsley. . . .

'Mrs. Vaughan used to make the most delicious puddings and sweets; and her orange jelly was unlike any I have eaten since. It really tasted of oranges.'

And in these words lie the secret of the good things that can be produced by becoming expert in English cookery. They will really taste of the chief ingredients of which they are made! And we are lucky to have in this book an orange recipe given us by Lady Beeton, wife of Sir Mayson Beeton, son of the real Mrs. Beeton who died at the early age of 29, two days after he was born.

Other recipes suitable for preparing dishes for luncheons, dinners and suppers will be found in Local and National Specialities, and suggestions for combining them will be found in some modern bills of fare for small dinners at the end of this book.

One more point is worth noting. It is never really necessary to add wine to English hot-pots, 'jugged' dishes or stews; even delicious syllabubs can be made without it from fruit juice and cream. Properly made according to the recipes the gravies and sauces here given have been voted by good judges to be the best they have ever tasted. Herbs, however, enter largely into our traditional national cookery.

The Pentecreme is a modern invention that helps us to use the old recipes, for with it butter can be emulsified by the addition of milk and becomes cream again. This makes a plentiful supply possible at a cheaper rate, and the 'gadget' soon pays for itself.

Much of our modern labour-saving kitchen equipment comes first from America, for the simple reason that American women wisely applied their college education at once to household problems.

APPETISERS AND FOOD ADJUNCTS

In the days of Queen Elizabeth the first step to a practical knowledge of cookery according to Gervase Markham (*The English Hus-wife*, 1615) was 'to have knowledge of all sorts of herbs belonging unto the kitchen; whether they be for the pot, for sallets, for sauces, for servings or for any other seasoning, or adorning, which skill of knowledge of herbs, she [the English housewife] must get by her own true labour and experience.'

Although Markham is frequently referred to as the first hack-writer in reality he wrote chiefly from his own experience. He was a country gentleman, belonged to a well-known Nottinghamshire family, and was not altogether lacking in ability to judge of what he writes. Much however of his cookery book he tells us is taken from 'a manuscript which many years agone belonged to an Honourable Countess, one of the greatest Glories of our Kingdom.' This means that although his book was first published in the reign of James I, the cookery he describes and the 're-ceipts' he gives belong to the great days of Elizabeth, Shakespeare, Drake and Raleigh; it was the food eaten by heroes, the men and women who made England and America, and we know they had inherited their skill from those who had lived in Britain from the earliest time. It is possible to trace the evolution of English cookery from prehistoric times to the present day.

Markham gives the first place in his book to salads, or, as he calls them, sallets, and says 'There be some simple, some compounded, some only to furnish out the table, and some both for use and adornation.'

This is proof of the importance attached to herbs and sallets in England at this period, and Markham's testimony is borne out by William Harrison who lived in the reign of Elizabeth and has given a detailed description of the home life of England. He says:

1. 'Such herbs, fruits and roots also as grow yearly out of the ground, of seed, have been very plentiful in this land in the time of the first Edward, and after his days; but in process of time they grew to be somewhat neglected, so that from Henry Fourth till the latter end of Henry VII and beginning of Henry VIII there was little or no use of them in England. 2. Whereas in my time their use is not only resumed among the poor commons I mean of melons, pompons, gourds, cucumbers, radishes, skirrets, parsnips, carrots, cabbages, navews, turnips and all kinds of salad herbs—but also fed upon as daintie dishes at the tables of delicate merchants, gentlemen, and the nobility, who make their provision yearly

from new seeds out of strange countries from whence they may have them abundantly.'

He further tells us that throughout the summer a dish of fresh salad was always the first served at the five o'clock supper, whilst brawn with mustard was the first dish at the 12 o'clock dinner from November to February.

It was in 1597 that Gerard published his famous *Herball*, which was 'principally intended for gentlewomen,' and in the preparation of which he was assisted by his wife; and it is a good augury for English cookery and the renewed prosperity it cannot fail to bring that *A Modern Herbal* has just been published containing the old traditions supplemented by modern science. See authorities at end of book.

Shakespeare and Gerard were friends, and it is delightful to think of those two walking and talking in the latter's garden in Fewter [Fetter] Lane, in Gray's Inn Lane and in the meadows near and far 'where Gerarde loved to trudge.'

Supported therefore by such unimpeachable authority we begin our inherited practical English luncheon, dinner and supper recipes with Markham's simple salads; the 'compounded' ones will be found in the section devoted to salads, page 220.

Simple Salads

Served in the 16th century and suitable for the modern table:

Chives	Onions
Radishes	Samphire
Boiled carrots and turnips	Bean-cods
Lettuce	Asparagus
Purslain	Cucumbers

and divers other herbs 'too tedious to nominate,' all of which may be served simply with a little vinegar, salad-oil and sugar, as a beginning to luncheon, dinner, or supper as they were in Elizabeth days.

Sugar as a Seasoning

It is a golden rule in cookery to add a little sugar to savoury and a little salt to sweet preparations. The important point is to gauge just the right amount. Neither the sugar nor the salt must taste: they must simply bring out the desired flavour of the preparations. For example; a piece of sugar added when boiling peas, and the salt added to a sweet cake.

Concerning Seasonings Generally

We very often condemn the flavourings in Old English Cookery because we don't know how to use them, and have never tasted them. Some herbs have to be used when *dried*, as for example pennyroyal in Worcestershire white puddings; others must only have the juice used and a very little of that: tansy is an example. It would take a cook, a chemist, and an epicure to make a really good practical cookery book.

The art of seasoning is perhaps the greatest art a cook can possess; it is at any rate most important. Every effort is made in this book to give approximate proportions, but in the end every cook must judge for him or herself.

'A little more, and how much it is;
A little less and what miles away!'

Our great-grandmothers not only made their own vinegar from flowers and fruit, but they also flavoured it variously when made: consequently the savoury dishes they prepared were delicious and never monotonous; some recipes for making vinegar at home are given, but many sauces can be made with bought vinegar.

Anchovy as a Seasoning

Until a hundred years ago essence of anchovy was frequently used to season meat dishes such as Melton Mowbray pork pies (page 45), Leicestershire jugged hare, and potted beef (page 51). When correctly used it cannot be tasted as anchovy any more than pepper and salt should be tasted, but it lends a subtly pleasing flavour to meat, when discreetly used.

These remarks are necessary because anyone looking through this book may jeer at recipes which contain unfamiliar seasonings and flavourings. Let them instead try them — nothing unusual has been inserted that has not first been tested.

THE ENGLISH KITCHEN SUPREME

In the delicacy and variety of its savoury and sweet flavourings the English kitchen is supreme. Unhappily these have been more and more neglected since early Victorian days, until now they are practically forgotten. They are worth reviving.

Mustard

Every day in the 16th century and earlier, brawn with mustard was the first dish served at the twelve o'clock dinner from November to February, and we are still noted for our love of mustard and its excellence.

But in those days the seeds were not ground into flour as they are to-day: they were used whole. The following is:

Gerard's Receipt

'The seeds of mustard powdered with vinegar, is an excellent sauce, good to be eaten with any gross meates, either fish or flesh, because it will help digestion, warmeth the stomach, and provoketh appetite.'

The black mustard, which is the best, grows wild in England and was most likely used as a condiment by the Saxons. It was cultivated in gardens in the 16th century, and in 1657 was cultivated in the neighbourhood of Tewkesbury, ground up and made into balls and sent to London

It was first prepared in its present form in 1720 by a Mrs. Clements, of Durham, who invented the process and kept it secret for many years.

Tewkesbury Mustard

The 17th Century Method

1. Have good seed, pick it and wash it in cold water, drain it and rub it dry in a cloth very clean, then beat in a mortar with strong wine vinegar and being fine beaten, strain it and keep it close covered.
2. Instead of vinegar it may be mixed with grape or apple juice, ale, buttermilk, white wine, claret or the juice of cherries.

Mustard Sauce to Bottle

As prepared by Richard Dolby, Cook at the Thatched House Tavern, St. James's Street, London, 1830

INGREDIENTS: Stock, 1 pint; shallots 2; salt ½ teaspoonful; pepper ¼ teaspoonful; mustard 4 teaspoonfuls.

METHOD

1. Put the stock on to boil.
2. Shred the shallots very fine.
3. Add them to the stock.
4. Also the pepper and salt.
5. Boil for half an hour.

6. Then dilute the mustard with a little of the stock and add it to the rest.
7. Stir it in well, bottle and use as required.

Delicious Mustard for Immediate Use

1. Take some mustard; 2. By degrees mix it quite smooth with new milk; 3. Add a little cream. Mixed in this manner it will keep; it is very soft and not in the least bitter.

Do not use cold water.

Never mix mustard with cold or hot water: use warm water.

Oxford Brawn Sauce

INGREDIENTS: Brown sugar 1 tablespoonful; made mustard, 1 teaspoonful; salt 1-3rd teaspoonful; pepper 1-6th teaspoonful· very fine salad-oil 3 or 4 tablespoonfuls; vinegar 2 tablespoonfuls.

METHOD

1. Mix the dry ingredients together.
2. Blend with the oil and made mustard.
3. Finally add the vinegar.

Home-made Vinegar

In these days when bought vinegar is so often unsatisfactory we might once more try to make our own at home. A friend writes from Gloucestershire: 'I think, perhaps, you may like to hear of a few old-fashioned methods, etc., of cookery known to me as a child in Worcestershire 45 to 50 years ago (1931) . . . I cannot now write down the actual recipes, but they were all easy to make. Many a time have I gathered primroses to make vinegar. We made all our own vinegar at home, and primrose was considered the most delicate in flavour. Gooseberry vinegar, too, was very good.'

Think what a poem a salad might be if 'dressed' with primrose vinegar. Fortunately another unknown friend has supplied the recipe: it was left, with a bundle of others, without the sender's name. If she sees this she will understand how much they are appreciated.

Primrose Vinegar

INGREDIENTS: Cold water; 30 quarts; brown sugar 12 lb.; primroses a peck; yeast (compressed yeast 1 or 2 ounces).

TIME: 10 minutes to boil; a few days to stand; a year to mature in the cask.

METHOD

1. Boil the water and sugar together for 10 minutes.
2. Before it is cold add a peck of primrose petals and
3. The yeast creamed with a little sugar.
4. Let it work a few days, stirring it often.
5. Then put it in a barrel with the primroses.
6. Keep it close and near the fire.
7. It must stand a year.

Rhubarb Vinegar

INGREDIENTS: Cold water 1 gallon; brown sugar 1 lb.; rhubarb 2 lb.; yeast ½ oz. compressed yeast.

TIME: 14 days to stand; about 14 days to work; 12 months in barrel; 12 months in bottle.

METHOD

1. Cut the rhubarb in pieces.
2. Put them in a tub with the sugar and water.
3. Let them remain covered up for 14 days.
4. Then boil up.
5. Strain the liquid through a hair sieve or cloth.
6. Then put the liquid in a barrel with the yeast creamed with a little sugar.
7. Let it work well.
8. It must then be made quite air-tight and remain near the fire 12 months.
9. Then bottle it and in 12 more months it will be fit for use.

Gooseberry Vinegar

INGREDIENTS: Gooseberries full ripe; to every pound of pulp 3 quarts water; to every gallon of liquor 1½ lb. brown sugar — *No yeast*.

TIME: 27 hours to stand; 12 months in barrel; 12 months in bottle.

METHOD

1. Crush the gooseberries.
2. Measure the pulp.
3. Boil 3 quarts of water for every quart of pulp.
4. Let the water get quite cold before you put the pulp into it.
5. Stir and stand 27 hours.
6. Strain through a sieve.
7. To every gallon of liquor put 1½ lb. brown sugar.
8. Stir well till the sugar is dissolved.
9. Put in barrel, and finish as before, except that it is *not* worked with yeast.

Verjuice

This is mentioned frequently in old cookery books. The following receipt is given in one published in 1830 sent by Mrs. Millington, of Preston, Lancashire. 'Take some crab apples when the kernels turn black, lay them in a heap to sweat; then pick them from the stalks and rottenness,

95

beat them to a mash, and press the juice through a bag of coarse hair cloth into a clean vessel; it will be fit for use in a month's time. If intended for white pickles, distil it in a cold still. It may be put into sauce when lemon is wanting.

Sugar Vinegar

INGREDIENTS: Water 1 gallon; sugar 2 lb. of the very coarsest; water a quart of cold to every gallon of hot; compressed yeast about ⅛ ounce; a piece of toast.

TIME: 9 days to work, 6 months to mature.

METHOD

1. Boil the water and sugar together.
2. Skim thoroughly.
3. Add one quart cold water for every gallon of hot.
4. When cool, but not cold, put in the piece of toast spread with the yeast creamed with a little sugar.
5. Stir for 9 days.
6. Then barrel it.
7. Place it in such a situation that the sun may lie on it.
8. Put a slate over the bung-hole. The best time to make it is March, and it will be ready in six months.

Spiced or Pickled Eggs

A good Shrewsbury, Shropshire, recipe

INGREDIENTS: Eggs 16; vinegar 1 quart; black peppercorns ½ oz.; Jamaica pepper (or allspice) ½ oz.; ginger root ¼ oz.

TIME: 15 minutes to boil the eggs; 10 minutes to simmer the vinegar; ready for use a month after making.

METHOD

1. Take 16 new-laid eggs, not more than 24 hours old.
2. Boil them for 15 minutes.
3. Lay them in cold water and take off the shells.
4. Put the vinegar with the peppers and ginger (which must first be bruised) into a pan.
5. Let all simmer for 10 minutes.
6. Now place the eggs in a jar.
7. Pour the vinegar and spices over them when cold.
8. Tie them down next day with a bladder. They will be ready for use in a month's time.

These are delicious with salads or cold meat.

To Pickle Elder Buds

1777

This old recipe was given in 1928 by Mrs. Monk, of The Yews, Burford, Oxfordshire. Mrs. Monk is the wife of the historian of Burford. Her account of cowslip gathering for making cowslip wine is delightful. She says she always dries her cowslips not only for cowslip tea but for wine, and 'when spread out on paper on the attic floor they smell like honey.'

INGREDIENTS: Elder buds; salt and water brine; vine leaves; allegar (the vinegar made from sour ale; ordinary vinegar may be used); a little mace; a few shallots; and some sliced ginger.

METHOD

1. Put the elder buds into a strong brine of salt and water.
2. Keep them there for nine days, stirring two or three times a day.
3. Strain them off the brine, but don't throw it away.
4. Put the buds into a preserving pan.
5. Cover them with vine leaves.
6. And pour the salt water over them.
7. Set them over a slow fire for some hours.
8. Then make a pickle for them of the vinegar, mace, shallots and ginger.
9. Boil this 2—3 minutes.
10. Strain the buds from the brine, and put them into a glass or stoneware jar.
11. Pour the pickle over them.
12. Tie them down and keep them in a very dry place.

N.B.—In the eighteenth century recipe at direction 4, we are told 'to put then into a brass pan, cover them with vine leaves and pour the water on them that they came out of; set them over a slow fire till they are quite green.'

[But Mrs. Monk did not tell me to do this; therefore the above recipe may be followed quite safely, and anyone who wants to make experiments and is not afraid of verdigris can experiment with the original directions. Personally I am afraid of brass for preserves and pickles, and always advise the use of stoneware, glass, and a wooden spoon. With the exception of heavy aluminium all metal and glazed ware should be studiously avoided. —ED.]

Pontac Sauce

Sent by Miss M. A. Sloane, of Enderby and Leicester, July 1931.

INGREDIENTS: Ripe elderberries 1 pint; boiling vinegar ¾ pint; salt ½ teaspoonful; mace or root of ginger; mace; peppercorns 40; cloves 12; shallots 4.

TIME: to stand 12 hours in cool oven; to boil the liquid 5 minutes; may be kept 7 years before using.

METHOD

1. Pour the boiling vinegar over the elderberries.
2. Let the jar stand all night in a cool oven.
3. Strain without pressure.
4. Boil the liquid 5 minutes with the root ginger, mace, peppercorns, cloves and shallots.
5. Bottle when cold, with the spices.

N.B.—Miss Sloane says 'I used to be told that it should be kept 7 years; ours was.'

Elderberry Sauce

This is a similar recipe given by Mrs. Brewitt of the Priory (Anne of Cleves House), Melton Mowbray, 1927. It is curious both these should come from Leicestershire and nowhere else, but I think the original in which there is no doubt claret was the principal ingredient may have been taken by Sir Charles Sedley or one of his friends from Pontack's Restaurant to his country house at Wymondham on the borders of Rutland, Leicestershire and Lincolnshire. Wymondham is not far from Melton Mowbray, and Little Dalby where the Brewitts lived is between that famous hunting centre and Quenby Hall; whilst Leicester is 7 miles further SW. from this still existing (1931) Elizabethan mansion.

The story of Pontack's Restaurant and its connections with Haut Brion, one of the world's three most famous clarets, is told farther on (page 318). Meantime here is the recipe for Mrs. Brewitt's sauce.

INGREDIENTS: Elderberries 2 quarts; boiling vinegar 2 quarts; mace 3 or 4 blades; bruised ginger a small piece; cloves a dessertspoonful; peppercorns 2 dessertspoonfuls; shallots 4 oz.

TIME: 12 hours in a cool oven; 10 minutes to boil up the liquid.

METHOD

1. Put the elderberries stripped from their stems into an earthenware jar.
2. Keep it in the oven through the night.
3. Next day pour off the liquid, put it in a saucepan with the mace, ginger, cloves, peppercorns, and shallots which must be finely chopped.
4. Boil up for 10 minutes.
5. Pour over the berries again.
6. Bottle all together, and cork securely. When needed the liquid should be drawn off the berries.

N.B.—There is a Pontac Ketchup given in Garrett's *Encyclopædia of Practical Cookery*, which is again similar to the above but contains 8 oz. boned anchovies to each quart of liquor, and in view of Miss Sloane's remark about keeping Pontac for seven years, it is interesting to note that the next recipe given is for what is actually called 'Seven Years Ketchup,' which, by the way, contains no elderberries but does contain 1 pint of claret, 1 quart of very old beer, 6 oz. boned anchovies, 1½ oz. peeled shallots ¼ oz. mace, ½ oz. cloves, and a little whole ginger root. Hot wine sauce or gravy was served with roasted ortolans at Pontack's, and this is given on page 158.

Mrs. Combers' Sauce

'Captain Charles Combers (born 1752), a member of the Quorn Hunt when on his way to Leicestershire stopped, as was his wont, to dine at The George at Bedford, then kept by a man named Harvey, where he ordered a steak, and when it was served Combers requested Harvey to let his servant bring from his buggy a quart bottle which contained an admirable sauce. Combers poured some of it into his plate and [having] mixed it with the gravy of the steak he asked Harvey to taste it, and the host pronounced it to be a most excellent relish.

' "Well, Mr. Harvey," said Combers, "I shall leave the bottle with you to use till my return, only be careful to reserve enough for me."

'On the next day Harvey had to provide a wedding dinner, and introduced the sauce which afforded such general satisfaction, that several smaller parties were made up and the contents of the bottle were soon exhausted.

'In due course Captain Combers returned, and having been told no more sauce remained, said, "never mind, I can make some more from my mother's recipe and, by the by, I'll give you a copy of it." He did so. Harvey made it in large quantities, sent it to different shops in London; advertised it as Harvey's sauce and by its extensive sale realized a large income — he subsequently sold the recipe for an annuity of £400 or £500 a year.'
                                            W. C. A. BLEW, M.A.
                                  The Quorn Hunt and its Masters.

And here is the

RECIPE

(as made by Richard Dolby, cook at the Thatched House Tavern, St. James's Street, London, S.W.1, in 1830).

INGREDIENTS: Anchovies 12; cayenne pepper 1 oz.; soy 6 spoonfuls; walnut pickle 6 spoonfuls; garlic 3 bulbs; cochineal $\frac{1}{4}$ oz.; shallots 2; vinegar 1 gallon.

TIME: 14 days to stand before straining and bottling.

METHOD

1. Chop the anchovies very small, bones and all.
2. Add the cayenne pepper, soy and walnut liquor.
3. Chop, but not too small, the 3 *bulbs* of garlic (not 3 *cloves* of garlic, each bulb or head is made up of several cloves) and add them.
4. Add the cochineal and the shallots chopped but not very small.
5. Finally add one gallon of vinegar.
6. Let it stand 14 days; stir it well twice or thrice every day; then pass it through a jelly bag; and repeat this till it is perfectly clear; then bottle it, and tie a piece of bladder over each cork

Lord Sandys' Sauce

This has been known for nearly 100 years as Worcestershire sauce — Its manufacture is not confined now to one firm but Lea & Perrin are the original makers. The story is that it was given to the founder of the firm as an unconsidered trifle by the second Baron Sandys of Worcestershire, who picked it up when he was in India. Its possibilities were not realized until 1838 when its owners began to make it on a large scale and the business developed so tremendously that Mr. Lea, the head of the firm, died a millionaire.

The following was amongst the recipes given by the anonymous friend before mentioned.

A Recipe for Worcestershire Sauce

INGREDIENTS: Capsicum 1 oz.; shallots 8 oz.; cinnamon 4 drams; garlic 6 oz.; cloves 2 oz.; nutmegs 2 oz.; cardamom 1 dram; soy 1 pint; mushroom ketchup 2 pints; vinegar (brown) 1 gallon. (16 oz. to each pint.)

TIME: boil one hour; stand one month.

METHOD

1. Bruise the shallots and garlic and boil for one half-hour.
2. Add the remainder of the ingredients and let them boil for another half hour in a close vessel.
3. Let the whole remain for a month, covered over.
4. Strain through a fine sieve.
5. And bottle the sauce.

The spices when drained off may be boiled in a few pints of vinegar which they will flavour, and which will be most useful for making pickles when once more strained through a hair sieve.

Sour Plums or Sweet Pickled Peaches

This recipe also hails from Yorkshire, via Ross-on-Wye, and is over one hundred years old.

INGREDIENTS: Ripe plums, damsons, peaches, nectarines, pears or green figs, but not over ripe 4 lb.; best white wine vinegar 1 pint; loaf (or lump) sugar $\frac{3}{4}$lb.; the white of an egg, cinnamon sticks $\frac{1}{4}$ oz.; $\frac{1}{2}$ oz. cloves

TIME: a short time on 3 successive days.

METHOD

1. Wipe the fruit (especially if you are using peaches, to get off the down).
2. Prick it all over with a needle.
3. Put into a large jar or bowl.
4. Boil the vinegar and sugar for 15 minutes and clear with white of egg (*see* p. 305).
5. Pour this over the fruit as hot as possible, cover tightly and stand till next day.
6. Then pour off the syrup and boil it up for half an hour.
7. Again pour over the fruit as hot as possible and cover close as before.
8. On the third day boil the fruit, syrup, cinnamon and cloves (tied in a muslin bag) all together, and when the mixture begins to boil all over, take off and tip out into the bowl.
9. Bottle when cold, and make air-tight (the old recipe says cover with bladder, but in 1932 we should use the special bottles made for fruit bottling).

Pickled Fruit

Mrs. Brewitt, Anne of Cleves House, Melton Mowbray, 1928

INGREDIENTS: Vinegar 1 pint; sugar (preserving) ¾ to 1 lb. according to the sweetness of the fruit; fruit, 1 lb.

TIME: varies according to the fruit.

METHOD

1. First put the sugar and vinegar together in a heavy aluminium, or into a Kenrick preserving pan and stand over the fire till dissolved.
2. Boil up.
3. Add the fruit.
4. Simmer until it begins to crack.
5. Bottle whilst hot.

N.B.—This is pickled fruit without spices. The vinegar for sweet pickled fruit may be spiced by adding a teaspoonful each of mace, pepper, ginger, and cinnamon, and a half teaspoonful of cloves to every quart of vinegar. Boil up and strain.

Plum Chutney

Melton Mowbray, 1927

INGREDIENTS: Plums (not quite ripe or only just so) 1½ lb.; tomatoes (also just ripe) ½ lb.; onions ½ lb.; cayenne pepper 1 teaspoonful; brown sugar ¼ lb.; salt 1 dessertspoonful; red chillies (if procurable); vinegar 1½ pints.

TIME: about 3 hours.

METHOD

1. Cut the plums in halves and remove the stones.
2. Peel the tomatoes.
3. Chop up the onions.
4. Stew all together in a heavy aluminium pan for 2 hours.
5. Then add the cayenne pepper, brown sugar, salt and the red chillies if you have them.

6. Add vinegar and cook gently for another ¼ hour.
7. When cool, place in well stoppered bottles.
8. Keep for a month or longer before use.

N.B.—It is best to cover the corks with melted wax.

Rhubarb Chutney

Mrs. Newcome

INGREDIENTS: Rhubarb 2 lb.; sugar 2 lb.; sultanas 1 lb.; vinegar 1 pint; salt 1 oz.; ginger 1 oz.; onion 1; pepper 1 teaspoonful.

METHOD

1. Peel and cut up the rhubarb; peel and chop up the onion finely.
2. Bruise the ginger and tie it in a piece of muslin, put all with the rest of the ingredients into a heavy English or Scottish aluminium saucepan or preserving pan and boil till it thickens.

Tomato Chutney

Melton Mowbray, 1927

INGREDIENTS: Ripe tomatoes 4 lb.; onions 3 large ones; Demerara sugar 1 lb.; salt ¼ lb.; pickling spice (cloves, cinnamon, peppercorns mixed) 1 oz.; cayenne pepper ½ teaspoonful; vinegar rather more than ½ pint.

TIME: to boil 1½ hours.

METHOD

1. Cut the tomatoes into slices.
2. Put them in a saucepan.
3. Slice the onions, and add them.
4. Add sugar, salt and pickling spice (tied in a muslin bag).

5. Then cayenne pepper.
6. Pour the vinegar over them.
7. Boil all together gently for 1¼ hours.
8. Stir to prevent burning.

Pickled Beetroot

Little Dalby

INGREDIENTS: Beets, vinegar; whole pepper 2 oz.; allspice 2 oz.; to 1 gallon vinegar.

TIME: to boil the beets about 1½ hours, to boil vinegar about 10 minutes.

METHOD

1. Boil beets till tender.
2. Peel and cut into rings about 1 inch thick.
3. Place in jars.
4. Have ready the vinegar cold, which has been boiled for 10 minutes with the pepper and allspice together.
5. Pour it on the beets which must also be cold. Cover with bladder to exclude from air. In a week they will be fit for use.

[N.B.—This is evidently a very old recipe although it is not dated, as covering with bladder was an old method. To-day we should use the latest modern bottle.—Ed.]

Green Tomato Pickle

Mrs. Stanley

INGREDIENTS: Green tomatoes 10 lb.; salt; vinegar 2 quarts; brown sugar 2 lb.; onions 1 lb.; cayenne pepper ¼ oz.; cloves ¼ oz.; cinnamon ¼ oz.; peppercorns ¼ oz.; apples 1 to 2 lb.

TIME: 24 hours to stand.

METHOD

1. Slice the tomatoes into a dish and sprinkle each layer with salt.
2. Let them remain all night.
3. Next day put in a preserving pan the vinegar, sugar, onions (sliced), pepper and spices.
4. Drain the tomatoes from the salt and add them.
5. Also the apples pared, cored and sliced.
6. Simmer all the ingredients till tender.
7. Bottle.

Cucumber Ketchup

'*A great addition to white sauce.*'—*Miss Turner*, 1857

INGREDIENTS: Cucumbers 6; large onions 1 dozen; (root ginger 1 oz.; white peppercorns 1 oz.; mace ½ oz. to every quart); salt.

TIME: 3 or 4 days in salt; 6 or 8 hours in a cool oven; then another hour to boil.

METHOD

1. Slice the cucumber and onions.
2. Sprinkle with salt and let them stand in a deep dish for 3 or 4 days.
3. Then put in a stewpot in a cool oven for 6 or 8 hours.
4. Strain it through a hair sieve and measure the juice.
5. Weigh out 1 oz. root ginger, 1 oz. white peppercorns, and ½ oz. mace for every quart, and
6. Boil the spice in the juice for 1 hour.
7. Strain through a hair sieve.
8. Bottle in pint bottles, and
9. Cork very tightly.

Tomato Ketchup

Tendring Hall, Suffolk, 1857

INGREDIENTS: Tomatoes, quite ripe; chilli vinegar; salt; garlic ½ oz.; or shallots 1 oz. to each quart.

TIME: bake for about 15 minutes; boil for 15.

METHOD

1. Bake quite ripe tomatoes till they are perfectly soft.
2. Rub the pulp through a sieve.
3. Add as much chilli vinegar as will make it a fairly thick cream.
4. Slice the garlic or shallot and boil all together for 15 minutes.
5. Take the scum off.
6. Strain it through a sieve to remove the garlic or shallot.
7. When cold bottle and cork it well.

N.B.—If when the bottles are opened it is found to have fermented, put more salt to it and boil it up again. The thickness when finished should be that of very thick cream.

Hot Tomato Sauce

Will keep for years

INGREDIENTS: Ripe tomatoes 1 gallon; red pepper 5 pods; salt 2 oz.; black pepper 2 oz.; allspice ½ oz.; vinegar 1 pint.

TIME: 3 or 4 hours.

METHOD

1. Peel tomatoes.
2. Cook with red pepper (chillies) till tender.
3. Rub through a hair sieve.
4. Stir the salt, pepper and allspice thoroughly into it.
5. Add vinegar.
6. Boil slowly for 3 or 4 hours.
7. Bottle while still warm and cork tightly.

Aromatic Spice

INGREDIENTS: Nutmegs 1 oz.; mace 1 oz.; cloves 2 oz.; white peppercorns 2 oz.; sweet basil, marjoram, and thyme, dried, 1 oz. each; bay leaves, dried, ½ oz.

METHOD

Pound all roughly, put between two sheets of strong white paper, and pinch the edges together to keep in the aroma. Dry in oven. Pound very fine; sift and bottle. Cork tightly.

2

SOUPS, SAUCES AND STUFFINGS

The Cook's Herb Patch

Chives, parsley, sage, thyme, mint, fennel, winter savory, sweet marjoram, sweet basil, and tarragon are the most useful to grow if space be limited; but there are others, and I cannot too strongly recommend all cooks to study Mrs. Grieve's and Mrs. Leyel's *Modern Herbal*.

A BUNCH OF SWEET HERBS, 1829

This is made up of parsley, sweet marjoram, winter savory, orange and lemon thyme; the greatest proportion of parsley.

A FAGGOT OF HERBS, 1895

By this is meant a few sprigs of fresh parsley, a sprig of thyme and a bay leaf tied together with twine. The equivalent to these in dried herbs would be a dessertspoonful mixed.

SWEET BASIL, AND SWEET OR KNOTTED MARJORAM

Both important ingredients in mock-turtle soup. Basil is good with tomatoes.

FENNEL

Used for sauce, for mackerel, and roach; also for garnishing pickled salmon.

MARIGOLD

For use in salads, soups, and stews. The flower petals may be dried for winter use in soups and stews.

SWEET MARJORAM

This herb gives a delicious flavour to soups, sauces and seasonings; and is nice (dried and powdered) sprinkled over roast pork just before serving.

WINTER SAVORY

This is so useful that it should always find a place in every herb garden. It is excellent for flavouring made dishes, stews, soups, savoury stuffings, and sauces.

ROSEMARY
This is used for stuffings, flavouring lard, etc.

CHIVES
These are easily grown and should be used all the year round. During the winter (or in flats without gardens) they can be grown in pots or boxes indoors. It is only the green grass-like leaves that are cut, and the more they are cut off to within about 1 inch of the soil the quicker others spring up; and the bulb-like roots send out offsets. They can be grown by division of the clumps of roots in the spring and autumn, and thrive on a rich soil.

N.B.—When making stuffing with herbs the cook should aim at having it look green and fresh, for which reason a little spinach juice colouring may sometimes be used with advantage. The stalks of parsley will also give a green colour; for this reason when chopping parsley for soups, sauce or butter where the contrast of white and green is required, only the leaves should be used.

Brewis

'This,' writes a Lancashire lady, 'dates from the "Hungry 'Forties" when we were very poor in Lancashire.'

Pour boiling water on a crust of bread; pour the water off and it is ready; season with salt and pepper. Serve it in a breakfast cup and eat it with a spoon.

Another kind of Brewis

'This,' writes Mrs. A. B. Gorton, 'was a great treat only obtainable after killing the pig, but in our village nearly every family had a pig. Soak oatcake in the liquor in which a piece of pork has been boiled, then mash it up with a potato masher and season with pepper and salt. It is said to be still eaten (in 1931) with black puddings, but if so probably only on the more out-of-the-way farms.'

Lady Westmorland's Soup

This is nothing more than the water in which young cabbage has been boiled according to the directions given on page 208 by Dr. Ellen Marion Delf (Mrs. Percy Smith). It is extremely good and delicate and tastes very much like chicken broth. It is not merely an economy but a luxury; one of the best of health and beauty drinks.

Clear Carrot Soup

As made and served in a celebrated Cambridge College

INGREDIENTS: Carrots; a little butter, sugar, and salt; clear stock; the juice of 3 or 4 grated outsides of carrots; a little boiled rice.

METHOD

1. Cut some carrots in fine match-like shreds.
2. Cook them for 5 minutes in a little butter.
3. Keep them as whole as possible.
4. Add sugar and salt.
5. Drain and put them into clear stock: just before sending to table squeeze the juice of 3 or 4 grated carrots rubbed through a tammy, add a little boiled rice, and serve.

Nettle Soup

Dr. William Fernie says: 'In 1890 a west-end vegetable dealer in London recognized the wholesome and nutritious properties of young nettletops when cooked for the table, and he arranged for a regular supply of the same on finding that a ready sale existed for these wares. If nettletops are taken as a fresh young vegetable in the spring and early summer, they make a very salutary and succulent dish of greens, which is slightly laxative; but during autumn they are hurtful. The true stinging nettle with a round, hairy stalk and which bears only a dull colourless bloom must be secured, and not a labiate nettle with a square stem.'

The soup may be made with some nettles left over from those that have been cooked as a vegetable (*see* p. 213).

RECIPE

INGREDIENTS: Young nettles, a panful; butter 1 oz.; flour 1 oz.; salt ½ teaspoonful; hot milk 1 pint; pepper to taste; dice of bread fried in bacon fat.

TIME: 20—30 minutes.

METHOD

1. Wash the nettles.
2. Throw them into a pan containing a pint of boiling water and a little salt.
3. Cook rapidly with the lid off for 10 minutes when they should be perfectly tender.
4. Rub the whole through a hair sieve.
5. Melt the butter in the saucepan, add the flour and cook together over low heat without browning, until it bubbles rather like a honeycomb.
6. Remove from fire and beat in the pint of hot milk gradually till quite smooth.
7. Return this white sauce to the fire, stirring all the time, boil up and boil for 5 minutes.
8. Pour gradually on to the nettles (stirring all the time).
9. Fry some dice of bread a delicate brown in bacon fat and keep them hot.
10. Return the soup to the saucepan, boil up very quickly and serve at once with the fried dice.

N.B.— Nettle soup made in this way retains all its vitamin C value, and is very delicious. More pepper and salt may be added to taste, and a dish of grated cheese may be handed round as well as the dice of fried bread.

18th Century Green Pea Soup

Made without meat

This Somersetshire recipe which makes a most delicious soup has been sent by Colonel Plomer, of Shrewsbury, who says 'once a year at least since about 1770 it has been, and still is, made in my family. If properly made I can vouch for its being jolly good.'

INGREDIENTS: Green peas 3 pints and young green peas 1 pint; water 5 pints, fresh mint; celery and cos lettuce; pepper; salt; butter ¼ lb.; cucumbers 2 large ones; onions 2 or 3; cos lettuce a large one; cucumber and cauliflower boiled separately to garnish if approved.

TIME: about 1 hour to 1½ hours.

METHOD

1. Boil up the water, put in the peas, a little fresh mint, a little chopped celery, and a cos lettuce shredded, pepper and salt.
2. Cook till tender (about 20 minutes).
3. Strain off the soup and rub the peas, etc., through a sieve.
4. Put the butter into a large pan, pare the cucumber, seed them, cut them in pieces about ⅜ inch thick.
5. Slice the onions.
6. Shred a large cos lettuce.
7. Cook all in the butter till tender.
8. Then put the sieved soup to them.
9. Add the pint of young green peas and let it all stew gently for ½ hour together.
10. Add a little flour rubbed down with butter to bind all together to a creamy consistency.

N.B.—It improves the colour and flavour if the cods (or shucks) of the young peas are boiled in a little water and added to it. The soup may be further garnished with sprigs of cauliflower and pieces of cucumber (cooked separately) and added at the last minute before serving.

Spring Soup

Mary Eaton, Bungay, Suffolk, 1823

INGREDIENTS: Green peas 1 pint; chervil; purslain; lettuce; sorrel, parsley; onions 3 or 4; butter about 1 oz.; warm water; yolks of eggs 3; a gill of good milk; pepper; salt.

METHOD

1. Put the peas with the vegetables and herbs (chopped up) in a stewpan with the butter.
2. Shake them over the fire for a few minutes.
3. Add warm water in proportion to the vegetables and stew till they are well covered.
4. Strain off the soup and pass the vegetables through a sieve.
5. Heat the pulp with three parts of the soup.
6. Mix the remainder with 3 yolks of eggs, a gill of milk, and the rest of the soup and thicken it over the fire.
7. When ready to serve add it to the soup.
8. Heat the soup and thickening together and season to taste.

Vegetable Water Soup

Mary Eaton, Bungay, Suffolk, 1823

INGREDIENTS: Cabbage ¼; carrots 4; parsnips 2; onions 6; turnips 3; celery root 1; parsley root, a small one; white beet leaves and chervil; peas ½ pint tied up in a piece of linen.

TIME: to cook 3 hours.

METHOD

1. Wash the vegetables but don't cut them up.
2. Put them in a saucepan holding about 2 quarts.
3. Add water to fill the saucepan 3 parts full.
4. Stew for 3 hours.
5. Strain off the broth and return it to the saucepan.
6. Add some salt.
7. Cut up some of the vegetables into dice with the peas, and use all these to garnish the soup.
8. Heat and serve.

Celery Soup (White)

Somersetshire, 1852

INGREDIENTS: Celery 2 heads; onion 1; mace 1 blade; peppercorns 12; white stock 1½ pints; egg yolk 1; cream 1 gill; salt, sugar.

METHOD

1. Wash and scrub the celery and cut it in pieces.
2. Boil it in slightly salted water, with onion peeled and cut up, mace and peppercorns, till the vegetables are soft.
3. Then drain off the water and rub the vegetables through a hair sieve.
4. Add to them the white stock.
5. Boil up, stirring all the time, and bind with the yolk of egg and cream beaten together.
6. Add a little soup to the beaten egg and cream and blend well before adding the mixture to the rest of the soup.
7. Add a very little sugar and serve.

109

The Judge's Circuit Soup

Worcester, 18th Century

This receipt was included in an old coverless exercise book sent by a
B.B.C. friend. It possesses no name but evidently, from the following
entry and other internal evidence, belonged to a Worcester cook and
caterer probably during the first half of the 18th century.

'This dinner,' runs the record, 'we — my daughter and I — dres't under
the Town Hall for the Corporation of Worcester; we had everything that
could be had for money that was nice, and was praised by all the Gentlemen as very elegant, the best they ever sat down to of the size.'

Unfortunately the bill of fare is not given, but there are 'receipts' for
dressing a turtle, for cooking two fine turbots, for lobster and shrimp sauce,
which were evidently featured. The directions have been modernized
without destroying the character of the soup.

RECIPE

INGREDIENTS: Veal, knuckle and lean part of leg; cloves, mace;
black pepper and white pepper; rice 4 oz.; water one quart.

TIME: 2 or 3 hours.

METHOD

1. Break the bones of the leg of veal and cut up the meat.
2. Put it into a pot and cover it with water.
3. Add cloves, mace, black and white pepper.
4. Let it stew gently two or three hours keeping it well skimmed.
5. Then put the rice in the quart of water, and boil till the water be chiefly gone.
6. Strain off your soup and thicken it with the rice and season to your taste.
7. 'Vermicelli is done in the same way, only when your soup is strained off then put in your vermicelli and let it boil a little while together instead of rice.'

Thick Oxtail Soup

1900

INGREDIENTS: Oxtail 1 large one; flour; water 2 quarts; onion 1;
carrot 1; turnip 1; celery 1 stick; herbs a small bunch; butter 2 oz.; plain
flour 2 oz.; lemon juice, a teaspoonful; sherry or claret 1 glass.

TIME: 3 hours.

METHOD

1. Cut the oxtail in pieces, wash and dry it; flour it and fry in the butter; put into a soup pot or saucepan.
2. Then prepare and cut up the vegetables and fry them in the same fat.
3. Put them also into the pot.
4. Pour 2 quarts of hot water over them.
5. Add the herbs, and simmer gently for 3 hours.
6. Strain.
7. Cut the meat off the large pieces of tail, and add them and the smaller pieces of tail to the soup.
8. Thicken in the usual way by melting the butter and cooking the flour in it; let it get brown but be careful not to let it burn; dilute it with some of the soup, return to the soup pot.
9. Give it a boil up, add the lemon juice and wine, and serve.

Pea Soup

Frome, Somersetshire, 1932

INGREDIENTS: Split peas ½ pint; onions 2; carrot 1; turnip 1; small head of celery; sprig of parsley; cold water 3 pints (the water in which ham or bacon is used is better if not too salt); salt 1 teaspoonful, pepper ¼ teaspoonful; sugar ½ teaspoonful; dripping 1 oz.

(1 oz. butter and 1 oz. flour to bind the soup and peas together just before serving.)

TIME: about 4 hours.

METHOD

1. Wash the peas and soak them in soft cold water for 24 hours (if the water is hard a little bicarbonate of soda may be put into it).
2. Drain, and put into a saucepan with the 3 pints of water or ham stock.
3. Put on to boil up.
4. Peel the onions and turnip, scrape the carrot, wash and scrub the celery, cut up into small pieces.
5. Scum the soup when it boils, and add the vegetables and all the other ingredients.
6. Boil until the peas are quite tender, and then press all the soup through a sieve.
7. Return it to the saucepan and stir till it boils up so that the peas do not sink to the bottom.
8. And to keep them equally distributed through the soup, melt the butter in another saucepan, add the flour, and cook together for a few minutes till it bubbles, then remove from fire and dilute with some of the soup. Return all to the soup pot and boil up.

Serve with dice of bread fried in bacon, and powdered dried mint.

Rice Soup

1823

INGREDIENTS: Rice 1 lb; cinnamon; water 2 quarts; sugar; nutmeg; eggs 3 yolks; a little white wine.

METHOD

1. Boil the rice with a bit of stick cinnamon in the two quarts of water.
2. Take out the cinnamon, add a little sugar and nutmeg, and let it stand to cool.
3. Beat up the yolks of the eggs in a little white wine and mix with the rice.
4. Set it on a slow fire, stir it well, and take it up as soon as it has come to a proper thickness.

Spinach Soup

Mary Eaton, Bungay, Suffolk, 1823

INGREDIENTS: Spinach 2 handfuls; turnip 1; onions 2; celery; carrots; parsley and thyme; butter the size of a walnut; good broth or the liquor in which meat has been boiled; hot water 1 quart; salt and pepper; butter ½ ounce and ½ ounce flour rubbed together; suet dumplings the size of walnuts.

METHOD

1. Wash the spinach, parsley and thyme, peel the carrots, turnip and onions, scrub and string the celery.
2. Shred all these vegetables and put them in a stewpot with the bit of butter the size of a walnut.
3. Add the broth or meat liquor and stir till the vegetables are quite tender.
4. Work them with the liquor through a coarse sieve with a spoon.
5. Return to saucepan, add a quart of hot water and boil all together.
6. Add the butter and flour kneaded together and stir till they are incorporated.
7. Have ready some small suet dumplings, add them to the soup, and serve at once piping hot.

N.B.—The suet for the dumplings must be perfectly fresh and should not be cut too fine.

Mock Turtle Soup from Sheep's Head

Frome, Somersetshire, 1852

INGREDIENTS: Sheep's head 1; water 3 quarts; turnips ½ lb.; carrots 5½ oz.; onions 7 oz.; peppercorns 3; mace 1 blade; cloves 3; allspice 3; salt 1 teaspoonful; bunch of herbs; celery 1 stick; butter 2 oz.; flour 2 oz.; ketchup, salt; cayenne to taste; lemon, juice of ½; glass of sherry or port. Forcemeat balls made of brains, bread-crumbs, pepper, a little chopped parsley, grated lemon peel, salt and 1 egg; fat for frying them.

METHOD

1. Clean the head.
2. Take out the eyes and throw them away; take out the tongue and cook it separately but in the same pot; take out the brains, wash and tie them up in a piece of pudding cloth and cook them also in the same pot.
3. Put the head and tongue in a pot with the water.
4. Bring slowly to boiling point.
5. Peel the turnip and onions, scrape the carrots, wash and string the stick of celery.
6. Remove the scum when it rises on the soup; and add a small cup of cold water to help it rise.
7. Slice the vegetables and put them in the soup with the peppercorns, cloves, allspice, salt and bunch of herbs (thyme, parsley, marjoram, and 1 bay leaf).
8. Simmer slowly till the tongue and

meat on the head are tender (the brains will only take about 10 minutes).
9. Strain off.
10. Take the meat off the bones.
11. When cold cut up the meat in rather large dice.
12. Take the fat off the broth and put the latter in a saucepan to get hot.
13. Melt the butter in a saucepan, add the flour and cook it a few minutes till it gets a golden brown, dilute it with a pint of the soup, boil up and return to the soup pot.
14. Boil up all together.
15. Add ketchup (either mushroom or walnut) to flavour, with salt, cayenne to taste.
16. Immediately before serving add the lemon juice and a glass of sherry or port.

Have ready some forcemeat balls made of the brains chopped up, and mixed with bread-crumbs, pepper and salt, a little chopped parsley and grated lemon peel and bind with the egg. They must be fried in hot fat, and drained well. Add them (also piping hot) to the soup.

Vegetable Marrow Soup

Another delicious Cambridge Soup

INGREDIENTS: Vegetable marrow; soup vegetables; flour 1 oz.; butter 1 oz. to every pint of white stock; a little boiling cream, ½ gill to every quart, or more if it can be afforded; pepper and salt.

TIME: 1 hour.

METHOD

1. Parboil the vegetable marrow.
2. Cut up some soup vegetables, carrot, turnip, celery, onion, and fry (without browning) for a few minutes.
3. Melt the butter in a pan and add the flour.
4. Cook together for a few minutes.
5. Dilute with boiling white stock.
6. Add the soup vegetables and marrow cut up.
7. Boil all together for 1 hour.
8. Rub it through a hair sieve.
9. Boil up.
10. Add the boiling cream and serve.

Herb Soup

An early 18th Century Worcester cook's recipe

INGREDIENTS. A knuckle of veal; part of a neck of mutton; a piece of brisket of beef (in these days the water in which a forehock of bacon, or ham, or a piece of silverside of beef has been boiled would make a suitable foundation, but would not be so delicate as if made with a knuckle of veal); lettuce; sorrel; endive; onions; sweet herbs; a ham bone; cloves; mace; and asparagus tops.

TIME: seven hours and a half.

METHOD

1. Put the knuckle of veal, part of a neck of mutton, and a piece of brisket of beef in cold water; bring it to boiling point and let the meat stew gently for 7 hours.
2. Skim well all the time.
3. Then add lettuce, sorrel, endive, onions, sweet herbs, and the shank of a ham bone.
4. Flavour with cloves and mace.
5. Boil up quickly for 20 minutes or half an hour.
6. Strain it, return the broth to the saucepan.
7. Chop fresh herbs and the tops of some asparagus.
8. Throw them into the soup and let it boil a little longer.

An Excellent Pea Soup

Early 18th Century

This is from the manuscript Cookery Book of the Worcester Caterer and Cook whose name is missing with the cover of his book. [His recipes are most excellent. Many have been tested in the Experiment Kitchen of the English Folk Cookery Association. — ED.]

Of this particular 'receipt' he says: Madam Parker told me she gave two guineas for it. She gave it me for a receipt I gave her for curing hams, which is also very excellent.

INGREDIENTS: Bacon 4 oz.; butter 4 oz.; green peas 3 quarts; a little milk, good broth 2 qts.; young peas 1 pint; bread cut into dice; pepper and salt and a little sugar to season.

TIME: about 1 hour.

METHOD

1. Put the butter and bacon in a saucepan over a very slow fire with the 3 quarts of peas to 'sweat' them, adding a little milk to prevent the peas getting dry.
2. Add two quarts of good broth (or stock).
3. Let them boil 10 minutes.
4. Strain them through a colander.
5. And mash them well with the broth.
6. If your soup be too thick add a little more broth.
7. Season to taste, blend by mixing a little flour with a little milk to a cream, stirring it into the soup and boiling it up.
8. When about to serve it, add the pint of young peas which must first have been boiled separately very green.
9. Don't boil it up afterwards.
10. Don't fry your bread – but dry it at the fire and cut it into dice.

Stock for Gravy or Gravy Soup

Mary Eaton, Bungay, Suffolk, 1823

INGREDIENTS: Lean beef 1 lb.; lean gammon of bacon 1 lb.; water 2 quarts; scraped carrots about 8 oz.; onions 6 oz. (peeled brings about 4 oz.); and scrubbed and stringed celery about 8 sticks.

METHOD

1. Slice and cut up the meat.
2. Slice the vegetables and add them to the meat.
3. Stew until the meat is quite tender but do not let it brown.

N.B. – 1. When thus prepared it will serve either for soup or brown or white gravy; if for brown put in a little brown colouring and put it on to boil for a few minutes.

2. The meat, if only boiled until it is tender, will make a delicious meat loaf (*see* p. 57) or potted meat for luncheon or breakfast (*see* p. 52).

Queen Henrietta Maria's Morning Broth

17th Century

This has been very kindly sent by Miss Prendergast (*see* p. 305).

INGREDIENTS: A hen; parsley, a handful; thyme, a sprig; spearmint our garden mint) 3 sprigs; a little balm; onion, half a large one; pepper; salt and a clove — water to cover the hen.

METHOD

1. Put the hen in a pot with enough cold water to cover.
2. Bring to boil.
3. Add the onion, herbs, pepper and salt and clove.
4. Simmer till the broth is reduced to less than a pint, and strain.
5. Remove any fat and serve broth in a porringer.

Chesterfield Soup

This is another University recipe

INGREDIENTS: Calf's tail; mushrooms; sherry 1 glass; ketchup.

METHOD

1. Make a good brown soup in the usual manner with calf's tail and mushrooms.
2. Add a little ketchup,
3. And the sherry.

Gloucester Clear Pheasant Soup

Another Cambridge soup of Victorian days

INGREDIENTS: Clear stock flavoured with pheasant; sherry 1 glass tiny forcemeat balls of pheasant, and some celery cut into peas.

METHOD

1. Put some clear stock flavoured with pheasant into a pot.
2. Add 1 glass sherry.
3. Garnish with tiny balls of forcemeat made of pheasant, and some celery cut into peas.

N.B.—Both the pheasant forcemeat balls and celery peas must be cooked before being put in the soup.

Mock Turtle

Mrs. Shaw, of Cheshunt, 17th Century

This is one of the Mayo family recipes sent by Mr. H. Mayo Leman, of Nottingham.

1. Take of lean mutton sufficient to make 3 pints of strong broth.
2. When cold take off the fat.
3. Then put in an anchovy chopt fine.
4. An onion chopt fine, the rind of half a lemon chopt fine, with the juice infused in a little thyme.
5. One dozen oysters if in season.
6. Half a teaspoonful of chian (cayenne) pepper.
7. Half a pint of Madeira wine and a little grated nutmeg.

N.B.—Into this soup you may put hash'd calf's head cut in squares, or chicken, what you like with forcemeat balls and whole hard-boiled eggs.

Scotch Broth

1900

INGREDIENTS: Scrag end neck of mutton 1 lb.; water 3 pints; carrot 1; turnip 1; small onions 2; celery 2 sticks; pearl barley 2 large tablespoonfuls; chopped parsley 1 dessertspoonful; pepper; salt.

TIME: 2 to 3 hours.

METHOD

1. Joint the scrag, cut off the meat, and cut it in pieces.
2. Remove all fat.
3. Put the bones and meat into the pan with the cold water and barley which should first be washed.
4. Bring to boil and let it simmer for 2 hours.
5. Strain and remove the bones, return the meat and barley to the pot, add the vegetables peeled, scraped, washed and cut into dice.
6. Cook another hour or until they are tender.
7. Season with pepper and salt.
8. Sprinkle in the parsley and serve piping hot.

Mutton and Barley Broth

INGREDIENTS: Scrag end of neck of mutton; cold water 3 pints; carrot 4 oz.; turnip 2 oz.; onion 6 oz.; celery 3 or 4 sticks; pearl barley parsley.

TIME: To cook 2 to 3 hours.

METHOD

1. Chop up the neck of mutton in very small pieces.
2. Put it into a pan with the water.
3. Bring gently to boiling point.
4. Skim, and add the vegetables cut up.
5. Simmer gently for 2 or 3 hours, adding a little water (as it lessens) to keep up the quantity.
6. Strain.
7. Leave till cold, skim off the fat.
8. Wash 2 oz. pearl barley, put it into the saucepan with the soup.
9. Bring to boiling point, and simmer till the barley is cooked (about 2 hours), season to taste.
10. Add some chopped parsley and serve.

Foundation White Sauce

The sender of this recipe was taught to make sauce and other things by Miss M. M. Mallock, sister of W. H. Mallock. Miss Mallock was one of the first educated women to train in cookery. (She was a student at the Birmingham School now closed, and is the author of *Economics of Modern Cookery or A Younger Son's Cookery Book*, 1896 and an article on 'Old English Cookery,' *Quarterly Review*, January, 1894.)

INGREDIENTS: Butter 1 oz.; plain flour 1 oz.; liquid about 11 liquid ounces (some flours take up more moisture than others); bay leaf 1; parsley and thyme 1 sprig of each; onion, turnip, celery, a small slice of each; cayenne; salt; lemon juice and a bit of butter the size of a nut.

TIME: about 20 minutes.

METHOD

1. Put the liquid (which may be all milk or half milk and half water, or white meat or fish stock according to the kind of sauce you want to make) into a saucepan with the bay leaf, herbs and vegetables, simmer with the lid on for 15 minutes.
2. Take off and strain, but keep the liquid hot.
3. Take a quart saucepan (you want a large one to enable you later on to have plenty of space to beat the sauce vigorously without splashing), put the butter in it and stand it over a low fire.
4. When the butter is melted, add the flour and stir with a wooden spoon; the cold flour will make the butter solid again, and the result will at first be a stodgy mass.
5. Keep on stirring it over a slow fire, and
6. The butter will gradually liquify again; and

7. The whole will bubble and form fascinating little holes.
8. When this happens remove the pan from the fire before the mixture colours.
9. Add the hot milk (or whatever liquid you are using) beating it in gradually with the wooden spoon to keep the sauce free from lumps.
10. When all the liquid has been beaten in this way, return it to fire and stir carefully with a wooden spoon (or whisk with a wire whisk) until the sauce boils.
11. Then boil 5 minutes.
12. Season with cayenne (which is the only pepper that will dissolve and keep the sauce white; white or black pepper will make it grey).
13. Squeeze in a little lemon juice.
14. Stir in the nut of butter to give the sauce a gloss, after this is added the sauce must not boil.

N.B.—A sauce made in this way is quite digestible because frying the flour in the butter, before the liquid is added, cooks it better than if it is merely diluted with liquid and stirred into boiling milk, etc. The above method is used also for thickening vegetable soups, and thus blending the vegetables into a homogenous cream instead of letting them separate from the liquid and settle at the bottom of the soup. The proportion of liquid added is merely greater according to the soup being thickened and blended.

If by any chance a beginner is doubtful at stage 10 whether the sauce be really free from lumps, she should put it through a gravy strainer before boiling it up, as a lump of flour mixed with liquid once boiled can never be smoothed out.

Foundation Brown Sauce

The method for making this is the same as above as far as stage 8 when, instead of removing the butter and flour mixture from the fire whilst still white, allow it to colour (of course without burning) until it is of a light coffee colour, and it may take 20 minutes or longer to achieve this. Then, instead of adding milk or a milk mixture, add stock (white or brown) or water and meat essence, according to the type of sauce you are making.

Brown Gravy with Meat

The same principle is followed when we make gravy in the pan in which meat has been 'roasted'(!) or baked in the oven; equal quantities of fat and flour are cooked together in the pan over a low gas or other heated fuel till brown. This is stirred all the time and care is taken not to burn the mixture. The liquid added is boiling water or (better still) stock. It is a good plan for this purpose to use the water in which vegetables and potatoes have been cooked. In this way all the valuable salts are used instead of being thrown down the sink.

Some 17th Century Sauces

1. *Oyster Sauce* with Roast Shoulder of Mutton, gravy, white wine, oyster liquor in which oysters have been parboiled, a few oysters, thicken with yolk of egg (the shoulder may be stuffed with oysters cut into bits, seasoned with pepper, salt, a little boned anchovy chopped fine, a few breadcrumbs, mingled with the yolk of one or two raw eggs and a little ham cut small). Garnish with slic't lemon.

N.B.—Oysters (with roast or boiled mutton, or mutton made into a pudding, pie or hot-pot) are a distinctive feature of cookery in this country dating from the days of the Romans.

2. *Sauce for Roast Shoulder of mutton without oysters*: Gravy, claret, pepper grated nutmeg; slic't lemon and broom buds. Garnish the mutton with barberries and slic't lemon.

3. *Sauce for Veal*. This may be made with the water in which carrots have been cooked, and may be flavoured with quinces cooked to a pulp and crab apple juice. To this should be added a little claret, sugar, lemon juice, nutmeg, pepper, salt, rose vinegar and a little ground cloves.

N.B.—It must be remembered that no spice should overpower another flavouring; they are used to make a fresh flavour. It is in this that a cook has scope to display genius.

4. The *Pork Sauces* are very like those used in the 20th century:
   (*a*) Gravy, chopped sage and onions boiled together, some pepper.
   (*b*) Apples pared, quartered and boiled in fair water, with some sugar and butter.

5. *For Pigeons*: Gravy and juice of orange, or gravy, claret wine and an onion stewed together with a little salt.

6. *Sauce for any land fowl or game, turkey, etc.* Stamp small nuts to a paste, with bread, nutmeg, pepper, saffron, cloves, juice of orange, and strong broth, boil them together pretty thick and strain.

7. *Sauce for Pork, Goslings, Chickens, Lamb or Kid:* Juice of green wheat (frumenty) lemon, bread and sugar.

A Very Good Irish Sauce

Mrs. Blagrove from Miss Wettin's Manuscript Book.

INGREDIENTS: Good strong gravy 4 spoonfuls; anchovies 4; horseradish a little bit; sweet marjoram, parsley, mace, a little bit of each; clove 1; peppercorns 5; nutmeg, a little bit; onion a small bit; melted butter (or white sauce) one pint; ketchup to make it brown; or for carp, a little red wine.

TIME: simmer together for 10 to 15 minutes.

METHOD

1. Wash and clean the anchovies.
2. Pull them to pieces.
3. Put them in the gravy with other flavourings.
4. Simmer all together till half is consumed.
5. Then strain it off.
6. Add it to the melted butter sauce.

N.B.—If you want it brown, add a little ketchup, or for carp or other fish a little red wine.

Nasturtium Seeds instead of Capers

INGREDIENTS: Pale vinegar 1 quart; salt 1½ ounces; shallot 1; whole pepper 6; cloves 3; mace and nutmeg and horseradish to flavour; young nasturtium seeds gathered as soon as the blossoms are off and before they get hard.

TIME: 10 minutes.

METHOD

1. Prepare the pickle by putting the vinegar, salt, spices, and shallot in an aluminium saucepan.
2. Bring to boiling point.
3. Boil 5 minutes.
4. Pour into a glass or stoneware jar.
5. Cover and leave till cold.
6. Strain off into another glass jar.
7. Keep closely covered with glass lid tied down with brown paper; no metal must go near vinegar.
8. As the nasturtium blossoms fall gather the seeds and drop them in the pickle.

Caper Sauce

This is a very old English sauce and admits of several variations. Well made it is delicious served with boiled mutton and various fish dishes for which recipes are given. English housewives pickled nasturtium seeds (*see* p. 120) for use instead of capers.

I

Make half a pint of Foundation White Sauce (*see* p. 117) using half milk and the other half some of the liquor in which the mutton or fish has been boiled; season and finish with a dessertspoonful of pickled capers, or nasturtium seeds, either of which may be cut in halves to make them go further. Don't boil after they are added.

II

Make half a pint of Foundation Brown Sauce and add the capers or nasturtium seeds as above.

Sharp Sauce

Make ½ pint Foundation Brown Sauce, season slightly with nutmeg, add gherkins and a few capers chopped fine; also 2 tablespoonfuls of Mrs. Combers' Sauce (*see* p. 99). The stock should be flavoured with onion and a little anchovy essence, and essence of beef may be added to the other ingredients. There is scope for individuality in making this sauce. Our great-great-grandmothers had imagination as well as skill, and loved to exercise both.

Reform Sauce

They used claret in the 17th century for some sauces; and later port wine. A glass of either of these may be added to a good brown sauce made with stock flavoured with ham or bacon, carrot, celery, onion, bay-leaf, thyme, peppercorns and a bit of mace; finish with a teaspoonful of anchovy, some of 'Mrs. Combers' Sauce and with two good tablespoonfuls of red currant jelly and you have the famous 'Reform Sauce.' Francatelli was chef of the Reform Club, London, in 1852, after he had been head of the Royal kitchens, and both this sauce and 'Reform Cutlets' are English, and his recipes are for dishes which this club made famous.

Anyone who does not want to spend time in making Mrs. Combers' sauce (*see* p. 99) can buy Harvey Sauce and use that.

Parsley Sauce and Fennel Sauce

This is simply Foundation White Sauce with chopped parsley leaves added. It mustn't boil afterwards, and the stems should not be used, as they will make the sauce green. Fennel Sauce is prepared in the sam manner (*see* p. 133).

Shrimp Sauce

Make ½ pint Foundation White Sauce, if possible with ½ fish stock and ½ milk, add 1 teaspoonful anchovy essence, 1 small pinch cayenne, a little lemon juice, and the picked shrimps.

Lobster Sauce

If using a fresh lobster pound the coral and spawn in a mortar with an equal proportion of butter and rub through a hair sieve. Add this to some Foundation White Sauce made as above with ½ milk and ½ fish stock; and season with the juice of half a lemon, a teaspoonful of anchovy and a pinch of cayenne pepper.

Oyster Sauce

Beard the oysters (saving their liquor); measure the latter and use it to make the white sauce, adding enough milk to make the right quantity of liquid, season with nutmeg, cayenne, anchovy and lemon juice — add the oysters and serve hot.

Mussels

These can be used for sauce instead of oysters; but a couple of well-beaten yolks of eggs should be blended with the white sauce, and a little cream is an improvement. Do not boil after the yolks, cream and mussels are added; simply heat up to simmering point, but don't let it even simmer.

Egg Sauce

Boil 2 or more eggs hard (i.e. for 6 minutes) and shell them; cut each into 8 pieces and put these into a well-made delicately seasoned Foundation White Sauce, using only milk for the liquid.

Mustard Sauce

Add a teaspoonful or more of made mustard (mixed with tarragon vinegar) a dessertspoonful of chilli vinegar, and a little anchovy essence to ½ pint Foundation White Sauce. Soft roes may be cut up and added.

Onion Sauce

Peel and slice 3 large onions, put them in boiling water and boil up the water and cook till tender, drain well, and stir them into ½ pint Foundation White Sauce made with ½ milk and ½ white stock. Heat through and serve, a little cream is an improvement. Suitable for roast mutton, rabbits and tripe.

N.B.—Onion sauce is more delicate if the sauce is rubbed through a wire sieve.

Celery Sauce

This is made in the same manner as onion sauce, substituting the white part of celery for the onions.

Mushroom Sauce

Add a dozen button mushrooms to ½ pint Foundation White Sauce made with half milk and half white stock, or to ½ pint Foundation Brown Sauce, add also some mushroom ketchup and boil for 10 minutes.

Truffle Sauce

Truffles are found in England in Hampshire, Wiltshire, Somersetshire and Gloucestershire (near Bristol) and other places; wash them and pare them but don't throw away the parings, wash them and put them in stock to flavour it; slice them into ½ pint Foundation Brown Sauce, add a glass of sherry, and boil for 10 minutes.

Bread Sauce

INGREDIENTS: Fine breadcrumbs 2 oz.; peeled shallot 1; cayenne pepper, salt, milk ½ pint; butter ¼ oz.; a little cream if possible, even a teaspoonful will make a difference.

TIME: to boil five minutes.

METHOD

1. Put all the ingredients (except the cream) together in a pan over the fire.
2. Boil 5 minutes stirring all the time.
3. Remove the shallot.
4. Add the cream and serve very hot.

Ham Sauce

INGREDIENTS: Lean boiled ham, shredded fine, 2 oz.; shallots 3 finely chopped, or a small quantity of chopped chives when in season; butter ¼ oz.; Foundation Brown Sauce ½ pint; lemon the juice of ½; pepper and chopped parsley.

TIME: 10 minutes

METHOD

1. Heat the ham, finely chopped shallots or chives in the butter over the fire for 4 minutes without browning them.
2. Add the brown sauce.
3. The lemon juice and pepper and boil for 5 minutes.
4. Stir in the chopped parsley, and serve with veal cutlets or any grilled meats.

The above hot savoury sauces are based on the English ones given by Francatelli (date about 1845).

Mr. Michael Kelly's Sauce for Boiled Calf's Head; Tripe or Cow-Heel

1823

Mr. Michael Kelly was composer and director of the music at the Theatre Royal, Drury Lane, and the Italian Opera in 1823. He was a friend of Dr. Kitchiner.

INGREDIENTS: Garlic vinegar 1 tablespoonful; mustard; brown sugar; and black pepper; 1 teaspoonful each; oiled butter ½ pint.

METHOD

1. Mix the dry ingredients with the vinegar; and
2. Stir into the hot oiled butter.

Mr. Michael Kelly's Sharp Sauce

INGREDIENTS: Capers 1 teaspoonful; minced parsley 1 tablespoonful; the yolks of three hard-boiled eggs; made mustard 1 tablespoonful; anchovies 6; oil 2 tablespoonfuls; vinegar 1 tablespoonful; shallot; vinegar 1 tablespoonful; cayenne pepper a few grains; gravy ½ pint.

METHOD

1. Pound the capers, mince the parsley, rub the hard yolks of eggs smooth with the mustard.
2. Bone and pound the anchovies.
3. Mix all the ingredients together and pound them in a mortar with the oil and vinegar.
4. When thoroughly incorporated add them to half a pint of good gravy; mix well, put the whole through a sieve and beat up thoroughly before sending to table.

Tomato Sauce for Present Use

Mrs. Calvert, Ockley Manor, Surrey, 1827

INGREDIENTS: Tomatoes, a little water, a few peppercorns, pepper and salt; cayenne; white vinegar; a small piece of butter.

METHOD

1. Put your tomatoes in a stewpan with a very little water and a few peppercorns tied up in a piece of muslin.
2. When quite soft, lift out the peppercorns and rub the tomatoes through a tammy or hair sieve.
3. Add pepper and salt, cayenne and white vinegar to taste.
4. Add a bit of butter, which is a great improvement.

Rules for Stuffings and Forcemeat Balls

Mary Eaton, Bungay, Suffolk, 1823

1. The ingredients should be so proportioned that no one flavour predominates.
2. Some dishes require a very delicately flavoured stuffing, while for others it should be full and high seasoned.
3. The consistence of forcemeats seems to be attended with some difficulty; they are almost always either too heavy or too light. They should be mixed perfectly smooth, and the ingredients thoroughly incorporated.

4. Forcemeat balls should not be larger than a small nutmeg. If for brown sauce, brown and fry them; if for white sauce, put them into boiling water, and boil them for 3 minutes; the latter are by far the more delicate.

5. Parboiled sweetbreads and tongues are the principal ingredients for stuffing or forcemeat. Besides these the following are used:

Yolks of hard-boiled eggs,
Flour, bread-crumbs,
Boiled onion, mashed potato,
Mutton, beef or veal suet, marrow,
Brains, and veal minced and pounded.
Garden herbs, and roots,
Parsley, thyme, spinach, marjoram.
Savory, tarragon, sage, chervil,
Basil, burnet, bay leaf,
Truffles, morels, mushrooms.
Leeks, shallots, onions and garlic.

Fish: Shrimps, prawns, crabs, lobsters, oysters and anchovies.

Spices: Pepper, mace, allspice, cinnamon, ginger, nutmeg, cayenne and cloves.

Bacon and ham.

Liquids: Meat gravy, lemon juice, essence of anchovy, mushroom ketchup, vegetable essences and essence of spices, milk, and egg.

Stuffing for Pike or other Fish

Mary Eaton, Bungay, Suffolk, 1823

INGREDIENTS: Fat bacon 1 oz.; beef suet 1 oz.; fresh butter 1 oz.; bread-crumbs 3 oz.; thyme and savory 1 teaspoonful; onion a small one; a few leaves of scented marjoram shred fine; boned anchovies 1 or 2; salt and nutmeg a little of each; pepper to taste. A few oysters will be an improvement with or without anchovies; and egg to bind.

METHOD

1. Chop the bacon and suet finely.
2. Also the fresh parsley, thyme and savory; the onion and anchovies, and sweet marjoram.
3. Pound all together, and season.

4. If you are using oysters mince but do not pound them, add them to the powdered mixture and
5. Bind with an egg.

126

Stuffing for Poultry

Mary Eaton, Bungay, Suffolk, 1823

INGREDIENTS: Beef suet (marrow is better) 4 oz.; bread-crumbs 4 oz.; parsley leaves 2 drams; sweet marjoram or lemon thyme 1½ drams; grated lemon peel 1½ drams; onion or shallot 1; all chopped as fine as possible; nutmeg, just a little; pepper ¼ teaspoonful; salt ½ teaspoonful; eggs 2; an ounce of cooked ham finely minced is an improvement.

Sufficient for a turkey poult; a very large turkey will take nearly twice as much.

METHOD

1. Finely chop the suet, herbs, etc.
2. Pound all the ingredients together thoroughly.
3. Beat up the eggs lightly and incorporate them with the rest of the ingredients little by little as you pound them.

Stuffing for Veal, Roast Turkey or Hare

Mary Eaton, Bungay, Suffolk, 1823

INGREDIENTS: Bread-crumbs 4 oz.; finely chopped beef suet 4 oz.; finely chopped parsley and sweet herbs 1 teaspoonful of each; anchovy 1 boned and minced; nutmeg; pepper ¼ teaspoonful; salt ½ teaspoonful; grated lemon peel, a little; raw egg or milk to bind.

METHOD

Pound all together and moisten with egg or milk.

Stuffing for Hare

Mary Eaton, Bungay, Suffolk, 1823

INGREDIENTS: Beef suet, chopped fine, 2 oz.; fine bread-crumbs 3 oz.; parsley 1 teaspoonful; marjoram and lemon thyme or winter savory half a teaspoonful each; grated lemon peel 1 dram; nutmeg ½ dram; finely minced shallot 1 dram; egg; pepper and salt to taste. The liver (if sound) parboiled and minced very fine.

METHOD

1. Pound the first ingredients.
2. Moisten with egg as usual.
3. Add the minced liver.

4. Put the stuffing in the hare and sew up.

Stuffing for Goose

Mary Eaton, Bungay, Suffolk, 1823

INGREDIENTS: Onions one or two, very finely chopped; bread-crumbs a large teacupful; pepper and salt a very little; half the liver parboiled; eggs 2, yolks only.

METHOD

1. Pound and incorporate as usual.
2. Put it into the goose but leave a

little room for the stuffing to swell.

Stuffing for Geese and Ducks

In Cheshire mashed potatoes are added to the stuffing for geese and ducks.

Good Forcemeat Balls

Miss Wettin

INGREDIENTS: Beef suet 1 lb.; veal $\frac{1}{4}$ lb.; bread-crumbs $\frac{1}{2}$ a pound; sweet marjoram; thyme; lemon peel; anchovy 1; nutmeg; salt; egg 1; flour.

METHOD

1. Skin and chop the suet.
2. Scrape the veal.
3. Chop the herbs and lemon peel.
4. Bone and chop the anchovy.
5. Grate in a little nutmeg and some salt.

6. Pound the suet with the bread.
7. Then put in the herbs, etc.
8. Add one egg.
9. And work up the whole with enough flour to make it roll out into balls.
10. Fry them in lard.

Currant Sauce for Sucking Pig

INGREDIENTS: Dried currants 1 oz.; water $\frac{1}{2}$ pint; bread-crumbs 1 oz.; cloves 1 or 2; nutmeg, grated, a very little; sweet wine, a wineglass; butter, a bit; sugar to taste.

METHOD

1. Boil the water for a few minutes.
2. Add the other ingredients and simmer for a few minutes.

3. Serve in sauce-boat.
4. For venison or hare use red wine not white.

FISH

To Bake a Codling

1777

1. Draw a codling, wash it well and dry it.
2. Take some oysters, some sweet herbs chopped small, some grated bread, the yolks of 2 or 3 eggs with some salt, pepper, cloves and nutmeg.
3. Mix these ingredients together, and use them to stuff the codling.
4. Lay it in a baking dish on a rack to keep it from touching the bottom.
5. Put into the dish some red wine.
6. Baste the codling well with butter before it is put into the oven.
7. When it is done pour off the liquor which is under the codling into a saucepan, with a piece of butter rolled in flour.
8. Let these boil together till of a proper thickness.
9. Add some shrimps or oysters and a little anchovy to flavour.
10. Heat up and serve.

N.B.—The codling lies best in the dish with its tail turned in its mouth. Bass may be cooked in the same manner.

A small salmon or trout is good baked in this manner.

(An epicure of the old school always insisted upon having his cod or codling rubbed all over with salt, placed in a dish in the larder, and kept there for at least two hours before cooking. The salt must be washed off before it is cooked. This method makes the flesh firmer.)

Baked White Fish, Bacon and Green Peas

Lancashire

Sea bream, fresh haddocks, rock salmon, codlings, fillets, etc., can all be made into a savoury nourishing dish if cleaned and put into a brown baking dish, floured and covered with rashers of bacon (or some breadcrumbs or bits of butter or clarified beef dripping may be sprinkled over the fish, and the rashers of bacon can be rolled and placed along each side). The dish is then baked in a good oven and will be done in about half an hour.

Bacon with fish is a favourite dish with fisher-folk, and at Blackpool green peas are always served with it.

Stuffed Fillets

Fillets of white fish, plaice, etc., are delicious placed flat on a board skin side upwards, brushed over with egg, a trimmed rasher of bacon or layer of veal or mushroom stuffing put on each, rolled up, dipped in egg and bread-crumbs and fried. A brown sharp sauce can be served with them. Both Mr. Michael Kelly's sauces are suitable (*see* pp. 124 and 125).

Steamed Fillets

Butter an enamel plate, arrange some plain delicate fillets on it. Put a little bit of butter on each, squeeze a little lemon juice over them, cover with a pyrex glass dish and stand it over a saucepan in which you are cooking potatoes. By the time the potatoes are cooked the fish will be ready. The use of a pyrex glass dish as a cover is convenient because the fish can be seen through it and its progress observed.

An 18th Century Cod Stew

1. Take a pound of large cod, and the sounds (which must be blanched, and if dried they must be boiled till tender), also the roe (blanched and washed clean) and the liver.
2. Cut the latter in round pieces.
3. Put them all into a stewpan, the large pieces of cod in the middle with a bunch of sweet herbs, a quarter of a pint of broth or boiling water, and half a pint of white wine.
4. Add some ground mace, an onion, some grated nutmeg, and some salt.
5. Cover them close, let them stew 5 or 6 minutes.
6. Then put in a dozen oysters with their liquor strained, and a piece of butter rolled in flour.
7. Shake the pan round till they are enough, and the sauce of a good thickness.
8. Take out the sweet herbs and onion.
9. Lay the fish in a dish and pour the sauce over it.
   [The thickening of the sauce with a piece of butter rolled in flour is interesting.—ED.]

Scottish Fish Custard, 1931

This comes through the *Woman's Leader* from Miss M. Barrowman, of Giffnock, Glasgow.

INGREDIENTS: Nice filleted fish (haddock) 1 lb.; eggs 3; milk 3 teacupfuls (¾ pint); ¼ teaspoonful salt.

TIME: ¾ hour in slow oven.

METHOD

1. Wash fish, and dry it.
2. Roll each fillet daintily and arrange nicely side by side in a pyrex fire-proof glass baking dish (or an ordinary pie dish).
3. Put the eggs in mixing bowl, and beat lightly.
4. Add milk, and salt.
5. Pour over arranged fish and bake in slow oven for 45 minutes.

Eels and Eel Pie

The Medical Research Council reported in 1928 that 'the body oil in eels (almost 30 per cent of their whole substance) contains not only Vitamin D, but almost as much Vitamin A as good cod-liver oil — a striking confirmation of the medieval notion that eels have high dietetic value.'

('Rediscovering what our grandmothers knew so well that we've forgotten 'em, and calling 'em by fresh names!')

Swan Song by John Galsworthy, page 84, July 1928.)

TO KILL EELS INSTANTLY

Dr. William Kitchiner, 1817

'To kill eels instantly, without the horrid torture of cutting and skinning them alive, pierce the spinal marrow, close to the back part of the skull, with a sharp pointed skewer; if this be done in the right place, all motion will instantly cease.'

Spitchcocked Eels

Dr. Kitchiner, 1817

1. Take two middling-sized silver eels; leave the skins on.
2. Score them well with salt, and wash them; cut off the heads.
3. Slit them on the belly side, and take out the bone and guts and wash and wipe them nicely, then cut them into pieces about 3 inches long, and wipe them quite dry.
4. Put 2 oz. butter into a stewpan with a little minced parsley, thyme, sage, pepper and salt, and a very little chopped shallot; set the stewpan over the fire; and when the butter is melted, stir the ingredients together, and take it off the fire.

5. Mix the yolks of two eggs with them, and dip the eel in, a piece at a time, and then roll them in bread-crumbs, making as much stick to them as you can.

6. Then rub a gridiron with a bit of suet, 'set it high over a very clear fire, and broil your eels of a fine crisp brown' (in 1932 we should grill them under gas or electricity); dish them up with crisp parsley, and send up plain melted butter in a boat, and anchovy and butter sauce.

Good and Inferior Eels

Kitchiner

'The yellow eels taste muddy; the whiteness of the belly of the fish is not the only mark to know the best; the right colour of the back is a very bright coppery hue; the olive coloured are inferior; and those tending to a green are worse.'

AN EXCELLENT SAUCE FOR EELS

Make ½ pint of good thick creamy white sauce (*see* p. 117) stir into it by degrees one tablespoonful of port wine, and 1 teaspoonful of mushroom ketchup, and 1 teaspoonful of the vinegar from pickled onions.

To Stew Eels

Ann Peckham, Leeds, 1767

Eels went out of fashion for many years because it was thought they had to be skinned alive, and the idea was revolting; but they can be killed instantly by piercing the spinal marrow (*see* p. 131).

INGREDIENTS: Some eels; fat for frying; gravy; claret; horseradish; an onion; a little mace; an anchovy.

METHOD

1. Cut the eels in what lengths you please.
2. Wipe them dry with a cloth and fry them.
3. Drain them free from fat.
4. Make some gravy hot.
5. Put a little butter into a stewpan, add a little flour.
6. Cook together till a nice brown.
7. Remove from fire and dilute with the gravy.
8. Add the claret, a very little horse-radish, an onion, a little mace and the anchovy.
9. Then put the pieces of eel in to simmer till they are cooked, but be careful not to let them cook too much.
10. Lift them out on to a hot dish and strain the sauce over them.

Elvers

THE WHITEBAIT OF THE WEST

*From Mr. Smith, late of Fisher's Tudor House, Gloucester, and
The Plough Inn, Cheltenham*

Elvers are immature eels, as slim as threads, that abound in the Severn at
Epney, below Gloucester. They are carried round in baskets and cried in
the streets of Gloucester. Washed clean with salt and water, floured and
fried in boiling fat, they are very nutritious. A plateful makes a complete
meal for a working man. The Germans buy them alive, carry them back
to Germany, and cultivate them.

Red Herrings

Great Yarmouth, 1823

1. Choose those that are large and moist.
2. Cut them open, and pour over them some boiling small beer.
3. Let them soak half an hour, then drain and dry them.
4. Make them just hot through before the fire, and rub them over with
cold butter.
5. Serve with egg sauce or buttered eggs; mashed potatoes should also
be sent up with them.

To Boil Mackerel

1826

'The season for this fish is May, June and July; when alive or very fresh
their sea-green colours are very brilliant and beautiful, their gills are a
fine red and their eyes bright; they are so tender that they carry and keep
worse than any other fish.'
1. Rub them with vinegar.
2. When the water boils put them in with a little salt.
3. Boil them gently a quarter of an hour.
4. Serve them up with fennel and parsley boiled for a minute or two,
chopped and put into a melted butter sauce, and gooseberry sauce—a
tureen of each.

Gooseberry Sauce for Mackerel

1749

1. Melt a little butter in a saucepan.
2. Add a dust of flour
3. Brown it.
4. Throw in some chives minced very fine.
5. When these have been heated together add some of the water in which the mackerel was boiled.
6. Add some salt and pepper.
7. And put in some small picked gooseberries.
8. Add a little sugar and keep simmering till the gooseberries are tender. Finish with a squeeze of lemon juice and a bit of butter.

N.B. – This is a recipe of Dutch origin.

To Broil Mackerel

1826

1. Wash them clean.
2. Cut off their heads.
3. Take out their roes (at the neck) and boil them in a little water, then bruise them with a spoon.
4. Beat up the yolk of an egg with a little nutmeg, lemon peel cut fine, herbs boiled and chopped fine, salt, pepper, and some crumbs of bread.
5. Make all these ingredients, roes included, into a stuffing or pudding.
6. Put it into the fish.
7. Flour them well.
8. And broil them nicely.
9. For sauce use a melted butter sauce with some walnut pickle.

Mullets as at Falmouth in 1881

INGREDIENTS: Red mullets; chopped parsley; shallots; grated cheese; wine. For sauce: tomato; spice; chopped ham; a few oysters; some capers.

METHOD

1. Butter a baking dish.
2. Clean but do not draw the mullet; lay them in the dish.
3. Sprinkle them with chopped parsley, shallot and grated cheese.
4. Add some white wine and bake.
5. Make a sort of tomato sauce with tomato, the liquor in which the mullet was baked, some butter and flour, season with a very little cayenne pepper and some salt, also a little spice.
6. Rub it through a hair sieve or tammy.
7. Cut some oysters in slices and put in sauce.
8. Also some capers.
9. Pour over the fish and send to table.

Baked Red Mullets

In the Chesterfield manner as understood at Cambridge

INGREDIENTS: Red mullets; chopped parsley; chopped shallots Harvey sauce, 1 glass; a little anchovy sauce; port wine 2 glasses.

TIME: to bake 1 hour.

METHOD

1. Butter an earthenware baking dish or (1932) a fireproof glass dish with a cover.
2. Clean, but do not draw the mullets, they are the woodcock of the sea, and are not drawn.
3. Put them in the dish, sprinkle with the parsley and shallots.
4. Add the Harvey sauce, anchovy sauce, and port wine and bake ½ hour.
5. Make a nice red sauce; add the sauce from the mullets and a little more wine, and pour this all over the fish, and garnish with truffles (*see* p. 123) and crayfish or lobster.

To Bake Pike

INGREDIENTS: Pike; veal stuffing; butter; claret; orange juice; a clove of garlic.

METHOD

1. Clean but do not scale the fish.
2. Put it into a Staffordshire baking dish (that has been rubbed lightly with a clove of garlic) with some salt butter and one or two glasses of claret.
3. Baste well, using plenty of butter.
4. Bake in good oven. When done squeeze some orange juice over the pike and serve in the dish in which it is baked, with the wine and butter in which it was cooked as sauce.

N.B.—Pike are best in November after the first frosts. They make excellent forcemeat balls for fish and fish cakes.

Lampreys and Lamperns

Both are caught in the Severn. Lamperns are in season from October to March, and Lampreys from Christmas till June.

Potted lamperns are a Worcester speciality and may be bought at George's (formerly Mountford's) Restaurant in the High Street, Worcester, and at their Cheltenham branch (1931). They are very delicious.

Bass

This very good fish is cooked in the same way as cod, either baked, boiled, or cut in slices and grilled (see page 129).

To Bake Plaice

1749

1. Mince some chives, shred some parsley very fine, cut some savoury herbs including sweet basil very small.
2. Mix them all together with some nutmeg, pepper and salt.
3. Rub inside of a baking dish well over with fresh butter, then strew the seasoning you have just made all over it that it may stick in great quantity on every part.
4. Choose some fine large plaice, clean them perfectly, cut off the heads and tails, and lay them regularly and evenly in the dish.
5. When this is done, pour in a gill of red wine (or water flavoured with tarragon vinegar).
6. Strew over them a little pepper, salt and grated nutmeg.
7. Drop in on them some melted butter in small quantity.
8. Cover with a large quantity of very fine bread-crumbs.
9. And bake them a fine brown.

To Poach Salmon

1. Place a thick slice of salmon weighing a pound in a fireproof glass baking dish that will just hold it comfortably.
2. Measure ½ pint water, add to it ½ a teaspoonful of salt, and 1 teaspoonful of tarragon vinegar.
3. Pour this over the salmon.
4. Put on the glass lid and bake it in a fairly hot oven until done. It is easy to know when it is ready because the flesh leaves the bone quite clean.

N.B.—This is a most excellent way of cooking salmon, the colour and white curd being both beautifully preserved, and if eaten hot no other sauce is required than the liquid in which it is cooked, whilst if required to be eaten cold as a salad it will keep delightfully moist. The thin part of the salmon is the greater delicacy, therefore serve a little of it with the thick part.

Baked Rolled Salmon

1777

INGREDIENTS: Half a salmon from the bone; oysters; parsley; crumbs of bread; pepper; salt; nutmeg and mace; butter; ½ pint of water; a teaspoonful of tarragon vinegar and a little salt, or a little wine, or wine and water.

TIME: to bake 1 hour.

METHOD

1. Take off the skin of the salmon.
2. And take off one side in one long fillet.
3. Make a seasoning with the oysters cut small, parsley chopped fine, and mixed with crumbs of bread and seasoned with the pepper, salt, nutmeg and mace.
4. Put your fillet flat on your board, with the skinned side next the board.
5. Brush the fish over with a beaten egg.
6. Spread it with the seasoning.
7. Roll it up very tight.
8. Put it into a deep baking pot.
9. Pour the seasoned water, or wine or wine and water, over the fish.
10. Put a few dabs of butter on top.
11. Cover it over either with a lid or paper.
12. And bake for one hour in a quick oven.

N.B.—Cod or fresh haddock or any other suitable fish would be nice if done in the same way. When salmon was more plentiful than now our ancestors had a number of interesting ways of cooking it, which might well be applied to the cheaper coarse sea fish we are urged to eat at the present day (1932).

Trafalgar Baked Trout and Salmon

INGREDIENTS: Salmon, or trout; plenty of butter and lemon juice; for sauce use fish stock; elderberry sauce; chopped parsley; chopped capers; lobster coral.

METHOD

1. Cut the salmon or trout into nice little collops or slices.
2. Skin them.
3. Bake in plenty of butter and lemon juice.
4. When cooked draw off the liquor and make a good sharp sauce with a little butter and flour and fish stock.
5. Strain.
6. Add some chopped parsley and capers, and some lobster coral.

Trout

Clean the fish, sprinkle with coarse oatmeal and grill them. They need no sauce but a little salt.

Grayling

These are found in many rivers; in Staffordshire, Izaak Walton's own county — Shropshire, Herefordshire, Worcestershire and Wiltshire.

They come in handy when salmon and trout go out as, although belonging to the same family, they are in season from June 16th to March 15th.

They are best grilled and should be sprinkled with powdered dried thyme.

Minnow Tansies

Izaak Walton, 17th Century

INGREDIENTS: Minnows; yolks of eggs; cowslip 'pips' (or flowers) or primrose petals; a very little tansy juice; and a little clarified fat in which to fry them.

METHOD

1. Wash the minnows well in salt, cut off their heads, tail them, and 'take out their guts.'
2. Blend them with a few cowslip pips or primrose petals, some yolks of eggs, and a very little tansy juice.
3. Season with pepper and salt, and
4. Fry them in a little fat as you would any other fritter.

Shad

The Severn is famous for its shad as well as its salmon, and great quantities formerly abounded opposite the Isle of Dogs in the Thames. It can be grilled and served with caper sauce; or stuffed with veal stuffing and baked with bacon; served with brown sauce sharpened with lemon juice or chopped pickled gherkins; or it may be boiled and served with the excellent Dutch sauce (*see* p. 143).

RECIPE

Mary Eaton, Bungay, Suffolk, 1823

INGREDIENTS: Shad; butter; salt; sorrel; chervil; onion, parsley; butter; cream; salt; pepper; nutmeg; or you may serve shad with stewed mushrooms; or brown sauce with capers, or nasturtiums, garnished with lemon.

METHOD

1. Scale the shad very clean, gut and wash them, dry them in a cloth.
2. Score them on their sides.
3. Rub them with butter.
4. Sprinkle salt over them, and
5. Broil (or grill) them a fine brown.
6. Boil the sorrel, chervil, onion and parsley all chopped fine in a little water; strain.

7. Melt a piece of butter in cream sufficient for your sauce, then
8. Put in your herbs.
9. Season with salt, pepper and a little nutmeg.
10. Toss it all up together to make it piping hot and pour over your fish.

Smelts

Mary Eaton, Bungay, Suffolk, 1823

1. When good and in season, they have a fine silvery hue, are very firm, and have a refreshing smell like cucumbers newly cut.
2. They should not be washed more than is necessary merely to clean them.
3. Dry them in a cloth, lightly flour them, and shake it off.
4. Dip them in plenty of egg, then into fine bread-crumbs.
5. Plunge them into a good pan of boiling lard.
6. Let them continue boiling and a few minutes will make them a bright yellow brown.
7. Take care not to take off the light roughness of the crumb, or their beauty will be lost.

How to Cook Soles and Similar Fish

1932

There is no need to egg and bread-crumb soles or similar fish, or to dip them in batter. They are delicious cleaned, wiped dry, brushed over with butter and grilled (*see* p. 31). Dish up on a plain white dish paper and garnish with a little finely chopped parsley arranged down the middle of the fish, some pieces of lemon and sprigs of crisp parsley at each end.

They may be served with chopped parsley and butter and lemon piped on top.

Sturgeon

1777

This old recipe says 'they are taken in the Severn and Tyne, some few in the Thames,' and they are occasionally caught now (but not in the Thames). People remember eating sturgeon as children, and they have been on sale in London occasionally, during the last ten years. This is a close fish, and tastes rather like veal when cooked. In case we get hold of some, it is just as well to know how to cook it. It can be boiled, baked, soused, or pickled.

To Boil Sturgeon

1. Take a piece of sturgeon; clean it well.
2. Put it into a vessel with 2 quarts of water, a pint of vinegar, a stick of horse radish cut into pieces, 2 or 3 bay leaves, some lemon, some whole pepper and a little salt.
3. Let the fish boil softly in this liquid till it is enough.

N.B.—This dish would do quite as well put into a modern oven, if the vessel had a lid to cover it; and in this case it would not require such a large quantity of water and vinegar, although the same proportions should be kept.

Sauce

1. Dissolve an anchovy in a very little water, and strain it.
2. Then put in a pot a very large piece of butter (2 oz.), roll it in flour (2 oz.) and melt it very smooth.
3. Add the anchovy water (¾ pint), 2 tablespoonfuls of mushroom ketchup, the same of white wine, the body of a small crab or lobster bruised (chopped small) and some shrimps.
4. Boil all together.
5. Squeeze in some lemon.
6. Pour some of the sauce over the sturgeon, and the rest in sauce boats.

N.B.—Or it could be served with oyster sauce.

('In England the sturgeon was at one time known as the royal fish, its consumption being confined to the King's table and those individuals or cities holding the royal permission to eat it. The law still stands though obsolete in practice.'—Artemus Ward, *Encyclopædia of Food*.)

How to Cook Whitebait

This is the recipe of Mr. Groves, a fishmonger

1. Take the whitebait out of the water.
2. Put them on the back of sieves to drain for about half an hour before cooking.
3. Lay a cloth on the table and flour it well.

4. Throw the whitebait off the sieves on the cloth and flour again.
5. Take up the two sides of the cloth, one in each hand, and shake the fish and flour together.
6. Put them into boiling fat without touching them with the hand.

Dressed Crab

1900

INGREDIENTS: 1 nice crab; bread-crumbs 1½ oz.; chopped parsley 2 teaspoonfuls; seasoning; cream 1 tablespoonful; lemon; juice of half; vinegar 2 teaspoonfuls; anchovy essence 1 teaspoonful; butter ½ oz.

METHOD

1. Take out meat from fish, reserve a little of the white meat from the claws for decoration.
2. Remove grey fingers from flesh.
3. Chop fish, add all the other ingredients to this and mix well.
4. Wash the shell and polish it with a little oil.
5. Place the mixture in the shell first breaking off the edges of the shell.
6. Garnish with some of the white flesh, chopped parsley, and coralline pepper.
7. Dish up on folded white table napkin or on a dish paper.
8. Garnish with a ring of the crab's legs, having the top joint cut off.

Crayfish

(ASTICUS FLUVIATILIS)

Mr. L. C. R. Cameron, author of *The Wild Foods of Great Britain* (1917) says: 'This is a species of small fresh-water lobster found in most chalk-streams, in the Bedfordshire Ouse, and in many ponds and other rivers, especially in those bordering on Cannock Chase in Staffordshire. I have caught them singly upon hooks baited with worms; but the best way to capture a number is to put a bit of "high" liver into a basket, which must be smartly lifted or they will escape over the edge. Small boys catch them singly on the Darenth in Kent by using empty round cigarette tins after the same manner.'

[They are found also in the Windrush, Oxfordshire; the Thame at Haddenham, Buckinghamshire, and the Exe, North Devon; and when we were young we used to catch a number in closely netted string-bags which we baited with the insides of a fowl and placed in likely places (amidst rocky stones for example near the bank of a stream in the cool of an August evening) sitting idly by for half an hour or so, dreaming, before we looked to see if we had had any luck. — ED.]

141

'First they must be dropped in boiling water for a few minutes,' says Mr. Cameron, 'when they will turn pink.' The meat is then picked from their shells.

HOW TO COOK THEM

1. The shelled fishes may be added to any green salad and tossed in a plain oil (3 tablespoonfuls) and vinegar or lemon juice (1 tablespoonful) dressing; season with pepper and salt.

2. They may be heated in a Foundation White Sauce (*see* p. 117) to which a little cream may be profitably added, seasoned with cayenne and salt, and flavoured with a little anchovy essence. They can then be put in deep scallop shells, covered with bread-crumbs, sprinkled with a little oiled butter and browned in the oven.

3. Or they may be eaten with Dutch sauce.

4. Or they may be made into a delicious soup. As, however, this is rather troublesome to prepare the recipe is not given here.

Buttered Lobster

Ann Peckham, Leeds, 1767

INGREDIENTS: One or more lobsters; gravy; melted butter; pepper; salt; and a spoonful of vinegar.

METHOD

1. Cut up the lobster small.
2. Put it into a stewpan with a little gravy, butter, pepper, salt and vinegar.
3. Set it over the fire till hot.
4. Heat the shells, and serve the lobsters in them.

Stewed Oysters

Mary Eaton, Bungay, Suffolk, 1823

INGREDIENTS: Oysters; mace, a bit; lemon peel; pepper, a few white ones; butter and flour; cream; sippets of toast.

METHOD

1. Open the oyster shells.
2. Separate the liquor from the oysters.
3. Beard them.
4. Strain the liquor into a stewpan, add the oysters, a bit of mace, lemon peel, and a few white peppers.
5. Simmer them very gently for 5 minutes, strain, take out the lemon peel, peppers and mace, return them and the liquor to the stewpan; put in some cream; and when that is hot through, add the flour rolled into the butter.
6. Simmer 5 minutes and serve piping hot.

N.B.—They may be served in the deep halves of oyster shells which must first be thoroughly washed and scrubbed; or they may be used to fill patty cases of puff pastry; or cases made of stale dinner rolls. (To make these, rasp the outside of the rolls, cut a piece off the top for a lid; scoop out all the crumb of bread leaving only a thin shell; brush over with yolk of egg, and bake in the oven till delicately coloured and crisp. The pieces cut off for the lids should be treated in the same manner. They can be kept in a tin and when required can be heated and crisped up in a few minutes and filled with stewed oysters, or any other delicious and delicate stew. They can be served with or without their lids).

These stewed oysters can be used also to stuff tomatoes. Do not skin the tomatoes, but cut off the top for lids, scoop out the flesh, fill with the stewed oysters, put on the tomato caps, place in a buttered dish and bake in a good oven for 15 minutes.

Plain Dutch Sauce

Francatelli, 1845

INGREDIENTS: White Foundation Sauce (*see* p. 117), a large gravy-spoonful; eggs, 4 yolks; nutmeg, grated, just a little; pepper; fresh butter 2 oz.; salt, a little, a little tarragon vinegar or lemon juice.

METHOD

1. Put the white sauce into a saucepan.
2. Add the yolks of eggs, nutmeg, pepper, salt, and fresh butter.
3. Stir briskly on the fire.
4. Pass through a hair sieve, or tammy.
5. Keep hot in saucepan in a pan of hot water.
6. Just before dishing-up add a little tarragon vinegar or lemon juice.

THE ROAST MEAT OF OLD ENGLAND

'The English principle is that our own meat and game shall be presented at table in the highest state of perfection attainable, so far as breeding, feeding, and keeping can accomplish it; each animal, when served, to be characterized by its own proper flavour, which is on no account to be masked or disguised by others, which are adventitious . . . Where meat is inferior or insipid, an opposite treatment is the better one , . . finely flavoured sauce is valuable for improving materials which do not possess their own distinctive fine qualities and flavours.

The Englishman loves the flavour of three- or four-year-old mutton (unhappily almost a tradition now), mature beef, the wildest game, both winged and ground; and he cares not how little of "sauce" is supplied— he demands only "gravy"; so that these are in fine condition, sufficiently, not over-kept, and simply cooked, for the most part carefully roasted.'

SIR HENRY THOMPSON, 1888.

THE TASTE OF THE FIRE

The well-known 'taste of the fire,' which is so much appreciated, is produced by actual carbonization of the surface of the food, and may be obtained by toasting, broiling or grilling. Even if no open fire be available for roasting, small birds, joints, chops, steaks, bacon, sausages, etc., can be toasted as a rule in a small Dutch or game oven in front of an ordinary gas or electric fire, and of course before a wood fire.

It is quite easy to stand a small Dutch or game oven on something that will raise it to the best position for cooking purposes. These handy little gadgets can be used in the dining-room or studio for impromptu little suppers.

GENERAL RULES FOR ROASTING

1. If you have a fire before which it is possible to roast, but have no spit or jack, two strong skewers put through the middle of the roast, one on each side with a strong piece of string tied round each end will do the trick. (This is a hint for campers, hikers and backwooders. Sir Walter Scott writing in 1820, in *Ivanhoe* says: 'Wild fowl brought in upon small wooden spits or broaches, "drip their fatness from the hazel broach"').

2. It is a good plan to turn the bird or joint upside down half way through the roasting process, so that the juices may be more evenly distributed. If skewered in the middle this can be achieved quite easily; with the old-

144

fashioned horizontal revolving spit this was not necessary. It was the perfect method of roasting.

N.B.—The old roasting and cooking arrangements in the Hall of the Brewers' Company, Addle Street, London. are complete and in a good state of preservation.

3. Before putting meat down to roast (or cook in any other way) joint it properly, preserve the fat by covering it with paper which should be tied on with fine twine (skewers let out the gravy, therefore too many should not be used). If there is more fat than you think will be eaten with the lean trim it off, for it will make an excellent pudding if finely chopped; or 'render' (melt) it down and clarify it for frying.

4. Put some dripping in the pan, baste the meat well at once, and every 15 minutes till the last half-hour; then take off the paper, sprinkle a little salt over the joint, baste it well with a little butter and dredge it with flour; let it cook for a few minutes longer till the froth arises then take it and dish it up.

5. Slow roasting is as advantageous to the tenderness and flavour of meat as slow boiling, of which everybody understands the importance. The warmer the weather and the longer the meat has hung the less time it will require to roast it.

6. Roasting should be done by the radiant heat of a clear glowing fire; meat may be 'roasted' in an oven or in a pot over the fire, but in both these cases it is in fact baked.

BASTINGS AND DREDGINGS

Our ancestors were very particular in their bastings and dredgings The following are given by Robert May in 1665:

'The Rarest Ways of dressing of all manner of roast meats, either flesh or fowl, by sea or land, and divers ways of breading or dredging meats to prevent the gravy from too much evaporating.'

DREDGINGS

1. Flour mixed with grated bread.

2. Sweet herbs dried and powdered, and mixed with grated bread.

3. Lemon peel dried and pounded, or orange peel mixed with flour.

4. Sugar finely powdered, and mixed with powdered cinnamon and flour or grated bread.

5. Fennel seeds, corianders, cinnamon, and sugar, finely beaten, and mixed with grated bread or flour.

6. For young pigs, grated bread or flour mixed with beaten nutmeg, ginger, pepper, sugar, yolks of eggs.

7. Sugar, bread and salt mixed.

BASTINGS

1. Fresh butter.
2. Clarified suet.
3. Minced sweet herbs, butter and claret, especially for mutton and lamb.
4. Water and salt.
5. Cream and melted butter, especially for a flayed pig.
6. Yolks of eggs, grated biscuit, and juice of oranges.

WILLIAM KITCHINER, M.D., 1817.

'ROASTING' IN THE OVEN

The general rules given above are the results of experiments made by Dr. William Kitchiner assisted by his own cook, Mrs. Elizabeth Lister, and Mr. Henry Osborne, cook to Sir Joseph Banks, President of the Royal Society; they apply also to 'roasting' in a gas oven in which the joint can be hung, or cooked in an uncovered tin.

'ROASTING' IN A SELF-BASTER

A baking tin, with a close-fitting cover in which there is a valve that opens and closes to enclose or let out the steam from the meat, has been on the market for some years. It is known as a Self-baster, and is made in block tin in varying sizes costing from 3s. 11d. upwards. It should be obtainable from any ironmonger and is always stocked by the Civil Service Supply Association, Strand, London, England. It can be used also for baking bread and cakes. Directions for 'roasting' meat, etc., are given with each tin. (Price in 1968: 31s. 3d.)

Its merits are:
1. When the valve in the lid is closed the contents of the tin require no further attention; the meat cooks in its own juices and steam; it does not require basting. When the valve is opened the meat browns.
2. The meat being covered, the fat does not splash the sides of the oven; this saves labour in cleaning; also it minimises the smell of cooking.
3. The meat is not exposed to the fumes of the gas when cooking in a gas oven.

The general rules for roasting given above can be followed or adapted with this exception: no paper is required to cover the fat, as the lid is sufficient protection.

POT-ROASTING

This is done in an iron pot (a gipsy kettle with a lid), which is slung over a good fire.
1. Put some dripping in the pot; make it hot.

2. Put in the meat, baste it as usual, put on the lid and stand it on, or hang the pot over, an even fire. It cooks as if it were in an oven. No paper is required to cover the meat.

3. Roasting on the same principle may be done in a 'Top-hat Cooker' placed over a low gas flame, electric or oil-cooker; the difference being that the 'Top-hat Cooker' is lighter in make than the iron kettle, and that the top-hat lid conserves the steam. Consequently, like the self-baster, it requires no attention when once set going.

TIME TO ALLOW FOR ALL ROASTINGS

Beef and mutton, 15 minutes for every pound and 15 minutes over.

Pork, lamb and veal, require 20 minutes to the pound and 20 minutes over.

Dr. Kitchiner says 'A noble sirloin of about 15 pounds will require to be before the fire for about 3½ or 4 hours. The fire must be well built, sound, and even.'

A thin piece will require a small brisk glowing fire.

The smaller the joint to be roasted the higher the temperature to which its surface should be exposed.

WHERE VISITORS CAN GET PERFECTLY ROASTED MEAT, POULTRY AND GAME

At 'Simpson's in the Strand,' 100 Strand, London, W.C.2, England. 'The meat literally melted in my mouth,' says Lady Margaret Campbell. The only fault to be found is that the portions served are too large for modern appetites, but if required smaller helpings can be cut at first and a second helping offered.

RECIPES

For all roasts follow the general directions given above according to the equipment you are using.

A SIRLOIN OF BEEF

If your joint be large and your family small, cut off the thin end and salt it; and cut out the undercut or fillet and cook it next day as 'Mock Hare'; thus you will get three dinners. It is the middle part of the sirloin that has the undercut.

MOCK HARE

1. Cut out the fillet from under the sirloin of beef, leaving the fat to cook with the joint.

2. Make some stuffing as for a hare; beef suet chopped fine 2 oz.; fine bread-crumbs 3 oz.; chopped parsley, a dram; shallot chopped finely ½

dram; chopped marjoram, lemon-thyme, or winter savory a dram; lemon peel grated a dram; nutmeg grated $\frac{1}{2}$ a dram, and the same of pepper and salt; the white and yolk of an egg.

METHOD

1. Mix all dry ingredients for the stuffing together, then
2. Blend with the egg, but be careful, the sizes of eggs differ; don't make your stuffing too thin; it must be stiff or it will be good for nothing.
3. You will only require half this amount, or even less, for your mock hare: the above quantities are for stuffing a real hare.
4. Put the stuffing on the beef, roll it up, tie it up with tape and roast in the usual manner. Serve with wine sauce and currant jelly.

RIBS OF BEEF BONED AND ROLLED

1. Many persons prefer the ribs to the sirloin.
2. Some cooks before they roll the ribs brush the meat with egg and sprinkle it with veal stuffing.
3. As it is a solid mass it requires steady and long cooking. Follow the general directions.—WILLIAM KITCHINER, 1817.

A LEG, HAUNCH OR SADDLE OF MUTTON

Hang in a cool airy place for four or five days at least; in temperate weather, a week; cold weather ten days. Follow general directions for roasting, and serve with currant jelly or prune sauce, and gravy (*see* p. 159).

SHOULDER OF MUTTON

Roast according to general directions and serve with onion sauce (*see* p. 123).

THE BLADE BONE BROILED

Dr. Kitchiner says 'The blade-bone of a shoulder of mutton is a favourite luncheon or supper relish, scored, peppered, and salted and broiled, or done in a Dutch oven.'

A CHINE OF MUTTON ROASTED

A chine of mutton was stuffed in similar fashion to the way a chine of bacon is stuffed to this day in Lincolnshire; lemon peel or orange peel chopped with here and there a clove (or in place of cloves, tops of rosemary) thyme, sage, winter-savory, or sweet marjoram all chopped and blended; roast it and baste it with butter; and serve with the following:

SAUCE

Mutton gravy, seasoned with nutmeg and boiled up with a little claret and the juice of an orange. Before dishing up rub the dish lightly with a cut clove of garlic.

ROAST LAMB

The usual accompaniments of roast lamb are green mint sauce, and a salad; and some cooks, about 5 minutes before it is done, sprinkle it with a little minced parsley.—WILLIAM KITCHINER.

HIND QUARTER

A quarter of a porkling is sometimes skinned, cut and dressed lamb-fashion, and served up as a substitute for it. The leg and loin of lamb should always be roasted together — the former being very lean — the latter very fat — and the gravy is better preserved.—WILLIAM KITCHINER.

FORE QUARTER

It is a pretty general custom, when you take off the shoulders from the ribs, to squeeze a Seville orange over them, and sprinkle them with a little pepper and salt.—WILLIAM KITCHINER.

ROAST VEAL

With those joints that are not stuffed send up forcemeat in balls or rolled into sausages, or fried pork sausages; bacon and greens are always expected with veal.—WILLIAM KITCHINER.

Oliver Cromwell was always much annoyed if his wife did not provide an orange to accompany roast veal.

BREAST OF VEAL

This makes a savoury relish for luncheon or supper. First boil it, then roll it in a cloth and press it between two dishes with a weight on top; when cold trim it neatly, egg and bread-crumb, and grill or brown in a quick oven.

'Breast of mutton is dressed in the same way.'—WILLIAM KITCHINER.

Stewed cucumber or cucumber sauce is delicious with both these joints.

TO ROAST VEAL IN PIECES

1. Cut some tender veal into squares the size of a hen's egg, season with pepper and salt, some ground cloves and fennel seed.
2. Arrange them on a metal skewer putting a slice of bacon the same size between each two pieces.

3. Wrap a piece of caul round each skewer and hang them on the hooks in a game roaster, and cook in front of the fire.

4. Serve with a good veal gravy or sauce.

MINT SAUCE WITH ROAST VEAL AND ROAST PORK

'This,' writes a lady from the Isle of Wight, 'is even better than mint sauce and lamb, or so I think; and I have tried it in Wales. Why only lamb I wonder?'

ROAST PORKER'S HEAD WITH MINT SAUCE

1826

INGREDIENTS: A fine young head; bread and sage stuffing (*see* p. 151) mint sauce, or a salad.

METHOD

1. Clean the head.
2. Take out the eyes and brains and tongue, cut off the ears.
3. Stuff the head with sage and bread (not onion) stuffing.
4. Rub over with butter.
5. Dredge with flour and roast (this would now be done in the oven).
6. Serve with mint sauce and salad.

PORK CHOPS WITH MINT

This recipe was published in the *Daily News* as one of a very fine series that appeared during the winter 1928–29. It was sent from Worcester.

METHOD

1. Mix half breakfastcupful of flour, half cupful of dried powdered mint, 1 teaspoonful salt, and a generous pinch of cayenne pepper. Pork chops rolled in this mixture and fried are excellent. The same mixture is used to dredge roast pork with instead of plain flour.

N.B.— 1. One of the features of Old English Cookery was the variety of 'dredgers' and 'bastings' used when roasting meat, etc. These might well be used to-day when meat is 'roasted' in the oven.

2. Mint was a favourite flavouring (*see* Yorkshire Mint pasty; and mint and sultana sandwiches and other recipes in this book—pp. 235 and 271).

ROAST PORK

The great thing is to be sure it is done enough.

Pease pudding is as good an accompaniment to roasted as it is to boiled pork.

LEG OF PORK

Score the skin in narrow stripes (some score it in diamonds) about a quarter of an inch apart; stuff the knuckle with sage and onions minced fine, and a little grated bread seasoned with pepper, salt and mixed with the yolk of an egg:

Sage ¼ oz.; onion ½ oz.; bread-crumbs 1 oz.; a little black pepper and salt, and ½ the yolk of 1 egg.

If you think the onion too strong parboil it. — WILLIAM KITCHINER.

Rub a little sweet oil on the skin with a paste brush or a goose feather; this makes the crackling crisper and browner than basting it with dripping; and it will be a better colour.

SPARE-RIB OF PORK

Mary Eaton, Bungay, Suffolk, 1823

1. Baste it with a very little butter and flour.
2. When done sprinkle with dried sage leaves crumbled.
3. Serve it with potatoes and apple sauce.

MOCK GOOSE

(or Leg of Pork roasted without the skin)

1. Parboil the leg.
2. Take off the skin.
3. Then roast it; baste it with butter.
4. Make a savoury powder of finely minced and powdered sage, ground black pepper, salt, and some bread-crumbs, rubbed together through a colander; you may add to this a little very finely minced onion.
5. Sprinkle it with this when it is almost roasted.
6. Serve with ½ pint of brown gravy in the dish and fried balls of the following stuffing:

GOOSE OR DUCK STUFFING

Green sage leaves 1 oz.; onions 2 oz.; both chopped finely; bread-crumbs 4 oz.; egg 1; a little pepper and salt, some add to this a minced apple. — WILLIAM KITCHINER.

N.B. — 'Make it a general rule never to pour gravy over anything that is roasted; by so doing, the dredging etc., is washed off, and it eats insipid.' — WILLIAM KITCHINER.

ROAST LOIN OF PORK

Stuff it with goose or duck stuffing made as on this page for Mock Goose; some of the savoury powder recommended for the Mock Goose may also be sprinkled on it.

How to Cook a Sucking Pig

This is one of our most esteemed traditional dishes, and the following is the way in which it was cooked when Charles Lamb sang its praises.

1. A sucking pig is in prime order for the spit when about three weeks old.
2. To be eaten in perfection it should be killed in the morning and eaten at dinner the same day. It loses part of its goodness every hour after it is killed; if not quite fresh no art can make the crackling crisp.

FOR THE STUFFING

INGREDIENTS: Bread-crumbs 5 oz.; sage a handful finely minced (about 2 oz.) and onion about 2½ oz.

TIME: a small three-weeks-old pig will be cooked in about 1½ hours.

METHOD

1. Mix them together with an egg, some pepper and salt, and a bit of butter as big as an egg; fill the belly of the pig with this, and sew it up; lay it to the fire, and baste it with salad-oil till it is quite done; do not leave it a moment; it requires the most vigilant attention.

CUT OFF ITS HEAD

Before you dish it up, cut off its head and part that and the body down the middle; chop the brains very fine with some boiled sage leaves, and mix them with good veal or beef gravy or what runs from the pig when you cut its head off. Send up also a tureenful of gravy (see p. 119).

Currant sauce is still a favourite with some (see p. 128).

Lay the pig back to back in the dish, with one half of the head on each side, and the ears, one at each end, which you must take care to make nice and crisp, or you will be scolded, as the good man was, who bought his wife a pig with only one ear.

When you cut off the pettitoes, leave the skin long round the ends of the legs. When you first lay the pig before the fire, rub it all over with fresh butter or salad-oil, ten minutes after, and the skin cooks dry — dredge it well with flour all over — let it remain on an hour — then rub it off with a soft cloth.

N.B. — A pig is a very troublesome subject to roast — most persons have them baked; send a quarter of a pound of butter and beg the baker to baste it well. — WILLIAM KITCHINER.

Roast Chicken or Fowl

Lancashire

In Lancashire a roast fowl is always stuffed, served with good gravy, rolls of bacon and bread sauce.

INGREDIENTS: of Stuffing: Bread-crumbs 2 tablespoonfuls; finely chopped suet ½ oz.; chopped parsley 1 teaspoonful; mixed herbs ¼ teaspoonful; lemon rind a grating; salt ¼ teaspoonful; pepper and cayenne; egg half a whole one, or the yolk of one and a little milk.

TIME: to roast fowl: ¾ to 1½ hours according to age.

METHOD
Mix all together and stuff the bird at the neck where the crop was.

Herefordshire

In Herefordshire farmhouses a piece of fresh pork (if available) is always roasted, and served with roast chicken.

Roast Duck

Mrs. Roundell, Nantwich, Cheshire

Ducks do not need hanging; in fact if required at once they may be cooked as soon as killed. Make a good brown gravy of the giblets.

TIME: ¾ to 1 hour; must be well-basted.

Duck and Green Peas

INGREDIENTS: Duck 1; onion 1; beef stock 1 pint; blanched sage leaves 4; blanched mint one dessertspoonful; pepper; salt; ½ an onion sliced; green peas 1 quart.

TIME: about 1 hour.

METHOD

1. Truss the duck for roasting.
2. Put the liver and a sliced onion inside, but do not stuff it.
3. Roast it for 20 minutes; then
4. Put it in a stewpan with the beef stock; put the sage leaves and mint, and halves of onion in a muslin bag and add this, season with pepper and salt.
5. Simmer for a quarter of an hour, and skim off all the fat.
6. Add the peas (not young peas).
7. Cover the pan closely, and
8. Simmer for twenty to twenty-five minutes more.
9. Give it one boil up.
10. Lay the duck on a large dish, and
11. Pour the peas and broth, just as they are, round it.
12. Lift out the bag of herbs and onions.

'Hindle Wakes'

Mrs. Kate A. Earp (Brighton) who sends this recipe says: 'We as a family in Lancashire called these fowls "Hindle Wakes" — why I do not know, unless it was, because old hens were sold at the "wakes" (fairs.)'

INGREDIENTS: An old boiling fowl; prunes 1 lb.; lemon juice (2 lemons); brown gravy.

TIME: to steam about 6 hours: to roast 1 hour.

METHOD

1. Wash lemon and pare the rind thinly and simmer it gently in ½ pint water for 15 minutes to extract the flavour.
2. Add to this water the strained juice of the 2 lemons.
3. Wash the prunes and pour the lemon juice, etc., over them.
4. Let them soak all night.
5. Next day stuff an old boiling fowl with the prunes; sew it up.
6. Steam for 6 or more hours till tender.
7. Then wrap in bacon fastened with skewer, and roast for one hour, serve with good brown gravy in the making of which use any of the lemon liquor that may not be soaked up.

To Roast a Hare

Worcester, early 18th Century

'Let him be well cleaned with the pudding thus:

'Sweet herbs, bacon, lemon peel, two anchovies and the liver (if sound) par-boiled all chopt fine, beef suet, bread-crumbs seasoned with what spice you please, mixt all together with butter and put into the belly, truss and roast him, basting him, with a quart of rough cider or milk. Put good gravy under him in the dish.'

Dr. Kitchiner's Recipe for Stuffing a Hare

1823

INGREDIENTS: Beef suet 2 oz. chopped fine; bread-crumbs 3 oz. parsley, 1 dram; shallot ½ dram; marjoram, lemon-thyme, or winter savory 1 dram; lemon peel 1 dram; nutmeg ½ a dram; pepper and salt ½ dram each; some egg. If the liver is quite sound, it may be par-boiled and added to the above.

METHOD

1. Blend the ingredients all together; and
2. Moisten the mixture with a little egg lightly beaten.
3. On no account must it be thin; if it is not stiff enough Dr. Kitchiner says it will be good for nothing. He also tells us most kindly that a middling sized teaspoon will contain about a dram.

Some Practical Notes

1. To ascertain the age of a hare, examine the first joint of the forefoot; if it is a leveret, you will find a small knob which disappears as it grows older. Then examine the ears; if they tear easily it will eat tender; if they are tough, so will be the hare, which is then only fit for soup or to jug.

2. When newly killed the body is stiff; when it becomes limp it should be cooked at once. It should not be paunched until it is to be cooked. It must be hung by the hind legs, but a basin should be put under the head to catch the blood; with care it may hang a week.

3. But a leveret must only hang a day or two.

4. When the hare has been paunched wipe the inside dry and line it with rashers of fat bacon, then put in the 'pudding' or stuffing, and close it up.

5. Mrs. Charlotte Mason writing in 1777 says: 'I have tried all the different things recommended to baste a hare, and never found anything so good as small beer.'

Dr. Kitchener believes in dripping. At the Red Lion Hotel, Fareham, Hants, which in the mid-Victorian period was noted for its good cooking, milk and butter were used for basting leverets.

As English cooking was notoriously good in the 18th century it would apparently be a good thing to try basting with a light beer, and cider seems quite a brain-wave — especially when we remember that our ancestors made a special point of 'bastings and dredgings.' (*See* p. 145).

How to Cook a Young Swan

Young swans were roasted in the 15th century in England, and they can still be bought in England to day.

On November 14th, 1931, the following advertisement appeared in the Personal columns of *The Times*.

'Cygnets (young swans) supplied dressed for dinner and banquets, or alive for ornamental waters — Master, Great Hospital, Norwich'; and here is a modern recipe for cooking them. It is one of Francatelli's, and in spite of his Italian name Charles Elmé Francatelli was an Englishman born and bred, and prided himself on that fact, but he had inherited a gift for cooking from his Italian forebears and also had the advantage of being a pupil of the great Carême. The English cook who only knows English cookery is at a disadvantage: 'He little knows of England who only England knows.'

'Cookery means the knowledge of Medea and of Circe and of Helen and of the Queen of Sheba.

'It means English thoroughness and French art and Arabian hospitality. . . .'

Norwich Cygnets

Francatelli, 1846—53

Procure a Norwich-fed cygnet (these birds are in best condition in September); stuff it with the following preparation:

INGREDIENTS: Rump steak 3 lb.; shallots 3; nutmeg; pepper and salt.

METHOD

1. Chop the steaks very finely.
2. Also the shallots.

3. Blend and season with pepper and salt, and
4. Use this mixture to stuff the bird.

TO COOK IT

INGREDIENTS: Well-buttered paper; flour and water paste; flour and butter; rich brown gravy; port wine sauce.

TIME: to roast, 4 hours.

METHOD

1. Truss as usual for roast poultry or game.
2. Wrap up in well-buttered paper and then encase the bird in a pastry made of flour and water rolled out.
3. Wrap up again in stout paper well greased and fastened with twine.

4. Roast for 4 hours.
5. Then remove all the coating.
6. Put down again and froth it with butter and flour in the usual manner.
7. Dish up with rich brown gravy.
8. Send to table accompanied by boatful of port wine sauce.

N.B.—Francatelli adds: 'Cygnets may be prepared for table according to the directions given for dressing wild geese.'

Port Wine Sauce

Dr. Kitchiner's recipe, 1822

INGREDIENTS: Port wine ¼ pint; unflavoured mutton gravy ¼ pint; red currant jelly 1 tablespoonful.

METHOD

Let it just boil up, and send it to table in a sauce-boat.

To Roast a Cygnet

WHICH MUST BE QUITE YOUNG

This is a family recipe belonging to Lady Grantham, Barcombe Place, near Lewes, Sussex. Her daughter, who sends it, says, 'I have used it in the good old days, and it is so good.'

INGREDIENTS: A young cygnet; powdered herbs; cloves and all-spice; beef dripping or good fat; water paste; flour and butter to baste; stuffing; gravy.

STUFFING: Rump steak 1½—2 lb.; chopped parsley; lemon rind; onion; pepper; salt and herbs; port wine ¼ pint. Good beef gravy: thicken with ½ oz. flour to every pint of stock; port wine; lemon juice; red currant jelly, a kitchen spoonful; pepper and salt.

TIME: Allow 15—20 mins. for each 1½ lb. in weight.

METHOD

1. Pick and draw as you would a goose.
2. Mix together powdered herbs, cloves and spice, and rub well into the bird inside and out.
3. Make the stuffing: mince the steak well, add the chopped parsley, etc., mix with the port wine and stuff the bird.
4. Truss the cygnet, being careful to sew both ends well over to prevent the gravy escaping.
5. Rub it all over with beef dripping or good fat.
6. Make a paste of flour and water.
7. Lay it over the breast, and
8. Tie the bird up in paper, and
9. Roast before a moderate fire or oven (see time above).
10. About 15 minutes before serving take up and remove paper and paste.
11. Put down again, flour well and baste with butter; and
12. Serve with gravy.
13. To make the gravy
14. Slightly thicken (see above ingredients) some good beef gravy.
15. Add the port wine, etc.
16. And serve very hot in a sauce-boat, putting a very little in the dish.

N.B.—It is quite a mistake to think that English people had only one sauce. In a small book called the *Compleat Servant Maid*, dated 1677, lent by Mrs. Loftus, Suffolk, there are a number of the special recipes used for different poultry, game, and meat; and it is interesting to observe that claret wine is given as the ingredient, not port (*see* Pontac Sauce, page 97).

Time for Hanging and Cooking Game

The best all-round book for Game Cookery and for directions for cooking freshwater fish is *The Sportsman's Cookery Book*, by Major Hugh B. C. Pollard. There is not space in the present book for any but the briefest instructions:

Pheasants: Must hang long; hang up by the tail feathers; in a good larder in clear, cold weather will keep 3 weeks. When the tail feathers 'give' the bird is ready to be cooked.

Baste well, roast for 45 minutes before a clear fire. Serve with good brown gravy, bread sauce, and celery boiled and covered with white sauce; or with braised chestnuts.

Partridges: Hang as long as possible. Time to roast 20 to 30 minutes; baste liberally; serve with bread sauce and fried bread-crumbs.

Grouse. Major Pollard says they 'require longer keeping than any other of the game birds, and hang from a minimum of three days to over a fortnight.' They are dry birds and must be larded with a piece of fat bacon, in addition to being well basted. Stuff them with red whortle-berries if you can get them. Time to roast 20 minutes. Fried bread-crumbs, bread sauce, brown gravy and watercress are the usual accompaniments.

Hazel Hens. Should have the breasts larded and well basted. Serve them with orange salad, or orange and pineapple. They also may be stuffed with cranberries or red whortleberries.

Wild Duck. Roast for 20 to 25 minutes.

Teal: For 15 minutes. For both serve orange, celery and watercress salad.

Grouse Stuffed with Bananas

Boodle's Club, 1923

1. Peel and cut up some bananas, mash and mix them with 2 level tea-spoonfuls of black pepper, 1 of salt, and 10 drops of lemon juice.
2. Use this to stuff either grouse or partridges, and roast them as usual.

Ortolans

Miss A. Vipan writing from near Bridport, Dorsetshire, March, 1931, says 'There are also a great many ortolans at Easton in Portland, but they are not much eaten nowadays.'

They were at one time a favourite delicacy, and this is the way they should be cooked:

1. Hang the birds till quite tender.
2. Pluck, singe and truss them like quails, but do not draw them.
3. Bind a vine leaf round each bird, fix them on a spit (or on the hooks of a game oven) and
4. Roast in front of a clear fire.
5. Put in the pan under each bird a slice of toast and baste them continually with butter. When the birds are cooked, place them on a hot dish with a piece of the toast under each, and serve with the following gravy:

Wine Sauce for Ortolans

1. Put into stewpan with a sufficient quantity of clear stock, a few strips of thinly pared orange peel, the juice of the orange.
2. A few basil leaves.

3. A wineglassful of port or claret.
4. Season to taste with salt and pepper.
5. Boil gently for 15 minutes, then strain and serve (*see also* pp. 97, 98).

To Roast Woodcock in the English Fashion

17th Century

1. Pull and draw them.
2. Truss and roast them.
3. Baste with butter.
4. Sprinkle them with bread-crumbs and flour.
5. Serve in a clean dish on the toast.
6. Send in good brown gravy.
   An orange and watercress salad can be served with them.

Snipe

Mary Eaton, Bungay, Suffolk, 1823

1. These birds will keep several days, and should be roasted without drawing, and then served on toast.
2. Butter only should be eaten with them, as gravy takes from the fine flavour.
3. The thigh and back are most esteemed.

Prune Sauce

Cre-fydd, 1863

INGREDIENTS: Prunes 1 lb.; water ½ pint; moist sugar 1 tablespoonful; rum or brandy 1 tablespoonful.

METHOD

1. Boil the prunes in the water till soft.
2. Add the sugar, rum or brandy.
3. Rub through a sieve, and serve in a sauce-boat

N.B. — Good with sucking pig, venison, or mutton.

5

OVEN COOKERY AND STEWS

OVEN COOKERY

Oven cooking and baked meats have always been a feature of good English cookery, from the days when an oven was dug in the ground and lined with stones to keep the earth from falling in, and heated with wood, seaweed, etc., along through the ages of public ovens to the oil, gas, and electric ovens of to-day.

The Manor Oven or as it used to be called the Town or Parish Oven was a prominent feature of domestic economy. It was not uncommon for the lord of the manor to provide a large oven for the baking of bread of the inhabitants of a parish, the ownership and charges for its use being reckoned amongst his manorial rights. In 1307 Melton Mowbray had one of them. When the oven was ready for baking a man paraded the streets blowing a horn.

Mr. Turner, English and French bread and biscuit baker, at the corner of London Street and Fitzroy Street, Fitzroy Square, in 1823 says:—

'Baking is one of the cheapest and most convenient ways of dressing a dinner in small families . . . I don't mean to deny the superior excellence of roasting to baking; but some joints, when baked, so nearly approach to the same as when roasted, that I have known them to be carried to the table and eaten as such with great satisfaction . . . I have been in the habit of baking them for the first families.'

The custom of sending the Sunday dinner to be baked at the baker's was kept up till nearly the end of the 19th century; it enabled the busy wife and mother, who was maid-of-all-work, to have a day's rest, and incidentally to go to church.

But the baker baked other things; Jane Austen in *Emma* refers to apples being sent to the baker's to be baked; and it was customary in Yorkshire for the baker to have special days for 'creeing' wheat for frumenty.

STEWING, BRAISING AND POACHING

Stewing: This is slow cooking (in more or less liquid) either over heat, or in the oven. It is in modern days (1932) frequently known as *casserole* cookery but is really the Old English method of stewing in earthenware jars and dishes. A casserole is merely the French name for a saucepan or stewpan. Cookery and the service of food is now a fine art, and food should be cooked and served in appropriate pots and pans; if you are cooking a French dish, by all means use a French casserole, and, if you like, serve the food in it, but if you are cooking an old English country dish cook and serve it in a Staffordshire or Nottinghamshire brown baking jar or pan and stand it on a homespun napkin placed on a dish of modern Staffordshire pottery. Clarice Cliff's designs are charming and whilst absolutely 20th century, carry on the English tradition.

Fireproof Glass Oven Dishes. The English fireproof glass oven dishes with and without covers, made in Sunderland and in Birmingham are an advance in cookery and table service. The food can be seen whilst cooking, and progress can be noted without lifting the lid, and it is never necessary to dish up the contents into another dish to send them to table. Food cooks particularly well in fireproof glass and as it is made in a variety of shapes to suit different food and methods of cookery it can be thoroughly recommended. It has stood the test of seven years' constant use in the E.F.C.A. kitchen; not one piece of a complete set has been broken.

Braising is merely a combination of frying in a very little fat and cooking afterwards in a very little liquid; the food cooks in its own juices. A proper braising pot has a lid on which hot charcoal may be put so that the cooking goes on between two fires — below and above; but braising, which is a very old form of cooking that came to us from the East, can quite well be carried on in a fireproof dish in any modern oven. It is possible to bake or braise out of doors by making a large hole in the ground, lining it with stones and putting the pot in it.

Poaching. This is simply cooking lightly in a small or larger quantity of liquid without actually boiling the food:

1. It may be placed in small tins in boiling water over the fire until the contents are cooked. In this case the tins must be covered with buttered paper, and they may sometimes be cooked in this way in a little water in a stewpan or frying-pan without a lid. The water should only reach about 3 parts up the tins, and great care must be taken that none gets in and touches their contents.

2. Fish may be placed in a fireproof oven dish with some cold milk or other liquid in the dish, either covering it or not as required; the dish may then be covered with a lid or buttered paper, and poached or gradually cooked in the liquid.

3. The third way of poaching is to place the food directly in boiling water as one does an egg; forcemeat balls can be cooked in this way if prepared for this purpose; so may dumplings.

Both the first and last of these methods of cooking belong more particularly to boiling, but oven poaching is so convenient that they are mentioned here with it. Even an egg may be poached in water in the oven in a covered fireproof dish; and there is no better way of cooking a slice of salmon.

Beef Olives

Worcester, 18th Century

'Cutt some square steakes of beef, wash them with some egg, season them lay on forcemeat. Role them up and tie them and either roast or stew them. Pour over them some good gravy with shallots, chopt fine in it. Garnish with pickles.'

BEEF OLIVES. A MODERN RECIPE

The Fanny Calder School of Cookery, Liverpool, 1904

INGREDIENTS: Rump steak 1 lb.; bread-crumbs 3 oz.; chopped parsley 1 dessertspoonful; finely chopped suet 1 oz.; anchovies 2 boned and chopped; lemon juice 1 teaspoonful; egg 1; seasoning; dripping 1 oz.; flour 1 oz.; water or stock 1 pint.

TIME: 1 hour.

METHOD

1. Cut the meat into thin slices about 3 inches long and 1½ inches broad.
2. Make a forcemeat with the bread-crumbs, parsley, suet, anchovies, lemon juice, egg, and season with pepper and salt.
3. Lay a little of this on each piece of meat, roll up and tie with a piece of string.
4. Put the dripping into a pan, when hot fry the meat rolls in it, turning over and over to brown them, and then remove from pan and drain.
5. Sprinkle flour into the pan, stir and brown it, being careful not to burn.
6. Add hot water (or stock) by degrees to avoid lumps.
7. Boil up and add seasoning, then put in meat and allow all to simmer gently for one hour in the pan or in a glass oven dish.
8. Remove string from meat, arrange on a hot dish with gravy poured round; or if stewing in the oven in a fire-proof dish send the olives up in the dish. Veal can be done in similar fashion.

Staffordshire Beef Steaks

1823

INGREDIENTS: Beef steaks; flour; pepper; salt; dripping; onions; boiling water; mushroom or walnut ketchup, a spoonful.

TIME: about 1½ hours or more according to the tenderness of the meat used.

METHOD

1. Beat the steaks a little.
2. Flour them and season with pepper and salt.
3. Fry them a nice brown, in a little dripping.
4. Lift them out, and place them in a fireproof glass oven dish (in former days they were put in a stewpan).
5. Fry some sliced onions, add a little flour to them, sufficient to take up all the fat.
6. Fry a nice brown but don't burn.
7. Pour enough boiling water over them to make a nice thick gravy (it must not be too thick).
8. Boil up, stir in a good spoonful of ketchup, and
9. Put all in the oven dish with the steaks.
10. Put on the lid, put in the oven and cook till tender.

Baked Liver and Onions

From a Yorkshire woman's scrap-book, 1931

INGREDIENTS: Liver; fat for frying; onions; pepper and salt; flour.
TIME: 1 hour.

METHOD

1. Peel the onions and throw them immediately into boiling water to remove the objectionable odour and taste.
2. Parboil the onions.
3. Cut up the liver in slices.
4. Dip in flour, pepper and salt.
5. Fry in boiling fat for a very few minutes.
6. Remove and place in an oven dish (with a cover).
7. Place the onions over the liver; put on the cover and cook very slowly in the oven until tender.
8. Make some gravy in the frying-pan, add to it any in the oven dish, thicken, and serve over the liver and onions.

Spiced or Hunter's Beef

From Miss Cullen, Dundee—a Boston, Lincolnshire, dish

INGREDIENTS: Beef, a small round; nutmeg 1; cloves ½ oz.; a little saltpetre; pepper and common salt; forcemeat; gravy 1 pint; butter.
TIME: to bake 4 hours.

METHOD

1. Take the bone from a small round of beef.
2. Salt it, using the nutmeg, cloves, saltpetre, pepper and salt (for proportions for salting meat *see* p. 59).
3. Stuff the hole from which you took the bone with forcemeat (*see* p. 125).
4. Bind the round lightly with tape.
5. Put it in a dripping tin (or earthenware pan) that will just hold it.
6. Pour over it the pint of gravy.
7. Put a little butter on top.
8. Cover with a piece of greaseproof paper.
9. And then with several folds of brown paper, or a close fitting lid.

Miss Cullen says: 'The gravy in the pan is fine, and useful for flavouring soups and sauces.'

If you don't want to keep the oven heated for so long, this joint will cook well in a fireless cooker, or over a low gas-jet if the latter is first covered with an asbestos mat and the pot stood on it. (An iron pot used for pot-roasting can be either slung over a wood fire made on the hearth, or placed on an open range or stove.)

How to Cook a Rather Coarse Piece of Beef

From a Yorkshire woman's scrap-book, 1931

INGREDIENTS: Beef — any coarse piece cut into a neat slab, thick ribs or similar piece; carrots; peas; small onions; pepper; salt; hot water; lentil flour.

TIME: about three hours.

METHOD

1. Prepare the vegetables and arrange them as a thick layer in a fireproof oven dish with a lid.
2. Place the meat on the vegetables.
3. Season with pepper and salt.
4. Hot water just enough to cover the meat.
5. Cook slowly.
6. Pour off gravy.
7. Remove fat.
8. Thicken the gravy with the lentil flour.
9. Pour over and serve.

Spanish Beef

A Woolrych family recipe

INGREDIENTS: Beef 4 or 5 lb. silver side of the round; with a loose piece of fat; stuffing made of bread-crumbs; pepper; salt; parsley and suet; onions 3 good-sized; cloves 9; bacon 3 thin rashers.

TIME: 3 or 4 hours to stew.

METHOD

1. Boil the fat separately.
2. Roll the beef round into a fillet, skewer and tie it round.
3. Have ready a seasoning of bread-crumbs, pepper, salt, parsley and suet.
4. With a sharp knife make 3 incisions in the beef.
5. Into these press the seasoning.
6. Have ready 3 good-sized Spanish onions into each of which stick 3 cloves.
7. Place 3 thin rashers of bacon and skewer the onions through them on top of the beef.
8. Then place the fillet in a stewpan — *not too large*, and without a drop of water or gravy.
9. Cover the pan with a wet cloth under the lid to keep in all the steam.
10. Place it at a distance from the fire until by listening you ascertain that the gravy is beginning to draw.
11. Gradually advance it – but on no account lift the lid.
12. Take the skewers out and pour the gravy over.
13. Serve the fat by the side.

Devilled Leg of Mutton

Another fine Cambridge College recipe, an excellent way of dealing with an undercooked leg of mutton

INGREDIENTS: Leg of mutton; devil seasoning (*see* p. 38); fresh butter; some good brown sauce (*see* p. 119); wine 2 glasses.

METHOD

1. Cut slices off an underdone leg of mutton.
2. Sprinkle them with devil seasoning.
3. Then with a little fresh butter, grill it under the gas (or by electricity or you can use a salamander), or it may be put into an oven hot enough to brown it.
4. Add the gravy that comes from it to some good brown sauce.
5. Put in 2 glasses of wine.
6. Pour this sauce round it and serve quite hot.

An Excellent Lancashire Hot-Pot

Manchester is noted for its hot-pots and has a special one of its own but the following excellent recipe hails from Bolton-le-Moors. The oysters may be omitted, but they are the correct thing in a real hot-pot. Another correct thing is to serve Lancashire hot-pot with a dish or glass jar of pickled red cabbage whatever recipe be used. This is traditional.

Bolton Hot-Pot

INGREDIENTS: 2 lb. middle neck of mutton; dripping 1 oz.; onion 1; flour 1 oz.; hot stock ¾ pint; pepper; salt and sugar; mushrooms 4 or 5; kidneys 2; oysters 20; potatoes 2 lb.

TIME: to stew in oven 2 hours.

METHOD

1. Cut the meat into chops.
2. Make the dripping hot in a pan, brown the meat in it.
3. Lift out and put into a brown Staffordshire pot that can be sent to table or, if you prefer it, a deep fire-proof baking dish with a lid.
4. Stew the onion and cook for a few minutes in the dripping.
5. Add the flour and cook it till it is nicely brown.
6. Add the stock (hot) to the pan and stir in the brown flour, as you would when making gravy.
7. Season to taste with pepper, salt, and a teaspoonful of castor sugar.
8. Slice the kidney thickly over the mutton.
9. Add the mushrooms peeled and, if large, cut to small size.
10. Add the oysters (all these are separate layers).
11. Peel the potatoes; cut them in thick slices and arrange them overlapping round the top of the meat, etc., with the knobbly ends in the centre to cover the contents of the pot completely.
12. Strain the thickened stock over the potatoes, put on the lid and stew in a moderate oven for 2 hours. Take off the lid during the last 15 minutes to brown the potatoes nicely.

Irish Stew

Stoodleigh Rectory Stew for the Hunting Season, 1892

When the meet of the Devon and Somerset staghounds was in the neighbourhood of Dulverton, Oakford and Stoodleigh, it was the custom of Mrs. Arthur Hillyard (wife of the Rector of Stoodleigh) to have a cold luncheon set from 12 to 3 o'clock in the dining-room, and it was also the custom to put on the fire, early in the day, a huge pot of what was known as Irish Stew, so that anyone could have a good plate of hot stew as well as cold meat and sweets. Only one servant remained in the kitchen on these days, one to wait in the hall and dining-room, and one man in the stables to attend to callers and their horses. Everyone else followed the hounds either on horseback or on foot. Even the children, their governess and nurse, would be packed into a wagonette and (driven by the coachman Charles) 'followed,' and shared in the excitement—part of which consisted in meeting friends. Here is the recipe for the famous white hunting stew.

INGREDIENTS: Fore quarter of mutton; twice the weight of the meat in potatoes (weighed after they have been washed and peeled); half the weight of the meat in Spanish or other mild onions; pepper and salt; water $\frac{1}{2}$ pint.

TIME: From $2\frac{1}{2}$ hours after it begins to simmer. A large quantity as above should be put on at 8.30 a.m. for a noonday luncheon, but a small quantity (1 lb. meat, 2 lb. potatoes, $\frac{1}{2}$ lb. onion, $\frac{1}{4}$ gill water) will do in 2 hours. The method is the same in both cases.

METHOD

1. Joint the mutton and cut the meat off the large bones in small neat thick slices, or collops; cutlet and similar bones should be left on the meat (or the meat on them if you prefer it).

2. Peel and slice the potatoes rather thickly, about $\frac{1}{4}$ or $\frac{3}{8}$ inch thick, and cut each slice in halves.

3. Peel and slice the onions quite thinly, and chop them slightly.

4. Put a layer of meat at the bottom of the saucepan.

5. On this sprinkle a layer of onion; then

6. A thick layer of potato.

7. Season all with pepper and salt and (if you have it) a little home-made mushroom ketchup, or you can add a sprinkling of chopped pickled mushrooms.

8. Pour the water over all and put on the lid, bring gently to simmering point and then cook on the hob for $2\frac{1}{2}$ hours or longer; it does not matter how long you cook it – the longer the better – and it will warm up excellently the next day.

9. Stir frequently to prevent burning on to the saucepan.

N.B.—The secret of making Irish Stew well is to add as little water as possible, only just enough as above to give it a start; the meat and vegetables cook in their own juices, and when done, the meat is embedded in a *very* thick gravy made of meat and vegetable juices thickened to a very thick creamy mash with the potatoes. There should be no liquid unabsorbed.

A Lancashire Way with Liver and Bacon

This also comes from Bolton-le-Moors

INGREDIENTS: Calf's or sheep's liver 1 lb.; fat bacon ¼ lb.; bread-crumbs ¼ lb.; chopped parsley 1 tablespoonful; salt; pepper; nutmeg; and (if liked) a few mushrooms; ½ pint water.

TIME: to bake in rather slow oven 45 minutes.

METHOD

1. Wash and dry the liver and cut into slices about ¼ or ½ inch thick.
2. Dip them in flour, and lay them flat side by side in a greased baking tin, or a fireproof glass dish.
3. Mix the bread-crumbs, chopped parsley, onion and chopped mushrooms together.
4. Season with pepper, salt and nutmeg.
5. Sprinkle this mixture over each slice of liver.
6. Place a thin rasher of fat bacon on top of each slice.
7. Pour the water round the liver in the dish and bake in a slow oven.

N.B.—If this is cooked in a brown Staffordshire baking dish or in a fireproof glass baking dish it can be sent to table in the same dish: this saves washing up and ensures the dish being piping hot as it should be. Potatoes baked in their jackets (*see* p. 215) are a delicious accompaniment to this dish.

Welsh Venison

This is another recipe from one of the great Cambridge colleges.

INGREDIENTS: A loin of mutton; sweet herbs; pepper and salt; vegetables and a brown braise (*see* p. 182), port wine 2 glasses; red currant jelly.

TIME: to braise, 2½ hours.

METHOD

1. Bone the loin of mutton.
2. Season it with powdered sweet herbs, pepper and salt.
3. Skewer it and tie it up tight.
4. Braise it in a brown braise for 2½ hours.
5. Lift out and keep hot; and
6. Reduce the braise to a half glaze, add 2 glasses of port wine.
7. Glaze your mutton, and send to table with hot red currant jelly.

167

To Stew Lambs' Tails

Miss Wettin's manuscript

INGREDIENTS: Lambs' tails 6; some good clear gravy; shallots 2; capers a few; flour; salt to taste.

TIME: to stew 4 hours.

METHOD

1. Blanch the lambs' tails in salt and water.
2. Put them in a cloth to dry.
3. Put them in good clear gravy, and
4. Stew them for 4 hours.
5. Chop the shallots finely and add them to the capers.
6. Dilute the flour with a little water and as the sauce boils thicken it.
7. Cook for about 5 minutes.
8. Season with salt and send to table.

[N.B.—This dish would be very much improved if the sauce were thickened in the ordinary way by cooking a little butter and flour together for a few minutes and diluting it with some of the gravy, then return it to the stew and boil up.—ED.]

Cornish Cutlets

As served in the University of Cambridge

INGREDIENTS: Veal cutlets; vegetables and bacon for braise (*see* p. 182) potatoes; egg; a little cream.

METHOD

1. Lard the cutlets.
2. Braise them.
3. Spread them on one side with potatoes mashed with a little egg and cream, and nicely seasoned.
4. Bake till brown. Send to table with tomato sauce.

'Love in Disguise'

An 18th Century Jest

INGREDIENTS: A calf's heart; bread-crumbs 4 oz.; finely chopped suet 2 tablespoonfuls; parsley chopped fine 2 teaspoonfuls; sweet marjoram

1 teaspoonful; lemon the grated rind of ½; minced ham 2 oz.; pepper ¼ teaspoonful; salt ¼ teaspoonful; made mustard ⅛ teaspoonful; egg 1; vermicelli 1 oz.; four or five slices of fat bacon; a piece of greaseproof paper. Gravy flavoured with tomato, and rather reddish in colour.

TIME: 2 hours.

METHOD

1. Break up the vermicelli into short lengths and simmer it in boiling stock for 10 to 15 minutes, lift out, drain, and let it get cold.
2. Remove all the pipes from the inside of the heart, clean it well, and let it lie in cold water for an hour.
3. Make the stuffing with the bread-crumbs, suet, parsley, sweet marjoram, grated lemon rind, minced ham, pepper, salt, made mustard, egg.
4. Wipe the heart dry, stuff it, wrap the rashers of fat bacon over it so that it keeps the stuffing in; skewer them on with small skewers.
5. Wrap the whole heart in grease-proof paper, spread thick with dripping or lard, tie round and put into a baking tin.
6. Bake in a good oven for 1½ hours, take out; remove the paper; brush all over with yolk of egg and roll in coarse bread-crumbs mixed with the cooked vermicelli which should be in quite short lengths to represent rough prickles.
7. Return to oven and cook for another half hour until nicely browned.
8. Dish up and serve with a good brown or tomato gravy.

Stuffed Breast of Veal

17th Century

Or as the directions were given in the 17th century 'To make a pudding in a breast of veal.' Don't be alarmed at the variety of ingredients in the stuffing: try them and see how good the mixture is. Remember that raw meat was once always used in mince-pies, and remember how good red-currant jelly is with roast hare, and cranberry sauce with turkey, and be courageous and enterprising.

INGREDIENTS: Part of a breast of veal; bread-crumbs 3 or 4 oz.; yolk of egg 1; cream a teaspoonful; currants washed and dried 1½ oz.; rosewater; ground cloves and mace to season; a very little saffron [it can be bought at the chemist's]; salt; beef-suet finely chopped 1½ oz.; dates 4 stoned and sliced; sugar; a piece of caul. For the sauce: gravy; claret; nutmeg; vinegar; butter; flour, and two or three slices of an orange.

TIME: 20 minutes for every pound (the joint being weighed after it is stuffed), and 20 minutes extra.

METHOD

1. Open the lower end of the breast of veal with a sharp knife between the skin and ribs, leave enough of the flesh on both sides, that you may put in your hand between the ribs and the skin.
2. Then make a pudding or stuffing of the bread-crumbs, currants, spice, suet, dates, sugar; mix well and blend with the yolk of egg, cream, rosewater and saffron.
3. Make the pudding pretty stiff.
4. Stuff the breast with it.
5. Wrap the caul over it to keep it in.
6. Skewer it and tie it with fine twine.
7. Bake in a tin basting it well, unless you put it in a self-baster when it will baste itself and only require turning over when half cooked.
8. Make the gravy or sauce in the pan in the usual manner, pouring off all the fat but one tablespoonful.
9. Shake in one tablespoonful of flour.
10. Let it brown, and avoid burning.
11. Dilute with a little hot water.
12. Then add a wineglassful of claret.
13. Some grated nutmeg, a little elder-berry vinegar, and two or three slices of orange.
14. Boil up and strain.
15. Put a little in the dish and the rest in a sauce-boat. Garnish it with slices of orange.

N.B.—An orange is the correct accompaniment to roast veal. It should be cut transversely, halved and quartered and handed round on a separate plate or dish.

ANOTHER WAY

If wished the veal can be parboiled before it is stuffed; and fresh sage leaves finely chopped and lemon instead of orange can be introduced into the stuffing. If parboiled it can be basted with sweet butter whilst roasting or baking, and can be sprinkled with fine white bread-crumbs.

ANOTHER KIND OF STUFFING

This may be made with a little minced lean of veal, some minced bacon, a little thyme, cloves and mace. Season with salt and pepper.

Savoury Veal

This is a Shrewsbury dish. E. C.

INGREDIENTS: Flour in a dredger; salt 2 teaspoonfuls; pepper $\frac{1}{2}$ teaspoonful; powdered sage $\frac{1}{2}$ teaspoonful; sweet marjoram $\frac{1}{2}$ a teaspoonful (also powdered); fillet of veal 2 lb. Butter $\frac{1}{2}$ oz.; flour $\frac{1}{2}$ oz.; and pepper and salt to season gravy.

TIME: to steam $1\frac{1}{2}$ hours; time to brown 10 minutes.

METHOD

1. Wring a clean pudding-cloth out of boiling water.
2. Dust it with flour, and then sprinkle it with the salt and pepper, powdered sage and sweet marjoram.
3. Wrap the veal up in this.
4. Steam for about 1½ hours, or until done and tender.
5. Take off the cloth.
6. Brush meat over with butter, dust with flour.
7. And put in a hot oven for 10 minutes to brown.
8. Whilst the meat is browning, make gravy of the water over which the meat was steamed, by adding salt and pepper to taste and ½ oz. butter rolled in ½ oz. flour, but not browned.
9. Boil up, send to table with the veal at once.

Veal Cutlets

1783

This is the recipe of Mr. John Farley, principal cook at the London Tavern in 1783. The tavern at that time was a new building. The site had been previously occupied by the White Lion Tavern, which was destroyed by fire in November 1765. It is stated in 1782 that 'the annual banquets of the officers of some 28 different regiments are held here in the month of May. There are likewise given here a very large number of the several entertainments of the different charities of London. 24 of the City companies hold their banquets here, and several balls take place annually. Masonic lodges are held here, and almost innumerable meetings, sales and elections for charities, alternate with the more directly festive celebrations of the London Tavern.' Therefore Mr. Farley's recipes may be taken as representative of the best English Cookery of that period.

INGREDIENTS: Veal, about the thickness of half a crown; yolk of egg; bread-crumbs; sweet herbs; lemon peel: lemon juice; butter for frying; gravy, a little flour.

TIME: about 15 minutes all told.

METHOD

1. Cut your veal into pieces of about the thickness of half a crown – as large as you please. Beat them.
2. Dip them in the yolk of an egg.
3. Strew over them some crumbs of bread mixed with a few sweet herbs, some grated lemon peel and a little grated nutmeg.
4. Fry them in clarified butter or fat.
5. When the meat is done, take it out and lay it in a dish before the fire.
6. Then shake a little flour into the pan.
7. Stir it round.
8. Put in a little gravy.
9. Squeeze in a little lemon, and
10. Pour it round the veal.
11. Make use of lemon in your garnish.

171

Sausages with Apples

1823

1. Fry the sausages.
2. Then fry some sliced apples with them.
3. Place the sausages in the middle of a dish with the apples round them.

Boiled Sausages and Baked Potatoes

1823

1. Put the sausages in boiling water and simmer for about 5 minutes.
2. Serve them up with poached eggs and roasted (baked) potatoes.

Pork Fillets

Another North of Ireland Recipe. Miss C. Clarke

INGREDIENTS: Pork cut thin as for beef olives; sage and onion; bread-crumbs; milk; pepper and salt to make a stuffing (*see* p. 151); apple sauce (*see* p. 119).

TIME: to bake 30 to 45 minutes according to the thickness of the fillets.

METHOD

1. Spread the fillets on a board.
2. Brush them over with egg.
3. Make sage, onion, bread-crumbs. milk, pepper and salt into a stuffing,
4. Spread on each fillet.
5. Roll up and tie.
6. Put into a baking tin.
7. Brush over with a little dripping.
8. Dust with flour.
9. Bake in hot oven.
10. Serve with apple sauce, mashed potatoes and a little brown gravy made in the pan (*see* p. 119).

To Stew Young Chickens

Worcester 18th Century

Mr. P. Morton Shand objects to the word 'stew,' but it is quite as good a word as 'ragout' and means exactly the same thing. A perfect 'stew' is as good as a perfect 'ragout.' The following is one of the 18th century Worcester caterer's recipes, and is evidently the same as a French *blanquette*; therefore I am rechristening it in deference to Mr. Morton Shand's sensibilities:

Young Chickens in a Blanket

INGREDIENTS: Young chicken; lemon peel; lemon juice; nutmeg; pepper; and salt; butter; flour; sippets of fried bread.

METHOD

1. Truss the chickens and put them into enough hot water to cover them.
2. Simmer till half cooked and keep well simmered.
3. Lift out, untruss and cut in quarters.
4. Add the thin peel and juice of one lemon to the broth, also a little nutmeg, pepper and salt.
5. Return the chickens to the broth and finish cooking.
6. Lift them out to drain, but keep hot.
7. Strain and measure the broth; for every ½ pint put 1 oz. butter into a clean saucepan, and when melted stir in 1 oz. flour; do not let it brown.
8. When it begins to boil withdraw from fire, add ½ pint of the hot broth and boil up.
9. Season with cayenne pepper (because it is the only pepper that dissolves and will not discolour the whiteness of the sauce), and salt.
11. If you have it add a little thick cream as it improves the colour, and a few button mushrooms are an improvement.
12. You may this way stew rabbits, partridges and veal.

N.B.—The 18th Century Worcester caterer says 'Serve up with sippets.' These were a regular feature of stews in middle-class cookery as recently as the '70's of the last century. They were then triangular pieces of toast arranged vandyke fashion round any stew.

Chicken Galantine

From Mrs. (Dorothy) Allhusen, Hampshire

INGREDIENTS: Fowl 1; veal cutlet ½ lb.; eggs 3; pistachio nuts; gherkins 3; rather fat bacon, 5 rashers; some truffle; nutmeg ½; some cold tongue; seasoning to taste. White sauce; 1 pint hot chicken broth; 1½ oz. butter; 1½ oz. flour; a little cream; salt; cayenne pepper; and lemon.

TIME: to braise about 2 hours, and time to be allowed for steaming 3 hours; total 5 hours.

METHOD

1. Make a good thick sauce with the butter, flour, and hot chicken broth in the usual way, adding a very little cream to make it workable.
2. Have a boiling fowl boned.
3. Cut it down the back and spread on a board skin side downwards. Cut off the legs and boil them gently with the fillet of veal.
5. Whilst this is being done, boil 3 eggs hard.
6 Skin some pistachio nuts.
7. And if you have any truffle essence add it.
8. Remove the skin from the chicken legs, and from the veal, chop roughly and put through a mincer.
9. Pound in a mortar with about ⅓ a teacupful of the good white sauce.
10. Then rub through wire sieve.
11. Spread some on boned chicken spread on board, alternately with the other ingredients.
12. Roll up.

173

13. Tie up in a cloth, and simmer in a white braise (*see* page 187), for about 2 hours; at the end of that time untie, roll up very tightly in a fresh cloth.

14. Place between two dishes with heavy weights on top till cold, or the galantine may be moulded in a tin mould shaped to represent a boiled chicken. In which case butter the mould well, arrange the skin and meat of the boned chicken in it pressing it down to fit the shape, and place the ingredients on it in alternate layers as described, pressing each down firmly until the mould is quite full and tightly packed. Then cover with a piece of buttered paper, put on the lid and steam three hours. Remove the lid; and put a piece of wood on it and a heavy weight and leave till cold. Then turn out, dipping the mould in hot water to loosen the galantine by dissolving the fat in the tin if there is any difficulty. A chicken mould of this description can be bought at Harrod's for 10s. 6d.

Whichever plan you choose the galantine, when turned out and trimmed, must be masked with ½ pint of the white sauce blended whilst hot with ¼ pint of strong savoury jelly.

A Delicious Stew of Pigeons

This is a very old English dish. In the Middle Ages every house of importance had its dovecot.

The following inherited recipe was the one used at the Red Lion Hotel, Fareham, Hampshire, in the middle of the nineteenth century, and is almost the same as that given by the 18th century Worcester cook and caterer — if anything his recipe is more simple.

INGREDIENTS: Young pigeons; stuffing made with crumbs of bread; sweet herbs; suet; lemon peel (chopt fine); cloves; mace; nutmeg; pepper and salt; some butter; bacon and mushrooms; stock; lemon juice and ketchup.

TIME: to stew till tender and this depends on the age of the birds.

METHOD

1. Make a stuffing with the above ingredients.
2. Stuff the birds and skewer and tie them up, i.e. truss them as for roasting.
3. Put the butter (about 1 oz.) into a stewpan.
4. Cut up the bacon into dice, also the mushrooms and put them into the butter directly it is melted.
5. Don't fry them but let them cook gently in the butter without browning for about 10 minutes.
6. Then strain the bacon and mushrooms off the butter, put them aside · and return the butter to the saucepan.
7. Now heat up the butter, flour the pigeons and put them in, breast downwards at first, and brown them nicely all over.
8. Lift out.
9. Make a good sauce with the butter by adding 1 oz. flour to every ounce of fat, browning the two together until coffee-coloured, remove from fire and dilute with 1 pint hot water or hot stock to every ounce of flour used, boil up, stirring all the time.
10. (The pigeons, etc., may be put in a fireproof glass oven dish, and finished as directed, but in the oven.) Put the pigeons back, also the

mushrooms and bacon, add a little of the vinegar from some pickled onions, a little browning if necessary, a little lemon juice and (perhaps?) some walnut ketchup or a little of Mrs. Combers' sauce.

11. Stew till tender.

12. Then lift out the birds.
13. Add some young tender peas cooked separately.
14. Remove the string and skewers from the birds, and return them to the gravy and peas.
15. Heat through and serve piping hot.

Jugged Pigeons

Worcester 18th Century

Different ways of cooking pigeons were formerly characteristic of English cookery, and were a valuable aid to the housekeeper who aimed at a wholesome variety.

INGREDIENTS: Pigeons; hard-boiled eggs; nutmeg; pepper; salt; bread-crumbs; suet; sweet herbs; lemon peel; water 1 pint; onion 1; sweet herbs a bundle; beer 1 glass; flour and butter.

TIME: till tender, depends on age—at least two hours.

METHOD

1. Pluck and draw the birds.
2. Boil the livers, chop them finely and make a stuffing with them, some yolks of hard-boiled eggs, nutmeg, pepper, salt, bread-crumbs, finely chopped suet, powdered sweet herbs, lemon peel, mix all together.
3. Stuff the birds and put them into a jug, with a pint of water, the onion, bundle of sweet herbs, and beer.
4. Put the jug into a pot over the fire and stop your jug close.
5. Let them stew until tender and strain off the gravy.
6. Put 1 oz. butter into a saucepan, melt it, add 1 oz. flour, brown both together.
7. Dilute with 1 pint of the broth, boil up and pour over the pigeons.
8. Serve up garnished with pickles.

N.B.—Pickles were a favourite garnish in England for hot dishes in the 17th and 18th centuries (and probably earlier) as Mr. Thomas J. Murray, an American writer on gastronomy, writing in 1892, says: 'Foreign writers call us a nation of pie-eaters, but should they call us a nation of pickle-eaters they would come nearer the truth. This is one of the customs brought over in the *Mayflower* which still clings to us.'

A Loaf of Mushrooms and Partridges

1744

INGREDIENTS: Bread, a round loaf; a hash of partridges or rabbits (*see* pp. 173 — 177); milk; egg; mushrooms a handful; ham 3 oz.; sauce (*see* pp. 117 and 118).

TIME: about 1 hour.

175

METHOD

1. Have ready a hash of partridges or rabbits.
2. Cut a piece off the top of the loaf for a lid.
3. Rasp the outside to remove the hard crust.
4. Take all the crumb out from the inside, leaving a thin shell.
5. Brush the outside of the loaf all over with beaten egg.
6. Put it in the oven to crisp and colour delicately.
7. Keep hot.
8. Whilst this is being done, peel some mushrooms and put them in a dish, cover with milk and put the lid on.
9. Bake for half an hour.
10. Drain off the milk, add a little brown gravy, and make it into a sauce in the usual way with butter and flour.
11. Add the mushrooms to the sauce and keep hot.
12. Have the partridge or rabbit hash very hot.
13. The baked shell of the loaf should be just ready.
14. Stand it on a hot dish.
15. Fill it with the hot hash.
16. Put on the lid of the loaf.
17. Pour the stewed mushrooms and sauce into the dish round the loaf.
18. Serve very hot.

VARIATIONS

Small dinner rolls may be prepared in the same manner baked crisp and filled with stewed mushrooms, or oysters, or chicken, or any other delicate savoury stew. It is a good way of using up left-over dinner-rolls, and of avoiding the time and trouble of making pastry.

Moor Fowl served with Red Cabbage

1826

These birds are common on all English rivers and lakes, and some people think the eggs superior to those of plovers.

INGREDIENTS: Two or more birds as required; red cabbage; pepper and salt; butter; flour; a glass of port wine; slices of fried bacon.

TIME: about 3 hours all told.

METHOD

1. Do not pluck the birds: skin them.
2. Leave them to soak for one hour in salted water.
3. Truss them as for boiling.
4. Put them on to stew in a little stock.
5. Simmer for half an hour.
6. Cut either a whole red cabbage or half or quarter (according to the number of people for whom you have to provide) in convenient pieces.
7. Add these to the birds; and cook till the cabbage is done (this will take about 2 hours).
8. Then season with pepper and salt, add a piece of butter rolled in flour.
9. A glass of port wine and stir till it thickens.
10. To serve lift out the cabbage on to a hot dish, arrange the moor fowl on it, strain the sauce over these, and garnish with small slices of fried bacon or, for a change, sausages.

A Dorsetshire Recipe for Cooking Rabbits

INGREDIENTS: A young rabbit; a little flour; pepper and salt; some thin slices of bacon; bread-crumbs ¼ lb.; sage, a small bunch; large onions 4; grated lemon peel, just a little; egg 1; milk 1 tablespoon.

TIME: to bake, quite 2 hours in a warm oven.

METHOD

1. Wash a rabbit.
2. Cut into joints.
3. Put it on a dish and flour well.
4. Then put into a baking dish with an edge, or a cake tin.
5. Put some thin slices of bacon on it.
6. Have ready in a basin the bread-crumbs finely grated, the sage finely cut, the onions also finely cut with the grated lemon peel, pepper and salt to taste, 1 egg and a tablespoonful milk, beat all these well together.
7. Place over the rabbit.

N.B.—This will require quite 2 hours to bake in a warm oven and should be a nice brown. If found likely to burn, place thin paper over it. To make more gravy, add a little water or milk. This is a delicious way of cooking rabbits.

'Pillar of Rice'

Another Tendring, Suffolk, recipe

INGREDIENTS: Rice; water or skimmed milk; cooked game; rabbits, pigeons or chicken; some good cold stock or gravy; pepper and salt; grated bread-crumbs; butter.

TIME: to bake 45 minutes in hot oven.

METHOD

1. Swell the rice gently with milk or water, season with salt.
2. Fill a piedish with the cooked game or whatever you want to use up.
3. Pour over some good well-seasoned stock or gravy.
4. Cover with a thick layer of the rice nicely domed.
5. Dust this over thickly with finely grated bread-crumbs.
6. Sprinkle with oiled butter and bake in good oven till hot through and nicely browned.

N.B.—When reheating game, poultry or meat of any kind, *cold* stock or gravy, not hot, must always be added to *cold* cooked meat.

Game in Glass Oven Dishes

And now here is a suggestion that may horrify epicures, but . . .

Roast any bird, poultry, pigeons, game, or wild-fowl, in the ordinary way.

Take it up, carve it either in joints, or if a small bird in halves, put it into a hot glass oven dish that possesses a lid, make the gravy and pour it over it, put on the lid, pop it in the oven to keep hot, and send it at once to table, piping hot.

This may not be orthodox but it is very practical for the servantless household and the bird (if undercooked) may be roasted in the morning, carved and put in the oven dish, the gravy poured over it, the cover left off and then in the evening the lid can be put on, the glass oven dish put into a hot oven for 15 or 20 minutes to heat through and finish cooking and sent to table in it.

Such dishes are a cross between a stew and a roast and are extremely good.

Lamb cutlets, mutton chops, beef steaks, pork chops, veal cutlets, jointed rabbit may all be cooked in similar fashion, but first they should be floured, browned in hot fat in a stewpan or frying-pan covered with gravy, and then baked for at least half an hour in the oven, the rabbit and pigeons may want 40 minutes to one hour—it depends on their age.

Another good idea is to introduce pickled onions into the made gravy instead of using ordinary ones sliced and fried; pickled walnuts and mushrooms are also good used in this way just as one would add olives.

By this simple plan it is possible to get a great deal of variety into ordinary dishes with practically no additional trouble. All one has to do is to strain the pickles from their vinegar and add them to the gravy; the little vinegar that clings to them will help to make chops, steaks, etc., tender.

Curry

This is a highly spiced stew which was prepared in England as long ago as the reign of King Richard II. Two 'receipts' for curry powders are given in the roll compiled by his master cooks about the year 1390. (Dr. Thudichum.)

But the greatest modern authority on curries and curry-making is Colonel Kenney Herbert.

The following directions are condensed from his chapter on curries in *Commonsense Cookery*, published about thirty years ago.

'In India there is a curry for almost every province'; we will be content with two, Madras Curried Chicken; and Ceylon Prawn Curry, as they are both representative but entirely different.

Madras Chicken Curry

INGREDIENTS: 1 small chicken; flour; onion 4 oz.; carrot 3 oz.; peppercorns 6; sweet herbs, a small bunch; salt, a saltspoonful; sugar half a teaspoonful; cold water. Milk of coco-nut or almond ½ pint (to make this infuse 1½ tablespoonfuls of desiccated coco-nut, or ground almonds in ½ pint of boiling milk, this is sufficient for 1 lb. of meat or fish). Shallots or mild onion 14 oz. finely chopped; clarified beef dripping or butter 1½ oz.; curry powder 1 tablespoonful; curry paste 1 tablespoonful; tamarind chutney 1 tablespoonful; broth one tablespoonful; salt 1 teaspoonful; sugar 1 teaspoonful.

TIME: about 2½ hours all told, including the making of the broth.

METHOD

1. Cut the meat off the chicken and make a good broth of the bones with 4 oz. onion (sliced), 3 oz. carrots sliced, 6 peppercorns, sweet herbs, salt, sugar, and cold water to cover. Bring to boil and simmer for about 1¼ hours, then strain and set aside to cool and skim.

2. Flour the chicken and put that aside till required.

3. Put the desiccated coco-nut or ground almonds into a small basin and pour over them ½ pint boiling water or milk; cover up and let soak till cold, then strain through a piece of muslin and squeeze dry. Put the infusion aside to use.

4. Put the clarified dripping or butter into a stewpan.

5. When melted add the finely minced shallots or mild onion and 'fry patiently' over a moderate heat, stirring the onions and shaking the pan every now and then, till the onions turn a nice yellow brown.

6. Whilst the onions are cooking put the curry powder, curry paste and chutney into a soup plate with a spoonful of the broth, the salt, and sugar, and mix to a paste.

7. Then when the onions are brown stir the mixture into the stewpan with them.

8. Cook for about 7 minutes briskly, if necessary adding a little more butter.

9. Add the chicken, a little broth (not more than ¼ pint) to moisten the whole, and stir about and cook for another 5 minutes.

10. Remove from fire and allow the curry to stand as it is for half an hour.

11. Then return to fire and stand it over a low heat, and add gradually sufficient hot broth to cover the chicken.

12. Increase the heat and stir till nearly boiling, then lower fire, put in half the coco-nut infusion, and

13. Simmer for 45 minutes with the lid of the pan not quite covering it.

14. The chicken should now be done. The remainder of the coco-nut infusion should be added, the whole brought up to simmering point once more and the curry is ready to be served.

N.B.—Colonel Kenney Herbert says 'an important point is the weight of the onions and their mincing; no thickening whatever should be used in a curry of this kind.' Stage 10 he says is important. 'Observe also', he says, 'the limited amount of broth; this gives the curry a nice juiciness; flavour is lost when a greater quantity of broth is expended.' He adds 'I have omitted green ginger because it is often difficult to get; when obtainable it should be grated like horseradish and then pounded with a little butter to a paste, a teaspoonful will be sufficient for a curry made with a pound of meat.

'Garlic is also left out because there is enough in the chutney.'

'A good curry paste is as essential in curry-making as powder, for it contains ingredients that cannot enter into a powder.'

'When cooked meat is used it should be cut into half-inch cubes, one-third fat to two-thirds lean. If rather underdone and juicy so much the better.

'When made with cooked meat the curry only requires 15 minutes cooking at stage 13.

'Never serve potato with curry.'

Serve in fireproof glass or earthenware bowls with the rice served in a separate bowl.

Ceylon Curry

This curry which was peculiar originally to places where the coco-nut is extensively grown and appreciated is sometimes known as Malay curry.

'Although best adapted for the treatment of shellfish, and ordinary fish associated with vegetables of the cucumber family, it may be used with chicken or any nice white meat.' It is a delicate stew rich with the nutty essence of the coco-nut, and very delicately flavoured with certain mild condiments. It ought to be by no means peppery or hot, though thin strips of sweet red and green peppers (capsicum) may be introduced if wished.

This curry may be made with prawns, scallops, shrimps, crayfish, crab, Dublin Bay crayfish, or lobster, with fillets of cucumber, vegetable marrow or egg-plant in slices, any firm-fleshed fish or tender chicken, with one of these vegetables.

Prawn Curry

INGREDIENTS: Fillets of cucumber 12, prepared as below; boiled prawns 1½ dozen; fish cuttings 1 lb. and water to make 1½ pint of fish broth; butter 2 oz.; finely minced onions 10 oz.; rice flour 1 tablespoonful; turmeric 1 teaspoonful; coriander powder 1 teaspoonful; cinnamon powder 1 teaspoonful; salt a saltspoonful; desiccated coco-nut 2 large tablespoonfuls; ground sweet almonds 1 large tablespoonful; grated or finely minced green ginger 1 tablespoonful.

To make the fish broth you will want 4 oz. onion; 2 oz. each of carrot and turnip; 1 oz. celery when in season all minced; a good bit of parsley; a sprig of marjoram or thyme tied in a bundle; a saltspoonful of pepper and two of salt; add to the fish broth and pounded prawn heads, bring to boil, simmer for half an hour then strain off the broth. The juice of half a lemon to finish the curry.

T I M E : 1½ to 2 hours including the preparation of the cucumber.

METHOD

1. Pare off the skin of one good-sized cucumber or two small ones, cut them into 1½ inch lengths, and split them in four lengthwise, thus producing four fillets to each slice, remove the seeds, drop each piece as prepared into a bowl of water; when all are finished put them into a stewpan with sufficient boiling water to cover them well, half an ounce of butter and a teaspoonful of salt; simmer them until they are done; then drain and use (they will take about 10 minutes to cook).

2. Pick a dozen and a half good-sized prawns.

3. Pound their heads and shells in a mortar, and with that and some fish cuttings and some water make 1½ pints of fish broth as directed above.

4. Put 2 oz. butter into an earthenware or aluminium stewpan, melt it.

5. Stir in the 10 oz. of onions.

6. Fry together gently till the onions begin to turn yellow.

7. Mix to a paste (in a soup plate) the rice flour, turmeric powder, coriander powder, cinnamon powder, and salt with a little milk.

8. Fry this with the butter and onions for 5 minutes.

9. Then moisten by degrees with the fish broth, mixing in with it the desiccated coco-nut, sweet almonds and green ginger.

10. Bring to the boil at once, and then simmer gently for half an hour.

11. Now place a roomy hair sieve over a bowl, and press all the liquid through it catching up the exhausted nuts, ginger, etc.

12. Wash out the stewpan, and return to it the contents of the bowl.

13. Slip into this the prawns and cucumber fillets.

14. Warm up to near boiling point.

15. Give it the juice of half a lemon, and the curry will be ready to serve.

N.B.—For uncooked chicken scallops or fillets of raw fish longer time will be required for cooking at stage 14:

1. Chicken (uncooked) must be simmered 25 minutes.

2. Raw fillets of fish 10 or 12 minutes.

3. Scallops will take about 25 to 30 minutes.

The fillets of chicken should be lightly tossed over the fire in a little butter and onion before being put into the curry sauce. The fish may be put in just as it is.

The scallops should be put into a basin of salted water and steeped for one hour; then rinse them in plenty of cold water, boil up and simmer slowly for 25 minutes, then add to the curry.

To Boil Rice for Curry

Colonel Kenney Herbert ('Wyvern')

Rice like macaroni must be plunged into boiling water and finished in the same way; but it will be well, perhaps, to give each step in detail:

1. For from four to six ounces of uncooked rice choose a four-quart, or even larger stew-pan; three-parts fill this with water, and set it on to boil, putting into it a dessertspoonful of salt, and the juice of half a lemon.

2. While the water is coming to the boil, sift on a sieve, but do not wash the rice. Rice for the English market is so carefully refined and winnowed that it does not require washing, and it is an advantage to keep the grains dry until they are plunged into boiling water.

3. Put a small jug of cold water within easy reach of the range.

4. As soon as the water boils freely, cast in the rice, and with a wooden spoon give it occasionally a gentle stir round.

5. Mark the time when the rice was put in, and in about ten or twelve minutes begin to test the grains by taking a few of them out with the spoon and pinching them between the finger and thumb.

6. When the grains feel thoroughly softened through, yet firm, stop the boiling at once by dashing in the jugful of cold water.

7. Empty the contents of the stewpan upon a large wire sieve, and drain off the water completely.

8. While it is draining, melt half an ounce of butter in the hot pan in which the rice was boiled, and when the latter has drained, return it to the pan; shake this well, set it on the corner of the hot-plate, and cover it with a clean napkin, so that it may dry, repeating the shaking every now and then to separate the grains.

9. The butter is put in to detach the grains which always adhere to the bottom and side of the pan: as this melts the grains will come away. Scatter them well with a two pronged fork. Never use a spoon.

The drying process will take from eight to ten minutes at the least, and must not be hurried. For this reason the cook should give herself full time for the operation. Even well-boiled rice will not come to the table satisfactorily unless it has been drained and dried as I have described.

A Brown Braise

Put some trimmings of fat meat, some onion, thyme, parsley, basil, marjoram, carrot cut into slices and mace; a bit of butter, a little stock, a bay leaf, and some celery in the stewpan. At the end of half an hour add a little stock and if liked a glass of white wine.

6

BOILED MEATS

Boiling Meat

Dr. Kitchiner says: 'This most simple of culinary processes is not often performed in perfection, because it demands a patient and perpetual vigilance, of which few persons are capable.'

'Though roasting and boiling are the most common, and generally considered the easiest and most simple processes of cookery, it requires more unremitting attention to perform them perfectly well than it does to make most made-dishes.

'That made-dishes are the most difficult preparations, deserves to be reckoned among the culinary vulgar errors — in plain roasting and boiling it is not easy to repair a mistake once made; the discretion and attention of a steady careful cook, must be unremittingly upon the alert.'

1. Put your meat into cold water, in the proportions of about 1 quart of water to a pound of meat: it should be covered with water during the whole of the process of boiling – but not drowned in it. The less water, provided the meat be covered with it, the more savoury will be the meat and the better the broth.

2. The water should be heated gradually; for instance a leg of mutton of 10 lb. should be placed over a moderate fire, which will gradually make the water hot (without causing it to boil) for about 40 minutes; if the water boils much sooner the meat will be hardened, and shrink up as if it were scorched; by keeping the water a certain time heating without boiling, its fibres are dilated, and it yields a quantity of scum.

When the pot is coming to a boil there will always, even from the cleanest meat and cleanest water, rise a scum to the top of it; proceeding partly from the foulness of the meat and partly from the water. This must be carefully taken off as soon as it rises.

3. When you have scummed well, put in some cold water, which will throw up the rest of the scum. The cleaner the top of the water is kept, the cleaner will be the meat.

Take care of the liquor in which you have boiled poultry or meat; in five minutes you may make it into excellent soup.

A good housewife never boils a joint without converting the broth into some sort of soup.

All the above is gathered from Dr. Kitchiner's remarks on the subject of boiling meat, based on careful tests and experiments made by skilled cooks.

Steaming

This method of cookery conserves all the 'goodness' of the food, but it is not suitable for green vegetables which must be cooked rapidly to conserve their vitamin value.

It can be carried out in various ways:

1. Small pieces of fish, eggs, etc., can be steamed in a buttered enamel plate covered and placed over a saucepan of boiling water; such a dish will cook over a pan in which potatoes are being boiled.

2. Puddings can be steamed in basins over a braise or small joint cooking in a 'Top-hat Cooker.' The basin, which must be covered, stands on a rack placed over the braise which supplies the steam. The Top-hat lid conserves the steam, and the whole contraption can be placed over very low heat and be left to cook all by itself.

3. In an ordinary steamer, either perforated or plain, the latter is the better, and there is much to be said for pressure cookery. That cannot be dealt with in this book, although it must not be forgotten as a modern development.

The 'Ideal' Steam Cooker is a very good make. It takes a little longer to steam puddings, etc., than to boil them, but when possible the difference in time is stated in recipes where steaming is an advantage.

Turkey — Yorkshire Fashion

INGREDIENTS: A turkey; some good forcemeat; a tongue; white sauce; turnips; carrots; cauliflower; peas, etc., as garnish.

TIME: to boil 2 hours.

METHOD

1. Truss the turkey with the feet inside.
2. Take out the breast bone, have ready a well-boiled calf's tongue.
3. Put it and some delicate well-made forcemeat inside the turkey in place of the breastbone.
4. Re-form the breast and truss the turkey correctly.
5. Boil up and simmer for 2 nours.

6. Pour over the bird some good white sauce made partly with the stock in which it has been cooked, and garnish with turnips, carrots, sprigs of cauliflower, peas, or any other suitable vegetable. A turkey cooked in this way is excellent served cold covered with a white sauce blended with aspic jelly.

Venison Roll

This recipe was given by an Aberdeenshire gillie's wife. It has been in the gillie's family for several generations and it is said that 'if eaten cold it ought to be rather dry: and then it is excellent.'

INGREDIENTS: Venison (any part) 1 lb.; fat bacon ½ lb.; bread-crumbs 4 oz.; onion, a slice; chopped parsley a dessertspoonful; salt, ½ teaspoonful; pepper ¼ teaspoonful or more to taste; egg 1.

TIME: to boil, 2 hours.

METHOD

1. Mince the venison and fat bacon finely together (put them through the mincer).
2. Mix in the bread-crumbs, onion, parsley, pepper and salt; blend well.
3. Beat the egg well and mix it with the dry ingredients to make them into a roll.
4. Put into a floured pudding cloth, tie up very tightly.
5. Put into a pot of boiling water and simmer gently for 2 hours. It can be served hot with gravy and red currant or rowan jelly.

N.B.—If it is to be used cold it is best to leave it in the cloth with a little pressure on top till it is to be served. It is a good plan in this case when it is first taken out of the pot to unroll the cloth and roll it up more tightly round the venison roll — which shrinks in cooking.

Sheep's Trotters

A Bolton lady writes: 'We eat sheep's trotters boiled in Bolton, it is a sort of ritual. When the Football Wanderers bring home the Cup, they are received with sheep's trotters decorated with white and blue ribbons.'

RECIPE 1830

INGREDIENTS: Sheep's trotters; stock; sweet herbs (see p. 105); a little flour, milk; pepper and salt; yolks of 1 or 2 eggs; some verjuice (see p. 95) [or lemon juice or vinegar].

TIME: sufficient to boil the feet till the bones can be taken out.

METHOD

1. Wash the feet well, changing the water repeatedly.
2. Put into some cold stock with a bunch of sweet herbs.
3. Boil up until the bones can be easily taken out.
4. Lift out herbs and return the meat to the saucepan.
5. Thicken the stock with flour, mixed with milk.
6. Season with pepper and salt.
7. Stir in the yolks of one or two eggs according to richness required, and
8. Sharpen with lemon juice or serve with vinegar. The eggs may be omitted.

Haggis

From the notebook of the Hon. Mrs. Hay Mackenzie, of Cromarty.

INGREDIENTS: A mutton paunch; the heart, lungs and liver of a sheep; salt; white and cayenne paper; nutmeg; onions; oatmeal a handful; beef suet 1 lb.; strong stock 1 glass; old whisky, or Athole brose (mixture of equal parts of whisky, cream and honey).

TIME: to boil ½ hour at first, then 3 hours.

METHOD

1. Wash the paunch and turn it inside out.
2. Boil the heart, lungs and liver together for half an hour; chop the meat very finely except half the liver which must be grated when quite cold.
3. Spread the chopped mixture on a table and season with the salt, pepper and nutmeg.
4. Chop the onions.
5. Add the grated liver.
6. And a handful of oatmeal.
7. Chop the suet and add that.
8. Mix all well together with the stock.
9. Fill the paunch, leaving plenty of room for the oatmeal to swell.
10. Sew it up.
11. Prick it all over with a needle.
12. Boil for three hours.
13. Serve with old whisky or
14. Athole brose.

N.B.—This is also Mrs. MacIver's recipe (Edinburgh, 1773) but she adds: 'Be sure to put out all the wind before you sew up the bag.' Mrs. MacIver was the daughter of a Highland laird impoverished through supporting Bonnie Prince Charlie. His daughter, a first-rate cook, turned her genius to account by setting up as a cookery teacher in Edinburgh. Her book, the property of one of her descendants (Mrs. MacIver Cruickshank of Nairn) would delight Mr. Morton Shand who regrets the substitution in Scotland of the term 'butcher' for the old Scottish word 'flesher'; Mrs. MacIver classifies all her meat receipts under the heading 'Flesh.'

Chicken and Rice

From a Yorkshire woman's scrap-book, 1931

INGREDIENTS: Boiling fowl one; water; milk ¾ pint; lemon rind and juice of one; Patna rice 1 breakfastcupful; flour 1½ oz.; butter 1 oz.; pepper and salt.

TIME: about 2—4 hours according to age of fowl.

METHOD

1. Cut up the fowl and cook it in water in the oven until tender, in a fire-proof oven dish with a cover.
2. Cook the Patna rice as for curry.
3. Heat the milk very slowly with rind of lemon peel to draw out the flavour.
4. Use it to make a good white sauce with 1½ oz. of flour, 1 oz. butter, salt and pepper.
5. Cook well.
6. Add lemon juice.
7. Drain fowl from liquid.
8. Serve with rice round it, and the creamy sauce poured over the rice.

N.B.—This is delicious and uses up quite old birds successfully. A rabbit can be cooked as above with rice and well made onion sauce used to mask it.

Rabbit and Rice with Onion Sauce

From a Yorkshire woman's scrap-book, 1931

Cook rabbit in the same way as chicken and rice (*see* p. 186), using wellmade onion sauce to mask it.

White Braise

Put some veal or pork fat trimmings cut in small pieces in a little cold water in a stewpan with a small bit of butter, onions, a faggot of thyme and parsley, a few blades of mace, the pulp of a lemon (that has all the white skin pared off) cut in thin slices; cook and keep stirring for a few minutes, add a little white stock. This is used for anything you want to look white.

White or Brown Cucumber Sauce

1. Cut the cucumbers as directed on page 181 (Method 1).
2. Peel as many small onions as you have pieces of cucumber.
3. Put all into vinegar and water for 2 hours. Drain.
4. Cook them in as much white stock as will cover them.
5. Add as much Foundation White Sauce (*see* p. 117) as you think proper. Or you can add Foundation Brown Sauce if you prefer it.

7

SAVOURY PIES AND PUDDINGS

Ruth Pinch's Beefsteak Pudding

Miss Acton, 1845

Ruth Pinch is a well-known character in *Martin Chuzzlewit*. She used 6 oz. butter for the crust of her pudding instead of 6 oz. suet, and moistened the flour, etc., into a paste with the well-beaten yolks of 4 eggs, mixed with a little water (an extravagant young woman, that!). Otherwise the ingredients and directions for making are the same as in Miss Acton's recipe.

For a basin that holds 1½ pints of water the following quantities will be required:

INGREDIENTS: Flour 1 lb.; beef suet finely minced 6 oz.; (or if you are a Ruth Pinch 6 oz. butter); flour 1 oz.; salt ½ teaspoonful; water ¼ pint (or the yolks of 4 eggs, and a little water); beefsteak 1 lb. (the 'skirt' makes an excellent pudding and is economical); salt ½ oz.; pepper ½ teaspoonful; water ¼ pint; mutton may be substituted for beef, and half a dozen or a dozen oysters interspersed with it.

TIME: to boil 3½ hours.

METHOD

1. Grease a basin, put a large pot of water on to boil.
2. Make the pastry with the flour, suet (or butter), salt, and water (or eggs!).
3. Roll it out and line the basin leaving a piece for the lid.
4. Cut the steak into convenient pieces, flour and season them with pepper and salt; put them in the pudding.
5. Pour in the ¼ pint of water, and put on the lid.
6. Tie over with a floured cloth, and boil as above.

Chicken Pudding

Staplehurst, Kent, 1837

INGREDIENTS: A good light suet crust; one chicken; some slices of cooked ham; a few button mushrooms if obtainable; parsley; pepper; salt; a thin steak of veal or fresh pork.

TIME: to boil 3 hours.

METHOD

1. Grease a basin.
2. Line it with a suet crust.
3. Cut up the chicken into convenient pieces and flour them.
4. Cut the ham into strips about ¾ inch wide and 2 inches long.
5. Chop up the parsley leaves (not the stalks) and scatter the ham, parsley, mushrooms if you have them, pepper and salt amongst the pieces of chicken until the crust-lined basin is filled.
6. Cover with a small thin steak of veal or fresh pork.
7. Pour a teacupful of cold water over all.
8. Cover with some of the suet crust.
9. Pinch the edges together.
10. Cover with a piece of buttered paper, then with a cloth and tie up securely.
11. Serve turned out of the basin.

N.B.—This is a very early mention of the use of a pudding basin, and at this time at Staplehurst in Kent where it was most certainly a farm-house delicacy it would equally certainly have been boiled in a closely-woven linen pudding cloth. Even to-day (1931) old-fashioned Kent and Sussex village folk declare that no puddings are so good as those boiled in a cloth.

But the cloth must be closely woven, wrung out in hot water, put inside a colander with its edges hanging over and well floured; the rolled-out crust is placed in this, and is thus hollowed out ready to be packed with whatever meat, etc., is being used. It is then gathered up and the edges pinched to another piece forming a lid. They make puddings of everything in Kent and East Sussex, just as they make pasties of everything in Cornwall. At Cranbrook in the Weald of Kent fresh gurnets brought by cart from Hastings where they had been caught in the early morning hours were in the boyhood of men still living made into much appreciated puddings, and boiled in a cloth.

Other Kentish and East Sussex Puddings

Pork, onion and apple; pork sausage pudding; beef steak and kidney; bacon pudding; rabbit pudding; partridge pudding.

'Donkey'

An old Fifeshire Recipe

Mrs. Burnet who sends the following says she remembers this savoury pudding being served in her childhood's days with cold meat, and that she and her household still enjoy it made in the same way, and served in the same fashion. It is distinctive dishes of this sort that never appear in ordinary cookery books that are so useful and interesting.

INGREDIENTS: Scotch oatmeal, a cupful or ½ pint; chopped suet 3 oz.; onion 1 large one; black pepper and salt; cold water.

TIME: to steam 3 hours.

METHOD

1. Chop the onion finely and
2. Blend it well with the oatmeal, suet, pepper and salt.
3. Mix with 1 pint cold water.

N.B.—Curious, but very good.

4. Put into a greased basin, leave plenty of room to swell.
5. And steam 3 hours.
6. Turn out and eat with cold meat.

Eel Pie

Richmond 1873

Mr. Aeneas Dallas of *The Times* (during the '60's and '70's of the nineteenth century) says: "This used to be a famous pie, but we hear little of it now.'

Here is the Richmond recipe:

INGREDIENTS: Puff pastry; Thames eels 2; hard-boiled eggs; shallots 2 small ones; butter ½ oz.; parsley a small faggot chopped; nutmeg; pepper; salt; and sherry 2 glasses; water. For the sauce: butter 2 oz.; flour 2 oz.; lemon the juice of a whole one.

TIME: to bake one hour; for preparation and cooking 1½ to 2 hours all told.

METHOD

1. Skin, cleanse and bone two Thames eels.
2. Cut these in pieces.
3. Chop the shallots; pass them in butter for 5 or 6 minutes and then add to them a small faggot of parsley chopped, with nutmeg, pepper, salt, and two glasses of sherry.
4. In the midst of this place the eels, add enough water to cover them, and set them on the fire to boil.
5. When they have boiled up, take out the pieces of eel and keep them hot.
6. Strain the stock in which they were cooked.

7. Melt the butter and add the flour in the usual way for a foundation sauce (*see* p. 117).
8. Add the strained stock, beat quite smooth, boil up and finish with the juice of a whole lemon.
9. Arrange the pieces of eel, and quarters of hard-boiled eggs in a piedish.
10. Pour the sauce over it, and when cold, roof the pie with puff pastry.
11. Bake in a hot oven at first, to raise the pastry and then in a cooler one, one hour all told.

Mr. Dallas adds 'And lo! a pie worthy of Eel-pie Island. It is a great question debated for ages on Richmond Hill whether this pie is best hot or cold. It is perfect either way.'

Mr. Dallas was a friend of Sir Henry Thompson and a frequent guest at his famous 'Octaves.'

Fish Roll

An excellent fish pudding from Leamington, Warwickshire. 'To be quite honest,' writes Miss Cullen, 'this is a war-time (1914—1918) emergency dish, for a meatless day, but it is too good to lose.'

INGREDIENTS: Cooked fish (herrings, pollock, or any kind of cheaper fish) ½ lb.; a little anchovy essence, pepper and salt; flour 4 oz.; fine oatmeal 4 oz.; suet 2 oz.; baking powder 1 teaspoonful; water to mix.

TIME: to boil 2½ hours.

METHOD

1. Flake fish, remove bones and skin.
2. Add a little anchovy essence.
3. Season with pepper and salt.
4. Make a light dough of the flour, oatmeal, suet, baking powder and water.
5. Roll out in an oblong.
6. Spread with the fish.
7. Roll up, pressing edges well together
8. Tie in a scalded floured cloth.
9. Boil gently for 2½ hours.
10. Serve with parsley sauce made of some of the water.

Hasty Haggis

A Lancashire Dish. Margaret B. Todd

INGREDIENTS: Dripping; onion; apple; oatmeal; currants; water; pepper; salt and sugar.

METHOD

1. Melt dripping in a frying-pan.
2. Add onion and apple chopped very small.
3. Also a few currants.
4. And a tablespoonful of water.
5. Scatter in some oatmeal when it boils.
6. Season with a dash of salt, pepper and sugar.
7. Fry quickly and serve very hot.

N.B.—Miss Todd says 'this is a cousin of the boiled haggis family — so is the Scotch white pudding made of oatmeal, fat, sometimes currants, boiled in a skin and then served with fried bacon.'

Herb Pudding

As made in springtime in Staveley Village, near Kendal, Westmorland
Mrs. S. Maud Garston, Burnside, Kendal, Westmorland

INGREDIENTS: Any kinds of edible young green herbs (wild ones) principally Easter ledges (*persicaria*) young nettle-tops, dandelion leaves,

191

lady's-mantle (*alchemilla*). (N. B.—Many other kinds are used but above make a delicious pudding.) Hard-boiled egg 1; raw egg 1; butter ½ oz.; pepper and salt.

TIME: to cook 30 to 40 minutes.

METHOD

1. Wash the leaves (several handfuls).
2. Put into boiling water and boil for 10 minutes.
3. Strain.
4. Chop up the leaves.
5. Add one hard-boiled egg chopped up small.
6. And one raw egg beaten up.
7. Add a little butter, pepper and salt.
8. Mix all together.
9. Put back in a saucepan. Heat through, then
10. Turn into a hot pudding basin to shape it.
11. Turn out and serve with the meat.

Herb Pudding

As made in Burnside Village, near Kendal, Westmorland, same as Staveley recipe, leaving out the raw egg and adding, when it is strained, some barley which has been boiled for two hours. About 2 tablespoonfuls of barley is sufficient, and of course strained.

N.B.—'Either of these recipes is very good. We made the Burnside one last spring (1930) and it was delicious. I heard of an old woman at Staveley, now passed on, who put an astonishing variety of herbs in her pudding.'—Mrs. E. MAUD GARSTON, Burnside, Kendal, Westmorland.

[In *Beauties of England and Wales*, 1814, we find the following: 'Garden vegetables, except onion and a few savoury herbs used in broth, were little known; but a mess made of the tender leaves of the alpine bistort (*viparum polygonum*) called here Easter-ment-gions, i.e. the sprout of the Easter month because it made its appearance about that season. Groats are the kernels of oats, divested of the inner and outer husk, and groats mixed with a small portion of young nettles, the leaves of the great bell flower, and a few blades of chives, all boiled together in a linen bag with the meat, was accounted a great delicacy to eat with veal in spring.' I have left the spelling and wording of this quotation unaltered.—ED.]

Pease Pudding

(*To serve with boiled pork*)

INGREDIENTS: Split peas 1 pint; butter 1 oz.; salt, pepper. (Or butter 1½ oz.; and eggs 3).

TIME: to boil the peas 2 to 2½ hours. To boil the pudding; without eggs 20 to 30 minutes; with eggs; 1 hour.

METHOD

1. Wash the peas, and soak them all night in plenty of cold soft water (if water be hard half a teaspoonful of carbonate of soda must be stirred into the water in which the peas are boiled).
2. Next day tie them up in a thick closely-woven pudding cloth giving them room to swell or they will be hard, but not too much or they will be watery, and if they are watery it is impossible to make them into a pudding.
3. Put them into a saucepan with cold water to well cover them; bring them to boiling point and boil them for 2 to 2½ hours.
4. Lift them into a colander, and let the water drain off, untie the cloth and crush the peas to a paste with a wooden spoon.
5. Stir in the butter, pepper and salt, tie up very tightly and boil for half an hour.
6. Turn the pudding very gently into a dish that it may not break, and serve it as hot as possible.

N.B.—'This is the common old-fashioned mode of preparing a pease pudding, and many persons prefer it to the more modern one which follows: i.e. making up with eggs.'

NEW METHOD
Miss Acton, 1845

INGREDIENTS: As above, but with butter 1½ oz.; and eggs to mix.

TIME: to boil 1 hour.

METHOD

1. Soak and boil the peas as above.
2. Drain the water well from them before the cloth is untied.
3. Rub them through a colander or sieve, mix the seasoning and the butter thoroughly with them.
4. Then add to them gradually 3 well-whisked eggs.
5. Tie the mixture tightly and closely in a floured cloth; and
6. Boil it for 1 hour.

Savoury Pudding

Another Yorkshire recipe received from Ross-on-Wye, dated ninety to one hundred years ago.

INGREDIENTS: Stale bread; milk; pepper; salt; sage; marjoram, nutmeg; onion; flour or oatmeal; egg one or two according to size of pudding.

TIME: to bake 30 to 40 minutes.

METHOD

1. Soak the bread in milk.
2. Mash with a fork.
3. Season with a little sage, marjoram, pepper, salt, grated nutmeg and chopped onion.
4. Add a handful of flour or oatmeal, and mix well with one or more well beaten eggs.
5. Spread about 1 inch thick in a greased baking tin.
6. Bake in a hot oven till a nice brown.

Season Pudding

Old Yorkshire

This has been kindly sent by Miss Esther Smith, Limpsfield, Surrey.

1. Break some pieces of stale bread into a bowl.
2. Pour on sufficient boiling water to soak the bread.
3. Cover with a plate till soft. Then mash up with a fork.
4. Add a handful of oatmeal, a chopped onion, mixed herbs, pepper and salt to taste, teaspoonful of baking powder, and sufficient milk to mix to a batter.
5. Bake in a greased Yorkshire pudding tin until brown and crisp on top.

Pork and Onion Dumpling

A Suffolk Recipe (Southwold)

To make a good family dumpling make a crust as follows, and line a large pudding basin with it:

INGREDIENTS: Flour ¾ lb.; suet 6 oz.; salt ½ small teaspoonful; about 1½ gills of cold water (all this is for the crust). To fill it: pork 2 lb.; onions 1½ lb.; pepper and salt to season; water 1 gill.

TIME: to steam 4 or 5 hours.

METHOD

1. Grease basin.
2. Make and roll out crust.
3. Line basin, reserving a piece of the suet pastry to cover the top.
4. Cut the pork into pieces, also the onions.
5. Arrange them in the crust-lined basin in alternate layers seasoning each.
6. When full add a gill of water.
7. Put crust on top.
8. Cover with greased paper and then tie up in a pudding cloth and steam 4 or 5 hours.

Partridge Pudding

'Said to have had its genesis in Saxon times in the district of Ashdown Forest, Sussex. It has the merit of simplicity being as easy to make as any ordinary beef steak pudding.'—H. J. G. PEVENSEY.

RECIPE

INGREDIENTS: Flour 1½ lb.; suet ½ lb.; water to mix crust; rump steak ¼ lb. thin slice; partridges, a brace of old ones; salt, teaspoonful; pepper ½ teaspoonful; good brown stock 1 pint.

N.B.—A few mushrooms, chopped parsley, and herbs are an improvement; and a glass of claret may be added to the stock with advantage, in the opinion of some people.

TIME: to boil 3 hours or more.

METHOD

1. Line a greased quart pudding basin with a thick suet crust made with the flour, suet and water, leaving enough for a cover.
2. Lay the thin slice of rump steak at the bottom.
3. Cut a brace of partridges into neat joints, season with pepper and salt.
4. Intermingle with mushrooms, parsley and herbs if you are using them.
5. Pour in the stock, but before doing so, mix in claret if you are using it.
6. Cover with the thick suet crust, pinch the edges together.
7. Tie a pudding cloth over the basin.
8. Plunge into boiling water and keep boiling 3 hours.

Plain Suet Puddings

1845

INGREDIENTS: Flour 1½ lb.; finely chopped beef suet ½ lb.; salt ½ teaspoonful; cold water to mix; or an egg and milk may be used to mix this pudding if a richer one be required, but it is quite good made with water. If required plain, to eat with hot meat, a ¼ teaspoonful of pepper may be added.

TIME: to boil 2 hours.

METHOD

1. Mix all together.
2. Make into a soft dough with water (or as above).
3. Shape in the form of a large sausage, roll up in a floured cloth.
4. Tie the ends tightly, put into a pan of boiling water and boil 2 hours.

N.B.—This pudding is delicious served plain with boiled or roast meat; and very much more so if it is cut in slices and browned in the pan in which the meat has been roasted. In old days when meat was really roasted it used to be cut in slices and browned in the pan underneath the meat. It makes an ideal dinner for small children if a slice be given them covered with some of the gravy that comes out of a joint when the first slices are carved.

Suet Pudding made with Bread-Crumbs

1845

1. Add ½ lb. fine white stale bread-crumbs to ¾ lb. flour.
2. And 10 to 12 oz. of beef-suet chopped extremely small.
3. A large half-teaspoonful of salt, and rather less of pepper.
4. Mix with 2 eggs and a little milk into a light elastic dough.
5. Make into a roll as before; roll up in a floured cloth, tie up the ends securely, put into boiling water, and boil for 2¼ hours.

Sussex Blanket Pudding

1826

1. Roll out either of the above doughs made without pepper about ¾ inch thick.
2. Spread with jam, or golden syrup to one inch of the edge.
3. Wet the edges, roll up the pudding, pinch the edges together, roll up in a floured cloth, tie the ends tightly and boil for 2 or 2½ hours.

Savoury Variations

1. This pudding is very good if the rolled-out dough be spread with a mince of fresh liver and bacon, a little onion, and parsley, all chopped, mixed together and seasoned. Finish as above. Serve with a thick gravy. It is an economical pudding as it does not take so much meat as a pudding made in a basin.
2. Sausage meat of any kind can be used.
3. It is a good way of using up the end of a ham. Cut off the meat and mince it, season with a little mace, and if there is no fat mix in a little finely minced bacon fat.

Any number of variations can be rung on this theme. Cooked meat can be used but the fresh is better because it has its natural gravy. If cooked meat be used a little gravy should be mixed with it to moisten it.

Sweet Variations

1. The suet crust may be spread with mincemeat.
2. It may be spread with chopped apples mixed with grated lemon peel, and sugar, a few bits of butter, and one or two tablespoonfuls of orange or quince marmalade.
3. Or with whole green gooseberries sprinkled with brown sugar.
4. Or with stoned cherries; or with red currants and raspberries, sprinkled in each case with sugar.
5. Or with stoned raisins and sugar and chopped candied peel.

A Proper Yorkshire Pudding

Mr. Dupuis Brown also says: The local preparation of Yorkshire pudding seems to have been quite a speciality, and I have never seen a faithful representation elsewhere. The joint of beef was suspended from the jack in front of the open range, and there was a strong tin table beneath it with a well in the centre to contain the gravy which was utilized at frequent intervals to baste the joint. The pudding was poured into shallow oblong tin dishes, locally termed 'dripping' pans which were placed on this table, their respective positions being occasionally changed in order to get full benefit of the roasting and to catch the dripping or the gravy from the joint. It was always thin and apt to be crisp if roasted too long. In London and elsewhere I have invariably found it very thick, resembling what we called in Yorkshire a batter pudding.

Surrounding three sides of this metal table was a fire screen lined with sheet tin and having two wings, in order to confine and reflect the heat.

RECIPE FOR PUDDING

INGREDIENTS: Flour, 4 tablespoonfuls; milk a little more than $\frac{1}{2}$ pint; a little salt; eggs 2; water one tablespoonful.

TIME: to bake in oven 15 minutes.

METHOD

1. One hour before you want to cook the pudding mix the flour and salt in a basin.
2. Mix in a little of the milk with the flour.
3. Drop in the eggs.
4. Beat up well, add a little more milk.
5. Cover the bowl and leave it aside for an hour (this allows the flour to swell).
6. Then put some dripping from the meat into some small shallow tins or small pyrex fireproof glass dishes, put them in the oven to get hot.
7. Whisk a tablespoonful of water well with the batter.
8. Divide it into 4 equal parts put in a hot oven for 10 to 15 minutes.
9. Brown them on the top shelf for 5 minutes and the result will be a puffy cup of crisp pudding the centre of which will be perfect for a little gravy, and in Yorkshire these puddings are served with it, before serving the meat and vegetables. But in Lancashire although the puddings are baked in shallow tins in dripping in the same way they are often served with castor sugar, after the meat and vegetables. Yorkshire pudding is served with any *roast*, not only roast beef but with roast mutton, pork, rabbit, hare, partridges, etc. In Durham it is served with roast duck or goose.

How to make Puff Pastry

Roberts, 1857

1. Weigh an equal quantity of butter and fine flour.
2. Rub into the flour one-third of the butter.
3. Make a hole in the middle.
4. To every pound of paste break in 2 yolks of eggs and a small pinch of salt.
5. Take water enough to make the paste of the same consistency as the butter which you must be very particularly careful about, otherwise the butter would break through the paste in working.
6. All the whey must be pinched out of the butter before it is used.
7. The paste which you have mixed should be worked with the palm of your hand at least a quarter of an hour.
8. Then let it remain covered with a cloth a quarter of an hour.
9. Roll out the paste round and
10. Put the whole of the butter in the centre and fold the paste over the butter.
11. Now dust the paste with a little flour and roll it into a square sheet and be careful the butter does not break through.
12. Then fold it up equally and leave it for 20 minutes.
13. Then roll it out and fold it again and so on until it has been rolled 4 times, allowing it to remain a short time between each roll, that the toughness of the paste may subside.
14. It is then fit for any purpose you may require, a piecrust, patties, or small pastry.

Rough Puff Pastry

INGREDIENTS: Plain flour ½ lb.; butter 6 oz.; (or 3 oz. butter and 3 oz. lard); lemon juice 1 teaspoonful; ¼ teaspoonful salt.

METHOD

1. Sift the flour and salt into a mixing bowl.
2. Break in the butter in pieces the size of walnuts.
3. Add the lemon juice and sufficient very cold water to mix well together into a stiff paste.
4. Flour the board.
5. Roll out three times.
6. If there is time let it stand in a cool place for half an hour, then use.

N.B.—This may be made with clarified dripping, but only 4 oz. must be used to ½ lb. flour.

A Cheshire Pork Pie

1747

This is one of the recipes of the famous Mrs. Glasse; it is not very explicit but as it is easy to adapt, it is given as she gives it; with this exception—the directions are split up, numbered, and one put on each line to make it a little more clear.

1. Take a loin of pork.
2. Skin it and cut it into steaks.
3. Season with salt, nutmeg and pepper.
4. Make a good crust.
5. Place in it a layer of pork.
6. Then a layer of pippins pared and cored, and quartered.
7. Add a little sugar to sweeten the pie.
8. Then another layer of pork.
9. Put in ½ pint of white wine.
10. Lay some butter on the top and close your pie.
11. If your pie be large it will take a pint of white wine.

[N.B.—It is quite evident from liquid being put in that this pie was made in a piedish, although the writer does not say so. Liquid is never put into a raised pie until it comes from the oven.—ED.]

Chitterling Turnover

This is a Suffolk recipe sent by Mrs. Osmonde, of Ealing, together with several other most interesting recipes connected with Suffolk country customs.

'The outside of the turnover,' she says, 'was an ordinary paste crust about 10 inches by 6 inches. The mixture was placed on one half, and the other half was turned over it, pressed down at the edges and the whole was baked in a brick oven at medium heat!'

Mixture to Fill

INGREDIENTS: Pig's chitterlings (or sheep's pluck; and in fact the heart, liver and lungs or lights of any beast used for food); sugar, spice, apples and currants.

METHOD

1. Clean chitterlings well.
2. Simmer till tender.
3. Chop finely.
4. Pare and core and chop some apples.
5. Wash and dry some currants.
6. Mix with the chitterlings.
7. Sweeten with sugar.
8. Season with spice.
9. Mix well and use.

Collier's Pie

From Mr. Colley A. Shorter, Burslem, Stoke-on-Trent, 1931

INGREDIENTS: Good flaky pastry; good fat grated cheese; Spanish onion (half); bacon; pepper and salt; one egg.

TIME: to bake: 40 minutes or more, according to size.

METHOD

1. Grease a plate.
2. Cover it with some good flaky pastry, fairly thick.
3. Put in a layer of good fat grated cheese to a depth of about one-eighth inch.
4. Grate over that half a Spanish onion.
5. Cover that with a layer of small dice of bacon.
6. Season with pepper and salt.
7. Cover the whole with another layer of pastry.
8. Brush with beaten egg.
9. Cook in oven.

Small Raised Mutton Pies

Gosfield Hall, Essex

The following recipe is taken from the dinner book for 1805, of John Simpson, cook to the first Marquess of Buckingham (George, third Earl Temple). A dish of these small mutton pies was one of the side dishes served on January 3rd, 1805, at Gosfield Hall. The recipe is equally good to-day: the pies can be made either in small shallow upright tins lined with pastry, and represent 'raised' pies, or, when made for sale, there is a small English-made machine that will stamp out the 'raised' crusts. The small 'raised' crusts, whichever way they are made, can in every case be filled with the following mixture and baked according to the directions given. Recipes for making rough puff pastry are given on pages 198, for raised crust or hot water pastry on page 45, and for short pastry on page 225.

INGREDIENTS: Small raised pie-cases with lids to put on top; meat off an uncooked neck of mutton or part of one; a gravyspoonful of stock; a little chopped shallot, mushrooms, parsley and thyme, pepper and salt; a little good thick brown gravy.

TIME: to bake, half an hour.

METHOD

Have ready the small raised pie-cases.

1. Cut the meat off the piece of neck of mutton.
2. Break up the bones and put them on to stew in a little water for stock.
3. Remove all skin and sinews from the meat and mince it very fine with a knife (don't put it through the mincer).
4. Chop some shallot (or a little onion), mushrooms, parsley and thyme and put them with the meat and a gravyspoonful of stock into a stewpan.
5. Add the mutton, and set it on the fire for 5 minutes, stirring all the time.
6. Take it off to cool.
7. When quite cool fill the pies.
8. Put on the lids, and put in an oven suited to the pastry you are using, a moderately hot oven is generally best for these small pies.
9. Bake for about half an hour.
10. When done cut off the tops or lids.
11. Have ready any of the chopped meat you may have left over after filling the pies; make it hot, mix it with a little good slightly thickened brown gravy, also made hot, and use it to fill up the little pies.
12. Put on the lids again, serve on a table napkin placed on a dish, and send to table piping hot. They are also very good cold.

Saucer Pies

Cumberland and Westmorland

Small saucers or large or small patty pans may be greased and lined with pastry, filled with the above meat mixture when it is quite cold, the edges of the pastry wet, the small pies covered with another piece of pastry pressed together, the tops brushed over with milk, or egg and milk, and baked in a good oven for half to three-quarters of an hour according to the size of the pie. Make a hole in the top crust when the pies come from the oven and pour in a little extra hot gravy by means of a funnel. This extra gravy is a great improvement; without it the meat in the little pies is frequently too dry.

Rook Pies

South Notts

INGREDIENTS: Young rooks; pepper and salt; beef steak; butter; flaky pastry for pie crust.

TIME: to bake 1½ hours.

METHOD

1. Pluck, draw and skin the young birds.
2. Cut out the back bone; it is bitter.
3. Season with pepper and salt.
4. Stew first to partly cook and let them get cold.
5. Lay a beef steak in the bottom of the dish.
6. Place the birds on it.
7. Pour a good deal of melted butter thickened with flour and diluted with stock over them.
8. Cover with a good flaky piecrust.
9. Brush with yolk of egg.
10. Bake in good oven for 1½ hours.

A Shropshire Pie

This recipe is supplied by a Shropshire lady who gives its date as 1778. She says in the letter that accompanied it:

There are two little things we always do in Salop, which I am told are curious and special to the county:

1. When serving roast duck it is 'the proper' thing to supply onion sauce (rich made with good milk or cream and very little onion) as well as apple sauce, though the bird is stuffed with sage and onion stuffing, and in Cheshire potatoes are added for stuffing goose and ducks!

2. Bread sauce (flavoured with a tiny onion boiled in it and removed, black and cayenne pepper, and salt) is still (1931) always served with a roast leg of mutton.

INGREDIENTS: Puff pastry; young rabbits 2; 2 lb. fat pork; pepper; salt; nutmeg; sweet herbs (some oysters if you have them) a little fat bacon; egg; 1 yolk (artichoke bottoms and cocks' combs if you have them); red wine ½ pint; water ½ pint.

TIME: to bake 1½ hours in a quick, but not too fierce an oven.

METHOD

1. Cut the rabbits in pieces and flour them.
2. Parboil the livers;
3. Cut up the fat pork into little pieces.
4. Lay your rabbits in a piedish.
5. Mix the pork with them.
6. Also some savoury balls made with the parboiled livers of the rabbits pounded, an equal quantity of finely minced bacon, a few white breadcrumbs, or mashed potato seasoned with some sweet herbs, nutmeg,

pepper and salt, you may add some chopped oysters if you have them, moistened with the yolk of an egg.

7. Also some artichoke bottoms cut in dice and some cocks' combs if you have them.

8. Grate some nutmeg over the meat.

9. Pour in half a pint of red wine and ½ pint of water.

10. Cover your pie with puff pastry ornament and brush over with yolk of egg.

11. Bake at first in a quick oven to raise and set the pastry; and then more slowly to finish cooking the rabbit.

Sussex Mock Pork Pie

This is sent by Mrs. K. Earp, of Brighton, and very much resembles the egg and bacon pie of the North.

INGREDIENTS: Short pastry; bacon 2 to 3 oz. for each person; eggs 1 for each person; mixed herbs ⅛ small teaspoonful; pepper and salt to taste.

TIME: 1 hour in good oven.

METHOD

1. Line a shallow piedish with either short or rough puff pastry.

2. Arrange pieces of bacon in it.

3. Dust over a pinch or more of mixed herbs according to size of pie.

4. Break one egg for each person.

5. Pour carefully in without breaking the yolks.

6. Add pepper and salt to taste.

7. Cover with pastry and bake till pastry is cooked.
Delicious hot or cold.

Salmon Pie

1823

1. Make some puff pastry.

2. Clean and scale a middling piece of salmon.

3. Cut it into 3 or 4 pieces according to the size of your dish.

4. Season it pretty high with mace, cloves, pepper and salt.

5. Put some butter at the bottom, and lay in the salmon.

6. Take the meat of a lobster cut small and pound it with an anchovy.

7. Melt as much butter as you think proper, stir the lobster and anchovy into it with a glass of white wine and a little nutmeg.

8. Pour this over the salmon, lay on the top crust, and let it be well baked.

Shrimp Pie

Mary Eaton, Bungay, Suffolk, 1823

1. Pick a quart of shrimps.

2. If they be very salt, season them only with mace and a clove or two.

3. Bone and mince two or three anchovies, mix them with the spice, and then season the shrimps.

4. Put some butter at the bottom of a shallow piedish. [A modern fire-proof glass pie-plate is just the thing.]

5. Put in the shrimps, and pour over them some more butter and a glass of sharp white wine.

6. Cover with a very thin delicate piecrust and bake until this is cooked. It won't take long.

Woof or Ling Pie

This excellent Yorkshire recipe is sent by a Scarborough B.B.C. friend. She writes: 'No fish except "woof" or ling is really satisfactory; "woof" is the local name for catfish (dory in some parts of Scotland, *not* John Dory!) It must be absolutely fresh. I would not buy it except on the coast where it has been landed. It is at its best from Easter until end of August.'

RECIPE

INGREDIENTS: Pieces of 'woof' or ling; pepper; salt; flour; bacon; hard-boiled egg; a little onion; milk ½ pint; pastry to cover.

TIME: to bake 1 hour.

METHOD

1. Grease a piedish.
2. Put in pieces of woof or ling cut not too thick.
3. Season with pepper and salt.
4. Sprinkle with a very little flour.
5. Add some small pieces of bacon.
6. Some slices of hard-boiled egg, and
7. A very little finely chopped onion.
8. Repeat till dish is full.
9. Pour the milk over all.
10. Cover with pastry.
11. Bake in a moderately hot oven – a pastry oven: this depends on the kind of pastry used. For puff paste the oven must be hot enough to raise it, and the pie can be finished baking in lower heat.

Miss Acton (1845) says: 'Raised pies may be made of any size and with any kind of meat, poultry or game, but they must be entirely free from bone.'

Woodcock Pie

INGREDIENTS: Woodcock or snipe (or both) 4; fat bacon ½ lb.; veal ¼ lb.; pepper and salt and a very little aromatic spice; 2 thick slices of uncooked carrot.

TIME: to bake 2 hours in a moderate oven.

METHOD

1. Pluck the woodcock, reserving 2 heads feathered to decorate the pie when cooked.
2. Singe and bone the birds reserving the trail; remove the gizzards.
3. Make a crust according to Mr. Wright's recipe for Melton Mowbray Pork Pie, or a firm short crust (see p. 200).
4. Put it into a collar mould (a tin that opens and is closed with a skewer).
5. Reserve 3 oz. bacon for the forcemeat; and use the rest for lining the pie, leaving a couple of pieces to cover the birds.
6. Make a forcemeat with the veal and 3 oz. of bacon, and pound all with the trail in a mortar, season with pepper and salt and a little aromatic spice (see seasoning p. 104).
7. Spread some of this inside each bird and pack them in closely, using a little forcemeat to fill up any crevices.
8. Cover with bacon and then with crust.
9. Make a hole in the cover and bake.
10. Clean the heads, remove the necks and replace them with a thick slice of uncooked carrot.
11. Fill up with a little clear gravy that will jelly when cold, and when sending to table put the heads on to the pie, using the pieces of carrot to keep them steady. Serve cold.

Truffles

If you live in a neighbourhood where truffles are found (see p. 123), you may put some slices on the birds before covering them with bacon: but many epicures think the more simple the ingredients used the better the birds retain their flavour.

A Royal Pie

In 1813, Lord Talbot, then Viceroy of Ireland presented King George III with 24 woodcock baked in a pie. Since then the custom has been followed of sending one to the reigning sovereign in England every Christmas. In 1929 such a pie was sent by Mr. James McNeill, Governor-General of the Irish Free State, to H.M. King George V, at Sandringham.

A Fourteenth Century Pie

This recipe was sent by Miss Ruth Mizen, Eriswell, Brandon, Suffolk, who says: 'I made this pie for a ball at Mrs. Hughes's. It was excellent. Please return it.'

1. Make a firm short crust (see p. 225) — using some eggs with the water to mix the flour and a little salt; but no sugar.
2. Roll it out but not too thin, and with it line a tin pie mould that opens and is kept closed with a metal skewer

3. Put in the middle of the pie 3 young partridges (boned) and
4. Round them put 6 fine quail boned and stuffed.
5. Round these put 12 larks, boned.
6. Cut a little bacon into dice and sprinkle them into the pie.
7. Put in some sour grapes and a very little salt.
8. And fill up with boned thrushes and other small birds.
9. Put in neither spice, nor cheese, nor water.
10. Ornament the top crust; make a hole in the middle; brush it over with yolk of egg, and bake in a very moderate oven, slowly for several hours according to size. Meantime make some good clear nicely flavoured game stock that will be a firm jelly when cold; strain it, and directly the pie comes from the oven pour it, hot, into the pie by means of a funnel placed in the hole in the middle of the lid.

N.B.—This pie may be eaten hot or cold. For a ball supper it will of course be eaten cold.

Good Friday Pudding

Gervase Markham, 1615

This is made with warm oatmeal 'mixt with eggs, milk, suet and pennyroyal, boyled first in a linnen bag, and then stript and buttered with sweet butter.'

8

VEGETABLES

How to Cook Asparagus
1845

1. With a sharp knife scrape the stems of the asparagus lightly but very clean, from within one to two inches of the green tender points.
2. Throw them into cold water as they are done, and when all are ready tie them in bunches of equal size, cut the large ends evenly, that the asparagus may all be of the same length, and put it into plenty of boiling water using 2 oz. salt to every gallon of water.
3. Directly the heads are tender lift out the asparagus and dish up on toast that has been quickly dipped in the water in which the asparagus has been boiled.

T I M E : to boil 20 to 25 minutes.

To Prepare Haricot Beans
Lady Rowley, 1857

1. Lay the quantity of beans you want to use in a day overnight in cold water.
2. Take them out about noon next day.
3. Put them in fresh cold water with one onion, salt and a piece of lard, and let them stew for 3 hours till tender.

TO SERVE WITH OIL AND VINEGAR

1 Drain them on a sieve.
2. Serve them up with plenty of chopped chives and parsley ready for mixing with oil and vinegar, pepper and salt.

TO SERVE WITH ROAST MEAT

1. Chop a middling size onion and a little parsley very small.
2. Stew them in 2 oz. butter for 5 minutes, add pepper and salt to your taste.
3. Put the beans that have been stewed till tender with this sauce.
4 Make them quite hot, and lay them under the meat; the gravy mixing with them will make them a proper consistency.

Or they can be served in hot tomato sauce.

Bubble and Squeak, or Fried Beef and Cabbage

Dr. Kitchiner's Recipe, 1823

'When 'midst the frying Pan, in accents savage,
The Beef, so surly, quarrels with the cabbage.'

INGREDIENTS: Slices of rather underdone cold boiled salted beef; butter; a cabbage; pepper and salt.

TIME: a few minutes to fry the meat, 15 to boil the cabbage and 2 or 3 to toss it in the pan.

METHOD

1. Put a bit of butter in the frying-pan.
2. Make it hot.
3. Pepper the slices of meat and frizzle them lightly in the hot fat, don't cook them too long or they'll be hard.
4. Have ready a cabbage boiled for 10 to 15 minutes not more.
5. Squeeze dry and chop small.
6. Take the beef out of the frying-pan, keep it hot in a plate over a saucepan of hot water.
7. Pepper and salt the chopped cabbage and toss it for two or three minutes in the frying-pan.
8. Pile up in the middle of a dish and surround with the frizzled beef.

Dr. Kitchiner amusingly gives four bars of music, the tune of Bubble and Squeak: beef, cabbage, cabbage, beef, in both the minor and major keys.

The Right Way to Cook Cabbage

Florence White, 1927

There is no doubt about the correct way to cook cabbage, because this is a culinary operation that has been dealt with scientifically by Dr. Ellen Marion Delf (Mrs. Percy Smith, D.Sc.) whose name is known all the world over in connection with the scientific tests she made for several years with various fruits and vegetables (particularly with orange and swede juice, cabbage and tomatoes) to discover their vitamin value and the best method of preserving it when they were cooked. She worked for five years at the Lister Institute, and later with the Medical Research Council, and has been now for some time Lecturer on Botany in the University of London. What she taught me is embodied in the following:

1. After washing the cabbage, cut it into quarters, remove any old leaves and cut out any tough stems.

2. Throw it into a saucepan of rapidly boiling slightly salted water.

3. *On no account must any soda, bicarbonate or kitchen soda of any kind be added:* it destroys all the vitamin value of the cabbage.

4. Boil rapidly with the lid off for 10 to 15 minutes; not a minute longer. Ten minutes is the best time. Lift out and drain; and press lightly. If the cabbage is properly boiled it will not be saturated with water but will be crisp yet tender, and light pressing will be sufficient to remove the superfluous water. When it is saturated it means it has boiled too long and is permeated with water. It then begins to sink and lose its colour. Old cabbage should never be cooked at all: it is worthless.

5. It is delicious served simply in this way with hot roast meat or any dish that has a good brown gravy, but if required as a vegetable with cold meat, or as a separate course, it may be chopped up finely [put through a mincer to-day] and blended with a good white melted butter sauce without being recooked or even reheated. The piping-hot sauce into which it is stirred well be sufficient to heat it through, and the saucepan can be stood in a pan of boiling water to preserve its heat until it is sent to table. But cabbage should not be kept waiting; it should be cooked and served immediately.

6. It has been proved conclusively and scientifically that rapid brief cooking at a comparatively high temperature preserves the value of the fugitive delicate vitamin C contained in any vegetable far better than slower cooking at a lower heat (*see* p. 74 *Report on the Present State of Knowledge of Accessory Food Factors* [*Vitamins*], compiled by a committee appointed jointly by the Lister Institute and Medical Research Council, 1927).

7. The water in which cabbage has been boiled in this manner should never be thrown away; it makes a delicate and delicious foundation for soups, sauces, and gravies (*see* pp. 106 and 119).

Forced Cabbage

Bath 1749

Mrs. Martha Bradley, who gives this dish, says 'this is a very cheap and elegant dish, and the young cabbages that are now (June) just coming into season are the fittest of all for it.'

1. Cut out the heart.

2. Throw the outside of one into boiling water, and let it scald till the leaves are pliant and manageable.

3. Then take it out and lay it on a sieve to drain and be ready.

4. Boil two hearts very well; boil 4 eggs hard; separate the yolks; chop the hearts of cabbages to pieces; cut very fine ½ lb. veal; ¼ lb. fine fat bacon; mix with the chopped cabbage; and then with the yolks of the eggs cut to pieces; mix with pepper and salt some grated bread and a very small quantity of grated cheese.

5. Make this stuffing into a ball, put it inside the scalded cabbage leaves.
6. Tie it up and put it on in a large saucepan in some very strong broth.
7. Let it simmer gently till it is done.
8. Then serve it up hot.
9. It is one of the dishes which requires no sauce, for its own sauce is within it, but some serve it up with gravy.

[N.B.—This recipe is a derivative of the Turkish Delma, for which Mrs. Ann Blencowe gives a recipe in her manuscript cookery book dated 1694, published by Mr. Guy Chapman 1925 (*see* p. 313).—ED.]

Stewed Red Cabbage

Mary Eaton, Bungay, Suffolk, 1823

INGREDIENTS: Red cabbage; ham a small slice; butter ½ an ounce; broth ¾ pint; vinegar 1 gill; salt, pepper, and a tablespoonful of pounded sugar.

TIME: to stew 3 hours.

METHOD

1. Cut the cabbage in quarters; wash.
2. Slice very thin.
3. Put into heavy aluminium stewpan with a small slice of ham, the butter and ½ pint of broth.
4. Stew 3 hours covered down.
5. When quite tender add a little more broth, salt and pepper, and add the pounded (castor) sugar.
6. Mix well and boil till the liquor has boiled almost all away.
7. Place on a hot dish.
8. Lay fried sausages on it and serve.

Champ

A North of Ireland dish, Miss C. Clarke

INGREDIENTS: Potatoes; hot milk; butter; cooked peas; small onions cooked; pepper and salt.

TIME: 30 to 45 minutes.

METHOD

1. Boil potatoes.
2. Mash them with hot milk and butter.
3. Cook peas and add them.
4. Cook the small onions and stir them in.
5. Season with pepper and salt.

N.B.—This is often served as a dish by itself.

To Fry Celery

Adam's Luxury and Eve's Cookery, 1744

INGREDIENTS: Celery a head; batter made with 1 egg; flour 2 oz.; salt; and a little Rhenish wine [in these days use milk]; butter or fat for frying; some good brown gravy, or sharp sauce (*see* p. 121).

TIME: to boil the celery ⅓ hour; to fry 10—15 minutes for a dishful.

METHOD

1. Boil the celery half an hour.
2. Let it cool.
3. Cut it up into convenient pieces.
4. Dip each piece into a batter made with 1 oz. flour, 1 egg, 2 good table-spoonfuls of milk, pepper and salt; beat the white and yolk separately, fold in stiffly whisked white last of all.
5. Fry each fritter in clarified butter or fat (deep fat frying).
6. And serve them with good brown gravy.

Chardoons

Adam's Luxury and Eve's Cookery, 1744

Chardoons, or Cardoons, as they are called now, 'are a wild thistle that grows in every ditch or hedge.' According to *Adam's Luxury and Eve's Cookery* several British thistles were eaten in former times as the green artichoke is now, after being boiled. The stalks also, stripped of their rind, were cooked in the same way as asparagus and eaten cold as salad, or as a vegetable. They were sometimes baked in pies. To-day they are cultivated on the Continent and in America and grown to a certain extent in England. Mrs. Charles Roundell, of Dorford Hall, Nantwich, Cheshire, strongly recommends the cultivation of the cardoon (*cynara cardunculus*) in our gardens in this country. It is 'grown in trenches like celery and banked up about October so as to blanch the stalks which are the edible portion.'

I

INGREDIENTS: One or two heads of cardoons, boiling water, pepper and salt and melted butter.

TIME: to simmer till tender, and this, Mrs. Roundell says, 'may take 2 hours or more according to their age and size.'

METHOD

1. Remove the rough outside of the stems.
2. Cut them up into pieces about 10 inches long.
3. Tie them up 20 in a bundle.
4. Throw them into boiling slightly salted water and boil them like asparagus.

II

Or they may be cut in small bits; 1, boiled as 'pease'; 2, drain; 3, toss them up with pepper and salt and melted butter.

III

WITH CHEESE

INGREDIENTS: Cardoons; brown stock; pepper; salt; juice of an orange; butter ½ oz.; flour ½ oz.; Cheshire Cheese 1 or 2 oz.

TIME: sufficient to cook the cardoons till they are tender, and to thicken the gravy, and 10—15 minutes to brown the dish.

METHOD

1. Prepare the cardoons as usual.
2. After they are stringed cut them into bits an inch long.
3. Stew them in brown stock or gravy till tender.
4. Season with pepper and salt.
5. Squeeze in the juice of an orange.
6. Thicken the liquid in the usual way with ½ oz. butter and ½ oz. flour to each ½ pint of liquid.
7. Put the cardoons and sauce together in a dish.
8. And cover all over with grated Cheshire cheese.
9. Then brown it all over with a hot cheese iron. (To-day we should put it in the oven for 10 minutes, or under the gas grill for 2 or 3 minutes.)
10. Serve up piping hot.

N.B.—This recipe would also be delicious made with celery, salsify, Jerusalem artichokes, cauliflowers, onions, rice and tomatoes; instead of cardoons.

Stewed Endive

Mary Eaton, Bungay, Suffolk, 1823

INGREDIENTS: Endive; a little strong gravy; pepper and salt; roast meat or potatoes; a little butter and flour kneaded together.

METHOD

1. Trim off all the green parts.
2. Wash and cut into pieces and boil until about half cooked.
3. Drain it well.
4. Chop it a little.
5. Put it into a stewpan with a little strong gravy, and stew it gently till quite tender.
6. Season with some pepper and salt.
7. Add the flour and butter five minutes before serving.
8. Stir well until thick and creamy.
9. Serve it up as sauce to any kind of roast meat; or it eats well with potatoes.

N.B.—Celery, carrots, cardoons, Jerusalem artichokes or cucumbers may each be stewed in the same manner; chopped parsley may be added to carrots.

To Stew Mushrooms

1. Do not wash them if gathered personally and taken straight to the kitchen. If bought they must be washed.
2. Wipe them carefully and peel them, putting the peelings in a little stock to flavour it. Take out the stalks, scrape them, and add them to the peelings.
3. Butter a covered shallow fireproof glass dish, stand the mushrooms in side by side.
4. Put a bit of butter and little pepper and salt in each.
5. Pour some top milk over them just to cover the bottom of the dish.
6. Put on the lid and bake in a good oven for half an hour without removing the lid.
7. The liquor round them can then be thickened with butter and flour in the usual way, and the mushrooms can be served in this sauce surrounded with sippets of toasted bread.

How to Cook Nettles

This is a Westmorland Recipe

INGREDIENTS: A panful of young nettles (*see* p. 107); boiling water; salt; butter, or a little cream.

TIME: to boil 10 minutes.

METHOD

1. Boil 1 pint water in a large saucepan.
2. Wash and pick the nettles.
3. Put them into the pan of boiling water, which should be enough to cover them.
4. Dress down and boil with the lid off for 10 minutes.
5. Strain, reserving the water for soup.
6. Chop up the strained nettles or mash them.
7. Put them back in the saucepan with a little pepper and salt and a little butter or cream.
8. Heat them through very quickly and serve at once.

N.B.—It is necessary to remember when cooking all green vegetables such as cabbage, etc., that plenty of water and rapid cooking for a short time preserves more of the vitamin C of the vegetable than longer cooking at a lower temperature, and soda must never be used, as the slightest pinch destroys the vitamin C absolutely (*see* p. 208).

Nettle Haggis

Another Westmorland Recipe

INGREDIENTS: Young nettles (*see* p. 107) boiling water; salt; oatmeal 2 or 3 tablespoonfuls; pepper; rashers of bacon.

METHOD

The same as the first 5 directions for boiling nettles as a vegetable (*see* p. 213).

6. Cut off the rind and rusty pieces of the rashers of bacon with a pair of scissors.
7. Fry them.
8. Pour the fat over the strained nettles.
9. Chop them up.

10. Put ½ pint of nettlewater in the frying-pan, and when it boils, sprinkle in the oatmeal, stirring all the time.
11 Season with pepper, and boil till it is of the consistency of properly cooked porridge (*see* p. 26).
12. Then stir in the chopped nettles.
13. Taste and see if it is sufficiently seasoned.
14. Serve very hot with the fried bacon.

Stewed Parsnips

Mary Eaton, Bungay, Suffolk, 1823

INGREDIENTS: Parsnips; milk and water, or milk; some good gravy; pepper and salt; butter ½ oz. rolled in flour ½ oz.

METHOD

1. Scrape, pare and boil the parsnips in milk or milk and water till fully half done.
2. Take them out, divide them into two down the middle and then across.
3. Put them in a stewpan with some good gravy.

4. Season with pepper and salt; and five minutes before they are taken up add the butter and flour to thicken the sauce.

N.B.—If you want to stew them white put them in broth and cream in equal quantities.

Stewed Peas

Mary Eaton, Bungay, Suffolk, 1823

INGREDIENTS: Old peas; butter a good bit; or a piece of beef or pork or bacon; pepper and salt if needed.

METHOD

1. Steep some old green peas in water (all night if they are not good boilers; otherwise half an hour).
2. Put them in a stewpan with just enough water to cover them and with a good bit of butter or a piece of beef, pork or bacon.
3. Stew very gently till the peas are

soft, or if meat be used, until it is tender.
4. If salt meat be used only season with pepper.
5. Otherwise add a little salt.
6. Serve the meat in a dish with the peas round them.

Potatoes Browned in the Pan

1884

Peel the potatoes, cut them in halves lengthwise and put them in the meat pan round the meat to cook and brown. They should be turned over once during the process.

Perfect Mashed Potatoes

Florence McCormack, 1931

INGREDIENTS: Old potatoes; cold water; salt; butter; hot milk; cayenne pepper (a very little).

METHOD

1. Peel and boil the potatoes in cold water with a little salt.
2. Drain off the water but don't throw it away.
3. Mash the potatoes.
4. Put on a little milk to boil.
5. Add some butter to the mashed potatoes, and mix it in.
6. Stir in the hot milk.
7. Whisk over the fire with a wire whisk till very light and creamy. Serve piping hot.

New Potatoes

1. These should be scraped and put into *boiling* — not cold — water with a little salt and a sprig of fresh mint.
2. Cook for 15 minutes.
3. Drain and dry on the stove with the lid tilted for a few minutes.
4. Put a piece of butter in them, and give the saucepan a shake to distribute it.
5. Serve piping hot in hot dish, and sprinkle a little chopped parsley over the potatoes at the last minute.

Potatoes Baked in their Skins

Scrub the potatoes quite clean, wipe them dry, and put them in a hot oven to bake for one hour, more or less, according to their size and the heat of oven.

Stewed Potatoes

Mary Eaton, Bungay, Suffolk, 1823

INGREDIENTS: Potatoes; cream; fresh butter and salt; or some good gravy; pepper and salt.

METHOD

1. Wash and scrub some good potatoes, half boil them in their jackets, putting them in cold water; let them boil for 10 minutes.
2. Drain them well.
3. Peel them.
4. Cut them into neat pieces.
5. Put them in a stewpan with some cream, fresh butter and salt, each proportioned to the quantity of potatoes, or into some good gravy with pepper and salt.
6. Simmer them gently until they are well done and be careful not to let them break.

Devonshire Stew

1837 *and still made in* 1931

INGREDIENTS: Boiled potatoes 1 lb.; boiled cabbage ½ lb.; boiled onions ½ lb.; pepper and salt; good beef dripping or butter.

TIME: to boil the vegetables 20, 15 and 30 minutes; time to fry about 10 minutes.

METHOD

1. Boil the potatoes and shred them.
2. The cabbage and shred it.
3. The onions (changing the water twice whilst cooking them), shred them also.
4. Mix all together.
5. Season with pepper and salt.
6. Put into a frying-pan with a lump of good beef dripping or butter.
7. And brown nicely.

Potatoes and Swede Turnips

1929

Mrs. Fowler, of Deepdene, Preston, says this Shropshire dish is excellent.

1. Choose a heavy swede, boil it till soft.
2. Boil also some good potatoes.
3. Mash all together with a little hot milk, butter, pepper and salt.
4. Serve very hot; it is delicious.

Potatoes, Parsnips and Cabbage

An Irish Country dish, 1750

1. Boil potatoes and parsnips till they are soft.
2. Mash them with new milk.
3. Add a cabbage boiled tender and cut very small.
4. Mix the whole over the fire with a slice of good butter, some pepper and salt, and eat it hot.

N.B.—This is recorded by Farmer Ellis, of Little Gaddesdon, Hertfordshire, and resembles the Irish dish 'Champ', and the Devonshire Stew, the recipe of which is dated 1837. All four are closely allied to the stoved 'taties of Aberdeenshire and Dr. Kitchiner's 'bubble and squeak.'

How to cook Salsify

Wash it well but do not scrape it; throw into boiling salted water; and, when tender, take out and peel. It can then be eaten with a good sauce.

T I M E : to boil, ¾ to 1 hour.

Baked Parsnips

Parsnips are excellent, scrubbed and baked in the same way as potatoes, and eaten buttered, with pepper and salt.

Swede Shoots

Miss Janet Esdaile writing from Fyfield, Milton-under-Wychwood Oxon., 1930, says:

'The other day my landlady served me with a delicious vegetable. It looked like very young and tender asparagus in the dish, but peach colour instead of pale green, and it had rather a strong smell. I was quite at a loss to identify it by colour and smell except that it reminded me of walking past a root field. Its taste was not unlike parsnips but not nearly so sweet and it melted in the mouth. It was swede shoots. My shepherd landlord told me he picked them off the sprouting roots when he unearthed the bury. They keep their delicate orange colour till they reach the light. They can only be had just at this time of the year (April) and round here the gentry consider them a great delicacy. "Us poor folk don't trouble about 'em," were his words.'

RECIPE

1. My landlady says she ties the shoots together in a bunch to keep them from breaking because they are so tender.

2. They are cooked like asparagus for 20 minutes to ½ hour in simmering slightly salted water.

3. Drained and served with melted butter and white sauce.

[N.B.—In the spring of 1882 children from the villages round Fareham, Hants, used to take swede turnip-tops round to the houses in the town. ED.]

Swede Turnip Tops

The Navew or Field Cabbage is sometimes found on the borders of fields and riversides in England but is probably a naturalized plant. Varieties of it have long been cultivated for their seeds or roots. The most valuable of these to the British farmer is called the Swedish turnip. It was first cultivated in England about 1781. It is a very good vegetable for the table when boiled being by some persons regarded as superior to the white kind. The green tops form a far better vegetable than those of the common turnip and are indeed superior in flavour and delicacy to any variety of the cabbage. If earthed up in the spring, they become blanched and in that state furnish the best substitute for seakale.

C. PIERPOINT JOHNSON, 1862.

[In 1882 I tasted these delicious swede turnip tops cooked. They still retained, after boiling, just a touch of orange colour in the thick stems and were perfectly delicious — much nicer than ordinary turnip tops. The blanched sprouts Mr. Johnson mentions as a substitute for seakale were evidently those served to Miss Esdaile at Fyfield.—ED.]

Seakale

1923

Seakale is cooked and sent to table in the same manner as asparagus, so are hop tops, young elder shoots, and the flowering stems of turnips.

Spinach as a Vegetable

Mary Eaton, Bungay, Suffolk, 1823

INGREDIENTS: Spinach; salt; butter; cream a spoonful.

METHOD

1. Wash and pick the spinach carefully.
2. Throw it into a suacepan with a little salt, and cover it close.
3. Set the pan on the fire, and shake it well.
4. When sufficiently done, beat up the spinach with some butter, but it must be sent to table pretty dry. A little cream is an improvement.

N.B.—It would look well, if pressed into a tin mould in the form of a large leaf, which is now obtainable (in 1823).

Cucumber as a Vegetable

Prepare and cook as on page 181 (Method 1). Serve with white or brown sauce.

9

SALADS

Some more Salads are to be found amongst the Appetisers

Salad Dressing

Boodle's Club, 1923

Rub the bowl with garlic, and break the lettuce; don't cut it with a knife.
1. Take 2 small saltspoonfuls of salt.
2. Cover this with dry mustard.
3. Cover this with white pepper.
4. Add 4 tablespoonfuls of olive oil.
5. Then one of best vinegar.
6. Mix well and toss the lettuce in it.

English Salad Sauce

Miss Eliza Acton 1845

INGREDIENTS: Hard-boiled eggs 2; salt 1 small saltspoonful; pounded sugar 1 large saltspoonful; cayenne a few grains; cold water 1 teaspoonful; sweet cream ¼ pint; chilli vinegar 1 tablespoonful; ordinary vinegar 1 tablespoonful.

METHOD

1. The first essential for a smooth well-made English salad dressing is to have the yolks of the eggs used for it sufficiently hard to be reduced easily to a perfect paste. They should be boiled at least 15 minutes, and should have become quite cold before they are taken from the shells. They should also be well covered with water when they are cooked, or some parts of them will be tough, and will spoil the appearance of the sauce by rendering it lumpy unless they be worked through a sieve, a process which is always better avoided if possible.
2. Mash up the hard-boiled yolks to a paste with the back of a wooden spoon.
3. Well mix in the salt, sugar and cayenne and blend with the cold water.
4. Stir in the cream by degrees.
5. Add the vinegar next, stirring the sauce briskly.

N.B.— The piquancy of this preparation — which is very delicate made by the directions just given — may be heightened by the addition of a little shallot vinegar, essence of anchovies, or tarragon vinegar; 6 tablespoonfuls of olive-oil may be substituted for the cream, but in this case the water should be omitted.

Potato Salad Dressing

Miss Acton, 1845

Miss Acton calls this the poet's receipt for salad dressing and adds 'as this salad is the result of great experience and reflexion it is hoped young salad makers will not attempt to make any improvement on it.'

1. Two well-boiled potatoes passed through a sieve.
2. A teaspoonful mustard; 2 teaspoonfuls salt; essence of anchovy.
3. About ¼ teaspoonful of very finely chopped onions (well bruised) must be incorporated with this mixture.
4. Add 3 tablespoonfuls olive oil, and 1 tablespoonful of vinegar, and
5. The yolks of 2 hard-boiled eggs mashed to a paste.
6. Stir up the salad immediately before dinner, and stir up thoroughly.

Sallets for Show Only

Gervase Markham, 1615

'They be those which are made of carrot roots of sundry colours well boiled, and cut into many shapes and proportions, as some into Knots, some in the manner of Scutcheons and Arms, some like birds, some like wild beasts, according to the art and cunning of the workman; and these for the most part are seasoned with vinegar, oil, and a little pepper. A world of other sallets there are, which time and experience may bring to our hous-wife's eyes, but the composition of them and the serving of them differetts nothing from those already rehearsed.'

To Make a Grand Sallet

Robert May, 1588—1660

This salad is described chiefly to show the different ingredients used.
1. Take a cold roast capon, and cut it into thin slices square and small (or any other roast meat, as chicken, mutton, veal or neat's tongue).
2. Mingle with it a little minced tarragon and an onion.
3. Then mince lettuce as small as the capon, mingle all together, and
4. Lay in the middle of a clean scoured dish:
5. Then lay capers by themselves, olives by themselves, samphire by itself, broom-buds, pickled mushrooms, pickled oysters, lemon, orange, raisins, almonds, blue figs, Virginia potato, peas and the like, more or less as occasion serves.

6. Lay them by themselves in the dish, round the meat in partitions.
7. Then garnish the dish sides with quarters of oranges and lemons or in slices.
8. Oil and vinegar beaten together and poured over it.
N.B.—On fish days a roast, broiled or boiled pike, boned, being cold, sliced as above.

OTHER INGREDIENTS SOMETIMES USED

1. The buds of all good sallet herbs, washed and swung in a clean napkin.
2. Dates, raisins, almonds, currants, figs.
3. Flowers, pickled or candied, such as violets, cowslips, clove-gilly flowers [old fashioned clove pinks] roses, primroses, borage, etc.
4. Leaves of spinach and sorrel, also red beetroot, white endive and chervil, corn sallet, Alexander buds [resembling celery].
5. Pickled mushrooms.
6. Some white cabbage leaves minced, and boiled cauliflowers.
7. Pickled grapes, gooseberries, barberries, red and white currants.

A Grand Sallet of Water Cresses

1. Watercress, finely picked, washed, and laid in the middle of a clean dish.
2. Sliced oranges and lemons finely carved one against the other in partitions, or round the dish.
3. Garnish with some Alexander buds, boiled or raw, currants, capers, oil and vinegar, sugar or none.

Salmagundy

This is a very delightful and useful eighteenth century salad. A very charming one was shown at the first exhibition of the English Folk Cookery Association, held at Kensington on January 16th, 1931. Any meat can be used. In this case it was simply corned beef and cold cooked vegetables of different colours, the whole surmounted by violets. The following recipe is for Mrs. Bradley's Salmagundy.

Mrs. Martha Bradley's Salmagundy

1749

1. Pick and wash three good lettuces, cut them as fine as threads and lay them at the bottom of a dish.
2. Cut the flesh from the breast of a couple of roasted chickens; it must be cut into thin slices as long and as broad as one's fingers and not thicker

than a shilling; spread them carefully over the lettuces in regular circles, leaving spaces between them.

3. Wash and bone and skin half a dozen fine anchovies, cut each into eight pieces, and lay them regularly between the slices of chicken.

4. Then cut the legs of the chickens into small square pieces like dice and cut a good lemon into square pieces in the same manner.

5. Boil 4 eggs hard; take out the yolks, mince them and mix them with some chopped parsley and 4 anchovies minced very small.

6. Boil some onions as big as walnuts till they are very white and tender.

7. Then pile up the minced anchovy and egg in the middle of the dish like a little sugar loaf; lay the onions round it and lay others thick round the edge of the dish.

8. When all is thus done, mix some oil and vinegar very well, beating it up with salt and pepper, and pour it carefully over the whole dish, then serve it up.

9. It is not only very soon ready for eating but makes a pretty appearance. There is as much nicety of hand shown in dressing up a Salmagundy as in anything.

Mrs. Glasse's Salmagundy

1747

1. Take 2 pickled herrings and bone them; a handful of parsley, four eggs boiled hard, the meat of one roasted chicken or fowl.

2. Chop all very fine separately, that is the yolks of eggs by themselves and the whites the same.

3. Scrape some lean boiled ham and hung beef very fine.

4. Turn a small china basin or deep saucer upside down in your dish.

5. Make some butter into the shape of a pineapple, or any other shape you please, and set on the top of the basin or saucer.

6. Lay round your basin a ring of shred parsley, then white of eggs, then ham, then chicken, then beef, then yolks of eggs, then herrings, till you have covered the basin and used all your ingredients.

7. Garnish the dish with whole capers and pickles of any sort you choose, chopped fine.

8. Or you may leave out the butter and put the ingredients in the basin and put a flower of any sort at the top, or a sprig of myrtle.

II

ANOTHER WAY

1. Mince veal or fowl very small, a pickled herring, boned and picked small, cucumbers minced small, apples minced small, an onion peeled

and minced small, some pickled red cabbage chopped small, cold pork minced small or cold duck or pigeons minced small, boiled parsley chopped fine, celery cut small, the yolks of hard eggs chopped small, and the whites chopped small.

2. And either lay all the ingredients by themselves separate on saucers, or in heaps in a dish.

3. Dish them out with what pickles you have, and sliced lemon nicely cut.

4. If you can get nasturtium flowers, lay them round it.

N.B.—This is a fine middle dish for supper; but you may always make Salmagundy of such things that you have, according to your fancy.

III

Salmagundy without Meat

FOR A MIDDLE DISH AT SUPPER

1. In the top plate in the middle, which should stand higher than the rest, take a fine pickled herring, bone it, take off the head, mince the rest fine.

2. In the other plates round, put the following things: in one, pare a cucumber and cut it very thin; in another apples pared and cut small; in another an onion peeled and cut small, in another two hard eggs chopped small, the whites in one — the yolks in another; pickled gherkins cut small; in another celery cut small; in another pickled red cabbage chopped fine.

3. Take some watercress clean-washed and picked, stick them all about and between every plate or saucer, and

4. Throw nasturtium flowers about the cress.

5. You must have oil and vinegar and lemon to eat with it.

N.B.—If it is neatly set out it will make a pretty figure in the middle of the table, or you may lay them in heaps in a dish; if you have not all these ingredients, set out your plates or saucers with just what you fancy and in the room of a pickled herring you may mix anchovies.

(Mrs. Glasse inserts the last Salmagundy as a Lenten dish.)

Herring Salad

INGREDIENTS: Bloaters 4; cold boiled potatoes; onions or shallots; herbs; parsley; chervil, tarragon; burnet; marjoram; hard-boiled egg; tomato; gherkins.

METHOD

1. Steep herrings, if dried, overnight.
2. Steam them and bone them.
3. Mash them with a fork with some cold boiled potatoes.
4. Season well with the uncooked onion or shallot, finely chopped.
5. Add herbs finely chopped.
6. Press into a mould, turn out and serve cold, garnished with slices of hard-boiled egg, tomato and gherkin.

N.B.—Any cold dried fish could be substituted for the herring, and green or yellow sweet peppers may be used instead of the gherkins, or pickled red cabbage makes another alternative.

Potato Salad

Mrs. Roundell, 1898.

Choose a waxy sort. Boil or steam. When cold cut in slices, and dress with oil and vinegar (*see* p. 219). Add some shredded celery, and chives or onion, and some finely minced parsley and tarragon.

10

SWEET DISHES

Short Pastry

FOR FRUIT PIES AND TARTS

INGREDIENTS: Plain flour 6 oz.; butter 4 oz. (or 2 oz. butter and 2 oz. lard) castor sugar 1 oz.; salt; and a little water.

METHOD

1. Rub the butter into the flour; add the sugar and salt, ½ teaspoonful of each.
2. Mix well.
3. Make into a firm paste quickly with a little cold water. Be sure not to make the paste too wet, because if you add flour to make it drier it will be hard, therefore only add a very little water at a time. This amount of flour will probably not take up much more than half a gill (2½ liquid ounces) at the most 3 oz., but as some flour takes up more than others it is impossible to state the exact quantity.

N.B.—If required for meat or any other savoury patties omit the sugar; and whether required savoury or sweet, if a richer crust be required the yolk of an egg can be blended with a little water to mix the paste. If a tenacious paste be required as for a raised meat or game pie made in a collar mould use the whole egg (one or two according to the size of the pie).

It is useful to know that *as a rule* ½ pint (10 liquid ounces) of water, or other liquid such as milk and eggs, will make 1 lb. flour into a firm dough, and that roughly speaking 1 egg beaten up will measure 2 liquid ounces. With this information calculations are easier.

Recipes for puff pastry and rough puff pastry will be found on page 198 and 199 and for a raised piecrust on page 45.

Apple Pie

This is one of our oldest English dishes, and one which is very often badly made. A horrible plan is frequently adopted in cheap or middle-class restaurants of simply stewing some apples, baking a sheet of pastry on a tin, and serving a wedge of it on the stewed apple and calling it apple pie. This is a direct insult to the real thing, and to the customer who knows better.

Mr. P. Morton Shand says (1927): 'English apple pie is of rare merit when achieved by a true cook, which is not too often,' and Abraham

SWEET DISHES

Hayward, Q.C., writing in *The Art of Dining*, 1852, says:

'The late Lord Dudley could not dine comfortably without an apple pie, as he insisted on calling it, contending that the term *tart* only applied to open pastry. Dining, when Foreign Secretary, at a grand dinner at Prince Esterhazy's, he was terribly put out on finding that his favourite delicacy was wanting, and kept on murmuring pretty audibly, in his absent way: "God bless my soul! No apple pie."'

FAMILY RECIPE

INGREDIENTS: Apples; water; sugar; cloves; lemon rind, rose petals if in season; or 2—3 fresh peach leaves. Short crust.

TIME: about one hour.

METHOD

1. Wash some apples.
2. Peel and core them and
3. Throw the peelings and cores into ½ pint of cold water.
4. Let them stew for half an hour, then
5. Strain off and let the liquor get cold.
6. Halve and quarter the apples, and if they are very large, cut the quarters in halves crosswise, but never cut thin slices because if you do, the juice will boil out before the apples are cooked, and the result will be tough and tasteless.
7. Pile the apples in a piedish making them high in the centre, add the sugar and the grated rind of half a lemon, which must of course be washed, also cloves if you are using them (some people don't like them, in any case do not use more than 4 for a large pie).
8. When it is cold strain the liquid from the peelings and cores and pour it all over the sugar.
9. cover the fruit with old-fashioned cottage rose petals, off which the white bit at the base has been nipped.
10. Make a short crust by rubbing 6 oz. butter and 2 oz. of pure lard into 1 lb. of good plain flour (not self-raising!), mix in 2 oz. castor sugar and the yolk of an egg well beaten with about ½ pint of cold water (*see* p. 225).
11. Roll out quarter inch thick.
12. Leave the pastry on the board or slab for ten minutes to recover (when pastry is rolled out, being elastic, it stretches, and if used at once, it frequently recedes from the edge of the dish).
13. Wet the edges of the piedish.
14. Cover the pie with pastry, being careful not to stretch it.
15. Trim the edges with a sharp knife, cutting them quite straight, and do not ornament at all (the reason for this is that in the old days a number of pies both meat and fruit, would be made at the same time on baking days and the fruit were distinguished by not being ornamented; consequently it became the correct thing not to ornament fruit pies, but to keep them perfectly plain). As a matter of fact they look very much nicer perfectly plain if the pastry is well made, and in baking rises and forms a good-shaped dome. This is achieved by putting them first into a hot oven, and lowering the heat to finish them off in a cooler one in order to cook the fruit.
16. When serving sift castor sugar over the top. Some people put a narrow strip of pastry on the rim of the pie-dish before putting on the cover at direction 14. If this is done the pastry strip must be wet first just as the dish was wetted.

226

Other Fruit Pies

Other pies of different fruit are made in a similar fashion.

All fruit pies are much nicer if served with Devonshire scalded or clotted cream which can be prepared anywhere if the milk be good.

It is the custom in some places where this cream is plentiful to lift the crust off a pie and cover the contents of the dish with a thick layer of cream. This is done not only for apple pie but also for chicken and parsley pie, and sometimes for a beef steak pie.

Scalded Cream

Mrs. Toogood, Knightshayes Dairy, Tiverton, Devon, 1887

1. Let the milk stand 24 hours in winter, and 12 hours in summer.
2. Place the pan on a hot hearth or over a 'copper' or boiler of water large enough to receive the pan.
3. It must remain on the fire or over the water till quite hot, but on no account boil, or there will be a skin instead of cream upon the milk.
4. When it is done enough, the undulations on the surface will begin to look thick, and a ring will appear round the pan, the size of the bottom.
5. The time required to scald cream depends on the size of the pan; and the heat of the fire; but the slower it is done the better.
6. When the cream is scalded, remove the pan into the dairy, and skim it the next day.
7. In cold weather it may stand 36 hours, and never less than two meals.

N.B.—Mrs. Toogood, along with other west country farmers' wives, made delicious butter with scalded cream, simply by beating it up with her hand. It was beautifully firm. She showed me how to scald the cream as above, and to make butter with it in this way. In days gone by the cream was scalded over peat fires, and this is said to have given the scalded cream a very fine flavour; this is the cream that Londoners call Devonshire clotted cream.   FLORENCE WHITE.

Almond Pastry

Mrs. Townley 1857

INGREDIENTS: Puff pastry; jam; egg; almonds; castor sugar.
TIME: about 20 minutes.

METHOD

1. Make some puff pastry.
2. Divide it into 2 parts.
3. Roll each out very thin.
4. Spread one piece with jam.
5. Cover with the second piece.
6. Brush over with a beaten egg.
7. Sprinkle with chopped almonds and castor sugar.
8. Bake in hot oven.
9. Cut into fingers when cold.

Baked Apple Pudding

This recipe, which was sent by Mr. M. W. Randolph, has been in the Wyndham family since 1740. It is as good to eat to-day as ever.

INGREDIENTS: Sharp apples ¾ lb.; sugar to sweeten; lemon 1; eggs 4, leaving out 2 whites; butter clarified ½ lb.; pastry; candied orange and lemon peel.

TIME: to bake in good oven ½ hour.

METHOD

1. Bake some apples and obtain ¾ lb. pulp which must be put through a hair sieve.
2. Add sugar to sweeten, and
3. The grated rind and juice of one lemon.
4. Beat two whole eggs and the yolks of the other two well together.
5. Add them to the apple mixture.
6. Cream the butter, and
7. Beat that in.
8. Mix all well together.
9. Lay a sheet of pastry on the bottom and sides of a greased piedish.
10. Pour in the mixture, and lay candied orange and lemon peel on top.
11. Bake as above.

Apples and Arrowroot

Lady Huntingfield's Receipt, 1865

INGREDIENTS: Arrowroot 2 oz.; castor sugar 1 oz.; milk 1 pint; butter 1 oz.; good baking apples 2; some apricot jam.

TIME: to boil 5 minutes — to bake half an hour.

METHOD

1. Make the arrowroot into a cream with a little of the milk.
2. Boil up the milk with the sugar.
3. Add the arrowroot and boil 5 minutes.
4. Pare, core and cut the apples round as for fritters.
5. Lay them in a piedish with a tea-spoonful of apricot jam on each.
6. Pour the arrowroot hot over them; and
7. Bake for half an hour in a fairly hot oven.

Old Yorkshire Apple Cake

LUNCHEON OR DINNER SWEET

Mrs. H. M. Willans, Tunbridge Wells

INGREDIENTS: Loaf sugar ¾ lb.; water 1 pint; apples 1½ lb. weighed after being pared and cored; lemon ¼ one, almond oil to oil the moulds

TIME: about 1 hour all told.

METHOD

1. Dissolve the sugar in the water and then boil up.
2. Boil the syrup to candy height (245°F.).
3. Add the pared, quartered and cored apples.
4. Wash the lemon and add half the rind grated.
5. Boil until quite stiff, keep stirring all the time; and
6. Pour into moulds which should first be brushed with a little almond oil (this can be purchased at any chemists).
7. Turn out when stiff and serve with custard or whipped cream as a luncheon or dinner sweet. It will keep good for years, and should be a pinkish colour when done.

[N.B.—This seems to be own sister to damson cheese! Mrs. Willans says it 'makes apple butter if not boiled so long.'—ED.]

Westmorland Pasties

Mrs. E. Maud Garston, Burnside, Kendal, who sent the recipes for Herb Puddings, says:

'All sorts of pasties are made in Westmorland; an apple pasty with some ripe elderberries on top of the layer of apple is very good.'

Apricot Pudding (Baked)

Adam's Luxury and Eve's Cookery, 1744

INGREDIENTS: Apricots 6 large ones; sugar to taste; eggs 4 yolks, 2 whites; a little cream; puff pastry.

TIME: to bake, about half an hour until the pastry is cooked and the pudding firm.

METHOD

1. Coddle (or steam) 6 large apricots very tender.
2. Break them small and sweeten to taste.
3. When they are cold beat in the eggs and cream.
4. Butter a dish or pie plate and line with puff pastry.
5. Put the mixture in the pastry; and
6. Bake it.

(Put it into a hot oven first to bake the pastry for 10 or 15 minutes, then lower the heat till the fruit mixture is firm.)

N.B.—This quaint little eighteenth-century book adds 'you may thus make any fruit pudding,' and the following more modern recipes are evidently derivatives, not only from the eighteenth-century recipe, but from a *Proper Newe Booke of Cokerye*, 1545.

Friar's Omelet

Red Lion Hotel, Fareham, Hants, 1873

INGREDIENTS: Large apples 6; butter 3 oz.; sugar 2 oz.; eggs 4 yolks; lemon grated rind of one, cloves to flavour; bread-crumbs 4 oz.; castor sugar

TIME: about 1½ hours to bake in slow oven.

METHOD

1. Bake the apples till tender.
2. Scrape out all the pulp.
3. Beat in 2 oz. butter and sugar and grated rind of lemon, also a little ground cloves (or if preferred – nutmeg).
4. Leave till cold.
5. Butter a piedish well.
6. Sprinkle thickly with white or brown bread-crumbs.
7. Beat the yolks of eggs into the apple.
8. Pour the mixture into the piedish.
9. Cover with white or brown bread-crumbs.
10. Put small pieces of butter on top.
11. Bake 1½ hours or till firm and set.
12. Serve hot.

Oxford and Cambridge Pudding

This is a pudding very much resembling Adam and Eve's apricot pudding, the only difference being that the fruit custard when baked is covered with a meringue made of one or two whites of eggs and one or two ounces of castor sugar. It should be noted that 1 ounce only of castor sugar should be stirred in lightly to each stiffly beaten white of egg when this meringue is required for covering a tart or pudding; but 2 oz. of fine castor sugar are required for each white of egg when making the cakes known as meringue. In both cases, however the meringue must be put into a very cool oven, otherwise it will be tough instead of crisp. It is therefore important that the pie or pudding should be cooked before the meringue is put on.

Apple Betty (or Brown Betty)

This well-known nursery pudding is evidently the simplest derivative of the 16th century borage and apple tart. In those days the pastry was used instead of a piedish, and a case made called a coffin. The Kentish pudding pies and the Deddington pudding pies are surviving examples of this old method of baking. To-day fireproof glass moulds are made in the same shape, and can be used for baked custards either lined with pastry or bread-crumbs.

Baked Rice Pudding

1887

Lady Bernard, wife of Sir Charles Bernard, Chief Commissioner of Burma, used to make a rice pudding as follows every day for her husband's tiffen. He said no one could make it as well as she did. The secret is slow, very slow and prolonged baking.

INGREDIENTS: Rice 2 oz.; milk 1 pint; sugar 2 oz.; butter or finely chopped suet 1 oz.; nutmeg.

TIME: to bake 4 hours.

METHOD

1. Wash the rice.
2. Put it in the bottom of a piedish.
3. Sprinkle the sugar over it.
4. Then the suet.
5. Pour in the milk.
6. Stir well.
7. Grate some nutmeg over the top and put the dish into a very slow oven.
8. If by any chance it looks as if it is getting too dry add a little more milk.

N.B.—Properly cooked the rice and milk at the end of 4 hours are deliciously creamy, and the top a 'symphony' in delicate gold and brown. A veritable poem of a pudding. Prepared in this way nursery children love it. It is its degenerate form that is so much disliked.

Bilberry Pies

Haworth, Yorkshire, 1867

These pies we may be sure were enjoyed by the Brontë Sisters, at Haworth Parsonage. Dr. Fernie tells us they are a feature of Yorkshire 'funeral teas'; they are first cousins to the famous American pies.

INGREDIENTS: Bilberries 1½ pints; castor sugar 4 oz.; baked apples 2; pastry; white of egg. Cream if obtainable.

METHOD

1. Mix the bilberries with 2 or 3 oz. of sugar.
2. Bake the apples in the usual manner, scrape out the pulp, sweeten it, and mix it with the bilberries.
3. Grease a pie-plate, and sheet it with short or puff pastry.
4. Fill it with the bilberry mixture; do not on any account add a drop of water.
5. Cover it with a thin sheet of pastry.
6. Brush with white of egg, dust this with castor sugar; or leave plain; bake (in quick oven at first to cook the pastry and afterwards in a slower one to cook the fruit).

N.B.—All fresh fruit pies, gooseberries, blackberries, raspberries and red currants, strawberries and raspberries, apple, peach, etc., can be made in this way.

Apple pulp is not always added to bilberry pies, but it makes them more juicy and some people consider it an improvement. It is frequently added in the same way and for the same purpose to blackberry pies.

To Make a Tart of Borage Flowers, Marigolds or Cowslips

Sixteenth Century

This very interesting recipe comes from a *Proper Newe Booke of Cokerye* a black-letter book in the library of Corpus Christi College, Cambridge. This copy belonged to Archbishop Parker, and was edited by Miss Frere, and republished in 1913.

1. Take borage flowers and parboil them tender.
2. Then strain them and
3. Mix them with the yolks of 3—4 eggs and sweet curds.
4. Or else take 3—4 apples and parboil them, and strain them and mix them with sweet butter and the yolks of eggs and a little mace and so bake it.

[N.B.— In those days it would be baked in a raised pastry coffin. To-day it would be baked in a fireproof glass piedish. — ED.]

Other flowers may be be cooked in exactly the same way; but it is advisable before using any part of a plant for food to study Mrs. Grieve's and Mrs. Leyel's *Modern Herbal.* (*See* Authorities.)

Buxton Pudding

INGREDIENTS: Flour 2 oz.; milk 1 pint; butter 3 oz.; sugar 6 oz.; eggs 6 (yolks only); peel of one lemon grated. Half these quantities will make a good-sized pudding.

TIME: to bake ¾ hour, in a moderate oven.

METHOD

1. Mix the flour with the milk and boil till thick.
2. Let it cool.
3. When almost cold stir in the butter and sugar, the yolks of the eggs and the peel of the lemon grated. Put it into a dish.
4. Bake as above.

Lemon Cheese or Curd

Miss L. M. Anstey sends this amongst a number of valuable recipes some of which have been in her family for many years. She says: 'This filling for lemon cheesecakes is taken from my mother's receipt book and must be a South-East Essex recipe. She was a Miss Angur, and was born at Burnham-on-Crouch in 1819. I have not met this mixture elsewhere. It should be used sparingly as it rises and spreads. It keeps good for several weeks. It is possibly much older than my mother's dates and may have come from my grandmother.'

INGREDIENTS: Powdered lump sugar ½ lb.; ground rice 2 oz.; butter 6 oz.; lemon grated peel and juice of one; eggs 2.

METHOD

1. Cream the butter.
2. Add the sugar.
3. And ground rice.
4. Then the grated peel and juice of the lemon; and
5. The 2 eggs well beaten.
6. Mix well together and put in jars.

Lemon Cheese for Cheesecakes

MS. Book, 1904

INGREDIENTS: Lump sugar ½ lb.; butter, 2 oz.; eggs 2; lemons, juice and rind of 1.

TIME: ½ hour.

METHOD

1. Beat the eggs well.
2. Put them into the top of a double saucepan.
3. Rub the sugar on the outside of the lemon (which must, of course, be first washed and dried) until you have taken all the essence, when this happens the sugar will be yellow and must be dropped into the eggs.
4. The lemon must then be cut, the juice squeezed, and strained, and beaten into the egg mixture.
5. Add the butter in bits.
6. Place this pan in the underpart of the double saucepan which must contain boiling water which must be kept simmering.
7. Stir all the time and cook very gently for ½ hour.

N.B.—This thickens as it gets cold and sets. It is used to fill tartlets, and is a delicious filling for jam sandwiches and layer cakes.

Rice Cheesecakes

INGREDIENTS: Puff Pastry about 6 oz.; butter 2 oz.; castor sugar 2 oz.; ground rice 2 oz.; egg 1; currants and cinnamon or other flavouring; sufficient for 12.

TIME: to bake 15 minutes, in a quick oven.

METHOD

1. Grease 12 patty pans and line them with pastry.
2. Make the mixture to fill these as follows: Cream the butter and sugar, add the ground rice, well-beaten egg, cinnamon, and a few currants.
3. Put a little of the mixture into each patty pan.

233

Egg Curry Cheesecakes

Mrs. Rycroft, a B.B.C. friend, writes from Cambridge: 'I wonder if you know of another truly delicious kind of cheesecake called "Egg Curry Cheesecakes"? The recipe was given me half a century ago and came from a family famous as cooks and housewives in their own neighbourhood. So far I have not met anyone who knows of it, but must have written it out scores of times for guests who have so much enjoyed those particular dainties during the last fifty years.'

RECIPE

INGREDIENTS : Butter ¼ lb.; fine white sugar ¼ lb.; yolk of 1 egg and whites of 2; currants 2 oz.; candied peel 2 oz.; and a little rum. Puff pastry to line patty pans.

METHOD

1. Cream the butter.
2. Beat in the sugar.
3. Add the yolk of 1 egg, and
4. The well-whisked whites of 2.
5. Mix in the currants, chopped candied peel and rum.
6. Butter and line some patty pans with puff pastry.
7. And put a little of the egg curry mixture into each.
8. Bake in a hot oven to raise the pastry.
9. And when this is cooked the mixture also will be done.

Marrow Pudding

This is a recipe from the Border Counties sent by Miss E. Cullen, of Dundee.

INGREDIENTS : White bread-crumbs 1 lb.; milk 1 pint; eggs 4; beef marrow 4 to 6 oz.; currants, 2 oz.; raisins 2 oz.; sugar to taste; a little ground cinnamon and nutmeg.

TIME : to bake about 1½ hours in a moderate oven.

METHOD

1. Grate the bread-crumbs.
2. Boil the milk.
3. Pour it boiling hot on the bread; cover to soak in.
4. Beat 4 eggs.
5. Chop the beef marrow, and add to bread-crumbs.
6. Clean and stone some currants and raisins, mix well with the bread.
7. Sweeten to taste.
8. Season with a little ground cinnamon and nutmeg.
9. Mix all well together and stir in the beaten eggs. Bake as above.

Yorkshire Mint Pasty

Mr. A. Dupuis Brown says: 'The Yorkshire "pasty," containing meat, fruit or jam, was very popular many years ago, but I cannot say if it was peculiar to that county — the jam "turnover" was made in most households then, and I have never found it elsewhere.'

The following was given by Miss Alice Jones, of Leeds:

TO MAKE OLD YORKSHIRE MINT PASTY

INGREDIENTS: Short pastry; currants, raisins; candied peel (chopped very finely); fresh mint leaves (chopped very finely); brown sugar; butter; nutmeg or spice.

TIME: to bake; according to size, and in a moderate oven.

METHOD

1. Roll out pastry about ¼ inch thick.
2. Cut into large rounds or squares.
3. On one half place a layer of currants, stoned raisins and candied peel.
4. Sprinkle with the mint.
5. Then sprinkle with brown sugar.
6. Add some more currants, etc.
7. Then some dabs of butter, grated nutmeg and spice.
8. Wet the edges of the pastry.
9. Turn the plain half over to cover the fruit, etc.
10. Pinch the edges together. Serve hot or cold.

Kent Lent or Pudding Pies

Sent by the same lady who sent the recipe for the Fourteenth Century Pie (see p. 205).

1. Boil 3 oz. good ground rice in just half a pint of milk.
2. Take from fire and stir into it 3 oz. butter and 4 oz. castor sugar.
3. Add to them 6 well-beaten eggs, a little salt and a flavouring of lemon peel.
4. When this mixture is nearly cold line some patty pans with puff pastry, and
5. Fill three parts full with the mixture.
6. Strew the tops with washed currants, just as they are, and put them in the oven.
7. Bake for 15 to 20 minutes in a quick oven.

Deddington Pudden Pie

'This was made for the Deddington Fair on November 22nd, known as "Pudden Pie Fair," but Deddington Fair is now no more.' A Deddington Pudden Pie was however made by Miss R. F. Fowler and exhibited at the first English Folk Cookery Exhibition organized by Miss Willans, M.B.E., in the lecture hall of the Gas Light and Coke Co., Church Street, Kensington, London, W. 8, England, on January 16th, 1931. The following recipe was published in the *Daily News* in 1930.

RECIPE

INGREDIENTS: Puff pastry; ground rice 4 oz.; milk 1 quart; eggs 3; lump sugar 6 oz.; lemon 1; currants 4 oz.

TIME: 10 to 15 minutes to boil and 15 to 25 minutes to bake in a moderate oven.

METHOD

1. Grease some large saucers and line them with puff pastry.
2. Make the rice into a cream with 6 tablespoonfuls of the milk.
3. Add the eggs well beaten to it.
4. Boil up the remainder of the milk with the lump sugar, and the thinly pared rind of a washed lemon.
5. When this boils add the rice mixture and keep stirring for 10 or 15 minutes; then
6. Lift out the lemon peel, and add the currants.
7. Pour into the lined saucers to within one inch and a half of the edge of the crust.
8. Bake in a moderate oven until the pastry is nicely coloured and the mixture set. They can be eaten hot or cold.

A Potato Pudding-Pie

Early 18th Century

INGREDIENTS: Potatoes ¾ lb.; butter 6 oz.; sugar 6 oz.; eggs 4 yolks and three whites; nutmeg grated ¼; a little brandy or any other flavouring you fancy; puff pastry.

TIME: 30—40 minutes, in a quick oven.

METHOD

1. Boil and peel the potatoes; then
2. Mash them with the butter and beat them well together.
3. Add the sugar.
4. Whisk the eggs well and beat them into the mixture adding the nutmeg and brandy as flavouring.
5. Sheet your dish with puff pastry, pour in your pudding.
6. Bake it in a quick oven till the mixture is set.

Orange Pudding

This and other recipes sent by Mr. H. M. Leman, of Nottingham, are taken from the old still-room books of his mother's family, the Mayo family of Cheshunt, Herts. He has purposely selected recipes with names attached that give them historical interest. This one is signed 'Mrs. Mayo, Cloak Lane.'

RECIPE

INGREDIENTS: Seville orange (or lemon) 1; Naples or sponge biscuits 2; butter ½ lb.; loaf sugar ¼ lb.; eggs 6; puff pastry.

TIME: to bake ½ hour.

METHOD

Butter a dish and line it with puff pastry; and make the mixture to fill it as follows:

1. Boil the thinly pared rind of the orange (or if they are not in season a lemon) until soft.
2. Beat it in a mortar with the juice of it.
3. Grate the biscuits very fine; add this to the orange peel.
4. Cream the butter and beat all together with the sugar which must be crushed and finely sieved (we should use castor sugar), add the yolks of the 6 eggs.
5. Pour into the puff pastry and bake for half an hour in a quick oven.

Pumpkin Pie

A Sussex Recipe.   Mrs. Creasey, Coolham, near Horsham

INGREDIENTS: Ripe pumpkin or marrow ½ lb.; apple ½ lb.; currants ½ lb.; mixed peel 2 oz.; sugar 3 oz.; a little spice (if liked). Enough good short pastry to cover (½ lb. flour 3 or 4 oz. lard and butter mixed or clarified dripping; ¼ teaspoonful salt; about 1 gill of water to mix).

TIME: to bake 1 hour in fairly good oven.

METHOD

1. Peel and seed the pumpkin or marrow and apple.
2. Chop them finely together.
3. Wash currants.
4. Add currants.
5. Also the mixed peel, sugar and spice.
6. Blend all together.
7. Put in a piedish and cover with a good crust.

This may also be made in a pie plate sheeted first with pastry. No water is required, but the pumpkin and apple must be chopped very finely.

Raspberry Tarts

1823

1. Roll out some puff pastry very thin and lay it in a greased patty pan
2. Put in the raspberries and strew some fine sugar over them.
3. Cover with a thin lid of pastry and bake the tart.
4. Mix a pint of cream with the yolks of 2 or 3 eggs well beaten, and a little sugar.
5. Cut open the tart, pour in the mixture, and return it to the oven for five or six minutes.

N.B.—Any soft fruit can be done in this way, also apples.

1. Line the dish with puff pastry.
2. Put in sugar and fruit.
3. Lay bars across and bake them.

N.B.—Currant tarts are done in the same way.

Barberry Tart

Gosfield Hall, Essex, February 5th, 1805

This is one of John Simpson's recipes.

RECIPE

Sheet a tartpan with puff paste, put preserved barberries in, and cross-bar it. For recipe for preserved barberries see page 308.

Red Gooseberry Pie

Old Folkestone Kent dish. 'This pie was always demanded by my wife's father on the Sunday following Folkestone Fair day. He always had it when a boy at Folkestone. It may have been a Fair day delicacy. He was born 1832.'—H. J. GLOVER, Pevensey.

RECIPE

1. The gooseberries must be the kind that turn red when ripe.
2. The pie is made in the ordinary way but the crust must be thick, as it has to be baked in a slow oven.
3. It must cook very slowly. The gooseberries turn red.

N.B.—This pie was probably made originally in a raised crust, as the Warden pies mentioned by Shakespeare and the Mansfield gooseberry pies that are still made (1931) and sold at Mansfield Fair every year. The old Shrewsbury simnel was also made in a raised crust of hot-water pastry just as the Scots bun is to-day.

Sorrel Tart

A Worcestershire lady writes (in 1931) 'In Lancashire they still use the fresh young leaves of wild sorrel (*Rumex Acetosa*) as a substitute for apple in turnovers. I have made it myself, and very good it is, with plenty of brown sugar and a little moisture on the leaves. Sorrel is in season between apples and gooseberries, i.e. in April and May.'

Suet Pasty

'All sorts of pasties are made in Westmorland. An apple pasty with some ripe elderberries on top of the layer of apple is very good, and so is the following suet pasty—one would hardly guess suet was used, it has such a nice and original flavour.'—Mrs. E. MAUD GARSTON.

RECIPE

INGREDIENTS: Pastry short crust; very finely shredded suet; brown sugar; grated nutmeg.

TIME: bake in hot oven till golden brown.

METHOD

1. Roll out the pastry thin.
2. And use it to cover a dinner plate.
3. Place on the pastry a layer of very finely shredded suet.
4. Sprinkle this thickly with brown sugar.
5. Grate a little nutmeg over the sugar.
6. Cover with a thin piece of pastry.
7. Bake in a nice hot oven till golden brown.

Cumberland Scrap and Currant Pasty

This recipe was given by Miss Elise Sprott, of the B.B.C.

'When the fat of a pig is rendered down for lard, the scraps or "scratchings" as they are called in Shropshire and Herefordshire, are chopped up and used in various ways. In Cumberland they use them as a filling for a pasty made as above, mixing the chopped scraps with brown sugar, currants and nutmeg or cinnamon and sometimes a little chopped apple.'

[As a child I have had in Surrey this particular pasty made as above with 'scraps,' apples, currants, etc. The cook was a Sussex woman.—ED.]

The 'scratchings' (which is the Shropshire word for the scraps left over after lard has been rendered down) are used in Cheshire to make very delicious cakes. The scraps are mixed with some flour and salt, made into a pastry with a little water rolled out, cut into rounds and baked. They rise a good deal and are crisp, somewhat resembling the flead cakes and pastry of Kent, but the last two are made with the flare of the pig before it is rendered down into lard, (*see* p. 328 for recipe).

In Shropshire and Hereford it is still the custom to flavour the rendered lard with rosemary by throwing in a piece of this herb during the process.

Sussex Pie

Sent by Miss Oonagh Woodlock, Liverpool

INGREDIENTS: Short crust pastry 6 oz.; cooked apples ½ lb.; sugar 3 oz.; raisins 2 oz.; currants 2 oz.; cinnamon ½ teaspoonful; mixed spice ½ teaspoonful.

TIME: to bake ½ to ¾ hour in moderate oven.

METHOD

1. Line a flan ring or pie plate with pastry.
2. Fill with cooked apples, sugar, raisins, currants, cinnamon and spice
3. Cover with crust.
4. Bake as above.

Treacle Custard

*This Southwold, Suffolk, recipe is over 100 years old
Sent by Mrs. Loftus*

INGREDIENTS: Short crust; egg 1; syrup 2 tablespoonfuls.

TIME: About 30 to 40 minutes.

METHOD

1. Grease a sandwich tin, or deep plate with the short crust.
2. Beat up the egg.
3. Warm the syrup so that it is liquid.
4. Beat up the egg and the syrup together.
5. Pour it into the pastry-lined tin or plate.
6. Bake in a slow oven till a golden brown.
7. Eat cold, when the mixture will set like a jelly.

Yorkshire Treacle Tart

This recipe was sent by Miss Milner Barry, Parkstone, Dorset

INGREDIENTS: Brown bread-crumbs ½ pint; mixed fruit ½ pint (such as currants, sultanas, and candied peel); lemon, the grated rind and juice of one; apple, one large one grated; mixed spice a pinch; ground ginger a pinch; treacle two tablespoonfuls. Short pastry.

TIME: to bake in hot oven 20 to 30 minutes.

METHOD

1. Grease and line a sandwich tin with short pastry.
2. Mix the bread-crumbs, fruit, lemon rind and juice, apple, spice, ground ginger and treacle all together.
3. Fill the piecrust with the mixture.
4. Cover with pastry and bake.

Lemon Mincemeat

Frome, Somersetshire, 1852

INGREDIENTS: Large lemons 2; finely sifted sugar 1 lb.; currants ½ lb.; stoned and chopped raisins ½ lb.; finely shredded beef suet ¾ lb.; cloves, mace and nutmeg to taste; candied fruits and chopped blanched almonds also to taste; brandy one or two glasses.

METHOD

1. Wash the lemons, cut them in halves, squeeze out the juice and strain it.
2. Boil the lemon skins in water till soft enough to pound to a paste. (N.B. - You must change the water several times to prevent their tasting bitter.)
3. Pound them to a paste, add the sugar and pound the two together.
4. Then mix in the rest of the ingredients and mix well, adding the brandy last of all.

Mincemeat

Mrs. Brewitt, The Priory, Melton Mowbray

INGREDIENTS: Apples 4 lb.; finely chopped suet, stoned raisins, currants, 2 lb. of each; granulated sugar 2 lb.; lemon the grated rinds of 3, and juice of one; mixed spice to taste; salt ½ oz.; brandy or wine, or both, to moisten.

N.B.—Do not let any flour of any kind touch the suet, or the mincemeat will ferment.

Apples Stuffed with Mincemeat

Mrs. Kermode (Douglas, Isle of Man) says: 'A dish I think we invented ourselves.'

INGREDIENTS: Good baking apples; mincemeat; butter; sugar.

TIME: to bake; according to baking quality of apples.

METHOD

1. Core but do not pare the apples.
2. Score round the waist.
3. Set on buttered plate.
4. Fill with mincemeat, butter and sugar.
5. Bake in moderate oven; the skin will come off in 2 caps.

N.B.—When coring apples that are to be stuffed, it is a good plan to replace the stem end of the core, as this will prevent the stuffing baking out on to the plate. They may also be stuffed with raspberry jam.

Baked Pears or Apples or Prunes

Eighteenth Century

Miss Margaret C. Cook says that pears or apples or prunes are perfectly delicious baked all night in the still warm oven of a stove that has been heated all day by a coal fire. In the morning the oven would be cold

1. Have a low earthenware pot or dish with a lid.
2. Pare the fruit carefully, and halve, and put into the pot.
3. Strew them with a little sugar according to taste.
4. Add flavouring also according to taste and quantity.
5. Pour over 1 tablespoonful water.
6. Cover with the apple or pear peelings pressed carefully down on top of fruit.
7. Put on the lid and put in the oven.
8. In the case of prunes — wash them first with boiling water, and then put into pot.
9. Flavour with one or two cloves and half an inch or an inch of stick cinnamon.
10. Add sugar to taste and about half a teacupful of water according to the amount of fruit.
11. Peel half a lemon and put the parings over the prunes in the same manner as for apples and pears.

Stewed Pears

'A dish always served at Barnstaple Fair-time in private houses or restaurants.'

Mrs. Maude S. Seldon, Braunton

INGREDIENTS: Pears 2 lb.; lump sugar 1½ lb.; lemon rind and juice of one; port or claret 1 wineglassful; water; cloves to taste; some sweet almonds.

TIME: cook till fruit is soft.

METHOD

1. Peel, halve and core the pears and throw into cold water.
2. Put them into a stewpan as soon as you have peeled them all, with the sugar, lemon rind, and juice, the wine and sufficient water to cover.
3. Simmer until the fruit is soft.
4. Colour with cochineal; and
5. When cold serve in a bowl or dish with blanched sweet almonds stuck into the fruit. A bowl of Devonshire cream should also be served with the pears.

Strawberries in Wine

Mary Eaton, Bungay, Suffolk, 1823

INGREDIENTS: The finest strawberries; castor sugar; Madeira or fine sherry (or better still, a bottle of home-made orange wine).

METHOD

1. Hull the fruit and put it in a Kilner fruit-bottling glass jar, or any wide necked bottle.
2. Sprinkle a very little sugar over each layer.
3. Fill up with the wine.
4. And fasten securely.

Strawberry Short Cake

A LUNCHEON SWEET

Mrs. (Dorothy) Allhusen, a Hampshire recipe

INGREDIENTS: Flour 6 oz.; sugar 6 oz.; a pinch of salt; butter 6 oz.; egg 1; strawberries 1 lb. or more; castor sugar; cream ½ pint; pistachio nuts.

TIME: to bake about 30 minutes in moderate oven.

The cakes should be made the day they are used.

METHOD

1. Mix the sugar and flour together.
2. Add a pinch of salt.
3. Rub in butter and mix with the egg.
4. Knead and make into two flat cakes the same size.
5. Bake on a flat lightly greased and floured tin in a moderate oven till firm to the touch.
6. Leave them on the tins till cold, then trim.
7. Take 1 lb or a few more strawberries, cut them in halves.
8. And place half the quantity evenly on one of the cakes.
9. Sprinkle well with castor sugar.
10. Place the other cake on top.
11. Then the rest of the strawberries and more sugar.
12. Whip the cream, but not too stiff and place on top. Sprinkle with pistachio nuts.
[N.B. – To prepare pistachio nuts put them in a small saucepan in cold water, and boil up; turn into a basin and the skin will come off easily.]

Poor Knights of Windsor

Berkshire

INGREDIENTS: Slices of stale bread about ½ inch thick; white wine and sugar, or milk and sugar; yolks of 2 eggs; fresh butter or lard; some jam, or sugar and cinnamon.

METHOD

1. Put some white wine and sugar or milk and sugar in a dish.
2. Put the slices of bread into it.
3. Turn them over.
4. Take them up carefully, one by one, and dip them in the beaten yolks of 2 eggs.

5. Have ready a little butter or lard boiling hot in a frying-pan.
6. Put the slices into it, fry a fine brown on both sides.
7. Drain and dish up on a hot dish.
8. Place a spoonful of jam on each, or if liked, strew on some sugar and ground cinnamon.

Pancakes

Somersetshire, 1852

INGREDIENTS: Plain flour 2 oz.; egg 1; milk 1 gill; salt a pinch; 2 oz. clarified fat for frying; castor sugar 2 oz.; lemon juice.

METHOD

1. Mix the flour and salt together, and make into a batter with the egg and milk.
2. Heat the frying-pan, add a little fat.
3. Make it quite hot, and pour in enough batter to cover the pan thinly.

4. When a golden brown on one side, toss or turn and fry the other.
5. Squeeze a little lemon juice over it, dust with castor sugar, roll up and serve dusted with castor sugar.

Mrs. Briscoe's Quire Pancakes

An 18th Century Recipe sent by Lady Gomme

INGREDIENTS: Good cream (or evaporated milk) 1 pint; eggs 4 yolks but 2 whites; flour enough to make a thick batter; nutmeg a little; powdered sugar and salt to taste; sack (or sherry) 2 kitchenspoonfuls; fresh butter half a pound.

TIME: 2—3 minutes to fry each.

METHOD

1. Beat the eggs and strain them.
2. Mix them with the cream.
3. Strew in as much fine flour by degrees as will make it a fine batter pretty thick.
4. Then grate in a little nutmeg.
5. Add powdered sugar and salt to your taste.

6. Then the sack (or sherry).
7. Melt the fresh butter, and when cool put it to the other ingredients and mix them well together.
8. Fry in a dry pan. Place one on top of the other; serve very hot.

They are called Quire Pancakes because they are supposed to be so thin that they resemble a quire of paper. [N.B. — I have not tried them.— Ed.]

Barford Pudding

This was a favourite pudding of Mr. Serjeant Woolrych who was born in 1795.

INGREDIENTS: Beef suet chopped 1 lb.; raisins stoned 1 lb.; flour 4 oz.; castor sugar 6 oz.; a little salt; half a nutmeg; eggs 5.

TIME: to boil 6 hours.

METHOD

1. Mix all well together.
2. Boil in a cloth which must be closely woven wrung out in hot water, well-floured, and tied very tight close to the pudding.

King George I's Christmas Pudding

This recipe is said to have been in the possession of the Royal Family from the days of George I.

INGREDIENTS: Suet 1½ lb. finely shredded; Demerara sugar 1 lb.; small raisins 1 lb.; plums 1 lb. (stoned and cut in half); candied citron peel 4 oz.; (cut in thin strips) candied lemon peel 4 oz.; candied orange peel 4 oz.; mixed spice 1 teaspoonful; nutmeg ½; salt 2 teaspoonfuls; bread-crumbs 1 lb.; sifted flour 1 lb.; eggs 1 lb. (weighed in their shells); new milk ½ pint; brandy 1 wineglassful.

TIME: stand after mixing for 12 hours in a cool place; and boil 8 hours.

METHOD

1. Mix all the dry ingredients together.
2. Beat the eggs to a froth.
3. Add ½ pint new milk, and the brandy.
4. Use this mixture to moisten the dry ingredients.
5. Stand 12 hours in a cool place.
6. Then put in buttered moulds which should be filled.
7. Cover with buttered paper.
8. Tie down with a cloth and boil 8 hours.
9. When required boil up for another 2 hours. Sufficient for 3 medium-sized puddings each weighing about 3 lb.

Mrs. D. C. Lysaght's Christmas Plum Pudding

(WITHOUT FLOUR)

Chepstow, Monmouth, 1931

INGREDIENTS: Raisins stoned 2 lb.; currants well washed 2 lb.; sultanas well cleaned in floured cloth 2 lb.; mixed peel 1 lb.; brown sugar 1 lb.; suet finely chopped 2 lb.; bread-crumbs 2 lb.; sweet almonds chopped and blanched 1 lb.; eggs well beaten 14; spice 1 teaspoonful; brandy ½ pint; not quite a quart of old beer.

TIME: stand all night, boil 8 hours for keeping, and then 2 hours before serving.

METHOD

1. Mix all these ingredients, except the brandy and beer, all together in a large pan and leave all night.
2. Stir again next day and add brandy and beer.
3. The mixture should be stiff and not too moist.
4. Place in buttered basins, cover with a piece of buttered paper and tie down with cloths.
5. Boil 8 hours for large puddings, and 6 hours for small.

N.B.—Mrs. Lysaght says the standing at least 12 to 24 hours is most important and makes all the difference to the lightness of the pudding; also the mixture, when beer and brandy are added, should not be allowed to become too moist.

Lord Barrington's Plum Pudding

1860

This recipe has been sent by the Lady Margaret Campbell, Vice-President of the English Folk Cookery Association.

INGREDIENTS: Eggs 3; milk ¼ pint; bread-crumbs one cupful; flour a large tablespoonful; a pinch of salt; white sugar 1 oz.; suet ¾ lb.; stoned raisins ½ lb.; currants just a few. If spice is liked — a little grated nutmeg may be added.

TIME: boil 4 hours.

METHOD

1. Beat eggs and milk well together.
2. Add the bread-crumbs, flour and salt, and one oz. of sugar and mix them in with the milk and eggs;
3. Cut the suet into small square pieces and stir it in.
4. Stir in the stoned raisins and the few currants.
5. When all are mixed together, tie it in a cloth and boil it as directed.

Sir Robert Walpole's Dumplings

1773

This has been very kindly sent by Mrs. MacIver Cruickshank, of Nairn. It is one of her grandmother, Mrs. MacIver's, recipes (1773).

INGREDIENTS: Suet 1 lb.; stale bread ⅜ lb.; currants 1 lb.; orange peel and citron ¼ lb.; cinnamon and sugar; eggs 6 or 8 but use only the whites of half the number, and all the yolks.

TIME: to boil about 1 hour.

METHOD

1. Shred the suet small.
2. Grate the bread.
3. Pick and clean the currants.
4. Cut the orange and citron peel small.
5. Mix all together, and season with cinnamon and sugar.
6. Make into a *stiff* paste with the eggs, it must be very stiff indeed.
7. You should have small nets, wrought of small pack-thread; put one about the size of an apple into every net; tie them close in the net; make them all of one size, except one for the middle, make it a little larger.
8. Put them into a pot of boiling water. They will take about one hour's boiling. If you have not nets, you may tie them up in pieces of clean rags; dish them, and pour beat-butter, wine and sugar over them.

Berkeley Pudding

A favourite pudding of the 3rd Earl of Normanton, Somerley, sent by his daughter, the Lady Margaret Campbell.

INGREDIENTS: Chopped suet 1 lb.; flour 4 oz.; bread-crumbs 12 oz.; eggs 3 whole ones; powdered cinnamon ½ a teaspoonful; mace ⅛ a teaspoonful, a small nutmeg grated; a little grated lemon peel; milk ½ pint.

TIME: boil rather more than 8 hours.

METHOD

1. Mix the dry ingredients together.
2. Beat up the eggs with the milk.
3. Blend with the dry ingredients.
4. Well butter a plain mould.
5. Pour in the mixture, and
6. Cover with buttered paper.
7. Put on the lid of the mould, put into boiling water over the fire and boil for 8 hours.

Plum Pudding without Eggs

Mrs. Martin, Frome, Somersetshire, 1852

INGREDIENTS: Plain flour, suet, currants, potatoes, and carrots, ½ lb. of each; moist sugar 1 tablespoonful; spice.

TIME: to boil 3 hours.

METHOD

1. Scrape the carrots and peel the potatoes.
2. Grate them.
3. Mix with all the other ingredients.
4. Put into a buttered basin.
5. Cover with a buttered paper.
6. Tie up in a cloth and boil as above.

Sir Charles Rowley's Plum Pudding
1857

This is a Suffolk recipe.

INGREDIENTS: Raisins ½ lb.; good beef suet ½ lb.; flour 7 oz.; sugar 2 oz.; eggs 2; a little salt.

TIME: to boil 5 hours.

METHOD

1. Cut the suet very large.
2. Mix the dry ingredients together.
3. Bind with the eggs well-beaten.
4. Put into a cloth wrung out of hot water and floured.
5. Boil as directed.

Sunday Pudding
Mrs. Arthur Hillyard, Stoodleigh Rectory, Tiverton, 1890

This pudding can be made some days beforehand.

INGREDIENTS: Flour 6 oz.; chopped suet 6 oz.; stoned raisins 6 oz.; currants 6 oz.; bread-crumbs 6 oz.; mixed peel 2 oz.; mixed spice 1 oz.; milk ½ pint; treacle 2 tablespoonfuls; flavouring.

TIME: to boil 5 or 6 hours the day it is made; then 2 hours the day it is eaten.

METHOD

1. Mix all well together.
2. Then put into greased basin.
3. Cover with buttered paper.
4. Tie up in a cloth.

Sunday Pudding
Frome, Somersetshire, 1852

INGREDIENTS: Plain flour 1 lb.; bread-crumbs ¼ lb.; finely chopped suet ½ lb.; raisins ½ lb.; currants ¼ lb.; sugar 2 oz. (or treacle, or Fowler's West Indian Syrup); eggs 3.

TIME: to boil 3 hours.

METHOD

Mix as usual, tie up and boil as above.

Vegetable Plum Pudding
From Miss Mary Smithson

INGREDIENTS: Potatoes ½ lb.; carrots ½ lb.; sugar 3 oz.; currants and raisins mixed ¼ lb.; flour ¼ lb.; suet 3 oz.; candied peel ½ oz.; egg 1; salt, 1 teaspoonful; a little nutmeg; a little milk if necessary.

TIME: steam 3 hours.

METHOD

1. Butter a pudding basin.
2. Peel and grate the potatoes (you want ½ lb. weighed after they have been grated).
3. Peel and grate the carrots (must weigh ¼lb. when grated).

4. Mix the potatoes and carrots, sugar, currants, raisins and all the dry ingredients well together; and
5. Blend them with the egg and milk.
6. Mix well.

Ginger Pudding

Burnham-on-Crouch, Essex

This is another of Mrs. Anstey's 'receipts', sent by her daughter. It is for a pudding made without any moisture except the fat from the suet and the melted sugar.

INGREDIENTS: Flour ½ lb.; suet finely chopped ⅛ lb.; sugar ½ lb.; ginger 2 large teaspoonfuls.

TIME: to boil 3 hours.

METHOD

1. Butter the basin well.
2. Mix the suet well into the flour.
3. Add the sugar and ginger.

4. Again mix well, put into basin; tie down and boil as directed.

To make a Gooseberry Boiled Pudding

Little Gaddesden, Hertfordshire. A receipt of 1750

This was a clever idea to save much of the expense of fruit at that period, by mixing green gooseberries in with the flour as we do raisins for a plum pudding. When boiled it was eaten with sugar and butter or sugar alone.

Fruit in Batter

Another Hertfordshire plan is to stir blackberries or gooseberries or plums into a stiff batter and boil in a closely woven linen bag or cloth. The cloth must be wrung out in hot water and well floured, and the batter must be as stiff as a fruit-cake batter or the fruit will sink.

Hunter's Pudding

Miss Anstey says: 'I do not know the origin of this receipt, which is from my mother's receipt book. She possibly had it from friends in Suffolk before her marriage in 1859. I have not met with this pudding out of the family.'

249

INGREDIENTS: Flour, a breakfastcupful ($\frac{1}{2}$ pint); suet a teacup ($\frac{1}{4}$ pint); sugar a teacupful; stoned raisins ($\frac{1}{4}$ lb.); milk 1$\frac{1}{2}$ pints; eggs 3.
TIME: to bake about one hour.

METHOD

1. Mix the flour, suet chopped fine, sugar and stoned and chopped raisins well together.
2. Beat up the eggs.
3. Mix with the milk, butter a piedish well.
4. Mix the eggs and milk with the dry ingredients.
5. Pour into the piedish.
6. Bake about one hour in moderate oven. When well set turn out of dish and serve with a sweet sauce. (*See* American Sauce, below).

American Sauce

To be served with batter cup puddings

This came from Ross-on-Wye, Herefordshire, with several other recipes accompanied by the remark: 'They are all from ninety to one hundred years old, and are Yorkshire.'

INGREDIENTS: Fresh butter 1 oz.; white sugar 4 oz.; sherry 1 small glass.

METHOD

1. Cream butter.
2. Add sugar.
3. Cream both together and add a small glass of sherry.
4. Beat to a whip.

N.B.—Lemon, orange or other fruit juice can be added instead of the sherry.

Wine Sauce for Sweet Puddings

Miss Acton, 1845

1. Boil gently together for 10 or 15 minutes the very thin rind of half a small lemon, about 1$\frac{1}{2}$ oz. sugar, and a wineglassful of water.
2. Take out the lemon peel, and stir into the sauce 1 oz. butter into which a large half-teaspoonful of flour has been smoothly kneaded.
3. Add a wineglassful and a half of sherry or Madeira, or other good white wine; and when quite hot serve the sauce without delay.

Port Wine Sauce

This is made in the same way, substituting port wine for white wine, and adding a dessertspoonful of lemon juice, some grated nutmeg and a little more sugar.

Orange rind and juice may be used for it instead of lemon.

Northamptonshire Pudding

From the Receipt Book of Lady Maria Elizabeth Finch
1786

Miss Joan Wake, author of *How to compile a History and Present-day Record of Village Life*, and Hon. Secretary of the Northamptonshire Record Society, says: 'I came across the following in a receipt book in a country house in North Wales last spring and printed it in the May number of the *Northampton County Magazine*.'

INGREDIENTS: Flour 1 quart; beef suet 1½ lb.; eggs 4, but the whites of only 2; cream enough to mix the pudding to a thick batter; a little salt (one teaspoonful).

TIME: to boil 2 hours.

METHOD

1. Clear the suet from all skin and shred very finely.
2. Rub it well into the flour.
3. Add a little salt.
4. Beat the 4 yolks and 2 whites of the eggs very well indeed.
5. Use them with sufficient cream to mix the flour, etc., into a thick batter.
6. Tie up in bag quite close and put it in when the water boils.

N.B.—This pudding may, of course, be steamed in a greased basin to-day.

Speech House Pudding

Forest of Dean

Miss Beaumont, of Sidmouth, Devon, says: 'This was given to a brother of mine at a little inn in the Forest of Dean. He thought the pudding good, and asked for the recipe. The name also is interesting.'

The Speech House was one of six old lodges, and from earliest times its site was used for holding the Forest Law Courts. An annual festival is held here, and Miss Beaumont adds 'I believe the oath was taken on a sprig of holly — or mistletoe? — instead of on the Bible as is usual. I have served the pudding very often when my sisters and I have been entertaining friends. It has always been new to them.'

INGREDIENTS: Butter 2 oz.; castor sugar 1 oz.; eggs 2; flour 2 oz.; raspberry jam 1 large tablespoonful; carbonate of soda ½ teaspoonful dissolved in a tablespoonful of milk; jam.

TIME: to steam 3 hours.

METHOD

1. Separate the yolks from the whites of the eggs.
2. Put the butter into a mixing bowl and beat it to a cream.
3. Beat in the sugar.
4. Beat the yolks of the eggs.
5. Stir in the flour.
6. Stir in the jam.
7. Have ready the whites of eggs beaten to a stiff froth.
8. Stir the carbonate of soda dissolved in a little milk quickly into the pudding; and
9. Equally quickly fold in the whites of eggs.
10. Fill a buttered basin or mould 3 parts full with the mixture.
11. Cover the top with buttered grease-proof paper, and
12. Steam 3 hours.
13. Turn out and serve.
14. It is an improvement to surround it with a little hot jam, or jam sauce.

Sussex Pond Pudding

'This was given us at Chailey, Sussex, by a nursemaid in 1880 or there-abouts. It was made for me boiled in a cloth (the correct way) in 1905 by an old cottage woman in the village of Westham. In Sussex cottages, steak and kidney puddings are still (1931) boiled in a cloth only.'—H. J. GLOVER.

RECIPE

1. Make a good suet crust, put in some currants, and a little sugar.
2. Divide in two and roll each piece into a rather thick round.
3. Put into the middle of one round a ball of butter mixed with sugar, using the proportions of $\frac{1}{4}$ lb. butter to $\frac{1}{4}$ lb. Demerara sugar.
4. Gather up the edges of the crust, and enclose the butter ball securely by covering the join with the second round of crust and pinching that up.
5. Put into a floured cloth, tie up rather tightly and boil 3 hours or more according to size.

N.B.—Mr. Glover says 'If you don't know this and think it uninteresting, try it. The melted butter and sugar make a delectable sauce just right for a cold winter's day.'

Caramel Cream

Trinity College, Cambridge

This recipe is given by Miss Eleanor L. Jenkinson, sister of the late Cambridge University Librarian in *The Ocklye Cookery Book* [1909]. Miss Jenkinson says: 'It is amusing to remember that this recipe, which came from a country house in Aberdeenshire in the 'sixties, was offered to the kitchens of Trinity College, Cambridge, by an undergraduate, and rejected with contempt. When the undergraduate became a Fellow, just thirty years ago (in 1879), he presented it again; this time it was accepted as a matter of course. It speedily became one of the favourite dishes of May week.'

INGREDIENTS: Cream 1 pint; castor sugar; four eggs, yolks only.

METHOD

1. Beat the yolks in a basin.
2. Boil the cream for a very short time.
3. Pour it on the yolks.
4. Pour the custard into the dish in which it is to be sent to table.
5. Allow it to become quite cold.
6. Strew it thickly with castor sugar, and
7. Brown it with a red-hot salamander.

N.B.—The sugar should make a hard surface like light brown ice all over the top, about an eighth of an inch thick.

The Ocklye Cookery Book is a collection of family recipes published in 1909 at the repeated request of friends, by Miss Jenkinson who acknowledges gratefully the help in preparing it she received from her cook.

Crystal Palace Pudding

1851

INGREDIENTS: Milk $1\frac{1}{2}$ pint; isinglass $\frac{3}{4}$ oz.; yolks of eggs 4; sugar; vanilla flavouring; dried cherries and other fruit; lemon jelly for lining the mould (a modern packet jelly will do for this).

METHOD

1. Line a plain mould with lemon jelly and decorate it with fruit.
2. Heat the milk and dissolve the isinglass in it.
3. Beat the yolks of eggs, add them to the milk and isinglass.
4. Sweeten to taste.
5. Heat all together until nearly boiling.
6. Add flavouring. Cool.
7. When nearly set pour into mould.
8. When quite cold cover with a little rather stiff liquid lemon jelly which should be quite cool when it is poured on.

The Dean's Cream

This is another favourite Cambridge pudding, an 18th century recipe used up to the time of the Great War.

INGREDIENTS: Sponge cakes; raspberry jam; orange marmalade; ratafias; sherry; brandy; cream $\frac{3}{4}$ pint; glacé cherries, pineapple, angelica.

METHOD

1. Spread some sponge cakes with raspberry jam.
2. And some with orange or apricot marmalade; arrange them in a dish alternately.
3. Add some ratafias.
4. Soak the cake with sherry.
5. Sweeten $\frac{3}{4}$ pint of cream, add a wineglassful brandy, whip till very thick, and
6. Pour over the soaked cake; decorate with cherries, pineapple and angelica.

N.B.—The cream and wine is the standard mixture for a solid sillabub, which in those days was generally used to top up trifles.

Cream Darioles

The following recipe is another very old English sweet beloved of Cambridge undergraduates in the 'eighteen-nineties.'

INGREDIENTS : To make the pastry: Ground almonds 2 oz.; sugar 2 oz.; flour 2 oz.; yolks of eggs 3; pinch of salt. To make the custard: eggs, milk (and cream if not too expensive, the original recipe says make a custard of cream and eggs); red currant jelly.

METHOD

1. Make the pastry with the ground almonds, sugar, flour, yolks of eggs and pinch of salt.
2. Butter some dariole moulds; line them with the pastry.
3. Fill with flour and bake.
4. Shake out the flour.
5. Make a good custard delicately flavoured.
6. Fill the almond cases.
7. Bake till set.
8. Leave till cold.
9. Turn out, and
10. Pipe round the edge with red currant jelly set with a little isinglass.

Mr. Aeneas Dallas, of *The Times*, a friend of Sir Henry Thompson and a great authority on gastronomic etymology says 'dariole' is not only one of the oldest words in our own language but one of the oldest of which we have any knowledge. It comes to us from the East, and a dariole originally meant 'something made in a dairy.' The above recipe is interesting because it is a correct recipe for a veritable dariole, being a custard baked in pastry. But in days gone by there was no tin used, the crust was raised and formed the 'coffin' or case for the custard. The tins were named after these custards not the custards after the tins. Darioles are mentioned in our earliest English cookery books.

Grassy Corner Pudding

The various colleges at Oxford and Cambridge are noted for their delicious cold and hot sweets and the following is one which will be longingly remembered by many, and recall undergraduate days. It has never appeared in print before.

INGREDIENTS : Jelly to line the mould; blanched and chopped pistachio nuts; strawberry cream; vanilla cream: isinglass.

METHOD

1. Line a quart mould with lemon jelly.
2. And sprinkle it thickly with the pistachios.
3. Let it set.
4. Make a cream of fresh or preserved strawberries rubbed through a sieve, sweeten, measure, and set with ½ oz. dissolved gelatine or isinglass to every ½ pint.
5. Blend with ½ pint thick cream, and whisk till cold and thick enough to stand up in points, but not set.
6. Make a second pint of cream flavoured with vanilla: dissolve ½ oz. gelatine or isinglass in ¼ pint hot water; when cool add ¼ pint pure milk, sweeten and then add ½ pint cream, blend and flavour with vanilla; now whisk ti'l it is the same consistency as the strawberry cream.
7. Use a spoonful of the two alternately to fill the mould.
8. Cover with some of the jelly used to line the mould.
9. Set on ice or in a cool place until required. Then turn out on to a dish or lace paper.

N.B.—If turning out on to a dish, it is useful to wet the dish, for then, if the cream is not quite in the centre when turned, it can easily be adjusted. If you have no refrigerator or ice cave 1¼ to 1½ oz. gelatine may be necessary to set 1 quart in hot weather. Any cream mixture can be used to fill the grassy jelly-lined mould. A plain chocolate cream flavoured with vanilla is very good and goes well, with the pistachio 'grass.'

A Hedgehog Tipsy Cake

18th Century

Gladys Langley, Acton, 1931

INGREDIENTS: A stale oval-shaped sponge or Madeira cake; fruit syrup, or wine to soak; apricot jam 2 tablespoonfuls; powdered chocolate a tablespoonful; raisins 2 for the eyes; sweet almonds 3 oz.; cream ½ pint; orange juice ¼ pint; or custard ½ pint; castor sugar 3 oz.; red currant jelly 2 tablespoonfuls.

METHOD

1. The day before this sweet is required cut the cake to represent the body of a hedgehog, fining off one end to represent the head and nose.
2. Place the hedgehog in the dish in which it is to be served, scoop a piece out of the middle of the back to form a cup.
3. Fill this with wine or sweetened fruit juice. (If a piece is not cut out it will be difficult to soak the cake thoroughly, but it must of course be replaced.)
4. Keep on pouring the syrup over and over the cake, which must be soaked through and through (wine may be used instead of fruit juice, and home-made orange wine is very good for this purpose).
5. Next day brush over with apricot jam and dust over with the powdered chocolate, stick in two raisins for his eyes.
6. Blanch the almonds, split them lengthwise, in three or four thin strips, and brown them in the oven.
7. Put one across each raisin eye to improve their appearance.
8. Stick the almonds into the cake beginning at the back and sloping them

255

backwards so as to present a fine backward sweep when the whole back and sides are covered.

9. Put 4 oz. orange and lemon juice, and 3 oz. castor sugar in a basin.

10. Add the half pint of fresh cream and whisk until very thick; this is a SOLID SILLABUB, and should be piled in the dish round the hedgehog; if cream is not obtainable make some custard. Finish by putting some red currant jelly just in front of the hedgehog to look as if he is eating it.

Rice Cream

INGREDIENTS: Ground rice 1½ oz.; milk 1 pint; lemon peel (1 lemon) cinnamon and sugar to taste; isinglass ½ oz.; cream ¼ pint.

TIME: about 45 minutes.

METHOD

1. Dissolve the isinglass in a little water.
2. Wash the lemon, and peel it very thinly.
3. Put the peel in the cold milk with a piece of cinnamon and sugar to taste; boil up and strain.
4. Make the ground rice into a cream with a very little cold milk.
5. Add it to the hot milk and boil up till it thickens, then for about 10 minutes to cook the rice.
6. Pour it on to the isinglass.
7. Add the cream, and whisk till cold and thick.
8. Put into a mould or moulds. Serve with stewed fruit, jam, or fruit syrup.

Rich Lemon Sponge

Mrs. Marshall

INGREDIENTS: Boiling water, 1 pint; isinglass 1 oz.; eggs 8; lemons 3; sweet wine 1 pint; sugar to taste.

TIME: 30 minutes to soak isinglass; about 10 minutes to cook.

METHOD

1. Pour the boiling water on the isinglass.
2. Let it stand half an hour.
3. Add the yolks of the 8 eggs but only the whites of 4.
4. Add the juice of the 3 lemons, but the thin rind of only 1.
5. Beat all together and add the wine.
6. Sweeten to taste.
7. Put into a saucepan, and stir over the fire till it begins to thicken.
8. Then strain into well wetted moulds.

A Cheaper Lemon Sponge

Tendring Hall, Suffolk

INGREDIENTS: Isinglass 1½ oz.; 1 pint water; the juice of 4 lemons; sugar and white wine to taste.

TIME: about half an hour.

METHOD

1. Dissolve the isinglass in the water.
2. Add the juice of the lemon, white wine and sugar to taste, and
3. Whip together until very thick.
4. Then put into moulds.

Lord John Russell's Pudding

This recipe for a very delicious iced pudding is from Rusley Lodge, Esher, 1863.

INGREDIENTS : Sufficient for a quart mould. Eggs 6 — yolks only; new milk 1½ pint; isinglass 1 oz.; loaf sugar 1½ oz.; cream ½ pint; brandy 1 wineglass; just a little ratafia essence; a little preserved pine-apple; citron, orange peel; a few dried cherries or any other dried fruit you like.

TIME : to whisk over fire about 20 minutes, ice for 6 hours.

METHOD

1. Put the yolks of the eggs beaten up with the milk together with the grated peel of the lemon, the sugar, and the isinglass into a stewpan; and
2. Whisk it well over a slow fire till the isinglass is thoroughly dissolved and the whole thick.
3. Add the cream.
4. Then the brandy.
5. Just a little essence of ratafia.
6. Let it cook and thicken but don't boil and then stir in the candied fruit.
7. Place it in a mould, put a piece of greaseproof paper over it large enough to cover the edges and keep the lid firmly on.
8. Put into an ice-cave, but if you have not one, make sure that your mould is hermetically closed so that none of the freezing salt can get into the pudding and stand it on ice mixed with freezing salt in a bucket; pack it all round and over with the same and cover with a blanket. Stand in a cool place.

Stone Cream

Mentioned in the 17th century, and sent by Mrs. Selwyn-Austen, Micheldever, Hants, who says: 'Individual glasses or stems can be used instead of a large dish.'

INGREDIENTS : Preserve of any kind; lemon, the juice and peel of half; white wine, a glass; isinglass ½ oz. and a little water; cream, 1 pint. Powdered sugar 2 oz.; decorations according to fancy.

TIME : must be made the day before it is required.

1. Put the preserve at the bottom of a dish or glass.
2. Pour over lemon juice and peel grated very fine, also the wine.
3. Dissolve the isinglass in the water.
4. Strain it.
5. Mix with the cream.
6. Add the sugar.
7. Just let it boil.
8. Stir until nearly cold.
9. Then put it into a jug with a small spout.
10. Pour gently over the preserve.

257

METHOD

N.B.—Mrs. Selwyn-Austen says: 'A sheet of gelatine weighing about ⅛ oz. is cheaper, but not so satisfactory as isinglass.'

From the *Letters of Maria Edgeworth*, published by Jonathàn Cape.

A Birthday Feast

To Miss S. Ruxton.

Edgeworthstown,
June 1st, 1805.

'. . . Cakes and syllabubs served in great abundance by good Kitty, formed no inconsiderable part of the pleasures of the evening. . . .'

Whip Sillabubs

An Essex recipe

'This,' Miss Anstey writes, 'is from my grandmother's receipt book She was a Kentish woman who went to Burnham on her marriage. She was born in 1784. We always had the above for parties in my childhood, but with rather less wine (as it was, it was potent enough) and it was served in old-fashioned custard cups of generous proportions.'

INGREDIENTS: White sweet wine ½ pint; brandy ½ glass; lemon juice a little; sweeten to taste; cream 1 pint.

TIME: 15 minutes to whip.

METHOD

1. Put the wine, brandy, juice of half a lemon into a large mixing bowl.
2. Sweeten to taste, remembering plain cream is to be added.
3. Add the cream.
4. Whip all together until very thick. Put into glasses.

Solid Sillabubs

18th Century

The recipe for these is given in the directions for making 'A Hedgehog Tipsy Cake' (*see* p. 255).

Lemon Whips

A very old recipe

This also is Yorkshire and reached this book by way of Ross-on-Wye. At Bath in the days of Beau Nash these were known as solid syllabubs.

INGREDIENTS: Castor sugar, 4 oz.; lemon, the juice of one, and half the grated rind; sherry 2 glasses; cream ½ pint.

TIME: Best made the day before; time to whisk about 15 minutes.

METHOD

1. Wash the lemon, grate the rind and put it into a large mixing bowl.
2. Squeeze the juice of the lemon; strain and put that also into the bowl.
3. Mix in the sugar.
4. Add the sherry, and when the sugar is dissolved, add ½ pint cream.
5. Whisk well till thick and serve in glasses.

N.B.—Next day there should be a clear liquid at the bottom of the glasses and the cream on top should be firm and spongy.

Strawberry and Raspberry Fool

Mary Eaton, Bungay, Suffolk, 1823

This is a luxury recipe; but we want all sorts of different recipes at different times in our lives, and this is distinctively English.

INGREDIENTS: Scarlet strawberries 1 pint; raspberries 1 pint; castor sugar ½ lb.; orange-flower water 1 tablespoonful; cream 1½ pints; some fine strawberries for decoration.

TIME: to boil 2 or 3 minutes.

METHOD

1. Bruise the strawberries and raspberries.
2. Pass them through a hair sieve.
3. Mix them with the sugar and orange-flower water.
4. Boil up the cream and stir it till it is cold.
5. Beat the fruit pulp and the cold cream together.
6. Stir them till they are well-mixed.
7. Put the fool into glasses or pile in bowls as you think fit.
8. Decorate with whole fresh strawberries.

Gooseberry Fool

This is made in the same way, but the gooseberries have to be stewed until they are soft enough to pulp; they should not, however, be rubbed through a sieve, because this process somewhat lessens their flavour. Just bruise them and whisk them to a smooth pulp.

Orange Jelly

Lady Beeton

Orange Jelly is one of the oldest English dinner sweets. Oranges were introduced into this country from Spain as early as 1290. They were reintroduced by Sir Walter Raleigh in the 16th century, and were cultivated by the Carews of Beddington, Surrey, in their garden, until the great frost of 1739–40 destroyed them. Their original home was Burma, whence they were taken to the Holy Land and introduced by the Moors into Spain in the 11th century. Orange jelly is a traditional dish for Christmas in Yorkshire. A friend writes: 'Christmas wouldn't be Christmas without orange jelly.'

INGREDIENTS: Leaf gelatine ½ oz. good weight; water 1 gill; loaf sugar ¼ lb.; oranges 4; lemon 1; sherry or Marsala ½ gill. Cream; lemon cheesecakes.

METHOD

1. Wash the oranges and dry them, pare one very thinly and steep the peel in the wine for 1 hour.
2. Soak the gelatine in half the water.
3. Stir over the fire until dissolved.
4. Strain on to ¼ lb. loaf sugar.
5. Add ½ gill hot water.
6. When sugar has melted, stir in the juice and pulp of the oranges, and juice of the lemon. Add the sherry or Marsala taking out the orange peel.
7. Turn into a moistened mould, and leave in a cool place to set.
8. Turn out carefully on to a glass dish and garnish with whipped cream. Serve with lemon cheesecakes.

N.B.—This jelly really tastes of oranges and has all the vitamins, because the juice and pulp are not cooked. It may be put into the emptied cleaned skins of half oranges and when set these may be again halved and form quarters of oranges. They were served in this way in the reign of Charles I.

Port Wine Jelly (1)

From Mrs. Anger's receipt book. Miss Anstey can remember her grandmother making it and giving it to an invalid in small teaspoonfuls.

INGREDIENTS: Wine 1 pint; isinglass 1 oz.; sugar candy 1 oz.; best gum arabic 1 oz.

TIME: sufficient to melt the ingredients and then to get cold.

METHOD

1. Put all the ingredients together in a saucepan.
2. Place over the fire and dissolve slowly
3. Put into moulds brushed over with almond oil (which may be bought from a chemist).

N.B.—When cold it is quite stiff. (See Whip Sillabubs, p. 258).

Port Wine Jelly (2)

Frome, Somersetshire, 1878

INGREDIENTS: Gelatine 1½ oz.; lump sugar ¼ lb.; port wine 1 pint; water ¾ pint; cinnamon ¼ inch; lemon ⅛ the peel grated; nutmeg.

METHOD

1. Put all the ingredients except ⅓ pint of the port wine into a saucepan.
2. Heat up till well blended.
3. Strain.
4. Add the other ⅓ pint of port wine.
5. Put into well-wetted moulds.
6. When cold turn out when required.

N.B.—In this way the jelly has both the flavour of the cooked and uncooked port wine.

Almond Puffs

1769

INGREDIENTS: Sweet almonds 2 oz.; orange flower water; eggs, the whites of 3; castor sugar 6 oz.

TIME: About 1 hour or longer in a very cool oven, till a delicate brown and crisp.

METHOD

1. Prepare a flat baking sheet, brush it over with oiled butter and when that is cold and set dredge it with flour; give it a knock to distribute the flour and shake out any that may be loose. [N.B.–This is quite the best and most simple way of preparing a tin for baking delicate cakes and biscuits; they come off quite easily – ED.]
2. Blanch the almonds, and pound them fine in a stone mortar with some orange flower water.
3. Beat the whites of the eggs to a very stiff froth (quite dry).
4. Add about one ounce of sugar, folding it in from the side so as not to break the egg froth.
5. Add the pounded almonds in the same way.
6. Then fold in the rest of the sugar.
7. Lay it in dessertspoonfuls in little round cakes on the tin and bake as directed.

N.B.—As these are rather soft and break easily it is a good plan to place a sheet of rice paper (which can be eaten) on the tin and bake the puffs on that; they can then be lifted out on the rice paper which can be cut out and broken away round them.

Chocolate Puffs

1769

INGREDIENTS: Castor sugar 2 oz.; unsweetened chocolate 1 oz.; egg the white of 1.

TIME: About 1 hour or more in a very slow oven.

METHOD

1. Prepare the tin as before for almond puffs.
2. Grate the chocolate.
3. Blend it with the sugar.
4. Whisk the white of the egg which must be new-laid (about 2 days old is best), to a stiff froth.
5. Fold in the chocolate and sugar, and keep on beating.
6. Drop the mixture on the tin in small spoonfuls and bake in a very slow oven.

Macaroons

1769

INGREDIENTS: Sweet almonds 2 oz.; castor sugar 2 oz.; rose water; eggs, the whites of 2; rice paper; a little extra castor sugar.

TIME: About 30 to 40 minutes.

METHOD

1. Blanch and pound the almonds using some rose water to prevent them oiling.
2. Add the sugar.
3. Whisk the whites of the egg very stiffly (quite dry) and blend all together.
4. Beat well and drop on rice paper as before.
5. Grate sugar over them and bake in very moderate oven.

N.B.—To-day we should use ground almonds.

Apple Fritters

Mrs. Roundell.

INGREDIENTS: Good cooking apples; water and juice of half a lemon; batter made with flour 4 oz.; butter 1 oz.; water in which the apples were soaked, 2 tablespoonfuls; brandy or lemon juice 1 dessertspoonful; the white of one egg; clarified butter for frying.

METHOD

1. Pare, core and slice the apples about ¼ inch thick.
2. Soak them in the juice of ½ lemon and ½ pint or a little more water according to the amount of apples, for 2 hours.
3. Make a batter by warming up 2 tablespoonfuls of this water sufficiently to melt the butter but do not make it too hot.
4. Add to it the brandy or lemon juice and use it to make the flour into a smooth batter.
5. Whisk the white of the egg to a stiff froth and fold it in the batter.
6. Drain the rings of apple, dip them in the batter, and fry them in butter: Cover with castor sugar and serve very hot.

11

SAVOURIES AND CHEESE

Scotch Woodcock

This recipe is taken from a manuscript cookery book belonging to Tendring Hall, Suffolk, and was given to the Editor of this book by Colonel Rowley. Its date is the second quarter of the nineteenth century and its contents represent very definitely the extremely good English cookery of that period. A note to the following points out: 'This is much approved by men.' It was originally served as a second course remove, but can now be used as a savoury for any suitable occasion.

RECIPE

INGREDIENTS: Bread 4 slices; anchovies 7 or 8; eggs 4; cream ½ pint; pepper and salt.

TIME: about 30 minutes all told.

METHOD

1. Toast the bread and butter well on both sides.
2. Wash and scrape and chop the anchovies and spread them between two slices of toast.
3. Have ready the yolks of the eggs well beaten with the cream and seasoned with cayenne pepper and salt.
4. Set them over the fire to thicken but don't let them boil.
5. Pour over the toast and send to table as hot as possible.

N.B.—The expense of this dish may be lessened by using the whole of the eggs and beating them up with ¼ pint of milk (and, if you have it, a *little* cream) but of course it won't be *quite* so good, and as in some houses and places cream is plentiful the original is given as it stands.

Mock Caviare

Dr. Hunter, York, 1806.

1. Take anchovies, parsley and chives or shallots.
2. Pound them in a marble mortar, with some olive-oil, salt and lemon juice.
3. Make a toast of white bread and spread the mixture upon it.
4. Cut it into neat pieces and serve it up.

N.B.—This is a very good substitute for caviare. The quantities of the different ingredients here are left to the discretion of the cook. The anchovy must predominate.

Mushrooms with Anchovy Cream

This also is a Cambridge College recipe of 1881

INGREDIENTS: Rounds of bread about 2 inches across; mushrooms; anchovies 9 or 10; cream 1 or 2 tablespoonfuls; pepper; salt.

METHOD

1. Cut some rounds of bread about ⅛ inch thick and 2 inches in diameter.
2. Fry them a golden brown.
3. Broil some mushrooms and put one on each piece of fried bread.
4. Wash 9 or 10 anchovies.
5. Chop them.
6. Rub them through a sieve.
7. Whip the cream.
8. Mix the anchovies with it, season with a little pepper and salt.
9. Just before sending to table put a piece of this mixture about the size of a walnut on each mushroom and serve.

Marrow Toast

1846

Charles Elmé Francatelli gives this recipe and adds 'Marrow toast used to be eaten every day at dinner by the Queen [Victoria] at the time when I had the honour of waiting on Her Majesty.'

INGREDIENTS: A marrow bone; boiling water; salt; pepper; chopped parsley; lemon juice; shallot, a mere suspicion; squares of hot crisp toast.

TIME: Sufficient to make the toast, chop the parsley and cook the marrow for a minute.

METHOD

1. Get the butcher to break the marrow-bone.
2. Cut the marrow into small pieces the size of a filbert.
3. Just parboil them in boiling water with a little salt for one minute.
4. Drain instantly upon a sieve, keep hot.
5. Season with a little chopped parsley, pepper and salt, lemon juice, and a mere suspicion of finely chopped shallot.
6. Toss lightly altogether, spread it out upon squares of hot crisp dry toast, and serve immediately.

A Tart of Artichoke Bottoms

A receipt of the Days of Queen Anne

1. Line a dish with fine pastry.
2. Put in the artichoke bottoms, with a little finely minced onion and some finely minced sweet herbs.
3. Season with salt, pepper and nutmeg.
4. Add some butter in tiny pieces.
5. Cover with pastry and bake in a quick oven.
6. When cooked, put into the tart a little white sauce thickened with yolk of egg and sharpened with tarragon vinegar.

A Tart of Claret Wine

Another recipe from the Days of Queen Anne

1. Take half a glass of claret wine, as much juice of ripe red gooseberries.
2. Add 2 crushed macaroons, and
3. The yolks of 4 eggs, and make this like cream;
4. Flavour with sugar, citron, grated cinnamon, a little salt.
5. Add also a small piece of butter.
6. Make a fine pastry, and line a dish with it.
7. Pour in the mixture, and bake as before.
8. Sprinkle orange flowers over it when you serve it.

A Delicious Savoury

18th Century

This is one of the recipes of Mrs. Raffald, the famous Manchester cook and caterer of Old Exchange Alley and the Officers' Mess at the Bull's Head. She was a Yorkshire woman, Doncaster born, and at the time of her marriage (about 1760) housekeeper to Lady Elizabeth Warburton at Arley Hall, Cheshire. Her cookery book was considered an indispensable wedding present, and it is still valuable as representing the best English cookery of the second half of the eighteenth century. Several of her recipes, suitable for modern tables, are included in this book. Dishes made from them were exhibited at the first English Folk Cookery Exhibition held in January, 1931.

To Make a Nice Whet Before Dinner

1. Cut some slices of bread half an inch thick.
2. Fry them in butter, but not too hard.
3. Then split some anchovies, take out the bones, and lay half an anchovy on each piece of bread.
4. Have ready some Cheshire cheese grated, and some chopped parsley mixed together.
5. Lay it pretty thick over the bread and anchovy.
6. Baste it with butter.
7. Brown it with a salamander (or it could be browned equally well under a gas or electric grill).
8. It must be done on the dish in which you send it to table.

A Fish Savoury (1)

INGREDIENTS: Cold cooked fish; a little milk; a little anchovy sauce; tarragon vinegar and cayenne pepper; squares of buttered toast; hard-boiled egg and parsley.

METHOD

1. Shred or chop the fish.
2. Moisten with the milk.
3. Season with anchovy sauce, tarragon vinegar and cayenne pepper.
4. Serve cold piled on squares of buttered toast sprinkled all over with chopped hard-boiled egg and parsley.

ANOTHER WAY OF SERVING

1. Cut off the top and core an uncooked very small tomato.
2. Cut the top off a hard-boiled egg, take out the yolk and mix a little with the fish.
3. Stuff the egg well with the fish mixture and put the white top on again.
4. Fix the point of the egg in the excavated tomato, and place the tomato and egg pyramids in a lettuce and cucumber salad.

A Fish Savoury (2)

From a Yorkshire woman's scrap-book, 1931

INGREDIENTS: The roes from 8 herrings; water; Patna rice ½ teacup (¼ pint); curry powder ½ tablespoonful; pepper; salt; butter 1 oz.; milk if necessary; dry toast.

TIME: 30 to 40 minutes.

METHOD

1. Cook the roes in water.
2. Drain.
3. Cook rice as for curry.
4. Moisten curry powder with water to a paste.
5. And fry in butter a few minutes.
6. Add rice and roe, etc., and cook for a few minutes.
7. Add a little milk if too stiff.
8. Serve on dry toast.

N.B.—The 8 herrings can be rolled and cooked in vinegar and water, in the oven for breakfast.

Cod's Roe

1. Buy a hard cod's roe from the fishmonger.
2. Tie it up in a cloth to prevent breaking and boil in slightly salted water for ½ hour or longer according to size.
3. Take out and allow to get cold.
4. Remove skin, cut in slices, dip in flour, or egg and bread-crumbs, and fry in shallow fat.
5. Fry also some small rolls of bacon, and serve one on each round of fried roe. If liked a piece of fried tomato may be put on the roe first and then the roll of fried bacon.
6. Send in with thin crisp toast and butter or home-made rye bread and butter.

Magdalen College Butter

Miss Eleanor Jenkinson, Ocklye, Sussex

INGREDIENTS: Parsley; anchovies 2; butter 2 oz.

METHOD

1. Boil a bunch of parsley till it is quite soft.
2. Press the water from it, and let it get cold.
3. Add 2 anchovies, well washed, boned and pounded, and 2 oz. of butter.
4. Mix all these ingredients together.
5. Rub them with a wooden spoon through a hair sieve.
6. Shape it into little balls.
7. Garnish with parsley, and serve on a cold dish.

N.B.—Freshly made dry toast (*see* p. 25) should be handed with it.

Anchovy Paste

From Mrs. Brewitt, Anne of Cleves House, Melton Mowbray

INGREDIENTS: Butter 4 oz.; yolks of eggs 4; anchovy essence 6 tablespoonfuls; cayenne pepper ¼ level teaspoonful.

TIME: 10 minutes.

METHOD

1. Cream butter.
2. Beat in the yolks of eggs.
3. Beat well.
4. Mix in the anchovy essence and cayenne pepper.

5. Place on fire but do not let it boil, keep stirring all the time till it thickens
6. Then remove, put into pots.
7. When cold pour clarified butter over it, or mutton fat.

Potted Shrimps

From a Cookery Book belonging to Miss Hope, dated 1797

INGREDIENTS: Picked shrimps 2 quarts; mace $\frac{1}{4}$ oz.; nutmeg $\frac{1}{2}$ of a $\frac{1}{4}$ oz. nutmeg and cloves, and salt as you please; butter 1 lb.

TIME: 10 minutes.

METHOD

1. Season the shrimps well with the spice and salt.
2. Put into baking dish.
3. Add the butter cut up.
4. Put in a cool oven for 10 to 15 minutes according to the heat of the oven.

5. Take them out and put into a colander to drain off the butter into a basin.
6. Pack the shrimps tightly in pots and when quite cold cover them with the butter which should be kept hot for this purpose.

Delicious as an appetiser with wholemeal bread and butter.

A CHEAPER RECIPE, 1830

METHOD

1. Season the shrimps with pepper, salt, a little powdered cloves and mace.
2. Sprinkle over them 2 oz. of warmed butter and stir in so that the butter lubricates the whole.

3. Put into a cool oven for 10 minutes.
4. Take out, stir the shrimps well, pack closely into small jars, and
5. When quite cold pour over clarified butter.

Bloater Paste

INGREDIENTS: Dried red herrings 16; fresh butter 1 lb.; ground mace 4 pinches; ground cloves 4 pinches; cayenne 1 teaspoonful; anchovy essence 4 teaspoonfuls.

METHOD

1. Pour boiling water on the red herrings and cook them for a few minutes, lift out and drain well; head, tail, skin and bone fish, discard roes.
2. Chop very fine.
3. Put all the flesh twice through the mincer.

4. Work the butter well in (if possible pound the mixture in a mortar).
5. Add the spices and anchovy sauce last of all.
6. Pot as usual.
7. When cold cover with oiled butter.

Devilled Biscuits, Dry

From Cre-fydd's Family Fare, 1865

The thin plain biscuits, known as cheese biscuits are the best for devilling. (1) Dip them twice into warm water. (2) Dredge them with cayenne (for six biscuits use a saltspoonful) and bake till quite crisp in a slow oven. Serve hot, either in a rack or piled on a napkin.

Devilled Biscuits, Buttered

Knead together an ounce and a half of butter; a saltspoonful of cayenne; and a saltspoonful of flour of mustard; dip the biscuits twice into warm milk; spread them with the butter, and bake in a slow oven till crisp.

Bath Olivers

These well-known biscuits invented by a Bath doctor in the eighteenth century are delicious plain or devilled.

Water Biscuits

Given by Lady Congreve, Crofton House, Titchfield to Mrs. (Dorothy) Allhusen

INGREDIENTS: Flour ¼ lb.; butter 1 oz.; baking powder ½ teaspoonful; salt, a pinch; cream 1 dessertspoonful; and cold water to mix. Buttered and floured baking sheet.

TIME: to bake 5 to 10 minutes.

METHOD

1. Rub butter well into flour.
2. Mix in baking powder and salt.
3. Make into firm dough with cream and cold water.
4. Roll out very thin.
5. Prick all over.
6. Bake in a good oven.

Dessert Biscuits

A Stroud lady sends this recipe which she says 'we always had made at home in the days when my father and his friends sat over their wine after dinner.'

INGREDIENTS: Flour 1 handful (about 2 oz.); butter the size of a walnut (about ¼ oz.); water a small teaspoonful.

TIME: to make — about 20 minutes.

METHOD

1. Rub the butter into the flour.
2. Add teaspoonful water and knead well together in basin.
3. Then place on board and roll flat over and over again till the dough is as thin as a wafer.
4. Butter and flour a flat tin (*see* p. 261).

5. Cut the biscuits in rounds and place them on it.
6. Bake in a very hot oven. They require watching as parts of the biscuit get brown quicker than others; these should be removed and put aside till all are done. Serve hot.

N.B.—Some people use milk instead of water, but for eating with good wines the plain water is best. The biscuits keep well in a tin box.

Devilled Almonds

Richard Dolby's way, 1830

INGREDIENTS: Jordan almonds ½ lb.; fresh butter 2 oz.; cayenne pepper and salt.

TIME: About 10 minutes.

METHOD

1. Blanch the almonds.
2. Wipe them dry.
3. Put the butter into a frying-pan.
4. Make it hot.
5. Add the almonds.

6. Fry till of a good brown colour.
7. Drain on a hair sieve.
8. Strew over cayenne pepper and salt and serve up hot, as a savoury.

Salted Almonds (Baked) 1900

INGREDIENTS: Jordan almonds ½ lb.; salad-oil 2 dessertspoonfuls; 2 dessertspoonfuls salt.

METHOD

1. Blanch the almonds.
2. Dry them.
3. Mix them in a basin with the salad-oil and salt.

4. Turn out on to a baking tin.
5. Bake in a very slow oven till a pale straw colour and quite crisp.

N.B.—To devil add a little cayenne, curry powder and mustard to the salt and oil.

Serve cold in sweetmeat trays or dishes, for dinner or cocktail parties.

Devilled Sardines

Frome, Somersetshire, 1890

INGREDIENTS: Sardines 1 box of 12; flour 1 oz.; stock or water ½ pint; Worcester sauce 1 teaspoonful; yolk of egg 1; cayenne pepper and salt; mustard one teaspoonful mixed with tarragon vinegar. Slices of toast.

METHOD

1. Remove the bones from the sardines.
2. Place the fish on slices of toast on a tin dish (or fireproof glass dish that can be sent to table). Heat in oven.
3. Pour the oil into a small saucepan; stir in the flour mixed with the stock or water.
4. Boil till the consistency of thick cream.
5. Add the other ingredients, beating them well in.
6. Pour a little of this sauce over the sardines.

Sandwiches

MINT AND SULTANA

This comes from Ventnor, Isle of Wight, 1931

Thin brown or white bread and butter spread with seedless raisins or sultanas put through a mincing machine, and sprinkled with fresh mint finely chopped.

Dandelion Leaves and Worcester Sauce

Mrs. Reginald Hindley, Cheshire, 1929

Thin slices of nicely buttered white bread, with just a speck of Worcester sauce spread on them, sprinkled thickly with finely chopped young dandelion leaves, and covered with a thin slice of brown bread and butter.

Emergency Rolls

Exhibited (Nov. 2nd—7th, 1931) at Barker's Stores by Miss Stuart Macrae, Director of Newnes-Pearson, and Editor of *Miss Modern*.

INGREDIENTS: Thin brown bread; asparagus tips; mayonnaise sauce; prawns; a little cream; grated Parmesan cheese; and coralline pepper. All the ingredients were canned or bottled except the bread.

METHOD

1. Open a small tin of asparagus tips, mash the tips in a basin, and wring them in muslin to squeeze out all the moisture, put the dry remains in a basin.
2. Open a tin of prawns, wash them and chop them very finely, add them to the asparagus.
3. Make into a soft paste that will spread with a little butter mayonnaise sauce and cream.
4. Put into a saucepan and scald but do not boil.
5. Leave till cold.
6. Meantime cut some thin brown bread and butter, using only a very

little butter which will spread more easily if it be creamed.

7. Spread each slice with the prepared mixture.

8. Dust this with finely grated Parmesan cheese and a little cayenne coralline pepper.

9. Cut off the crusts. To keep:

10. Roll up in greaseproof paper and place on a table napkin dipped in cold water and wrung out quite dry.

11. Place another damp table napkin over them.

N.B.—These are excellent with other light refreshments for Bridge parties or they may be served either as appetisers or savoury.

Celery and Cheese Rolls

1. Take some delicate white centre sticks of a head of celery.
2. Put a little potted cheese along the hollow of each.
3. Roll up in thin home-made wholemeal bread and butter.
4. Leave the tiny tips of leaves peeping out at one end in as many rolls as possible.

Asparagus Rolls

These are made in the same way, but instead of celery a cooked head of asparagus is dipped in cold Dutch sauce and rolled up.

This may be varied by using various savoury butters.

Marrow Bones

1846

This also is Francatelli's recipe — but if you want to see marrow bones served as they should be, go to the Mitre, Oxford. They make a speciality of them.

INGREDIENTS: Marrow bones from the centre of a round of beef or from any part of the legs or shins; flour and water paste; a deep stewpan of hot water; crisp toast.

TIME: about half an hour.

METHOD

1. Saw the bones in half crosswise.
2. Chop the thick ends into shape so as to make them stand upright.
3. Cover the open end of each with a paste made of flour and water.
4. Place the bones upright in a deep stewpan containing hot water reaching half way up the bones.

5. Cover the stewpan with a lid and cook them in the boiling water for about half an hour.
6. Remove the paste.
7. Envelope each bone in a napkin or cut paper.
8. Send to table accompanied by hot crisp dry toast.

Onions and Cheese (1)

This is a Lancashire (Bolton-le-Moors) Sunday supper dish eaten with slices of currant bread. (For recipe for Lancashire currant bread *see* page 68.)

INGREDIENTS: Onions; milk; salt; grated cheese.

METHOD

1. Boil the onions in milk, or milk and water with a little salt.
2. When done drain but do not drain too dry.
3. Chop them up and stir grated cheese in them.
4. Return to pan, reheat, then serve.

Onions and Cheese (2)

The Devonshire Way.

This has been sent in from Plymouth. The onions are either boiled or baked, seasoned with salt and pepper, served whole or cut in halves with butter on them, and eaten with bread and uncooked cheese. Miss McNaught, who had them at a friend's house, says they are delicious.

Cheese Toast

INGREDIENTS: Squares of buttered toast; bread-crumbs 1 table-spoonful; milk 2 tablespoonfuls; egg 1; made mustard; salt and cayenne; grated cheese 2½ oz.; chopped parsley.

TIME: a few minutes in a hot oven.

METHOD

1. Make the milk hot.
2. Soak the bread-crumbs in it.
3. Beat the egg and mix with it.
4. Season highly with made mustard, salt and cayenne.
5. Stir in the grated cheese.
6. Spread on the squares of toast.
7. Place in the oven to brown.
8. Sprinkle a little chopped parsley over each and serve.

Cheese Rice

INGREDIENTS: Rice 4 oz.; water 1½ pints; cheese 2 oz.; milk ½ pint; butter ½ oz.; cayenne pepper and salt to season.

TIME: to cook rice, 20 minutes; bake dish ½ hour.

METHOD

1. Boil rice slowly in water till tender.
2. Drain away any water that is not absorbed and use for something else.
3. Grate cheese.
4. Make the milk hot.
5. Add cheese and butter.
6. When dissolved add the rice and season highly with cayenne and salt.
7. Butter a piedish.
8. Fill with the mixture.
9. Sprinkle with grated cheese and bake for ½ hour.

Mrs. Forbes' Cream Cheese

1. Let your pan of milk remain unskimmed for several days until the milk under the cream becomes quite thick.
2. Then take off the cream and put it in a coarse calico or linen cloth.
3. Tie it up and hang it to drain for 2 or 3 days until it ceases to drip.
4. Then take it out, season it with a little salt, and put it in another clean cloth, tying it in the centre close to the cheese, so as in pressing the cheese will be round and flat.
5. Then put it between two boards with a weight on top for 24 hours when it will be fit for use.

Whole Milk Cheese

This may be made with ordinary milk in exactly the same way. The only difference is the thick milk curd underneath the cream is tied up with the cream, and only the whey left to drip. This whey is most delicious and makes a refreshing drink.

or

In small flats and houses where there is no larder or dairy accommodation any household milk that may be left over and turns sour can be at once put in a perfectly clean aluminium saucepan, stood on an asbestos mat over a low gas ring (or on the hob of a coal fire or even in a warm corner of a wood fire!) anywhere where it is subjected to very moderate heat (it must on no account boil or even simmer). Gradually the whey will separate from the curds; when this happens a coarse linen cloth or fourfold cheese muslin must be put into and over a colander, the curds and whey poured in, and the cloth tied up and the cheese hung up to drain and finished in exactly the same way as Mrs. Forbes' Cream Cheese.

N.B.—A very little cream mixed with this sour milk cheese improves it considerably, and it is very nice if celery salt be used instead of ordinary salt.

Potted Cheese

Richard Dolby, Cook at the Thatched House Tavern, St. James's Street, London, S.W.1., England

INGREDIENTS: Cheshire, Cheddar, Gloucester or North Wiltshire cheese (the very best) 3 lb.; best butter ½ lb.; sherry a large glass; ground mace nearly half an ounce.

METHOD

1. Pound the cheese and butter together in a mortar.
2. Mix the sherry in gradually.
3. Add the mace.
4. Mix well, pot it; and pour over it clarified butter.

N.B.—A little made mustard may be added if preferred instead of the sherry or in addition to it. The addition of a little curry powder, or cayenne will also vary it.

With Stilton cheese a little port wine may be added instead of sherry. This probably is one of the most individual cookery preparations we have, as so much depends on the cook's palate.

12

WINES, etc.

'Irish Wine'

Maurice Healy, K.C.

'Dean Swift,' says Mr. Healy, 'writing to Stella on the 17th October, 1710, said: "I dined to-day with your Mr. Sterne by invitation and drank Irish wine." His cousin puts a note to this that the author was referring to claret — the Dean nearly always named the wine he drank — but when he was associating wine with Ireland it is always of claret he is speaking.'

The following practical directions for serving this wine are given by Mr. Healy in a pamphlet on Irish wine that was printed for private circulation only, and these excerpts are made with his permission:

'1. No claret should be drunk before it is at least a dozen years old and it is at its best for about 12 to 35 or 40 years.

'2. Watch your claret as it pours; if the bubble is purple it is very young and probably not fit to drink; if red the wine is ripe; if of that lovely brown sometimes described as onion-peel, it is probably 35 to 40 years old and you may anticipate a really great wine.

'3. Always decant your wine yourself.

'4. Take it from your cellar at least twenty-four hours before you intend to drink it.

'5. Uncork it from one to eight hours before drinking; the older the wine the longer it should be allowed to mature.

'6. Stand it, as the experts tell you, not in the room in which it is going to be drunk, but in a room a little warmer than that in which it is going to be drunk. We drink our claret too cold in most places in England.

'7. Don't boil it of course, but raise it gradually to a temperature a degree or two above that of your dining-room.

'8. Draw your cork carefully, and do not break it if you can help it, you can then dispense with a decanting funnel, whereas if you break it you will probably have to use muslin as well, and you will kill your wine.

'9. Warm your decanter, but don't make it warmer than your wine.

'10. Then take your bottle, and holding it so that a light shines through the shoulder, pour its contents gently but firmly from the one receptacle to the other.

'11. When about a wineglassful is left in the bottle you will see the sediment coming along. Stop pouring, take your decanter to the dining-room, and leave it with the stopper out.

'12. And then drink its contents out of big thin glasses, white glasses with no tricks of ornament.

N.B.—It is very difficult to get drunk on claret—it can prompt a kind but hardly a violent act—when it is gone it leaves regrets, but only for itself, and never for its effects.'

Cider

The Ministry of Agriculture sends the following communication:—

'Genuine cider is probably the healthiest and most refreshing of all fermented drinks and has been brewed in Europe almost since the dawn of history.

'History relates that the apple tree was known and appreciated by the Aryan races of Northern Europe long before their separation into the Slavonians, Germans, and Celts. The apple tree was to them as the date tree was to the Austrians, Babylonians and Assyrians, and the vine to the Persians, Greeks and Romans. When the Ancient Britons came to settle in this country they brought with them a few apple trees and it is thought that the Phoenicians taught them to manufacture the drink now known as cider.

'It was not, however, until the end of the seventeenth century that cider orchards began to be planted on any considerable scale in this country. The reason for the wider interest taken in cider at that time was the cessation of the import of foreign wines as a result of Continental wars.

'To the consumer National Mark cider offers a guarantee of a pure, refreshing and inexpensive beverage, with recognized health-giving properties. For the first time the public can be assured that their cider is manufactured only with sound English fruit under hygienic conditions, and of a definite high standard of quality. Young and old can drink it with safety. Climatic conditions do not allow of the production in these islands of the wine of the grape, but in cider our orchards provide a vintage of another kind more appropriate to our own needs; and in asking for National Mark Cider the discerning public will be obtaining a truly national beverage of great attractiveness and will be assisting in a great national development which promises to have far-reaching effects in promoting the advancement of British agriculture and the general well-being of the whole nation.'

No recipe is given because the process is too complicated for home use, and those who wish to make cider can get directions elsewhere.

Nettle Beer

Leicestershire, 1927

INGREDIENTS: Water 1 gallon; sugar 1 lb.; whole ginger bruised 1 oz.; nettles 2 or 3 handfuls, also a few dandelions, and some comfrey.

METHOD

1. Boil the water.
2. Add the well-washed nettles, dandelions, and comfrey. Boil for 15 minutes.
3. Strain off the liquor.
4. Boil it up with the sugar and ginger; strain again; cream 1 oz. compressed yeast, put it on a piece of toast, and lay it on the liquor when lukewarm.
5. Let it stand till next morning near the fire covered with a cloth.
6. Then carefully take off the scum and bottle taking care not to disturb any sediment.

N.B.—Dr. Fernie says: The true stinging nettle with a round hairy stalk, which bears only a dull colourless bloom, must be secured, and not a labiate nettle with a square stem.—1905.

To Make Mead

Mrs. Calverley

INGREDIENTS: Water 1 gallon; honey 1 pint; loaf sugar ¼ lb.; the white of eggs; lemon, the peel and juice of one; yeast sufficient to work it (1 oz. compressed yeast to the gallon).

METHOD

1. Blend the water, honey and sugar together.
2. Stir in the whites of 2 eggs beaten to a froth.
3. Boil it as long as any scum rises.
4. When lukewarm add the yeast and let it ferment.
5. Add the peel and juice of a large lemon.
6. And when it has done working, bottle it.

N.B.—Very good.

'The Gossip's Bowl'
Lamb's Wool

This is a very old English drink, and the recipe is sent by Mr. S. Taylor of Haverthwaite, Ulverston.

INGREDIENTS: Ale 1 quart; white wine any kind 1 pint; nutmeg ½; moist sugar to your taste. Roasted crab apples.

METHOD

1. Make the ale and wine hot.
2. Add sugar and nutmeg.

3. Roast some crab apples, and float them on the hot ale.

This is the drink referred to by Shakespeare: —
'When roasted crabs hiss in the bowl.'

Love's Labour Lost, Act v., Sc. 2.

Also, in *Midsummer Night's Dream*, Puck says: —
'And sometime lurk I in a gossip's bowl,
In very likeness of a roasted crab,
And when she drinks, against her lips I bob.'

Act ii., Sc. 1.

General Forbes' Ginger Beer

Tendring Hall, Suffolk, 1857

INGREDIENTS : Water 3½ gallons; bruised ginger 3 oz.; lemons 2; loaf sugar 3 lb.; cream of tartar 1 ounce; yeast 2 tablespoonfuls (or 1 oz. compressed yeast); 1 egg white.

TIME : ½ hour to boil, 2 nights to stand.

METHOD

1. Bruise the ginger and boil it for ½ hour in water.
2. Wash the lemons and slice them and put them in a pan.
3. Add the cream of tartar and the sugar broken up.
4. Strain the ginger-flavoured water over the lemons, etc.

5. When lukewarm work (i.e. ferment) it with the yeast put on a piece of toast.
6. Let it stand 2 nights.
7. Take off the scum.
8. Whisk the white of an egg in the ginger beer before bottling it.

IV

COUNTRY AND SCHOOLROOM TEAS

These words conjure up pictures of the great halls of country houses with logs blazing and sizzling on the hearth; a table large enough to allow a man who hates afternoon tea to sit and spread scones with butter and home-made jam; a singing kettle; piping hot toast; and home-made cakes, dogs lying warming themselves in blissful happiness, never even troubling to stir as well-known footsteps are heard outside, and members of the houseparty and other friends come in, one after the other, exhilarated but tired after a splendid run with some well-known pack, or a day with the guns.

Or in summer time long trestle tables literally weighed down with cups and saucers and good things for tea out of doors for the consolation or encouragement of rival cricket teams; or between sets of tennis.

Or in farmhouses where one knows a good tea will be spread if one calls in at the right time.

Or — perhaps best of all? — schoolrooms in town or country where the best toast is to be had, and a cut-and-come-again cake of which one never wearies.

Only recipes for the homely favourite cakes, buns, jams and jellies and school tuck are given here, directions for making home-made bread, etc., will be found on page 62; potted meats and fish must be sought amongst the dinner savouries, ham and sausages amongst the breakfast dishes and some especially good things will be found amongst Local and National Specialities, whilst how to make Devonshire scalded or clotted cream cannot be divorced from apple pie although it is associated indelibly with Cricket Teas at Knightshayes, Tiverton, Devonshire when Blundell's School played some other Eleven, and whether they won or lost Blundell's boys piled thick rich cream on to thick slices of plum cake, or trickled golden syrup over substantial slices of bread and cream which they called 'thunder and lightning,' or stuck a spoonful of luscious strawberry jam in the centre of a split Chudleigh already thickly spread with scalded (or as Londoners call it, clotted) cream before closing it with another half on top and digging their strong white teeth well into the chosen 'tuck.'

At Canterbury Huffkins can be provided instead of Chudleighs; at Hawkshead where Wordsworth went to school there may still be bought

Whigs such as he loved and a special pastry cake filled with a sort of mincemeat resembling Cumberland Currant pasty. In Oxfordshire Banbury Cakes are the order of the day, and if you want to taste the real thing you must visit Miss Brown's shop at Banbury. She will tell you that some people say the original recipe for these cakes was brought by the Crusaders from the East; anyhow they are good, and it is interesting to note that Eccles cakes, Cumberland currant pastry, Chorley cakes, Coventry godcakes, Banbury cakes, Hawkshead cakes, Yorkshire 'Sally Sly', are amongst our oldest traditional Feasten Cakes, and that their only rivals to first place are the Darioles or Maids of Honour, or curd cheese-cakes for which Devizes, Melton Mowbray, Clee in Lincolnshire, York-shire and Richmond (Surrey) are particularly noted.

Again in *Memories of Three Reigns*, Lady Raglan acts as our gastronomic historian and gives us a vivid picture of country house teas in England in 1873.

'That tea-time! That was always a delightful hour in the country when we would gather beside a blazing log fire and retail to each other the news of the day. At one country house I remember that this meal was always served in the billiard room, because the men for what reason I could never imagine, liked to play billiards whilst we had tea.

'Everything was home-made, the bread and the cakes and the scones. And there was a particular delicacy associated with this place which I particularly loved. It was ginger jumbles, which were served all hot and crisp and sticky like treacle.'

Speaking of schoolroom teas she says:

'In those days hostesses used to encourage their cooks to become expert in some special dish which guests would afterwards associate with that particular house. My aunt's cook was famed for her gooseberry fool, and so we children used to be indulged with this particular delicacy at her tea parties served to us in dainty cut-glass cups.'

There is one instruction given in the recipe for making cakes that may well alarm us in 1932, and that is the length of time we are told to beat eggs! Moderns have neither the time nor the helpers necessary for such feats of valour, but we wished to know what effect such prolonged energy had on the cake. So we tested the recipe for an 18 lb. wedding-cake that took us about four hours to make, and found that the prolonged beating and whisking of the eggs really made a better cake, that in short it was quite worth while.

So it might be; but life is not long enough, and there are other things worth doing. We therefore rang up Miss Caroline Haslett of engineering fame and asked her if she knew of a small electric gadget that would whisk one or more eggs. She did, and now we make this self-same cake in less than one hour!

All we have to do is to put an egg or more in a basin, adjust the whisk, regulate the speed indicator, stick the plug into its fitment in the wall, and the egg whisks itself, while we sit down and read, or sew, and listen to B.B.C. talks, or music.

So the past and the present have clasped hands and never the twain shall part; and arm-aching produced by whisking eggs, whipping cream, or making sillabubs is known no more. But the invention is American. Those cousins of ours are so clever.

I do not, however, see why I am not to use a useful gadget that we have not invented or made as yet in England simply because it is made in America; therefore I use my electric egg whisk gaily; after all, it is worked by English electricity, which, without it, would not be used.

Rich Plum Cake

MS. 1904

This is a most delicious cake of the Dundee type, and is suitable for a birthday, wedding or Christmas cake.

INGREDIENTS: Butter ½ lb.; castor sugar ½ lb.; eggs 6; flour ½ lb.; currants ½ lb.; peel ¼ lb.; blanched almonds ¼ lb.; cherries ¼ lb.; stoned raisins ½ lb.; sultanas ½ lb.; cream of tartar 1 teaspoonful; bicarbonate of soda ½ teaspoonful; salt ¼ teaspoonful; brandy or rum 2 tablespoonfuls or if preferred 2 tablespoonfuls of orange juice; if a dark cake be required a little black coffee may be added, but don't use any that has chicory in it. These quantities are sufficient for a 4 lb. cake.

TIME: to bake 2½ to 3 hours, but the cake should be made 3 weeks at least before it is required, and it will keep much longer.

METHOD

1. Prepare cake tin which should measure 7½ inches in diameter and 2¾ in, in depth, by brushing the inside with sweet olive-oil; then line with buttered greaseproof paper.
2. Divide the flour into three parts.
3. Sift the cream of tartar and bicarbonate of soda with one part of the flour.
4. Leave one part plain.
5. Chop up the peel and almonds; cut the cherries and raisins in quarters, wash and clean and dry perfectly the currants and sultanas, and mix them all together with the third part of the flour; this helps the fruit not to sink to the bottom of the cake.

Now having everything prepared;
6. Cream the butter.
7. Add sugar and cream again.
8. Add one egg at a time, beating each in very thoroughly, adding a teaspoonful of the plain flour after the third egg and each of the others to prevent curdling.
9. Add colouring and liquid flavouring; beat all in very thoroughly and lightly.
10. Then sieve in the flour that you mixed with the cream of tartar and bicarbonate of soda and salt and the rest of the plain flour if any be left.
11. Add the fruit (stir in well but lightly) and put into cake tin; make the centre a trifle lower than the sides,

and smooth the top lightly with the knuckles of the hand dipped in milk.

12. Tie a double strip of brown paper round the outside of the tin and stand it on a flat tin covered with a double piece of brown paper. This will prevent the burning of the bottom and outside of the cake.

13. Put on the centre of the shelf in the centre of the oven, the heat of which should be moderate 350° F. or No. 5 in the Junior New World Cooker.

14. Bake for 2½ to 3 hours.

Wedding Cake

MS. 1904

The following ingredients are mixed and baked in the same way as above, but as they weigh about 16 lb. instead of 4 lb. they will have to be baked in three tiers, the lower one 9½ in. in diameter will take longer to bake, the middle one 7½ in. (as above) and the third 6 inches in diameter will take less time. They can be baked on three separate days, using 1 lb. 2 oz. butter for the lowest cake; ½ lb. butter for the middle; and 6 oz. butter for the top; the other ingredients being used in corresponding proportions.

RECIPE

INGREDIENTS: Butter 2 lb.; castor sugar 2 lb.; eggs 16; flour 2 lb.; currants 2 lb.; raisins 1 lb.; sultanas 1 lb.; dates ½ lb.; prunes ½ lb.; almonds ½ lb.; mixed peel 1 lb.; cherries ¾ lb.; brandy ¼ pint; sherry or rum ¼ pint; maraschino 2 tablespoonfuls; essence of lemon 1 tablespoonful; vanilla 1 teaspoonful; carbonate of soda 1 tablespoonful; ground mace 1 teaspoonful; ground cloves ½ teaspoonful; cinnamon ½ teaspoonful; salt ½ teaspoonful.

Almond Icing

For a three-tier cake of the above size the following amounts of ingredients will be required for the almond icing:

INGREDIENTS: Ground almonds 2½ lb.; icing sugar 3¾ lb.; the yolks of 8 eggs; 1 tablespoonful of rum; one teaspoonful of orange flower water, and 1 teaspoonful of vanilla.

METHOD

1. Mix as usual to a stiff paste.
2. Brush the cake all over with apricot jam.
3. Roll out a length of almond icing the size and height of the sides of the cake; roll out a piece the size of the top and put these on.
4. Press down and,
5. Roll smooth with a rolling-pin, and with a sharp knife trim the edges sharp.

Royal Icing

For the white or Royal icing to cover these three almond-covered tiers you will want the following:

INGREDIENTS: Finely sifted icing sugar 2½ lb.; whites of eggs 8; orange flower water 1 dessertspoonful; acetic acid mixed with a spot of blue, a few drops.

TIME: to whisk: 20 to 30 minutes.

METHOD

1. Sift the sugar.
2. Whisk the whites of the eggs which must be new-laid (preserved eggs won't do as the whites have lost something of their strength).
3. Add the sugar gradually to the whisked whites, and beat all together vigorously with a wooden spoon, adding the orange-flower water, and acetic acid when half way through; the acid toughens the icing and makes it more workable and consistent, and better for holding the two upper tiers and easier to pipe, and the blue prevents a yellowish appearance.

N.B.—I always get both acetic acid and blue mixed together from a reliable chemist; Lewis and Burrows, of Earl's Court Road, London, S.W.5, England.

Old English Plum Cake

From South Notts.

INGREDIENTS: Flour 2 lb.; butter 6 oz.; lard 4 oz.; cream of tartar 2 teaspoonfuls; bicarbonate soda 1 teaspoonful; currants 1 lb.; raisins ½ lb.; mixed peel ½ lb.; moist sugar ½ lb.; eggs 3; milk ¾ pint.
TIME: 2½ to 2¾ hours to bake.

METHOD

1. Sift 1½ lb. flour.
2. Rub in butter and lard.
3. Sieve cream of tartar and bicarbonate of soda with the other ½lb. flour; and
4. Blend all the four together.
5. Wash, pick and stone the fruit, cut peel finely and add to the flour.
6. Whisk the eggs, stir the milk to them, and
7. Use to moisten the cake.
8. Beat it up well and quickly.
9. Have a greased cake tin lined with paper ready, put in the mixture.
10. Bake in a good oven for 2½ to 2¾ hours reducing the heat towards the end, and putting a folded paper over the top.

An Interesting Fruit Cake

Miss Rawlins, Burford, 1906

NGREDIENTS: Butter 10 oz.; castor sugar 6 oz.; plain flour 1 lb.; cream of tartar 1 teaspoonful, bicarbonate of soda ½ teaspoonful; salt

¼ teaspoonful; bitter and sweet almonds mixed and finely chopped
1 oz.; currants ½ lb.; sultanas ½ lb.; plums ½ lb. (stoned and each cut into
four); nutmeg ½ grated; eggs 6; brandy 1 wineglassful.
TIME: to bake 2 hours in hot oven.

METHOD

1. Cream the butter.
2. Then add sugar and cream again.
3. Sift the flour, cream of tartar, carbonate of soda, salt and nutmeg together.
4. Mix them into the creamed butter and sugar.
5. Prepare the fruit and mix that in.
6. Whisk the eggs well.
7. Add the brandy.
8. And with them mix the cake.
9. Put into an oiled and paper-lined cake tin and bake as above.

N.B.—This cake must be made three weeks before it is used, and will
keep 3 months. It makes a very good birthday cake if iced and decorated.

Ripon Plum Cake or Christmas Cake

Mr. Herbert M. Bower's recipe

INGREDIENTS: Butter 18 oz.; castor sugar ¾ lb.; 7 eggs; dried and
sifted flour 18 oz.; currants 1 lb.; sweet almonds 2 oz.; candied citron
peel as much as you please; lemon whisky 1 wineglass.
TIME: to bake about 1½ to 2½ hours in a quick oven.

METHOD

1. Beat the butter to a cream before the fire.
2. Add sugar and beat together until quite white and smooth.
3. Separate the whites from the yolks of the eggs.
4. Beat the whites to a stiff snow.
5. Mix both together a little before adding the butter.
6. Beat them all well together; then
7. Mix the flour in lightly with your hand, then the currants (washed and dried the day before), the almonds blanched and shredded, the citron and lemon whisky.

N.B.—Mix very lightly with the hand, for if much beaten after the
flour is added the cake will be heavy; keep it near the fire all the time of
mixing.

Have ready a cake tin lined with paper, pour in the mixture and bake
in a quick oven as above.

Cake made for Peggy Lovet's Christening, May 15th, 1744

This recipe was sent by Miss E. Lovet, of 'Brynhyfryd,' St. Asaph, North Wales.

INGREDIENTS: Flour 4 lb.; powdered sugar 1½ lb.; cinnamon ¼ oz.; nutmeg ¼ oz.; eggs 13, leaving out 6 whites; milk 1½ pints; yeast 1½ pints (or 1½ oz. compressed yeast creamed with sugar); brandy ¾ pint; ale ¾ pint; butter 2 lb.; currants 4 lb.; candied lemon peel 6 oz.; candied orange peel 6 oz.; candied citron peel, 6 oz.

METHOD

The same method as for the 18th Century Bride Cake (*see* p. 330).

Yule Cake, Whitby

Lady Robinson, who sent this recipe along with several exhibits for the first English Folk Cookery Exhibition held on January 16th, 1931, says: 'It has been a great privilege to obtain this recipe. An old lady regales her friends who call upon her between Christmas and New Year's Day with this cake and a glass of cherry brandy.'

INGREDIENTS: Plain flour 1½ lb.; butter ¾ lb.; moist sugar ½ lb.; cinnamon ½ oz.; ½ nutmeg grated; raisins ½ lb.; currants ½ lb.; unlimited candied lemon peel and almonds; eggs 3; 1 glass of brandy, and a little cream sufficient to make the whole into a paste.

TIME: to bake in a moderate oven 3 hours.

METHOD

1. Rub the butter into the flour.
2. Mix in the dry ingredients.
3. Mix well.
4. Beat up the eggs very well with the brandy.
5. Mix with the dry ingredients.
6. Work into a dough with a little cream.
7. Press into a flat tin—it will half fill.
8. Cut it half through each way into small squares.
9. Bake in a moderate oven for 3 hours.
10. Turn out of the tin on to a wire pastry tray when you take it from the oven; and
11. When cold break into rough pieces where the knife indicated before cooking.

Maude's Sultana Cake
MS. 1912

INGREDIENTS: Butter 4 oz.; brown sugar 6 oz.; eggs 3; flour 12 oz.; sultanas 4 oz.; cream of tartar ½ teaspoonful; bicarbonate of soda ¼ teaspoonful.

TIME: to bake about 1 hour.

METHOD

Usual creaming method (*see* below Common Pound Cake).

Great-Grandmother's Pound Cake

Mrs. Wickens, Burford, 1928

INGREDIENTS: Butter 1 lb.; sifted loaf sugar (castor sugar) 1 lb.; eggs, the yolks of 10 and the whites of 5; flour 1 lb.; a wineglassful of brandy if liked.

TIME: to bake, in moderately hot oven, about 1½ to 2 hours.

METHOD

1. Cream the butter.
2. And then with the sugar.
3. Whisk the eggs well together; and
4. Add them gradually, adding a tea-spoonful of flour between every 3 or 4 eggs to prevent curdling.
5. Sieve in the rest of the flour very lightly, and stir but do not beat it in.
6. Bake as above.

Common Pound Cake

Miss Anstey says: 'This was, I think, in my grandmother's receipt book, and was modernized by my mother. The original "receipt" had, I believe, volatile salts instead of baking powder' (*see* Whip Sillabubs p. 258).

INGREDIENTS: Flour 1 lb.; butter ½ lb.; currants ½ lb.; fine moist sugar ½ lb.; milk ½ pint; baking powder 2 teaspoonfuls; eggs 3; half a grated nutmeg.

For a commoner one you may double the quantity of flour and baking powder, and add more milk.

TIME: to bake 1½ to 2 hours in a moderate oven.

METHOD

1. Cream the butter.
2. Add the sugar and beat well.
3. Beat in the eggs one at a time.
4. Sift in the flour and nutmeg, beating well.
5. Dissolve the baking powder in the milk and beat that in.
6. Beat all well together.
7. Pour into a buttered and floured tin, and bake in a moderately hot oven.

Madeira Cake

MS. 1904

INGREDIENTS: Butter ½ lb.; castor sugar ½ lb.; plain flour ½ lb.; eggs 5; candied citron peel 2 thin slices to put on top. Castor sugar for sifting over cake.

TIME: to bake 1 hour in a moderate oven.

METHOD

Usual creaming method (*see* p. 287). Sift castor sugar thickly over cake before putting into oven, and without taking it out of the oven place the thin slices of candied peel over the top when the cake has just set.

Preserved Ginger Cake

MS. 1904

This is made in the same way and the same proportion of ingredients, but 6 oz. preserved ginger cut into dice are added and some of the syrup as flavouring. The top may be covered afterwards with a little white glacé icing made with 6 oz. icing sugar and a little warm water and decorated with crystallized ginger.

A Plainer Madeira Cake

Kensington, 1921

A very good cake mixture for all ordinary purposes may be made with the following:

INGREDIENTS: Butter 8 oz.; castor sugar 8 oz.; eggs 4; milk 1 gill; flour 1 lb.; ground rice or cornflour 4 oz.; cream of tartar 2 teaspoonfuls; bicarbonate of soda 1 teaspoonful; salt ½ teaspoonful; grated rind and juice of one lemon.

METHOD

As above, but beat up the eggs with the milk which should be slightly warm. This mixture can be used to make Victoria sandwiches, jam rolls, jam fingers, and all sorts of shapes for fancy cakes; boats for children's parties, foundations for birds' nests, hearts, diamonds, etc., and any small cakes that can be dipped in different coloured sugar and water icings. The birds' nests may be piped round the edge with stiffly whipped cream or with white of egg stiffly whisked and castor sugar, finished with finely cut split almonds and filled with marzipan eggs. The boats may be provided with paper sails of ordinary note-paper and set to float on a sea of jelly.

A Children's Birthday Cake

The above may be converted into a fascinating birthday cake for the very young by cutting it into three or four layer slices and spreading a different kind of jam on each layer. A layer of strawberry jam, one of lemon curd and one of greengage jam make a good combination of flavours, and charm by their different colouring.

The cake when put together can be simply iced with a water and sugar icing (many children don't like almond paste) into which roses holding little candles, and other suitable decorations may be fixed.

Cherry Cake

MS. 1904

INGREDIENTS: Butter 7 oz.; castor sugar 6 oz.; eggs 3; plain flour 6 oz.; rice flour 2 oz.; glacé cherries 3 oz.; and 6 for the top; also a little angelica, grated peel of 1 lemon; carmine; 6 oz. of icing sugar and a little warm water for the icing.

METHOD

1. Usual creaming method.
2. Colour a delicate pink.
3. Cut the cherries in quarters before adding; bake in a moderate oven.
4. When cold cover with a pink or white water-and-sugar icing and decorate with a bunch of cherries and leaves of angelica. Stalks can be piped to the cherries with a fine lettering pipe, or a border of cherries with leaves cut out of angelica can be put all round the edge of the cake. This is very effective.

Chocolate Cake

MS. 1904

INGREDIENTS: Butter 2 oz.; sugar 2 oz.; flour 2 oz.; egg 1; grated chocolate 1½ oz.; vanilla essence.

TIME: 30 minutes to bake in a *moderate* oven if made into one large cake; in a *hot* oven if small cakes are made.

METHOD

1. Prepare cake tin by brushing it over with liquid clarified butter and dusting this with plain flour; give it a knock to distribute it and shake out any that may be loose.
2. Cream butter.
3. Add sugar.
4. Cream both together.
5. Beat in egg.
6. Mix flour and chocolate together, and
7. Sieve in other ingredients.
8. Stir well; and
9. Add vanilla essence.
10. Bake in a moderate oven if a large cake.
11. When cold this cake may be improved by splitting it in two, spreading the lower half with some stiffly whipped cream flavoured to taste, and covering it with the top half.
12. The cake may then be brushed over with apricot jam and completely covered top and sides with chopped almonds or other nuts that have first been blanched, then chopped and browned in the oven.

Or it may be covered with a white sugar-and-water icing made by mixing 6 oz. sifted sugar with a little warm water to the consistency of thick cream, and pouring it over the cake; some halves of walnut placed on top before the icing sets make a good finish for those who like walnuts. And if they are used a few, chopped, may be mixed with the cream layer filling.

Marmalade Cake

Mrs. Wickens, Burford, 1928

INGREDIENTS: Self-raising flour ½ lb. (or plain flour ½ lb. mixed with 1 small teaspoonful cream of tartar; ⅛ teaspoonful of bicarbonate of soda and ¼ teaspoonful salt); butter 2 oz.; sugar 1 oz.; egg 1; marmalade 3 tablespoonfuls; a little milk if necessary.

TIME: to bake: 1¾ hour in Junior New World Cooker the first hour in No. 5 (350° F.) and turn down to No. 3 for the last ¾ hour.

METHOD

1. Rub the butter into the flour.
2. Add sugar.

3. Add marmalade, beaten up with well-beaten egg.
4. If necessary add a little milk.

Jam Roll

MS. 1904

INGREDIENTS: Butter 2 oz.; castor sugar 2 oz.; eggs 2; 1 tablespoonful hot water; plain flour 4 oz.; cream of tartar ½ teaspoonful; bicarbonate of soda ¼ teaspoonful; salt ⅛ teaspoonful; vanilla essence.

TIME: to bake in rather hot oven 15 to 20 minutes.

METHOD

1. Cream butter and sugar together.
2. Separate yolks from whites of eggs.
3. Add the yolks to the butter and sugar and whisk well.
4. Sieve the flour with the cream of tartar, bicarbonate of soda and salt, and
5. Add to the egg mixture; add the flavouring and hot water.
6. Have ready the whites of the eggs stiffly whisked and fold them in.
7. Have ready a shallow baking tin lightly brushed with oiled butter and

dusted with flour (*see* Almond Puffs p. 261, and Chocolate Cake p. 289).
8. Pour the mixture in, spread level and bake.
9. Turn out on to a paper sprinkled with castor sugar.
10. Cut off the edges of the cake very quickly.
11. Spread with warm jam and roll up quickly, using the paper to help this proceeding.
12. Leave rolled up in the paper till cold, standing it on a wire pastry tray.

Lunch Cake

Bolham, Tiverton, 1887

INGREDIENTS: Plain flour ½ lb.; lard 3 oz.; sugar ¼ lb.; currants ¼ lb.; candied peel 1 oz.; a little flavouring; ¼ teaspoonful salt; cream of tartar 1 teaspoonful; bicarbonate of soda ½ teaspoonful; egg 1; and milk to mix.

TIME: to bake ¾ to 1 hour.

METHOD

1. Rub the lard into the flour.
2. Add all the dry ingredients.
3. Mix well and make up with the egg and milk.

4. Bake as above in a moderately hot oven.

A Very Good Luncheon Cake

Burford, 1898

INGREDIENTS: Plain flour 1 lb.; clarified dripping (or half lard and half butter) ½ lb.; ground rice ½ lb.; cream of tartar 2 small teaspoonfuls; bicarbonate of soda, 1 small teaspoonful; salt ¼ teaspoonful; sugar 4 oz.; sultanas ½ lb.; eggs 2 (preserved eggs will do); milk about ½ pint, more if required.

TIME: to bake, 1 hour in moderate oven.

METHOD

1. Rub the fat into the flour.
2. Sift the ground rice, cream of tartar, bicarbonate of soda, and salt together.
3. Blend it with the flour.
4. Add the sugar and sultanas.

5. Beat up the eggs with half the milk and use it to mix the cake, adding the rest of the milk as required.
6. Put into a greased and floured tin, and
7. Bake as above.

Beer Cake

Miss Heath, of Lyghe, Tonbridge, sends this and two other recipes which are over a hundred years old, but which she has recently had made and eaten, and knows to be good. She says: 'With regard to the decline of English cookery, my mother who was born in 1826 used to say that 'when kitcheners came in good cookery went out.' I think she meant that with the open range of her youth, bread, cakes, etc., had to be baked in a brick oven and meat roasted on a spit in front of the fire, not baked, and fried things were fried, not as is too often the case now (1931) baked; also food could not be kept warm indefinitely as in an iron oven.'

Meat was roasted however on a spit turned by a jack fixed to the kitchen chimney shelf and wound up by a key as late as 1867. Houses within 4 miles of Bow Bells, London, were provided with these ranges, although comparatively newly built, that is to say, after the accession of Queen Victoria and before the exhibition of 1851.

RECIPE

INGREDIENTS: Flour ½ lb.; butter 3 oz.; sugar (moist) 3 oz.; currants 3 oz.; egg 1; beer ¼ pint; bicarbonate of soda ½ teaspoonful.

TIME: to bake 1 hour in a moderate oven.

METHOD

1. Cream the butter.
2. Add the flour, sugar and currants.
3. Beat up the egg with the beer.
4. Dissolve the soda in it.
5. Add it to the mixture, mix well and keep stirring till it is put into the oven.

Rich Seed Cake

Mrs. Martin, Frome, 1852

INGREDIENTS: Butter 1 lb.; eggs 6; castor sugar ¾ lb.; flour 1 lb.; caraway seeds 3 oz. (or, if *seeds* are disliked, flavour with caraway essence).

TIME: to bake in moderate oven 1½ to 2 hours.

METHOD

1. Cream butter.
2. Add sugar and cream again.
3. Sift in flour.
4. Add seeds, mix well;
5. Whisk eggs well with wheel whisk, and
6. Fold into cake.
7. Whisk altogether with Scotch wire whisk for 10 minutes.
8. Have ready a tin lined with buttered paper.
9. Pour in; and
10. Bake as above.

Plain Seed Cake

MS. 1904

INGREDIENTS: Butter 4 oz.; plain flour 12 oz.; castor sugar 8 oz.; cream of tartar ½ teaspoonful; bicarbonate of soda ¼ teaspoonful and a little salt; eggs 3; milk two tablespoonfuls; a few caraway seeds (or a few drops of caraway essence).

TIME: to bake in a moderate oven about 1 hour.

METHOD

1. Rub the butter into the flour.
2. Add sugar, cream of tartar, bicarbonate of soda and salt; mix well.
3. Beat up the eggs and milk.
4. Add them to the dry ingredients to make them into a thick cake batter.
5. Pour into a lined cake tin.
6. Bake in a moderate oven about 1 hour.

Nell's Rice Cake

'This is a Devonshire recipe, given to my cousin,' says Miss Anstey, 'by a very old friend, about 1870.'

INGREDIENTS: Ground rice ½ lb.; fine white sugar ½ lb.; eggs 5.

TIME: to bake in slow oven about 30 to 40 minutes.

METHOD

1. Mix the ground rice with the sugar.
2. Beat the eggs well.
3. Sift in the rice and sugar; and
4. Beat all well together for 20 minutes.
5. Put into a lightly buttered tin, dusted with rice flour and sugar mixed, and bake in slow oven.

[N.B.—This makes an excellent sponge layer cake or a jam sandwich —Ed.]

Portland Cake

(A cut-and-come-again cake that keeps moist as long as there is any left.) This recipe of his mother's is contributed by Mr. Stanley Bennett.

INGREDIENTS: Baker's dough 2 lb.; flour 1 lb.; lard ¾ lb.; butter (or margarine) 6 oz.; mixed candied peel 4 oz.; moist sugar 2 lb.; nutmeg 1 large one; currants and sultanas ¾ lb.

TIME: to bake 2 to 2½ hours in moderate, rather slow oven.

METHOD

1. Put the dough into a warm basin.
2. Add the lard, and butter and work them in.
3. Mix in the candied peel, moist sugar, nutmeg, currants and sultans.
4. Add the flour.
5. And mix well together.
6. Three parts fill warm greased tins.
7. Stand in warm place to prove till well risen about 1 hour.
8. Bake in rather slow oven.

Dough Cake

Mrs. Wickens, Burford, 1928

INGREDIENTS: Flour 2 lb.; butter ½ lb.; sugar ½ lb.; currants ½ lb.; warm milk 1 pint; compressed yeast 1 oz.

TIME: to rise; over one hour; to bake 1 to 1½ hours in hot oven which may be gradually slackened.

METHOD

1. Rub butter into flour.
2. Add the dry ingredients and mix well.
3. Cream the yeast with a little of the sugar.
4. Mix it with the lukewarm milk; and
5. Stir it into the flour etc., and make it into a light dough.
6. Stand in a warm place to rise for more than an hour, then bake as above.

Welsh Bun

Mrs. Perowne, from Lampeter, S. Wales

INGREDIENTS: Butter ½ lb.; sugar ½ lb. or less; currants or sultanas ½ lb.; flour (plain) 1 lb.; milk, warm and new ¼ pint; bicarbonate of soda 1 teaspoonful; eggs 3, a little more milk may be added if necessary.

TIME: to beat 15 minutes; to bake 3 or 4 hours in slow oven.

METHOD

1. Beat the butter to a cream.
2. Separate the yolks from the whites of the eggs.
3. Beat the yolks and add them to the butter.
4. Then the sugar.
5. The fruit.
6. The flour.
7. Lastly, add the whites well-beaten and sprinkle in the soda.
8. Beat for 15 minutes.
9. Bake immediately in a greased tin in a slow oven for 3 or 4 hours.

[N.B.—I have not tested this recipe.—ED.]

Bath Buns, 1904

INGREDIENTS: Flour ½ lb.; salt ½ teaspoonful; butter ¼ lb.; castor sugar 2 oz.; compressed yeast ½ oz.; half teacup lukewarm milk; eggs 2; candied peel 1 oz.; sugar from the candied peel; and 4 lumps roughly crushed, a few currants.

TIME: to rise 10—15 minutes; to bake in hot oven 10—15 minutes.

METHOD

1. Rub the butter into the flour.
2. Add 1½ oz. of castor sugar.
3. Cream the yeast with the other ½oz.
4. Beat up the eggs and add to the luke-warm milk.
5. Blend with the yeast.
6. Pour this into the flour and make into a soft dough.
7. Mix it very thoroughly and set to rise in a warm place.
8. Divide into 8 portions.
9. Knead lightly and shape into buns

folding a little crushed candied peel sugar into the centre of each.
10. Put on to a greased and floured baking tin.
11. Brush with water and sprinkle with crushed lump sugar and a few currants.
12. Set in a warm place to rise for 10–15 minutes.
13. Bake in a hot oven for about 10–20 minutes according to size.

N.B.—Sugar nibs can be bought for putting into Bath buns and sprinkling on them.

Bath Buns

Early 18th Century

INGREDIENTS: Butter 1 lb.; flour 1 lb.; flour ½ lb.; eggs 8; sack (sherry) 1 tablespoonful; rose water 1 tablespoonful; yeast 6 tablespoonfuls (or 1 oz. compressed yeast) caraway comfits ¼ lb.; and sugar 6 oz.

TIME: to rise, ½ hour; to bake, ½ hour in a hot oven.

METHOD

1. Work the pound of butter into the pound of flour to make a paste, add the sugar.
2. Put it aside whilst you make the following sponge.
3. Warm the half pound of flour.
4. Add to it 8 well beaten eggs, the wine, and rose water and yeast; (if using compressed yeast it must be creamed with a little sugar).
5. Mix all these well together till smooth.
6. Set it in a warm place to rise ½ hour.
7. Now take the butter paste you made and work the sponge into it with a spoon.
8. Add the caraway comfits, keeping some of them out to strew on the top of the cakes.
9. Lightly butter and flour some tins and put the buns on them; one kitchenspoonful makes a cake.

Belvoir Castle Buns

1869

These buns were made at Belvoir Castle and were greatly liked by the Duke of Rutland, who often asked for them. The recipe has been preserved and handed on through the interest the head kitchenmaid at that period took in her job.

INGREDIENTS: Flour, plain 2 lb.; sugar 6 oz.; butter 5 oz.; currants 6 oz.; milk 1 pint; yeast 1 oz.

TIME: to rise, just 2 hours; then half an hour; and 10 minutes to bake.

METHOD

1. Place the flour in a basin.
2. Add the butter and rub it in till the mixture looks like bread-crumbs.
3. Mix in the sugar.
4. Place the yeast in a small basin, cream it with a little sugar.
5. Take 1 gill of the milk, let it boil and add it to the remainder of the milk.
6. Add this to the yeast and pour it in the centre of the flour.
7. Stir in the flour from the sides.
8. Cover the basin with a clean towel and
9. Set in a warm place and let it rise for 2 hours.
10. Knead it and divide into 6 pieces.
11. Weigh out the currants and well wash and dry them.
12. Roll out the dough very thinly, and
13. Over each piece sprinkle some of the currants.
14. Fold it up and cut into strips, and turn them upside down on a buttered and floured tin.
15. Let them rise for 30 minutes, and
16. Bake for 10 minutes.

Revel Buns

(*See also* pp. 324 and 325)

'My old aunts gave me this recipe. The buns were very rich, but very good. Something like the more modern Easter cakes, but much richer. I do not know why they must be baked on sycamore leaves, but as a child I should not have thought them right if they had not had the imprint of the leaf under them.'

Mrs. MAUDE S. SELDON,
Braunton, N. Devon.

INGREDIENTS: Flour 1½ lb.; Devonshire cream ¾ lb.; butter ½ lb.; currants 6 oz.; sugar 1 lb.; egg 1; new milk ¼ pint; saffron a large pinch; yeast 1 oz.; ground cinnamon 1 teaspoonful; salt a pinch.

METHOD

1. Rub the butter into the flour.
2. Add the sugar.
3. Set the saffron (in a piece of muslin) in some of the milk in a saucepan and warm to extract the flavour.
4. Warm the cream in a cool oven.
5. Mix the yeast in a basin with a little sugar and a wineglassful of warm water.
6. Add the cream to the flour, butter and sugar and mix lightly with a spoon.
7. Add the milk, the whisked egg, and the cinnamon.
8. When the yeast is ready add it to the other ingredients.
9. Also the saffron milk.
10. Lastly the currants.
11. Keep the mixture, covered in a warm place for 12 hours.
12. Bake in small flat cakes on sycamore leaves, in a moderate oven.
13. When cold, powder with sifted or castor sugar.

296

Easter Cakes, 1904

These somewhat resemble Shrewsbury Cakes

INGREDIENTS: Flour ¾ lb.; butter 8 oz.; sugar 5 oz.; currants 3 oz.; cream of tartar ½ teaspoonful; bicarbonate of soda ¼ teaspoonful; salt a pinch; egg 1.

TIME: 10—15 minutes.

METHOD

1. Rub the butter quickly and lightly into the flour.
2. Add the sugar and currants, cream of tartar and bicarbonate of soda and salt.
3. Beat the egg.
4. Mix it in with the flour, using a knife.
5. Gather the mixture into one piece.
6. Turn out on to a floured board.
7. Roll out thinly about ⅛ inch.
8. Then cut out with a round, fluted cutter.
9. Lay on a greased and floured baking tin.
10. Bake in a moderately hot oven 10 or 15 minutes.
11. Take out, sprinkle with castor sugar.
12. And lay on a sieve to cool.

N.B.—These cakes must be watched while baking as they catch easily, and only require to be a faint brown.

To Make Shrewsbury Cakes

From a family receipt book kept from 1630 to 1750

This interesting recipe has been sent by Colonel Plomer from Shrewsbury, who says they are generally known to-day as

SHREWSBURY BISCUITS

INGREDIENTS: Flour 1 lb.; sugar 1 lb.; butter 1 lb.; caraway seeds ½ oz.; some nutmeg; eggs 3; sack (sherry will do) 3 tablespoonfuls; rose water 3 tablespoonfuls.

TIME: about 20 minutes in a rather cool oven.

METHOD

1. Rub the flour, butter, sugar, caraway seeds and nutmeg well together.
2. Beat the eggs well, and add the wine and rosewater to them (you will want less than 8 oz. of liquid all told for this quantity of flour, especially as the quantity of butter is large).
3. Mix the liquid with your paste a little at a time so as not to overdo it, and roll it out.
4. Cut it into what shapes you please.
5. Bake them upon slightly greased and floured tin plates.
6. Prick them with a pin.
7. 'Let your oven be not too hott.'

Hard Cakes

Old Yorkshire recipe used at farm tea-parties from Miss Esther A. Smith, Limpsfield, Surrey.

INGREDIENTS: Flour 1 lb.; butter and lard 10 oz.; baking powder 1 teaspoonful; volatile salts, ½ teaspoonful; salt to taste; cold water to mix.

TIME: 15 to 25 minutes.

METHOD

1. Sieve the flour, baking powder and volatile salts.
2. Rub the fat in.
3. Mix to a stiff paste with cold water.
4. Roll out to ⅛ of an inch.
5. Stamp or prick all over with a fork.
6. Cut out with round cutter.
7. Bake in moderate oven.

Fat Rascals

Yorkshire

INGREDIENTS: Plain flour 1 lb.; butter ½ lb.; moist sugar 1 oz.; currants ¼ lb.; salt ¼ teaspoonful; a little milk and water; a little castor sugar.

METHOD

1. Rub the butter into the flour.
2. Mix in the currants (well cleaned and dried) also the sugar and salt.
3. Mix all well together.
4. Make into a firm dough with a little milk and water.
5. Roll out half an inch thick.
6. Cut into rounds with the top of a tumbler.
6. Dust with white sugar, and bake in a quick oven.

Fried Cakes

Mrs. Brewitt, 1927

INGREDIENTS: Flour, self-raising flour, 3 oz. (or 3 oz. plain flour and ½ teaspoonful baking powder); currants just a few; milk enough to mix stiffly. Clarified fat for frying.

TIME: about 10 minutes.

METHOD

1. Mix stiffly.
2. Roll out.
3. Cut into rounds.
4. Fry in clarified fat.
5. Scatter sugar on top.
6. Stand on clean cloth on a pastry tray to dry.

Brandy Snaps

INGREDIENTS: Butter 2 oz.; flour 2 oz.; Demerara sugar 2 oz.; syrup 2 oz.; lemon juice ½ teaspoonful; vanilla ½ teaspoonful.

TIME: About 15 minutes.

METHOD

1. Put all together in a pan and boil for 5 minutes, except flavouring.
2. Add these.
3. Put on greased and floured tin in strips, a little apart.
4. Bake in a moderate oven till perforated and a nice colour.
5. Allow to stand 2 minutes and then curl round a wooden stick; or shape round a spigot into cones.

[N.B.—Londoners and Southerners used to buy these in rather large flat rounds which were sometimes slightly curled, and called them 'jumbles' sixty years ago.—ED.]

Eliza Acton's Gingerbread Biscuits

These have been tested by Mrs. Woods and found 'very good indeed.' She adds 'I leave the paste all night and find it a better method.'

INGREDIENTS: Treacle ¾ lb.; butter ½ lb.; flour 1 lb.; brown sugar ½ lb.; ginger ¾ oz.

TIME: to bake about 30 to 45 minutes.

METHOD

1. Mix the flour with the brown sugar and the ginger.
2. Melt the treacle and butter together.
3. Pour hot on to the flour mixture.
4. Make into a paste; leave all night.
5. When quite cold roll out thin as for biscuits with just as much flour as will prevent it sticking to the board.
6. Cut into rounds and bake on greased and floured tins in a gentle oven.

Ripon Parkins for November the Fifth

Mr. Herbert M. Bower's recipe.

INGREDIENTS: Medium oatmeal ¾ lb.; flour ¾ lb.; butter 2 oz.; lard 2 oz.; brown sugar ¼ lb.; treacle 1 lb.; milk 2 tablespoonfuls; bicarbonate of soda 1 teaspoonful; ground ginger 1 tablespoonful.

TIME: to bake in slow oven about 1½ hours.

299

METHOD

1. Rub the lard and butter into the flour.
2. Blend the flour, oatmeal, ginger and sugar all together.
3. Melt the treacle and mix that in.
4. Finally, dissolve the soda in the milk and add that.
5. Mix well, bake in a dripping tin, and cook in a slow oven.
6. When done cut into squares; or the parkin may be rolled out and cut into rounds.

Ripon Ginger Cake

(For all Seasons)

Mr. Herbert M. Bower's recipe

INGREDIENTS: Plain flour ½ lb.; fine oatmeal ½ lb.; treacle ½ lb.; butter ¼ lb.; castor sugar 2 oz.; ground ginger 2 oz.; bicarbonate soda 1 teaspoonful.

TIME: to bake about 2 hours in a moderate oven.

METHOD

1. Sieve the flour and bicarbonate of of soda together 3 times.
2. Mix in with it the oatmeal and ground ginger.
3. Cream the butter and sugar together.
4. Warm the treacle and add that.
5. Add the flour, oatmeal, and soda you have sieved.
6. Mix well, put in a lined cake tin and bake in a moderate oven about 2 hours.

Gingerbread Cake

Mrs. Macpherson-Grant

INGREDIENTS: Flour 1½ lb.; treacle (golden syrup) 1 lb.; butter or lard ½ lb.; preserved ginger or peel ¼ lb.; sugar ½ lb.; eggs 3; milk 1 gill; bicarbonate of soda, 1 teaspoonful.

TIME: to bake in moderate oven 2¼ hours.

METHOD

1. Sieve the flour and ground ginger together into a basin.
2. Shred the peel finely and add the flour.
3. Put the butter, treacle and sugar into a stewpan to dissolve.
4. Beat the eggs in a small basin.
5. Mix the flour and ginger with the treacle, butter and sugar.
6. Put the bicarbonate of soda into another small basin and add the milk lukewarm to it.
7. Mix this with the other ingredients and beat *well*.
8. Turn the mixture into a greased tin and bake.

Eliza Acton's Gingerbread, 1845

Mrs. Woods, of Glaston Rectory, Uppingham, says: 'In the opinion of the members of this household the gingerbread is the best ever tasted; but it must be kept in a jar or tin, to mature, before using. I use golden syrup instead of treacle.'

INGREDIENTS: Eggs 5; treacle 1¼ lb.; pale brown sugar 6 oz.; flour 1 lb.; butter 6 oz. (not margarine); ground ginger 1 oz.; lemons, grated rind of 2.

TIME: to bake, about 2 hours.

METHOD

1. Beat eggs well.
2. Add warmed syrup gradually, beating all the time.
3. Add sugar in same manner.
4. Add butter, which must be warmed but *not* hot.
5. Add the ginger to the flour and sift the two together. Add to egg mixture.
6. Beat till bubbles appear in batter, then add flavouring.
7. Bake in greased shallow tin in slow oven.

Lancashire Parkin

This has been very kindly sent by Mrs. Stocks, of Durham

INGREDIENTS: Oatmeal (medium) 1½ lb.; treacle 1 lb.; brown sugar ½ lb.; butter or margarine ½ lb.; ground ginger 1 teaspoonful; ground allspice one teaspoonful.

TIME: One night to stand; 2 hours to bake.

METHOD

1. Mix the dry ingredients together.
2. Heat the treacle and butter sufficiently to melt the latter.
3. Mix well.
4. Leave to stand all night.
5. Next day put into a shallow baking tin (well greased) and bake in a cool oven for about 2 hours. It is done when the parkin springs back when an impression is made with the finger.

Yorkshire Parkin

This is another 'very old' Yorkshire recipe sent from Ross-on-Wye, Herefordshire.

INGREDIENTS: Medium oatmeal ¾ lb.; plain flour ¼ lb.; treacle 1 lb.; raw sugar ½ lb.; ground ginger 1 teaspoonful; mixed spice ½ teaspoonful; bicarbonate soda 2 teaspoonfuls; lukewarm water 2 tablespoonfuls.

TIME: to bake 20 minutes.

METHOD

1. Warm treacle together with the butter.
2. Mix the oatmeal, sugar, ginger and allspice with the treacle and butter.
3. Dissolve the bicarbonate of soda in the warm water and mix that in well.
4. Drop in spoonfuls on greased and floured tins (see p. 261); and
5. Bake quickly in a hot, but not too hot oven.

Another Gingerbread or Parkin

(A really nice old family recipe)

Mrs. Millington, Preston

INGREDIENTS: Fine oatmeal 1 lb.; flour (plain) 1 lb.; golden syrup 1 lb.; bicarbonate of soda 2 teaspoonfuls; butter ¼ lb.; brown sugar ⅓ lb.; ground ginger ¼ oz.; egg 1; a little milk.

TIME: bake in a moderate oven for about one hour.

METHOD
The same as for Sponge Parkin or Gingerbread (see p. 303).

Another Gingerbread or Parkin

(MADE WITH WHOLE WHEATMEAL)

Mrs. Millington, Preston

INGREDIENTS: Plain flour (2 breakfast cups) 1 pint; whole wheatmeal ½ pint; sugar ½ pint; treacle 2 tablespoonfuls; butter 1 tablespoonful, ginger 2 teaspoonfuls; bicarbonate soda 1 teaspoonful; egg 1.

N.B.—Double quantities for a very thick parkin, and bake in a large dripping tin.

TIME: bake in a moderate oven for about 1 hour.

METHOD
The same as for Sponge Parkin or Gingerbread (see p. 303).

Mother's Parkin

(from Sheffield)

Mrs. Millington, Preston

INGREDIENTS: Fine oatmeal 1 lb.; baking powder 2 dessertspoons; lard ¼ lb.; golden syrup or treacle, enough to mix it; ground ginger 2 teaspoons; mixed spice 1 teaspoonful.

TIME: moderate oven 1 hour.

METHOD

1. Rub the lard into the oatmeal.
2. Mix in the baking powder, spices and ginger.
3. Take the lid off a tin of syrup or treacle and warm tin till the treacle runs.
4. Mix it with the oatmeal into a stiff mixture.
5. Put into a greased dripping tin and bake in the centre of a moderate oven.

N.B.—It burns quickly if the oven is too hot. No other liquid is used in this at all but the syrup or treacle.

Sponge Parkin or Gingerbread

Mrs. Millington, Preston

INGREDIENTS: Plain flour ½ lb.; fine oatmeal ½ lb.; black treacle ½ lb.; brown sugar (demerara or raw) ¼ lb.; butter and lard mixed ¼ lb.; mixed spice 1 teaspoon; powdered ginger 1 teaspoon; nutmeg, just a grating; bicarbonate of soda, 1 teaspoon; milk ½ teacupful.

TIME: bake in a moderate oven for about 1 hour.

METHOD

1. Rub the butter and lard into the flour.
2. Stir in oatmeal.
3. Add the other dry ingredients.
4. Then the syrup (slightly warmed).
5. Slightly warm the milk and dissolve the soda in it.
6. Stir it into the mixture.
7. A beaten egg may be added (the mixture must be quite light and fairly moist, so it is safer to use an egg than more milk).
8. Grease a large meat roasting or a Yorkshire pudding tin.
9. Pour in the mixture.
10. Bake as above.

Parkin

This is eaten in Lancashire and Yorkshire on November 5th and the following recipe comes from Bolton-le-Moors:

INGREDIENTS: Medium oatmeal 8 oz.; plain flour 8 oz.; butter 8 oz.; black treacle 8 oz.; nutmeg, mace, ¼ teaspoonful each; ground ginger ½ teaspoonful; bicarbonate of soda 1 teaspoonful; a little cream about 1 tablespoonful; salt ½ teaspoonful.

TIME: to bake 1¼ hour in a moderate oven.

METHOD

1. Mix the oatmeal, flour and salt well together in a mixing bowl.
2. Rub the butter into it.
3. Mix in the spice and baking powder.
4. Warm the treacle and cream and use them to blend all the dry ingredients.
5. Leave all night.
6. Next day bake in a flat dripping tin in a moderate oven for 1 to 1¼ hours. Some people add candied peel, which should be chopped very finely. This parkin will keep a long time, and improves with keeping, but should *not* be kept in a tin, or it will get dry.

Loaf Gingerbread

Another of the receipts of Mrs. Anger, of Burnham-on-Crouch, Miss Anstey's grandmother.

INGREDIENTS : Flour 2 lb.; treacle 2 lb.; butter ½ lb.; sugar ⅓ lb.; ginger 1 oz.; volatile salts ½ oz.; milk 2 teaspoonfuls.

TIME : to bake about 2 hours in moderate oven.

METHOD

1. Mix the flour, sugar and ginger together.
2. Melt the treacle and butter together, and
3. Use to mix the flour.
4. Dissolve the volatile salts in the milk.
5. Mix that in.
6. Pour into well-greased shallow tins.
7. Bake slowly in moderate oven.
8. When cooked and cold cut into squares.

Home-made Jams and Jellies

It is impossible in a book of this size to give as many recipes as one would wish for the many delicious jams and jellies we have in England. Fortunately, however, there is a cheap and thoroughly reliable publication available. This is *The Domestic Preservation of Fruit and Vegetables* (*see* pp. 376, 377).

The following is an example of the directions given:

Strawberries

'It has been pointed out that pectin occurs in the cell-walls of the fruit, and that the fruit has to be broken down to a certain extent before the pectin can be brought into solution. The most popular strawberry jam, however, is that in which the berries remain whole. In this case, therefore, it is necessary to add pectin in sufficient quantity to give the desired set. Strawberries are also low in acid, and it is necessary to increase the acidity. This deficiency in pectin and acid can be remedied by adding gooseberry juice or red-currant juice as both these juices are rich in pectin and acid.' If neither of these juices is available a small quantity of fruit pectin (Certo is good) and lemon juice, or tartaric acid may be used.

INGREDIENTS : Strawberries 5 lb.; gooseberry juice 1 lb.; sugar 6 lb.

METHOD

1. Weigh the jam pan.
2. Put the strawberries and sugar in it.
3. When the sugar is dissolved add the gooseberry juice.
4. Boil until the jam weighs 10 lb, (now you see why the pan has to be weighed: when the jam is ready the pan with the jam in it must be weighed; and the total weight if the jam is ready should be 10 lb. plus the weight of the pan). The jam must be stirred gently from time to time to prevent burning.

N.B.—Strawberry jam should be allowed to cool slightly before being filled into jars; this causes it to thicken somewhat, and if the jam is stirred just before pouring it into the jars the berries will remain suspended throughout instead of rising to the surface.

To Clarify Loaf Sugar

1. Take as much sugar as you require.
2. Put it in a pan capable of holding about double the quantity to allow room for it to boil.
3. Add ½ pint water to every lb. sugar.
4. Beat up with it some whites of egg and set it on the fire until the scum rises.
5. Then throw a very little water in to prevent its boiling over.
6. Let the scum rise three times before you skim it, throwing a little water in each time.
7. The fourth time skim it very clear and then let it boil for 20 minutes or until it comes to 235°F.
8. Strain it through a silk sieve, or napkin.
9. This syrup can be used for all kinds of soft ripe fruit, as it is of a proper strength, and will prevent the fruit breaking. It may be kept in bottles for flavouring ices.

N.B.—It is also useful for cocktails.

Queen Henrietta Maria's Marmalade of Cherries

17th Century

'To make a fine marmalade of cherries with juice of raspes and currans as Madam Mancy made it for the Queen.' This has been sent by Miss Prendergast of Eastbourne. The Queen was undoubtedly Henrietta Maria, Charles I's queen, as it is recorded by George Hartman, Steward to Sir Kenelm Digby, and Sir Kenelm Digby was her Chancellor and friend at court and in exile. Hartman published a good many 'receipts' in 1648, and later after Sir Kenelm's death, many of which he probably obtained, when in his service (see p. 374).

INGREDIENTS: Cherries, stoned, 3 lb.; juice of rasps ½ lb.; juice of red currants ½ lb.; fine white sugar 1 lb. (or 'peradventure a little more if to keep all the year').

METHOD

1. Put the stoned cherries, juice of 'rasps', juice of red currants and sugar altogether into the preserving pan;
2. Boil them quickly directly the sugar has dissolved, especially at first.
3. Skim them all the while as the scum riseth.
4. When you find them of a fit consistency with a firm clear jelly mingled with the cherries, take them from the fire, and
5. Bruise the cherries with the back of your spoon.
6. When cold put them in pots. 'It is', says George Hartman in *The True Preserve*, 1682, 'a very fine sweetmeat.'

Orange Marmalade

Mrs. Calvert, Ockley Court, Surrey, 1827

INGREDIENTS: Lump sugar 6 lb.; Seville oranges 3 lb.; water 3 quarts.

TIME: to boil 1 hour after the whole has been prepared.

METHOD

1. Wash the oranges and cut them as thin as possible into short chips keeping out the seeds and hard roots of the division of the oranges in the raw state.
2. Dissolve the sugar in the water.
3. Clarify the sugar (*see* p. 305).
4. Throw in the orange chips, pulp and juice.
5. Let it all boil one hour as quickly as possible, when the chips will be found quite tender and clear, and the marmalade ready to put into pots. While boiling it requires constant attention

Marmalade

Another of Miss Heath's grandmother's recipes, 1823 (*see* pp. 51 and 291).
1. Put the oranges into the preserving pan.
2. Cover them with water, and boil until they are quite tender and clear when cut.
3. Pour off the water in which they were boiled and set it aside.
4. Cut the oranges in thin slices removing the pips.
5. Weigh them and allow 1¾ lb. preserving sugar to every pound of pulp.
6. Boil the sugar in the orange water till a little sets, when put on a plate.
7. When put in the fruit and boil again till done. It will take only about 15 minutes longer.

Quince 'Marmalet'

This is the Worcester cook's recipe, early 18th century

INGREDIENTS: Quinces 1 lb.; loaf sugar 1 lb.; water 1 pt.; a little brandy and some thin paper.

TIME: till tender.

METHOD

1. Wipe and peel and cut in quarters and core the quinces and throw them into cold water to keep their colour.
2. Put the peelings and cores in cold water and boil them till tender.
3. Strain off the liquid.
4. When it is cold put the peeled quinces into it, weighing one pound of the fruit and 1 lb. of loaf sugar to 1 pint of liquid.
5. Boil all together till they are tender, keeping them close covered.
6. 'Beat them till they be of a right thickness.'
7. Pour it into your pots and, when cold, cover with brandied paper.

Green Tomato Marmalade

Melton Mowbray, 1927

INGREDIENTS: Green tomatoes 6 lb.; sugar 4½ lb.; lemons 2 (juice and rinds); root ginger 1½ oz.; chillies ⅛ oz.; candied peel 2 oz.

TIME: to boil about 1½ hours.

METHOD

1. Stalk, wash and quarter the tomatoes.
2. Put them in a bowl.
3. Cover with sugar.
4. Add juice and rind of the lemons.
5. Leave for 24 hours.
6. Next day place in preserving pan.
7. Add the ginger and chillies tied up in muslin.
8. Boil till tender about 1½ hours.
9. Take out the ginger.
10. Put in 2 oz. candied peel finely sliced.
11. Boil up quickly and, when it sets, put into pots.

Apple Butter

A Somersetshire Recipe

INGREDIENTS: Apples, any kind (windfalls will do, crabs and especially Siberian crabs are, if anything, superior to orchard apples); sugar ¾ lb. to 1 pint of sieved apple pulp; lemon juice and grated peel to flavour.

TIME: about 2 hours.

307

METHOD

1. Wash and dry the fruit quickly.
2. Do not pare the apples.
3. Cut them in quarters.
4. Cut away any unsound bits and if necessary the core, but not if it is quite good.
5. Put into a preserving pan, cover with cold water.
6. Stew to a pulp.
7. Press through a hair sieve.
8. Throw away what won't go through, and measure the pulp; and weigh out ¾ lb. preserving sugar for every pint of apple.
9. Return pulp to pan and boil for about one hour till quite thick; then
10. Add the sugar and lemon juice and grated peel (about ½ lemon to each quart of pulp, but this is a matter of taste) and when it is dissolved boil up again quickly for a short time till stiff enough to spread without running. Put into jars and when cold cover with paraffin wax, or in the old-fashioned way with a piece of paper dipped in brandy. Tie down.

N.B.—It is an improvement to use half cider and half water when stewing the fruit for pulping (direction 5); cinnamon and cloves may be added as a flavouring with the sugar instead of lemon. If properly made this will keep a couple of years or more.

Barberries

Barberries are one of England's good things that are now frequently neglected. They are far too acid to eat in their natural condition but, preserved with sugar, they have a very fine flavour, and may be commended to users of curry as a very good substitute for tamarinds. Several 17th century recipes have been sent from Hurdcott House, Wilts, as well as the following; all are intensely interesting as survivals of bygone days and might well be used to add to the variety of modern meals. Barberries were candied in bunches in addition to being made into jam and jelly. Barberry 'drops' were another delicacy.

Preserved Barberries

1826

INGREDIENTS: Barberries and preserving sugar, equal weights; a kettle (i.e. a pan) of boiling water.

TIME: 24 hours to stand and then 15 minutes to boil up.

METHOD

1. Stand the fruit and preserving sugar in a stoneware jar in a pan of boiling water and keep the latter boiling till the sugar is melted and the barberries are quite soft.
2. Take out the jar and let the fruit remain in it all night.
3. Next day turn it into a preserving pan, and boil up for 15 minutes.
4. Put into jars, tie close, and set them by for use.

Barberry Jam or Jelly

METHOD

1. Pick the barberries from the stalks.
2. Put them in a Nottingham (brown earthenware) jar, cover them, and bake in a slow oven till soft.
2. Pass then through a sieve.

3. Weigh them, and weigh out an equal amount of powdered sugar.
4. Mix them well together.
5. Put into a preserving pan and boil up for 15 minutes.
6. Pot as usual for use.

Jelly

METHOD

1. Pick the barberries.
2. Bruise them slightly and put them in a preserving pan with just enough cold water to cover them.
3. Boil up and simmer until the fruit is very soft.
4. Put into a jelly bag; (or into a cloth suspended across two kitchen chairs placed back to back) and let the juice

drip all night into a pan placed underneath.
5. Next day measure the juice, and weigh out one pound of preserving sugar to every pint of juice.
6. Put into preserving pan and, when the sugar is dissolved, boil up quickly for about 5 minutes or until it jellies when tested on a plate.

Blackberry, bilberry or whortleberry preserves and jam may be made in the same way.

Crab Apple Jelly

Mrs. Brewitt, 1927

INGREDIENTS: Crab apples, a panful; lemon 1 large one; and loaf sugar 1 lb. to every pint of liquid.

TIME: 20 minutes to half an hour.

METHOD

1. Rub the apples with a cloth; don't peel them, but they may be cut in halves to see if they are quite sound at the core.
2. Put in preserving pan. Cover with water.
3. Boil up and simmer till the fruit is a pulp.
4. Pour into a jelly bag and leave to drain till next day.

5. Measure the liquid.
6. Weigh out 1 lb. loaf sugar to every pint of liquid, add also the lemon juice.
7. Put it into the preserving pan.
8. When the sugar is dissolved, boil it up quickly until it becomes stiff, about 20 to 30 minutes.
9. Put into glasses and tie down.

Hawthorn Jelly

INGREDIENTS: Red haws, water, sugar.

METHOD

1. Pick and stalk the haws.
2. Wash them.
3. Put into a preserving pan with a breakfastcup (½ pint) water to every 1 lb. of fruit.
4. Simmer till soft.
5. Mash.
6. Strain
7. Make into a jelly as above.

N.B.—When making jelly let the juice drip all night; you will then get every drop there is.

Green Fig Jam

Green figs in England are as a rule associated with West Tarring, near Worthing, where there is a famous fig garden in which one particular tree is said to have been planted by Thomas à Becket. It is not so generally known that there are many fig trees at Rochester and in the neighbourhood. The fruit is very fine and ripens in September. Fresh green figs make an excellent jam or sweet pickle. They may also be preserved whole.

INGREDIENTS: Ripe green figs 1½ lb.; rhubarb 2 lb.; lemon 2 (rind and juice; preserving sugar 3½ lb. (Alternatively: 3 lb. fresh green figs; 1½ lb. preserving sugar; rind and juice of 2 lemons.)

METHOD

1. Wipe the figs and remove stems.
2. Cut them in quarters lengthwise.
3. Wipe, skin and cut up the rhubarb.
4. Put both into a double boiler or stoneware jar.
5. Cover with the sugar.
6. Don't add water.
7. Place the top of the double boiler or the stoneware jar in hot water which must be kept boiling.
8. And cook till the fruit is quite soft.
9. It may then be rubbed through a wire sieve.
10. Put into a preserving pan.
11. Wash the lemons.
12. Grate the rinds and squeeze the juice.
13. Add grated rind and juice to the fruit.
14. Stir well; and
15. Boil rapidly for 10. 15 or 20 minutes till sufficiently thick to jelly (test on plate).
16. Pot and tie down.

Gate House Tea Room, Rochester, Kent.

Pickled Green Figs

INGREDIENTS: 4 lb. barely ripe figs; strong salt and water; 2 lb. sugar; 1 pint vinegar; ½ oz. broken cinnamon and ½ oz. cloves.

METHOD

1. Wipe the figs, leave stems on.
2. Place in strong salt and water.
3. Next morning rinse well in fresh cold water.
4. Dry gently with soft muslin.
5. Pack closely together in glass jars.
6. Put the sugar and vinegar in a heavy British aluminium saucepan.
7. When dissolved add the spices tied up in muslin.
8. Bring to boil.
9. Simmer 5 minutes.
10. Remove spices, boil up the vinegar.
11. Pour boiling over the figs.
12. When cold put on glass lid and tie down closely with strong brown paper.

N.B.—No metal except heavy British aluminium must go near vinegar; use a wooden spoon. The fruit must be kept covered with the vinegar.

Gate House Tea Room, Rochester, Kent.

To Preserve Peaches in Brandy

Mrs. Ann Blencowe

INGREDIENTS: Peaches; clarified sugar; brandy.

METHOD

1. The peaches must be ripe, but not too ripe; you must put them into boiling water in order to peel them. Let them continue there until you find the skins will easily come off.
2. Skin them and fling instantly into fresh water.
3. Take them out of that and put them into clarified sugar and give them one boiling.
4. So let them cool in the sugar that it may soak well into them.
5. Then put them upon a sieve or a plate with holes.
6. Reboil the sugar until it will stick to your finger.
7. Repeat this method 3 times both in relation to the peaches and sugar.
8. After which the peaches so prepared must be put into glass bottles, which are to be filled after this manner: ½ brandy and ½ the syrup made by boiling the peaches in sugar and so they are to be kept for use.

Preserved Rhubarb

1875

This is best made in the autumn.

INGREDIENTS: Rhubarb 7 lb.; loaf sugar 7 lb.; lemons 2 juice and peel; bitter almonds blanched 2 oz.

TIME: to boil about ¾ hour.

METHOD

1. Peel and cut the rhubarb into 1 inch pieces.
2. Put over the fire till the juice is extracted.
3. Add the sugar; grated peel of the lemons and their juice; and
4. The almonds blanched and slightly powdered or bruised.
5. Boil it till it is a good rich colour and quite thick.
6. Pot as usual.

311

N.B.—If half rhubarb and half apple be used the jam will be firmer, and the grated rind and flesh (free from all white skin) of 4 oranges can be used instead of the lemons.

Sugar Boiling Degrees

Those who wish to boil sugar successfully should most certainly study the instructions in *Skuse's Complete Confectioner*.

But it is useful for many purposes to have a quick reference for the different degrees.

N.B.—Moisten 7 lb. sugar with 1 quart water. It must not boil till the sugar is all melted.

1. *Smooth* is reached when the thermometer registers 215–220°F. This degree is suitable for crystallizing and making gum goods and liqueurs.

2. *Thread:* 230–235°F.:

3. *Feather or blow:* 240–245°F.: suitable for candying fruits and for making fondants and creams.

4. *Ball or pearl:* 250–255°F.: suitable for coco-nut and other candies, coco-nut ice and grain sugars generally.

5. *Crack:* 310–315°F.: this is required for all kinds of drops, rocks, toffees and clear goodies.

N.B.—There is a very good article on sugar-boiling in the *Encyclopædia of Practical Cookery*, edited by Theodore Francis Garrett, and William A. Rawson (1890). There are in it also a number of clearly stated recipes for making confectionery of every kind.

Papers, Boxes and Packing

It may be useful to many people both in England and abroad to know that every kind of paper and cardboard equipment for packing sweets can be obtained (1931) from Mr. F. G. Kettle, 127 High Holborn, London, W.C.1. Thermometers for sugar-boiling, frying and baking can be obtained from Messrs. Short and Mason, aneroid makers, Walthamstow, England, or may be ordered through any household ironmongers or kitchen equipment stores. Ask for Taylor's Home Set.

To Candy Cowslips or any Flowers in Bunches

Mrs. Eales, Confectioner to King William III and Queen Anne

1. Steep gum arabic in water [N.B.—Be careful to buy the gum at the chemist's.—Ed.]

2. Wet the flowers with it.
3. Shake them in a cloth to remove superfluous moisture.
4. Dip them in fine sifted sugar.
5. Hang them on a string tied across a chimney that has a fire in it.
6. They must hang 2—3 days till the flowers are quite dry.

To Sugar all Sorts of Small Fruits

Another of Mrs. Eales' receipts

1. Beat the white of an egg.
2. Dip the fruit in it.
3. Let it lie on a cloth that it may not be wet.
4. Then take fine sifted sugar and roll the fruit in it till it is quite covered with sugar.
5. Lay it on a sieve in a stove, or before a fire to dry it well.
   N.B.—It will keep a week.

Honeycomb Cakes of Cowslips

Another of Mrs. Eales' receipts

1. Take about ½ lb. fine sugar.
2. Sift it through a hair sieve.
3. Wet it a little more than for a candy with a little water.
4. Boil it almost to candy height (245°F.)
5. Then put in the petals of the flowers.
6. Boil them a little in the candy or it will be too thin
7. Then put in card coffins.

[N.B.—To-day we should pour the candy into little tin moulds first brushed over with a little almond oil.—ED.]

Caramel Oranges

This is from the *Receipt Book of Mrs. Ann Blencowe*, daughter of John Wallace, mathematician and cryptographer 1616—1703. She was born in 1656. In 1675 she married John Blencowe, who represented Brackley, Northants, in Parliament from 1690—1695, and was raised to the Bench in 1696. This receipt book has remained in the possession of her descendants; and a limited edition was published in 1925 by Guy Chapman, Adelphi, London.

These caramel oranges resemble exactly the same dainties that were recently and still are served in London at all smart dinners.

Ann Blencowe's Receipt

INGREDIENTS: Oranges; fine sugar ½ lb.

METHOD

1. Peel the oranges; split them in quarters; do not break the skin.
2. Lay the quarters before the fire, and turn them until the skin is very dry.
3. Take ½ lb. sugar sifted through a hair sieve.
4. Put in a brass or silver pan.
5. Set it over a slow fire, keep stirring till the sugar is melted and looks pretty clear.
6. Then take it off the fire and put in the orange quarters.
7. Put in one at a time; take out again as fast as you can with a silver spoon; and
8. Lay them on a dish which you must butter, or the fruit will not come off. The sugar will keep hot enough to do any plateful.

N.B.—1. You may do roasted chestnuts the same way, or any fruit in summer; but first lay the fruit before the fire or in a stove, to make the skin tough. If any wet comes out the sugar will not stick to it. It must be done just when you use it: it will not keep.

2. This rule-of-thumb method is all very well for the experienced cook, but in these days we have sugar thermometers and can cook the sugar to the exact degree required for all this sort of thing. It should be boiled to the crack 310°—315°F.

3. It is much better to oil the tins or dishes, in which caramel sweets are placed to dry, with almond oil instead of butter. The almond oil can be bought at the chemist's and is not expensive.

Toffee Apples

These are a favourite fairing and delight children immensely. Take the flower bud off the apple without breaking the skin, also the stalk, and put a small wooden skewer about two or three inches long where the stalk was, then dip the apple into the caramel as above and let it dry.

The skewer, of course, is held in the hand, whilst the toffee apple is being eaten; but it is useful also when drying the toffee, because the skewers can be stuck in a bowl of heavy sugar and the apples can hang over the side to dry.

These apples are sometimes called 'treacle apples,' because the caramel soon melts when held by little hot hands, and becomes treacle-like.

Caraway Seeds and Other Comfits

Charles Elmé Francatelli, 1862

'The manufacture of comfits embraces various very complicated processes. It forms in itself a special branch of confectionery, and this is so true that there exist in this country, and also on the Continent, not only distinct establishments, but even particular towns where comfits are manufactured wholesale. For instance I will name Bristol in England and Verdun in France.'

UTENSILS REQUIRED

1. An untinned copper comfit pan: it should have a handle over the top and one in front of the pan. 2. A chafing dish or portable gas stove to place underneath. 3. A beading funnel with a pointed wooden stick adapted to stop the upper hole of the funnel (this is called a spigot). 4. This funnel is used to pearl comfits, or in other words to coat kernels, aromatic seeds or certain whole spices of which comfits are usually made.

Almond Comfits

INGREDIENTS: Gum arabic 6 oz.; loaf sugar $3\frac{1}{2}$ lb, Jordan almonds 1 lb. for this amount of sugar.

METHOD

1. Scald, skin, wash, wipe, and thoroughly dry the almonds in the oven.
2. Clarify the sugar.
3. Dissolve the gum arabic in hot water, but not too thin.
4. The chafing dish under the comfit pan must contain live embers of charcoal if you are not using a gas stove.
5. The syrup, quite hot but not boiling must be kept near, at a slow heat.
6. Put a sixth part of the syrup into a sugar pan with a sixth part of the dissolved gum.
7. Boil this to the thread degree (230°–235° F.).
8. Then swing the comfit pan over the chafing dish, put the almonds (or caraway seeds) in it, stir them round until they are hot.
9. Add a tablespoonful of the gum, stir all together until the gum has dried on the almonds.
10. Add another spoonful of gum and shake or dredge in a little starch powder to give them another coating.
11. Next use the coating funnel to give a coating with the boiled sugar and gum.
12. This done, the almonds must be detached and separated from each other by shaking the pan to and fro with the front handle.
13. When perfectly dry, turn them out upon a cane sieve and riddle off any fragments of sugar.
14. Clean out the comfit pan and repeat the charges of gum, starch, and sugar five times more, cleaning out the pan each time.
15. Put the comfits to dry in slow heat till next day.
16. Almond comfits require six more coatings in the manner described, that is to say twelve in all.
17. But caraway comfits can be made with only six coatings.

315

TO COLOUR COMFITS

The colour must be added in a liquid or powdered state when giving the two last charges or coatings.

TO FLAVOUR COMFITS

A few drops of any kind of essence such as vanilla, orange, lemon, rose, cinnamon, etc., may be added to the syrup.

N.B.—Comfits may be made of almonds, pistachio kernels, filberts, cherry kernels, caraway seeds, coriander seed, cinnamon, angelica, aniseed.

Caraway Comfits

To succeed with any degree of perfection in making caraway seed comfits it is safest to make not more than a tablespoonful of seeds at a time; these must first be heated in the comfit pan, by stirring them over the chafing dish or portable gas stove with a wooden spoon and then giving the charges of sugar and gum as directed.

About six coatings will be sufficient to render them of the size of an oval pea; called in Cornwall 'lambs' tails.'

N.B.—The method for making almond comfits, or sugar coated almonds, and caraway seed comfits is the same: but of course less sugar, etc., will be required for the latter.

Bull's Eyes

Garrett's Encyclopædia of Practical Cookery, 1890

INGREDIENTS: Moist sugar 7 lb; water 1 quart; oil of peppermint sufficient to flavour.

METHOD

1. Put the sugar and water into a pan and boil to the *crack* (310°–315° F.).
2. Remove the boiler from the fire.
3. Stir in slowly enough oil of peppermint to flavour.
4. Pour the whole out on to an oiled slab.
5. Cut off a piece from the mass.
6. Pull it over a hook fastened in the wall till it becomes a light brown.
7. Pull it into lengths about ½ inch in thickness.
8. Lay them on the remainder of the sugar, then fold the whole over and commence working, slightly rolling it and bringing the two ends together each time.
9. Run it through a ball machine or form it into ball shapes, and when quite cold bottle or pack away in tins.

N.B.—The slab must be kept warm during the operation of working, should a slab not be at hand the sugar mass may be turned out on to a board, where it will keep warm for a long time without additional heat.

Barley Sugar

This is Francatelli's recipe, 1862

INGREDIENTS: Loaf sugar 1 lb.; water 3 gills; lemon 1; essence of lemon a few drops; oil of almonds; a marble slab; a sugar boiling thermometer.

METHOD

1. Put the sugar with the water on the fire to boil.
2. Skim it; and
3. Boil it to the *crack* degree (310°–315° F.).
4. Add the juice of the lemon and a few drops of lemon essence.
5. Give the sugar a boil.
6. Cool the bottom of the pan in cold water.
7. When the first heat has subsided, pour the sugar on a marble slab very slightly smeared with oil of almonds.
8. As the sugar spreads, lift it up all round in a heap with a knife.
9. As soon as it has cooled a little, cut off portions the size of a finger.
10. Roll them in the form of round sticks.
11. Twist them so as to resemble cords.
12. Place them on a baking sheet slightly oiled, to become cold and stiff.

N.B.—Keep in well-stoppered glass jars in a dry place.

Toffee

Mrs. Brewitt, 1927

I

INGREDIENTS: Brown sugar 1 lb.; butter ¼ lb.; golden syrup ½ lb.; lemon essence, and a spot of vinegar.

METHOD

1. Boil till it sets hard when dropped in water.
2. Pour in a greased tin.

[N.B.—It is much better to brush the tins over with oil of almonds instead of butter.—ED.]

II

INGREDIENTS: Nestlé's milk 1 tin; Demerara sugar 1 breakfastcupful; golden syrup 1 tablespoonful; butter 1 oz.

TIME: ½ hour.

METHOD

1. Put sugar, butter and syrup in saucepan over fire to melt.
2. When melted add the milk.
3. Stir till it boils.
4. Boil 20 minutes.
5. Pour on tins, brushed with almond oil which can be bought at the chemist's.

Burnt Almonds

1826

These are made with unblanched almonds.

1. Rub them well in a cloth to clean them properly.
2. Weigh out an equal weight of powdered loaf sugar.
3. Put the sugar and almonds in a frying-pan with a very little water.
4. Keep them on the fire, stirring continually, until they crackle and fly about, and the sugar begins to colour.
5. Stir them about gently to gather the sugar, and leave them in the pan to dry about two hours on the stove or any moderate heat.

'Pontack's'

'In Plantagenet days,' says Mr. Maurice Healy, K.C., 'there were only six houses in the City of London licensed for the sale of Bordeaux wine. One of these was in Lombard Street. It was a hostelry known before the Great Fire as the "White Bear," or "Great Bear." It was at this house that Pepys first drank Haut Brion (which he called Ho Bryon). . . After the Great Fire, Monsieur de Pontac who owned the Château Haut Brion, set up an eating house on the site of this hostelry, which under the name of Pontack's became the most famous eating house of Stuart days.'

V

LOCAL AND NATIONAL SPECIALITIES

Flummery

1615-1895

As flummery and frumenty are sometimes confused (even by the learned who should know better) it is necessary to introduce this old English dish with a few words of explanation.

Gervase Markham writing on 'Skill in Oatmeal,' in 1615, says: 'lastly from this small oatmeal, by oft steeping it in water and cleansing it and then boyling it to a thick and stiff jelly, is made that excellent dish of meat which is so esteemed of in the west parts of this kingdom, which they call in Cheshire and Lancashire Flamery or flumery. . . .

'Some eat it with honey which is reputed the best sauce; some with wine, either sack, claret, or white; some with strong beer or strong ale, and some with milk.'

And Dr. Thudichum, one of our greatest authorities on the history, science and practical import of the art of cookery says:

'Flummery signifies an *acid* jelly made originally from the husks of oats; in Scotland it is known as Sowans. The name is now applied to any starch jelly made from cereals, wheat flour, rice, ground rice, sago, potatoes, etc., the liquid used to develop it being either fruit juice, milk, or even cream.'

RECIPES

Oatmeal Flummery

1823

1. Steep in cold water, for a day and a night, three large handfuls of very fine oatmeal.
2. Add as much more water, and let it stand the same time.
3. Strain it through a fine hair sieve, and boil it till it is as thick as hasty pudding, stirring it well all the time.

4. When first strained, put to it one large spoonful of white sugar, and two of orange flower water.

5. Pour it into shallow dishes, and serve it up with wine; or it will be very good with cream and sugar.

Rice Flummery

1826

1. Boil with a pint of new milk, a bit of lemon-peel, and cinnamon; sweeten it.

2. Mix with a little cold milk 3 oz. ground rice.

3. Stir it into the boiling milk, flavour with almonds, add a bit of butter.

4. Boil till it thickens (stirring all the time) and leaves the sides of the saucepan.

5. Pour it into a mould and leave till cold.

6. Turn out and serve with cream or custard, or stewed fruit, or any kind of sweet preserve.

CORNWALL

A Cornish Fairing

Miss M. W. Rogers (Marazion) writes: A proper and complete fairing included:

> Gingerbread biscuits,
> Caraway comfits (lambs' tails),
> Candied sticks of Angelica and
> Almond comfits,
> Macaroons.

The last are quite different from the English variety, much thicker and softer and crumbly, not tough. They are very good and can still be obtained from Messrs. Treleavor of Truro, and Hasselyn of St. Ives.

The Cornish Pasty and the Hoggan

Miss M. W. Rogers (Marazion) writes: The Cornish pasty is one of the few forms of English cookery that conserves all the value of the food. It contains meat, turnip and onion, with the pastry joined at the side. The *hoggan* is made without potato, and joined across the top.

Are They Phœnician Delicacies?

Mr. John Pollock says 'In my youth every knowing man and boy put a meat pasty in his pocket when going for a day's tramp or hunt on Dartmoor. But what of the form of the pasty? Why this; it was not unlike two Phrygian caps put together at their base. In other words it was like a quarter moon with somewhat blunted horns—in fact the emblem of Astarte, goddess of the Phœnicians.'

RECIPE

Cornish Pasty

St. Ives, 1922

INGREDIENTS: Flour ½ lb; lard or dripping 3 oz.; a pinch of salt; water to make a fine dough about 1 gill (2½ liquid ounces). Uncooked beef steak ½ lb.; uncooked calf's liver ¼ lb.; uncooked potatoes 2; onion 1 large one; turnip 1 medium sized one; carrot 1 large or 2 small ones. Pepper and salt.

TIME: to bake 1 hour; at first in a good oven to raise the pastry and then in a very moderate oven to cook the meat and vegetables.

METHOD

1. Roll out the dough fairly thin, cut in squares.
2. Chop the steak and liver finely, mix together and season.
3. Peel or scrape, and slice the potato, onion, turnip and carrot. Mix and season the vegetables.
4. Put a layer of vegetables on half of each square of pastry and some of the chopped meat on top.
5. Brush the edges of the pastry with white of egg, fold the plain half over the meat and pinch the edges well together.
6. Bake as above.

N.B.—It is important to close the edges neatly and closely, so that no steam escapes, and to use uncooked meat and vegetables. The contents cook in their own juices, so after the first few minutes require a very moderate oven. The above amounts make 2 large or 3 medium-sized pasties.

CUMBERLAND

Burnet Wine

A Cumberland Recipe

INGREDIENTS: Burnet heads 4 pints; water 1 gallon; sugar 3 lb.; raisins 2 lb.; yeast 1 oz.

TIME: to boil 20 minutes; to infuse 2 weeks. To be kept one year before using all told.

METHOD

1. Boil the heads in water for 20 minutes.
2. Strain.
3. Add sugar and raisins.
4. When cool, but not cold, add yeast creamed and dissolved in a little of the wine.
5. Let it stand 2 weeks.
6. Remove scum as it rises.
7. Strain into stone jar.
8. When finished working, close down tightly.
9. At the end of 3 months draw off and bottle.

Clipping-time Pudding

Mrs. Wivell of the Keswick Hotel and Armathwaite Hall

'In England on the day they began to shear their sheep a plentiful dinner was provided for the shearers and their friends. A table also, if weather permitted, was spread in the open air for the young people and children. The washing and shearing of sheep is attended with great mirth and festivity.' (Sir Henry Ellis, Principal Librarian of the British Museum, 1841.)

Tusser in his *Five Hundred Points of Husbandry*, under 'The Ploughman's Feast Days,' has the following lines: —

SHEEP SHEARING

'Wife, make us a dinner, spare flesh, neither corne,
Make wafers and cakes for our sheepe must be shorne;
At Sheepe shearing, neighbours none other things crave,
But good cheere and welcome like neighbours to have.'

The 'cakes' here mentioned were curd cheesecakes which are one of our great national delicacies. The 'Clipping Time Pudding' of Cumberland which Mrs. Wivell describes, is famous. It is a rich rice pudding: and every farmer's wife has her own cherished recipe which resembles more or less closely the following early eighteenth century 'receipt.'

A Fine Rice Pudding

Mrs. Martha Bradley, Bath, 1745

1. Clean some rice, blanch it in water and then set it in milk proportionate to the quantity of the rice; put in some salt at first, and when it is half boiled break in a large stick of cinnamon, let it boil some time longer with this, and then add some fine sugar powdered.
2. When the rice is boiled tender, and the whole is thick, take it from the fire.

3. Pick and wash half a pound of currants, and stone the same quantity of the finest raisins of the sun.

4. Beat up 6 eggs using only three of the whites, mix them with the rice and milk, and then put in the currants and raisins and stir all well together.

5. Break a pair of good beef marrow bones, take out the marrow, cut it into small square pieces, and stir them in; then put it into a dish, and send it to be baked. This is very delicate and fit to appear on any table.

N.B.—Suet may be used instead of marrow, but it is far inferior.

Rum Butter

The recipe for this Cumberland delicacy was given in 1929 by Mrs. Irwin, landlady of the Pennington Arms Hotel, Ravenglass, Cumberland, one of the most famous cooks in a county noted for its good cooking and notable cooks. Mrs. Irwin exhibited Rum Butter, Cumberland shortbread, and currant pasty at the First Exhibition of the English Folk Cookery Association (*see* p. 348) and here is her recipe. Rum butter makes a delicious filling for layer cakes or Tunbridge Wafers; and is quite the best sauce for Christmas and similar plum puddings, resembling in effect the equally famous American Hard Sauce.

INGREDIENTS: Sugar 2 lb.; fresh butter 1 lb.; rum 2 small glasses; nutmeg and cinnamon to taste.

[N.B.—The best sugar for the purpose is a pale soft Barbados, not the dark coarse stuff which is sometimes sold as Barbados. In London if one asks for Barbados sugar one sometimes gets one and sometimes the other, and I have not yet had time to find out *which* is really Barbados sugar properly so called. I shall be pleased if anyone will send this information. But I have tried both varieties, and the dark variety is far from nice for making rum butter, it is too strong and coarse. The pale soft sugar rather like soft fine sand is excellent; failing this a soft castor sugar may be used.—Ed.]

METHOD

1. Beat the butter up with your hand.
2. Beat in the sugar.
3. Then the rum, nutmeg and cinnamon.
4. Put into one large basin and smooth the top.
5. It must on no account have a rough and rocky appearance.

Old Cumberland Custom

Rum butter is sometimes called 'Sweet Butter'; a bowl of it is always prepared before the coming of a baby; it is offered to visitors and there are many curious folk customs connected with it, one of the most amusing being that 'a small piece is put in the baby's mouth as its first taste of earthly food.'

DERBYSHIRE

Bakewell Tarts

An early nineteenth century recipe still used in Derbyshire

INGREDIENTS: Eggs (4 yolks and 3 whites); castor sugar ¼ lb.; butter ¼ lb.; some rich pastry.

METHOD

1. Line some patty pans with rich pastry.
2. Cover the bottom with a thin layer of strawberry jam; now make the following mixture.
3. Put the butter into a brass or aluminium pan.
4. Let it boil up.
5. Skim it carefully.
6. While boiling stir into it the eggs and sugar beaten up together; again beat all well together.
7. Place a thick layer of this mixture on the strawberry jam.
8. And bake until it is delicately brown.

NORTH DEVON

Barnstaple Fair Gingerbread

Mrs. Maude S. Seldon writes from Braunton, N. Devon: —

'At Barnstaple (six miles from here) where I lived all my married life there is an annual three days' Fair, held in the middle of September with an opening ceremony in the Guild Hall, at which hospitality is freely dispensed in the shape of specially prepared spiced ale, toast soaked in the ale, cheese and the usual Fairing sweets and gingerbread. I enclose a recipe for the gingerbread, but the spiced ale is made from a very old recipe which is closely guarded and only handed from one burgh official to another and is not available to the public. Any member of the public is welcomed at this old ceremony, and can taste the spiced ale, and it is worth attending one of these Fair openings — not for the ale — but to see the old borough silver which hardly ever sees daylight except on that day.'

RECIPE

INGREDIENTS: Treacle 6 oz.; flour 6 oz.; butter 5 oz.; sugar 6 oz.; ground ginger 1 teaspoonful.

TIME: 30 minutes in a very slow oven.

METHOD

1. Warm the treacle.
2. Rub the butter into the flour.
3. Add the sugar and ginger.
4. Mix well.
5. Blend with the warm treacle.
6. Drop small pieces on a well-greased tin.
7. Bake at once in a very slow oven.

Revel Buns

(As made by Sam Hook (Colebrooke, N. Devon), a baker living there about 1824). Mrs. I. M. Pope who sends this recipe says the buns were celebrated in the neighbourhood, and the 'receipt' has been copied from S. Hook's own book now in the possession of a lady living in Copplestone, Devon. A revel was an anniversary feast to celebrate the dedication of a church; called a 'wake,' in the North of England.

INGREDIENTS: Flour 1 bushel; butter 16 lb.; cream 7 quarts and a pint; brown sugar 3 quarters; saffron 1 oz; milk 3 pints; eggs 36; currants 1 lb.; nutmeg 1; lastly crushed sugar 1 quart to sprinkle over them.

[N.B.—I think this must be crushed cooked sugar such as one gets out of candied peel; it is very good crushed and sprinkled over Bath buns.—Ed.]

METHOD

None is given, S. Hook being a qualified baker did not need to note method and his ingredients which are for a large quantity of buns are simply given here for other qualified bakers and cooks who may like to make them for sale, in which case they would probably sprinkle the buns with the sugar nibs, supplied for making Bath buns.

DEVONSHIRE

Devonshire Junket

Miss M. M. Mallock, Wincanton, Somersetshire

This is quoted from Miss Mallock's cookery book *Economics of Modern Cookery*. Miss Acton writing in 1845 gives similar information, but in her day bottled rennet was unobtainable and the inner lining of a calf's stomach was used. Writing in 1896 Miss Mallock says: —

According to the more old-fashioned Devonshire practice, junket is made by preference in a china bowl and is usually covered thickly with scalded cream and sprinkled with cinnamon or nutmeg.

Formerly a strip of the inner lining of a calf's stomach, previously cleaned and salted, was laid in the milk to curdle it, and in farmhouses and out-of-the-way country places this is often done still; but the 'essence of rennet' which is sold ready prepared in bottles, is now more commonly used. Thus made, for a moderate-sized junket we shall require:

INGREDIENTS: Milk 1 pint; sugar to sweeten; rum or brandy (to flavour, if liked) 1 or 2 tablespoonfuls; essence of rennet, 1 large teaspoonful.

METHOD

1. The temperature of the milk when the rennet is added to it is the first thing to attend to. This must be 'milk' or 'blood' warm (about 98°F.).
2. It must be sweetened and flavoured *before* the admixture of the rennet, while *after* this it must remain absolutely undisturbed till firmly set.
3. It will set best in a room of ordinary temperature.

'Unless there should be any fault in the rennet, failure to set may be taken as a sign that the milk has been used too cold, while should it have been too hot, a broken curdled appearance will be the result. When well made, junket should cut into smooth shiny slices like jelly

'If while otherwise good, it has a noticeably salt taste, this will be owing to too much rennet having been put in it.

'In the absence of scalded cream to cover it, a spoonful or two of raw cream poured over the top when set is an improvement; and the surface should then be very lightly dusted with cinnamon powder and castor sugar mixed in equal parts.

'Tightly corked and kept in a cold place, essence of rennet will remain good some time; but the fresher it is the better, and small-sized bottles, therefore, are best to get.

'Junket is not a thing that improves by keeping after being once cut, as the whey then separates and runs out of it. Thus if the quantity likely to be eaten is doubtful, it is a good plan after mixing the milk with the rennet to pour it at once to set in little cups or glasses.'

TO SUM UP

1. Mix the flavouring and sugar in the bowl.
2. Pour on them the milk heated to about 98°F.
3. Add the rennet.
4. Stir in well.
5. Then let it remain *undisturbed* until set.

DEVONSHIRE, SOMERSET AND WALES

Laver

We English folk don't know our wealth — we used to be called a nation of shopkeepers but we are not nearly so good at discovering marketable products as the French, and nothing like as good at marketing and advertising those we do know.

Laver is a case in point. It is an edible seaweed that abounds on our Western coast. Before the invasion of French chefs in 1848 it was common enough in London; Mr. Aeneas Dallas of *The Times* in the '70's says:

'The French know it not — and for that matter indeed they are far behind England and Holland in their knowledge of all marine products. When French cookery took form there were no railways and the great metropolis of cooks was too far away from the seaboard to enable them to do justice to sea fish. . . .

'Laver — the true purple laver — and other seaweeds are wonderfully nutritious, and may be had for the gathering. According to recent scientific research laver is rich in iodine. If we had had the business acumen of the French we should have made it as famous as truffles of Perigeux. There is a charm about it,' continues Mr. Dallas,' which ought to have kept it in the front as one of the distinctions of English cookery.'

It is not too late, for, although neglected for years, it is once more on sale in London, and indeed has always been served in a few exclusive clubs and private families. It is prepared at the place where it is gathered, Braunton in particular is one, and it was exported as a pickle in earthen pots from Watchet in Somersetshire in 1797.

It is first steeped in water to reduce its saltness, and a little carbonate of soda is added to remove any bitterness. It is then stewed in fresh water till it is as tender as spinach. It is then ready to be made up and served in the following ways, and it is in this preliminary form it can now be bought in London.

AS AN ADJUNCT TO ROAST MUTTON

1 lb. of the prepared laver is put into a heavy aluminium or nickel stewpan with 3 oz. of fresh butter and stirred over a quick heat with a wooden fork, spoon or spatula. A little lemon juice may be squeezed into it. When Seville oranges are obtainable the juice of one is delicious with it; try also tangerine. It must be served boiling hot over a spirit lamp or hot-water dish. A chafing-dish is excellent for the purpose as it provides both.

AS A BREAKFAST DISH

It may be blended with cooked oatmeal, made into cakes and fried in fat as a breakfast dish in the same manner as potatoes. It is so made up and sold for this purpose by the coast-dwellers in Wales.

AS A SALAD

The prepared laver is very good eaten cold as a salad with oil, vinegar and pepper and a dash of sugar.

GLOUCESTERSHIRE

Gloucester's Royal Pie

'A Lamprey Pie embellished with gilded ornaments was sent annually as a Christmas present from the Corporation of Gloucester to the Sovereign of the realm down to the time of Corporation reform in 1830.

The custom was revived in 1893 by the Mayor of Gloucester, Mr. John A. Matthews, at his own cost.

The pie was made by Mr. John A. Fisher, of Tudor House, Gloucester, and one was sent to Queen Victoria in her Diamond Jubilee year; it weighed 20 lb., was oval in shape, the crust garnished with truffles and crayfish on gold skewers, and aspic jelly; on the top was a gold crown and sceptre and at the base were four gold lions.

The gold skewer heads were in the form of crowns and on either side of the pie was a white silk banner, on one of which was the Gloucester coat of arms and on the other two lampreys entwined with the inscription beneath 'Royal Lamprey Pie, Gloucester's Ancient Custom from the Norman Period to the Victorian Era.'

[N.B.—These particulars were given to me by Mr. Smith, head of the kitchens of the old Plough Inn at Cheltenham in 1928. When an apprentice he helped to make this pie, and he told me of a pamphlet Mr. Fisher had written on its history, which visitors may see in the Gloucester Public Library.—ED.]

Gingerbread Husbands

These were Hampshire fairings: they represented figures of men made of gingerbread pressed into wooden moulds, then baked and gilded. Just imagine a child's joy in the gingerbread husband, and her grief when the gilt wore off! They were the consistency of crisp Parliament gingerbread.

KENT

Flead Cakes

A Kent Delicacy

'In days gone by,' writes a friend who was the daughter of a farmer in the Weald of Kent, 'cakes and scones would be made from buttermilk, and the flour for them and the bread would be made from the farmer's own wheat sent to the mill to be ground. Bacon, ham, and sausages were all cured and made at my old home. Twice a year a pig would be killed, in March and October, cured and salted for home consumption. Lard also was put down; jams, fruit jellies and pickles were made. We were,' she adds, 'particularly noted for our pickled walnuts.'

This is her recipe for Flead Cakes:—

INGREDIENTS: Flead 1 lb. (this is called flare by London butchers); household flour 1½ lb.; a little salt; water to mix.

METHOD

1. Free the flead from all the skin and veiny pieces; cut in thin flakes.
2. Place the flour in a bowl, add the flakes of flead and the salt, mix all together.
3. Make into a stiff dough with a small quantity of cold water.
4. Turn on to a floured pastry board.
5. Take one end of a rolling-pin and then just beat as hard as you can, turning over as required, but handling as little as possible, and working quickly.
6. Let it rest about 15 minutes, then repeat; do this three times.
7. After the third beating and rest, roll out to about an inch in thickness, cut in any shape fancied and bake in a quick oven.
8. Have ready some kitchen paper 'rucked up' on a large dish, then turn cakes on to this, allow to cool in the warm kitchen. Then store in tins. They will keep a long time.

SECRETS OF SUCCESS

1. Use nice thick flead and allow it to hang as long as it will keep fresh and sweet.

2. Take plenty of time in making and bang well. 'My mother used to say,' adds the sender of this recipe, 'that the only time we might lose our tempers was when we were making flead cakes.'

[As a tiny girl of four in 1867 I remember helping my mother to make these cakes, my share being to bang a piece of dough with a wooden hoop stick. It was a pure joy. She was the daughter of a Weald of Kent yeoman who grew hops, but at that time we were living in London within 4 miles of Bow Bells.—ED.]

3. The flead and flour must be thoroughly incorporated, but on on account must the cakes be rolled out more than once. This is important, as rolling out makes them too much like pie-crust. A properly made flead cake should be different from that, eating light and crisp. It should rise to twice the height it was before making. Care should be taken also not to open the oven door too soon; they are rather apt to go down a bit if cold air invades the oven during the raising process.

N.B.—'It is a very funny thing,' continues this lady, 'but it is not everyone who can make these delicious cakes; even good cooks fail miserably sometimes, and give up trying.' I never can understand why, unless the hand is too hot. Always as far as possible, keep the hands cool, and touch the paste as little as possible.

KENT, HAMPSHIRE, WILTSHIRE

Wafers

These appear to be as much a South Country dainty as girdle scones and pikelets are of the North of England. They were made for Mothering Sunday and Mrs. Baverstock of Horseshoe Cottage, Chilbolton, Stockbridge, Hants, still makes them and exhibited some at the first Exhibition of the English Folk Cookery Association in 1931. They require wafering irons or tongs for making them and Mrs. Baverstock lent her tongs or irons to be exhibited at the Winchester Museum in 1930. The Victoria and Albert Museum also has specimens of wafering and goffer tongs or irons. Mid-Lent or Mothering Sunday was sometimes knows as Wafering Sunday.

And here is a recipe dated 1769: —

1. Take 2 tablespoonfuls of cream; 2 tablespoonfuls of sugar, the same of flour, and one tablespoonful of orange flower water.

2. Beat them well together for half an hour (here the modern electric whisk would come in useful).

3. Make your wafer tongs hot; pour a little of your butter in to cover your irons.

4. Bake them on a stove fire, and as soon as they are baked roll them round a stick like a spigot. As soon as they are cold they will be very crisp. They can of course be kept flat.

5. They are proper for tea, or to put upon a salver to eat with jellies.

Romary's Tunbridge Wells Wafers

Anyone who has neither the time nor facilities for making wafers can buy them from Romary, Tunbridge Wells, Kent, England. This firm was established in 1862 and makes these delicate and delicious English wafers from old English recipes. They have lately acquired Freeman's Norwich Hollow Biscuits. This firm has made biscuits 'By Appointment' for Queen Victoria, King Edward VII, and now makes them for His Majesty King George V.

There are Ginger wafers, Royal wafers, water biscuits, Old English stone-ground wheaten wafer biscuits, etc., all unique and delicate eating, quite different from the ordinary biscuits however good; and distinctively English.

LANCASHIRE

An Eighteenth Century Bride Cake

Manchester, 1769

This is Mrs. Raffald's recipe. Mrs. Raffald was one of our most famous English cooks. She was a Miss Whittaker of Doncaster, and trained as a housekeeper; 'but finding servants generally so ignorant in dressing meat, and a good cook so hard to be met with, put me upon studying the art of cookery more than perhaps I otherwise should have done. Always endeavouring to join economy with neatness and elegance, being sensible what valuable qualifications these are in a housekeeper or cook; for what use is their skill if they put their master or lady to an immoderate expense in dressing a dinner for a small company, when at the same time a prudent manager would have dressed twice the number of dishes for a much greater Company, at half the cost?' Her last situation was as housekeeper to the Lady Elizabeth Warburton of Arley Hall, Cheshire, eldest daughter to the 11th Earl of Derby. Miss Whittaker married the head gardener, Mr. Raffald, and went with her husband to live in Manchester where he joined his brothers in a florist and seedsman's stall in the market place whilst his wife took a confectioner's shop at the corner of Old Exchange Alley. There she received pupils, the daughters of the principal local families who paid well for the privilege. They worked in the kitchen of the establishment and received lessons in cooking and confectionery, etc. They were taught how to pluck poultry, skin hares, etc., no less than to cook them afterwards, and to carve them when placed on the table. These particulars are taken from the *Manchester Collectanea*, vol. ii, Chetham Society, 1862, and the editor says: 'The influence she exercised in her own day, in securing attention to the duties of a good housewife, and in including the culinary art amongst the homely and useful accomplishments of the young ladies of an extensive district, it is scarcely possible to overrate.' She was an enterprising woman at any rate. She superintended arrangements for public and private dinners and was celebrated for these achievements. She took the Bull's Head Inn in the market place and ran that so well that the officers of the regiments stationed at Manchester had their mess table at the Bull's Head, and on her removal to the King's Head, Salford, the officers' mess removed thither also.

The shop at the corner of Old Exchange Alley is no more, but the Bull's Head Inn in the Market Place was still there in 1930. In addition to all her domestic activities, she lent aid in money and influence to public projects with such effect, that it is said Manchester without her would have been left without a newspaper. Her biographer adds :—'If therefore the city shows its appreciation of female merit by erecting a statue to commemorate it, the first claim is undoubtedly that of Elizabeth Raffald. Her cookery book appeared in 1769 and young married ladies would say, "I have got Mrs. Raffald's book, and I would not be without it for a good deal. I don't think I could have got up a dinner without it." '

[The presentation copy signed by Mrs. Raffald given to Lady Elizabeth Warburton's daughter is still to-day a valued possession of a descendant. The popularity of the following recipe may be gauged by the fact that I have found it in three manuscript recipe books of the period and later, into which it has been copied by notable housewives and cooks in Leicestershire, Somersetshire, and Berkshire.—Ed.]

Recipe for the Bride Cake

This was given by the Misses Hope, Henfryn, Reading

INGREDIENTS: Fine flour, well dried, 4 lb.; fresh butter 4 lb; loaf sugar, pounded and sifted fine, 2 lb.; mace ¼ oz.; nutmeg ½ oz.; eggs 32; currants 4 lb. (picked and dried well); sweet almonds, blanched and cut lengthwise very thin 1 lb.; citron 1 lb. shredded; candied orange peel 1 lb shredded; candied lemon peel 1 lb. shredded; brandy ½ pint (8 liquid oz.).

TIME: It will take 3 hours baking [in one of the old-fashioned brick ovens. Personally I should think it would take much longer. One made of one-fourth the quantity took 2 hours to bake in a moderate oven.—ED.]

METHOD

1. Work the butter with your hand to a cream.
2. Beat in your sugar for 15 minutes.
3. Beat the whites of the eggs to a very strong froth.
4. Mix them with your sugar and butter.
5. Beat the yolks for 30 minutes at least.
6. Add them.
7. Then put in your flour, mace and nutmeg, keep beating it well until your oven is ready.
8. Put in your brandy.
9. Beat currants and almonds lightly in.
10. Tie three sheets of buttered paper round the bottom of your hoop to keep the mixture from running out.
11. Put in a layer of cake mixture and a layer of half the candied peel, then another layer of cake and a layer of the rest of the candied peel.
12. Cover with the remainder of the cake mixture.
13. After it has risen and coloured, cover it with paper.
14. It will take three hours baking.

TO MAKE ALMOND ICING FOR BRIDE CAKE

INGREDIENTS: Jordan almonds 1 lb; rose-water; eggs, the whites of 3; loaf sugar, beat fine, 1 lb.

METHOD

1. Beat the almonds very fine with a little rose-water to prevent oiling.
2. Whisk the whites of the eggs to a strong froth.
3. Mix your almonds with the eggs lightly together.
4. Add the fine sugar by degrees.
5. When your cake is done enough, take it out and lay your almond icing on and then put it in to brown.

TO MAKE SUGAR ICING FOR BRIDE CAKE

INGREDIENTS: Double-refined sugar 2 lb.; fine starch 2 oz.; eggs, the white of 5.

TIME: to beat ½ an hour after all the ingredients are blended.

METHOD

1. Beat the sugar with the starch in a pestle and mortar.
2. Sift it through a gauze sieve.
3. Beat the whites of the 5 eggs with a knife upon a pewter dish for half an hour.
4. Beat in your sugar a little at a time, or it will make the eggs fall and will not be so good a colour.
5. When you have put in all your sugar, beat it half an hour longer.
6. Then lay it on your almond icing and spread it even with a knife.
7. If it be put on at the time the cake is taken out of the oven, it will be hard by the time the cake is cold.

EDITORIAL NOTE

As an experiment, the above cake mixture was made in the kitchen of the English Folk Cookery Association, the method being followed exactly, modern ingredients being used; for example, ground almonds replaced the whole almonds for the almond icing; castor sugar, the beaten loaf sugar, and modern icing sugar for double-refined loaf and starch. Only a fourth of the quantities given was used. This made a cake weighing five pounds three ounces and cost without labour and fuel 5s. 6½d. It was baked in a slab cake tin measuring 11½ ins. by 9 ins. and 2½ ins. in depth. The amount of cake used covered the tin to the depth of 1½ ins. and rose during baking to the height of 2¼ ins. This cut up into 48 pieces about ¾ inch in thickness by 3 inches in length. It proved an excellent cake, flavour good, texture fine and delicate. The beating of the egg yolks for half an hour made them thick, creamy, and light. The labour would have been so arm-aching that we promptly obtained a small electric gadget that would do the beating for us. It is an American invention; nothing of the kind is yet made in England. It appears that in the eighteenth century wedding cakes were not decorated, but were left plain white. If any reader has different information on this point the Editor of the present book would be glad to have it and to insert it in future editions.

LANCASHIRE

Bury Simnel Cake

Mrs. Huggins, The Rowans, Four Oaks, Warwickshire, writes in March, 1931: 'Mid-Lent or Mothering Sunday is kept in Lancashire (even now I believe) by children visiting their mothers and taking the present of a cake, the time-honoured Simnel cake.

'The following recipe has been handed down for many generations — possibly for centuries — in the family of a pastry cook of Bury, and was at one time a trade secret. It is the recipe of the original cake.'

Mrs. Huggins came to know of the English Folk Cookery Association through *The Women's Leader*, in which paper small money prizes were offered by the founder for local recipes. One was awarded to Mrs. Huggins.

INGREDIENTS : Flour 2½ lb.; butter ½ lb.; lard ½ lb.; salts of ammonia 1 oz.; sugar 1½ lb.; almonds ¾ lb. a few bitter ones, if liked; currants 4 lb.; nutmeg ½ oz.; cinnamon ½ oz.; candied lemon peel ½ lb.; eggs 5; a little milk if necessary.

TIME : to bake in a slow oven for about 1½ to 2 hours or more according to the size and thickness of the cake.

METHOD

1. Rub the butter and lard into the flour.
2. Pound the salts of ammonia and mix well.
3. Then mix in, well, all the other dry ingredients,
4. And blend them with the eggs into a *stiff* dough which should be made into the form of a batch loaf about 18 inches and more across, 2½ to 3 inches thick and round in shape.

Eccles Cakes

Lancashire

Eccles cakes, Banbury cakes, Coventry Godcakes, Hawkshead cake and Chorley cakes all belong to the same class. They consist of pastry, short or puff as the case may be, round as in the case of Eccles and Chorley, which are much about the same size, and in the case of the Hawkshead cake which is as large as a plate; but at Coventry taking the form of an isosceles triangle, and at Banbury made in the oval shape of a rather wide shuttle.

Each and all are filled with a special mixture partaking of the character of the mincemeat we put in pies at Christmas time.

Here is a recipe for Eccles cakes. These have been made for the Eccles 'wakes' from time immemorial:

'When racing and fighting were all at an end,
To an ale-house each went with a sweetheart or friend;
Some went to Shaw's, others Phillip's chose,
But me and my Moll to the Hare and Hounds goes.

(*Chorus*)
With music and cakes
For to keep up the wakes
Among wenches and fine country beaux.'

A pretty story is told about these cakes. It is said Mrs. Raffald (*see* p. 330) gave her own recipe as a wedding present to a servant who had served her well and was going to live at Eccles, and that the girl made and sold the cakes so successfully that she made a fortune.

Bradburn's, Eccles, to-day is advertised as 'The only Old Original Eccles Cake Shop. Never removed. On the Site of these Premises Eccles Cakes were first made. Rebuilt 1835.' [They are at any rate about the best I have tasted, and those sold at the old cottage opposite Eccles Cross where Williams Deacon's Bank now stands were made and baked at Bradburn's. The cottage had no ovens].

RECIPE
Lancashire, 1904

INGREDIENTS: Some short pastry. For the filling: currants ¼ lb.; finely chopped peel 1 oz.; allspice and nutmeg ½ teaspoonful; sugar 2 oz.; butter 1 oz.

TIME: to heat and cool mixture about 20 to 30 minutes; to bake cakes 10 to 15 minutes in a hot oven.

METHOD

1. Put all the ingredients for the mixture into a pan and heat for a few minutes, then turn into a basin to cool.
2. Roll out short pastry (this is nicest if made of lard) to about ¼ inch thickness.
3. Cut into rounds.
4. Place a good tablespoonful of the mixture on each round.
5. Gather up the edges, turn over and press with rolling-pin into flat cake; make a hole in the centre of top crust.
6. Place on baking sheet 10 to 15 minutes in a hot oven.
7. Sprinkle with castor sugar when cakes are cooked.

[Mr. Lyle, Manager of Bradburn's Original Eccles Cake Shop, Eccles, Lancashire, England, exhibited some Eccles Cakes at the first Exhibition of the E.F.C.A., 1931.—ED.]

Fig or Fag Pie

This is a Mothering Sunday delicacy in some parts of Lancashire. At Blackburn and district, for example, it was the custom for people to visit their friends on this day, when they would be given 'fag-pie' and egg flip. At Burnley the custom is kept up on the fifth Sunday in Lent.

In some villages Palm Sunday (the Sixth Sunday in Lent) is known as 'Fig Sunday.' 'At Edlesborough, Buckinghamshire, the children procure figs, and nearly every house has a fig-pudding. For some days beforehand the shop-windows of the neighbouring town of Dunstable are full of figs, and on Palm Sunday crowds go to the top of Dunstable Downs, one of the highest points in the neighbourhood, and eat figs. Nor is the custom confined to Buckinghamshire; until quite lately people used to assemble on Silbury Hill on the same Sunday and eat figs, and fig-puddings were much in vogue.'—P. H. DITCHFIELD, 1896.

The custom of observing 'Fig Sunday' prevails in the counties of Bedford, Bucks, Hertford, Northampton, Oxford, Wilts, and in North Wales. At Kempton in Hertfordshire, it has long been the custom for the people to eat figs — 'Keep warsel' — and make merry with their friends on Palm Sunday. More figs are sold in the shops on the few days previous to the festival than in the rest of the year. Probably it is connected with the withering of the barren fig tree, the account of which immediately follows the narrative of the triumphal entry into Jerusalem. (Same authority and date.)

RECIPES

Fig or Fag Pie

INGREDIENTS: Short pastry; figs ½ lb.; water: cornflour; mixed spice ½ teaspoonful; a few currants; treacle, a dessertspoonful.

METHOD

1. Line a piedish, or plate, with short pastry.
2. Put the figs in a saucepan with just enough water to cover them.
3. Stew until tender.
4. Thicken the liquid with cornflour.
5. Add the spice, currants and treacle.
6. Mix well, put into the piecrust and bake a nice brown.

[N.B.—If wished the mixture may be covered with pastry, and a covered pie be made.]

Mrs. Hart's Fig Pudding

Worcester

INGREDIENTS: Bread-crumbs ½ lb.; figs ½ lb.; moist sugar ½ lb; suet 6 oz.; nutmeg ½; eggs 2; wine sauce.

TIME: to boil 4 hours.

METHOD

1. Mince the figs very very small.
2. Also mince the suet very very fine.
3. Mix bread-crumbs, figs, sugar, suet, nutmeg all together very well.
4. Moisten with the eggs which should first be well beaten.
5. Put in a greased mould or basin, cover well with greased paper and steam 4½ hours.
6. Turn out and serve with wine sauce.

LEICESTERSHIRE

Curd Cheesecakes

Mrs. Brewitt, Melton Mowbray

At the Whitsuntide Feast at Melton, it is said enough cheesecakes are made and eaten to pave the whole town. Mrs. Brewitt has kindly given her recipe. She is very generous, and all she gives is good.

INGREDIENTS: Well-drained dry curd 1 lb; eggs 8 (but only use 5 of the whites); butter 6 oz.; castor sugar 6 oz.; ground ginger; grated lemon peel; a few currants; a little cream. Some short crust or puff pastry to line the patty-pans.

METHOD

1. Press the curd and butter through a sieve.
2. Add the flavouring, eggs, a few currants and a little cream.

3. Have ready some patty-pans greased and floured as usual (*see* p. 261) and put a little of the curd mixture in each. Bake in a quick oven.

Elderberry Syrup

LITTLE DALBY

Mrs. Brewitt, Melton Mowbray

To every pint of pure juice, add 1 lb. of lump sugar and boil ½ an hour Add a few cloves to flavour, then bottle.

Elder Flower Wine
or English Frontignac

Bottesford, Leicestershire

INGREDIENTS: Whites of egg 6; lump sugar 16 lb.; water 6 gallons; raisins 8 lb.; elder flowers ¼ of a peck; yeast ¼ pint or 1 oz compressed yeast; lemons 4.

TIME: about a week.

METHOD

1. Whisk the whites of eggs.
2. Put them and the loaf sugar to the water.
3. Boil up, skimming it well.
4. Stone and chop the raisins.
5. Put them to the boiling liquid.
6. Add the elder flowers, well rinsed.
7. Infuse these last, do not boil them.

8. When new-milk-warm, put the yeast to the liquid, stirring it well.
9. Next day put in the juice of 4 lemons and the thin rind.
10. Let it ferment in the open crock or pan, covered with a cloth to keep out the dust, 3 days; then
11. Strain and cask it.

The Story of Stilton Cheese

Leicester, March 15th, 1931

This contribution came from Leicester but the sender gave no name. If he or his family see this they will know how much it was appreciated.

'The writer has read with much interest the notice of this cheese by Miss White, which appeared in to-day's issue of the *Observer*.'

'Born in the county of Leicester 80 years since, he has "eaten" Stilton more or less, all his life.

'He well knows the names mentioned by Miss White — Quenby Hall and Village, Little Dalby, Wymond House, all in the centre of the famous "Quorn" country, and has known many farms which in years gone by made glorious Stiltons, and has seen the great open Market Place of the County City of Leicester at the annual Cheese Fair in September in years gone by, and now never to return, filled with "stacks" of Stilton and the famous yellow Leicestershire cheese with their makers prepared to sell them.

'I am wondering whether Miss White in the course of her researches has heard of the Stilton known as "Slipcoat"?

This was so called for the reason that in some cases, the Stilton, after being made and set in the cheese room to mature, for some reason, begins to "effervesce" as it were, and, "slipping its coat" overflows in a mass, whilst still white, creamy and immature.

'It was not exposed for sale in that form, but to some palates it was more delicious than when mature, and many times in the past, has the writer been indebted to farmer friends for a generous gift of "Slipcoat", a pleasant memory even now, though so trivial.

'WITH APOLOGIES.'

Leicester,
    15/3/31.

LINCOLNSHIRE

Grantham Gingerbread

This is the name given to the round puffy white gingerbread biscuits of which Blunden says in the *British Baker*, tons are sold as fairings at Fair time. He also tells us these biscuits should be almost hollow, slightly dome-shaped and should be baked a pleasing fawn tint. In Norfolk this dome shape is not required. The white buttons as they are called there, must rise and fall back in the oven, leaving peculiar cracks on them. They are sometimes rolled in sugar to keep this process.

INGREDIENTS: Plain flour 1 lb.; castor sugar 1 lb.; butter or margarine 6 oz.; ground ginger 1 teaspoonful; eggs 3; vol (ammonia) 3 drams; enough milk to mix into a dough that can be rolled out.

TIME: to bake about 1 hour in a very slow oven.

METHOD

1. Rub the fat into the flour.
2. Mix in the sugar and ginger.
3. Dissolve the 'vol' in a little milk.
4. Make a well in the flour, drop in the eggs.
5. Mix with a knife, adding, as the eggs get mixed in, the milk and 'vol' and finally more milk to make a stiff but pliable dough.
6. Roll out ½ inch thick.
7. Cut into rounds 2½ inches across.
8. Bake in a very slow oven.

MIDDLESEX

Johnny Cake and Mr. London Bun

In the old days when wheaten cakes were a luxury, they were associated with special feasts and each had a story. Lady Gomme, the first President of the English Folk Cookery Association, relates most charmingly the sad adventure of a Johnny Cake. It was customary it appears for the housewife when she made bread to take a piece of the dough and shape it as a boy or man with currants for his eyes and mouth; currants also were used to represent the buttons on his coat.

One day when a cottager made her batch of bread, she was unexpectedly called away and jokingly left her baking in charge of a Johnny cake. Time passed and she did not return, and the story goes Johnny becoming hot edged nearer and nearer the open door first one leg, then his arm, then his head, then the other arm touching the ground each time till finally he had turned a complete 'cart wheel' and began another and another which carried him out of the house, and when the house mother returned she saw Johnny rolling over and over in this way down the street and tripping up all who tried to catch him. From that day a Johnny cake was often called 'the little cake that ran away,' and housewives watched them carefully lest they jumped out of the oven and rolled out of the door. Johnny cakes are still made not only in private households but for sale in London shops, and one interesting cake which can be bought at a baker's in the Cambridge Road, Kilburn, represents a boy running away and in the act of turning a cartwheel, but the young saleswoman knew nothing of the old legends. When made of bun dough they are known as 'Mr. London Bun.'

339

SPECIALITIES

Mrs. E. Nelson Fell of Oxford writes in March, 1931: I was an American child of English descent brought up in New York — in about 1863. 'Johnny Cake' was the common name of an excellent bread made in flat shallow tins. . . . We had a song — for exercise I suppose — which I remember standing in the nursery and singing as we jumped in time, placing our hands, simultaneously one before us and one behind our backs. The song was:

> "Give me some Johnny Cake, thick, thick, thick,
> And a piece of butter, quick, quick, quick,
>   Peter stands *at* the Gate
>   With his knife *and* his plate
> Waiting for butter to put on his Johnny cake
>   Come Butter come
>   Come Butter come."

'At the refrain we jumped twice as fast.' It is an old English churning song; and this American connection is most interesting. So also is the recipe for the cake sent by Miss Wyld of Tunbridge Wells, Kent, and she remarks: 'This is a family dish that I have never met with elsewhere on household tables. It was introduced into our family in the 'sixties or 'seventies by Canadian relatives. It may be as well to add that its flavour certainly is more or less "caviare to the general": you either regard it as a very special treat or as a penance!'

INGREDIENTS: Plain flour 1 cupful or ½ pint; maize (or Indian corn) meal ½ pint; salt, a pinch; butter 2 oz.; bicarbonate of soda 1 small teaspoonful; egg 1; milk, enough to mix (about ½ pint); sugar to taste (if liked) but it is not in the original recipe.

TIME: to bake 40 minutes in hot oven.

METHOD

1. Work the butter into the flour.
2. Mix in all the other dry ingredients.
3. Separate the yolk from the white of the egg.
4. Whisk each separately add sufficient milk to make the dry ingredients into a firm dough.
5. Half-fill a well-buttered shallow cake tin and bake in a really hot oven for 40 minutes, or till well risen. If a steel fork inserted comes out clean, the cake is done. It should be eaten warm ; it is nice also cold, or can be successfully rewarmed in the oven. In any case spread with butter as if it were bread.

MONMOUTHSHIRE

Frumenty

Mrs. Pickersgill, a B.B.C. friend, writes from Newport, Monmouthshire: 'Your talk on "Frumenty" was both helpful and interesting. The wheat can often be bought at a corn shop instead of the baker's, if people would just enquire. I have a recipe which is very good if a savoury be required.'

INGREDIENTS: Hulled wheat, cree'd (stewed) to a jelly; cheese grated; tomatoes sliced; salt and pepper.

TIME: to bake 20 to 30 minutes in a good oven.

METHOD

1. Butter a pie dish.
2. Skin some tomatoes by pouring boiling water over them.
3. Grate some cheese.
4. Season the stewed or 'cree'd' frumenty with salt and pepper, and put it into the dish.
5. Then a layer of sliced tomatoes.
6. Season this also with pepper and salt.
7. Cover with grated cheese.
8. Sprinkle with butter; and
9. Bake till nicely browned.

[N.B.—This is a very good example of an old English dish being modernized by an English (or Welsh) woman to suit present tastes and customs.—ED.]

NOTTINGHAMSHIRE

Cowslip Vinegar

South Notts

Another of Miss Cullen's excellent recipes.

INGREDIENTS: Cowslip 'pips' 2 pints; white wine vinegar 1 pint; lump sugar 1 lb.; brandy 1 wineglassful; soda water.

TIME: 3 days to infuse. 1 hour to boil.

METHOD

1. Gather the cowslips on a dry day.
2. Pick all the flower 'pips' from the stalks.
3. Put them into a basin.
4. Pour on white wine vinegar.
5. Let them remain 3 days to infuse.
6. Wet a piece of muslin with vinegar.
7. Strain off the liquor from the 'pips' into a stone jar; add 1 lb. lump sugar to every pint of liquor.
8. Stir from time to time until the sugar is dissolved.
9. Then cover the jar.
10. Set it on the fire in a saucepan of boiling water.
11. Let it boil for one hour.
12. Add one wineglassful of brandy to each pint.
13. Bottle when cold and seal the corks.
14. Dilute it with soda water as a cooling drink.

Aunt Lucy's Home-made Wines

Harby, Nottinghamshire

'Everything Aunt Lucy made was so good,' says Mrs. Herbert Watson, who has given the following series of formulae.

I

GINGER WINE

INGREDIENTS: Water 1 gallon; ginger 2 oz.; sugar 3½ lb.; raisins 1 lb.; oranges 2; lemon 1. (For method *see* p. 345).

II

COLTSFOOT WINE

INGREDIENTS: Water 1 gallon; coltsfoot flowers 2 quarts; sugar 3½ lb.; oranges 1 and lemon two-thirds.

TIME to stand 2 or 3 days.

METHOD

1. Boil the water and pour it on the flowers.
2. Let them stand 2 or 3 days, stirring each day.
3. Then strain.
4. Boil the liquid with the sugar.
5. Add the juice of the orange and lemon.

III

ORANGE WINE

INGREDIENTS: Water 1 gallon; oranges 8; sugar 3½ lb.; compressed yeast 1 oz.

METHOD

1. Boil the water and sugar together.
2. Squeeze the juice from the oranges.
3. Pour the boiling water on to the juice.
4. When cool (luke-warm) cream the yeast.
5. Put it on a bit of toast.
6. Float the toast on the wine to work it.
7. Then put into a barrel with the thin peelings of the oranges, being careful not to put in any white.

IV

BLACKBERRY WINE

INGREDIENTS: Blackberries 1 gallon; boiling water 1 gallon; lump sugar 3½ lb.

TIME: (1) Stand 24 hours. (2) Keep in barrel a year, then bottle.

METHOD

1. Bruise the berries.
2. Pour the boiling water over them
3. Let the mixture stand for 24 hours, stirring occasionally; then
4. Strain on to the sugar.
5. Let it stand until dissolved, then put into barrel and keep there until the following October.

V

SLOE WINE

INGREDIENTS : Sloes 1 gallon; boiling water 1 gallon; lump sugar 4 lb.; ½ a lemon.

TIME : 3 or 4 days before putting into barrel.

METHOD

1. Pour the boiling water on the sloes.
2. When cool enough for the hands, mash them well up.
3. Let them stand one day.
4. Strain on to the sugar.
5. Boil the sliced lemon in a little water and add it.
6. Let it stand until the sugar is melted.
7. Then put it into the barrel; and
8. In a few days bung it down.

VI

DAMSON WINE

INGREDIENTS : Water 1 gallon; damsons 1 gallon; sugar 3½ lb.

TIME : Let it stand first 8 or 9 days; then one day; then a week; keep for a year.

METHOD

1. Boil the water and pour on the damsons which must be well bruised.
2. Let them stand 8 or 9 days, stirring every day.
3. Strain off.
4. Add 3½ lb. sugar.
5. Let it stand one day or more, stirring occasionally until the sugar is dissolved.
6. Then put into barrel.
7. Let it stand a week, then cork down tightly.

OXFORDSHIRE

Banbury Cakes

Gervase Markham, Cottam, Nottinghamshire c. 1568-1636

A recipe 'To make very good Banbury cakes' is given by Markham in his *English Hus-wife* (1615) but it is so involved that although interesting as a record of cakes made in Elizabethan days it is useless in its original form. The following has therefore been extracted for modern use without destroying its character.

[I have not yet tried it. — ED.]

343

SPECIALITIES

OLD RECIPE

1615

INGREDIENTS: Currants 1 lb.; ground cloves, mace, cinnamon, and nutmeg 2 teaspoonfuls; flour 2 lb.; butter 2 oz.; sugar 8 oz.; salt 1 teaspoonful; compressed yeast 1 oz.; cream ½ gill; milk ½ pint; egg 1.

METHOD

1. Wash and dry the currants.
2. Rub the butter into the flour.
3. Cream the yeast with a little of the sugar, and add the remainder to the flour with the salt; mix well.
4. Heat the milk and cream together till lukewarm (they must not be too hot); mix them with the yeast and well beaten-up egg and use them to make the flour into a dough.
5. Work all together for one hour or more.

6. Divide the dough into two.
7. Put one half to rise in a warm place, whilst you mix the currants and spices well in with the other.
8. Then put the currant dough to rise, whilst you roll out the other very thin.
9. Now make your cakes any size you please with the currant dough, and cover each one with the thinly rolled out plain dough. Slash each across the top and bake in a hot oven according to size.

Anyone who wants the best Banbury cakes ever made can buy them from E. W. Brown, 'The Original Cake Shop,' 12 Parson Street, Banbury, Oxfordshire (1931).

A MODERN RECIPE

1929

This is the same type of cake as those sold by E. W. Brown, and as will be noticed it differs considerably from Markham's cake which seems to be more like the old Shropshire Simnel. There were of course any number of local variations of different cakes similar in type; those of E. H. Brown at Banbury are an instance of the survival of the fittest, and deserve the name of Banbury cakes.

INGREDIENTS: Rough puff or puff pastry; butter 2 oz.; currants ¼ lb.; mixed peel 2 oz.; allspice ½ teaspoonful (or nutmeg); sugar 1 oz.; cinnamon ¼ teaspoonful; rum.

METHOD

1. Melt the butter and mix in the other ingredients, a little rum is a great improvement but not absolutely necessary.
2. Roll out the pastry into a thin round.
3. Place some of the mixture in the centre lengthwise.

4. Turn the sides over the mixture, pinch the pastry together, and shape into an oval.
5. Turn over, flatten with a rolling-pin, make 3 slashes across the top.
6. Brush over with white of egg and dust with castor sugar.

[N.B.—Banbury Cakes were exhibited by Miss Brown at the first English Folk Cookery Exhibition held in 1931.—ED.]

Dandelion Wine

Given by Mrs. Wickens of Burford

INGREDIENTS: Water 1 gallon; dandelion heads 3 quarts; sugar 3 lb.; ground ginger ½ oz.; lemon 2; oranges 2; a little yeast; ½ lb. raisins.
TIME: 1 hour to boil; a few days to work or ferment.

METHOD

1. Boil the dandelions in the water for ½ hour.
2. Strain them from the liquor.
3. Add the sugar and ginger to the latter.
4. Boil with lemon and orange peel for ½ hour.
5. Put in crock or tub to cool, add lemon and orange juice.
6. When cool enough, put a little yeast on toast, and leave to work (or ferment).
7. Then put into cask with a few stoned raisins.

Ginger Wine Without Boiling

Mrs. Wickens, Burford

INGREDIENTS: Cold water 4 gallons; root ginger ¾ lb.; lump sugar 14 lb.; raisins 2 lb.; lemon 6; sweet oranges 6.
TIME: 1 week; 9 months.

METHOD

1. Bruise the ginger.
2. Chop the raisins finely.
3. Wash the lemons and oranges and dry and slice them.
4. Put altogether in a crock with the sugar.
5. Then add the cold water, stir every day for a week.
6. Bung down.
7. Will be fit for use in 9 months.

SHROPSHIRE

Shropshire Fidget or Fitchett Pie

This pie was used a great deal in old farmhouses as a supper dish for harvesters. The recipes given here are taken from the cookery book compiled by the Shropshire Women's Institutes (Brown and Brinnand, Ltd., printers, Shrewsbury, price 1s.), Mrs. Dale, Fordham and Cardiston W.I., says her recipe is excellent made with chops cut from the scrag end of a neck of mutton. The recipe given by Mrs. Tudor, Weston Rhyn W.I. was her mother's. Mrs. Wood of the same Institute gives a similar recipe.

Mrs. Dale's Fidget Pie

INGREDIENTS: Potatoes 1 lb.; apples 1 lb.; bacon or ham (home-cured) ½ lb.; pepper; a very little salt; sugar if apples are sour; about ½ pint stock, and short crust to cover.

TIME: to bake about 1½ hours in the bottom of a fairly hot oven.

METHOD

1. Put a layer of rather thickly sliced potatoes into a pie dish; then.
2. A layer of bacon or ham cut into dice or small slices about ¼ inch thick, and then
3. A layer of apples, peeled and sliced and dipped in sugar if very sour.
4. Repeat the layers until the dish is quite full.
5. Add the stock; and
6. Cover with a rather thick good short crust.
7. Bake for one hour first at the top and then at the bottom of a fairly hot oven.

Mrs. Tudor's Mother's Recipe

INGREDIENTS: Potatoes; apples; onions; pepper and salt; bacon; a teacupful of water.

METHOD

1. Put a layer of sliced potatoes in the bottom of a piedish; then
2. A layer of sliced apple; and
3. A layer of sliced onions.
4. Season with pepper and salt.
5. Then add a layer of sliced bacon, cut in small fingers.
6. Repeat till dish is full, having the bacon on top.
7. Pour ¼ pint water over it, cover with a dish and put it in the oven to cook the vegetables and fruit; then
8. When cold, cover with a good pie-crust and bake till the pastry is cooked.

SOMERSETSHIRE

The Pie Man, Bath

Mr. John Hatton, Spa Director, The Pump Room, Bath, sends the following interesting particulars supplied by an old Bathonian:—

The 'Pie Man' stood on the Boro' Walls, between Cater's and Ship and Teagles, close to the pavement by Cater's.

He had a brightly polished case of stout tin standing on 4 legs and fitted with three drawers.

In one he kept meat pies, the other mince pies, the third had a small charcoal fire arrangement which kept the pies hot.

He announced his presence by fairly quietly repeating quickly, 'All 'ot all 'ot all 'ot,' about five times very rapidly. (Try it and you get the effect.)

He sold them at the recognized price of the day — one penny each. But with boys, who tossed with him (halfpennies) or with men who tossed (pennies); if they lost he took the money, if they won they had a pie. I think the meat pies were 2d. as the men generally took meat pies, but if they did not choose they had mince pies.

But, as I have said, you could also buy.

I should not like to say how many halfpennies of mine he had. Another curious fact was, he always 'called' and took care to see they were not tossing with a coin on edge under the hand, by pressing your two hands together before calling.

He disappeared, I think about 1893. I remember him from 1880. As I told Mr. Taylor, he bought the 'stale pies' from Fisher's. By 'stale' is meant pies more than a day old. I do not think confectioners are so particular to-day, but in my youth all confectionery was half price the day after the buns, tarts, and pies were made.

This links up the mutton pies of England with the old Nursery rhyme:

'Simple Simon met a pieman going to the Fair,
Says Simple Simon to the pieman "Let me taste your ware." '

Sally Lunn's Tea or Breakfast Cakes

Bath 18th Century

Take one pint (16 oz.) of milk, quite warm, a quarter of a pint of thick, small beer yeast (or 1 oz. compressed yeast creamed with a little sugar), put them into a pan with flour, from 2 lb. sufficient to make it a thick batter; cover it over; and let it stand till it has risen as high as it will — that is, about two hours; add two ounces of lump sugar, dissolved in a quarter of a pint (4 oz.) of warm milk; and a quarter of a pound of butter rubbed into the rest of the flour very fine; then knead the dough lightly and let it stand for half an hour. Then make up into cakes and put them on tins. When they have stood to rise, bake them in a quick oven.

The late Dr. King, of Bath, told his daughter Miss King, Principal of the Bath Domestic Training College, that the correct way to eat Sally Lunn's cakes was to split them, spread them with very thick scalded cream — not butter — and eat them very hot.

Gingerbread Valentines

These were a Bath delicacy made at one time by Mr. Fisher, but he gave up business and sold the remains of his stock and equipment to Mr. Taylor, of the Red House Restaurant, Bond Street, Bath; and Mr. Taylor gave the wooden moulds to Mr. John Hatton, Director of the Spa, for the Pump Room Museum, where they can now be seen.

Some were courteously made, and gilded by Mr. Taylor especially for the First English Folk Cookery Exhibition 1931. At this Exhibition Lady Gomme also showed some wooden moulds for moulding gingerbread and other cakes that she had bought at Lewes in Sussex.

The First English Folk Cookery Exhibition

January 16th, 1931

This was organized in a hurry by Miss E. Willans, Principal of the Advisory Department of the Gas Light and Coke Company, and Vice-President of the E.F.C.A. It was held in the Lecture Hall of the Gas Light and Coke Company, Church Street, Kensington, London, W.8. England; and in spite of the shortness of notice (and impossibility of transporting many meat dishes, etc., from a distance) 32 English Counties were represented, and the Exhibition though small was a great success.

Frumety or Fermety

A lady writes from Weston-super-Mare, Somersetshire (1930): 'About 40 years ago — rather longer perhaps — country women in shawls and sun-bonnets used to come in to the market in this town in little carts bringing basins of new wheat boiled to a jelly, which jelly was put into a large pot with milk, eggs and sultanas and lightly cooked, was poured into piedishes and served on mid-Lent Sunday and during the ensuing week.'

Sedgemoor Easter Cake

This was sent in by Mrs. Wyatt, of Huish Episcopi, near Langford, on behalf of the Women's Institute, and was exhibited at the first English Folk Cookery Exhibition, 1931.

INGREDIENTS: Flour ½ lb.; butter ¼ lb.; castor sugar ¼ lb.; currants ¼ lb.; mixed spice ½ teaspoonful; ground cinnamon ½ teaspoonful; egg 1; brandy 2 tablespoonfuls.

METHOD

1. Rub the butter into the flour.
2. Add sugar, currants, spice and cinnamon.
3. Well beat the egg and mix with the brandy, and then mix with dry ingredients.
4. Roll out about half an inch thick, cut in rounds, and bake in a moderate oven for about 20 minutes.

STAFFORDSHIRE

Staffordshire Yeomanry Pudding

INGREDIENTS: Rich pastry; raspberry jam; eggs (4 yolks and 2 whites) castor sugar ½ lb.; butter ⅓ lb.; almonds ground 1 oz.

TIME: to bake in slow oven 1½ hours — bake first in a quick and then in a slow oven.

METHOD

1. Butter a piedish.
2. Cover the inside with rich pastry.
3. Spread a spoonful of raspberry jam over the pastry on the bottom of the dish.
4. Beat well the yolks and the whites of the eggs together.
5. Cream the butter.
6. Add the sugar.
7. Mix in the almonds.
8. Blend with the beaten eggs.
9. Pour the mixture over the raspberry jam.
10. Bake it first in a quick oven to cook the pastry and then in a slow one to cook the pudding (time altogether 1-1½ hours).

SUFFOLK

Fermenty or Fromity

Mrs. Osmonde, Ealing, says: 'I am sure flummery and fromity were quite distinct in Suffolk. Furmenty was made from new wheat, crushed and sodden all night in milk and water, baked or boiled with honey and cinnamon. It was eaten during the twelve days at Christmas, December 25th to January 6th. Some was placed in a plate outside the door at night for the "Pharisees" (fairies). This custom seems to show that frumenty was eaten before Christianity came.'

Sugar Beer for Harvest

Another Suffolk recipe from Mrs. E. L. Osmonde, Ealing

'This was a light effervescent drink much used in harvest time for the harvest men's elevenses and fourses (11 a.m. and 4 p.m.). Eaten with it was a bread cake made of yeast bread with lard shortening, currants, sugar and spice.'

Mrs. Goodman's Recipe

INGREDIENTS: Hops 1 cupful (½ pint); water 1 gallon; honey or sugar to sweeten; toast 1 slice; 1 tablespoonful brewer's yeast, or ½ oz. compressed yeast creamed with sugar.

TIME: 24 hours.

METHOD

1. Boil the hops in the water for 2 hours.
2. Then strain them out.
3. Add honey or sugar enough to sweeten the liquid.
4. Pour the mixture into an earthen vessel.
5. Float a slice of toast on top with a spoonful of brewers' yeast on it (if you can't get brewers' yeast, cream ½ oz. of compressed yeast and use instead).
6. Cover with a cloth and leave standing all night.
7. Next day, take out the toast, skim the froth off and the mixture is ready for drinking.

N.B.—Mrs. Osmonde says 'It did not keep very long, so the quantities were limited to a 3 or 4 days' supply; but it was very refreshing.'

Fourses Cake

This is a cake made of yeast bread, lard, currants, sugar, and spice, eaten by Suffolk harvesters at 4 o'clock. One was included in the collection of local and ceremonial cakes shown by Lady Gomme at a Conference of the Folk Lore Society held in London in 1892. Sugar beer was drunk with it (*see* p. 349).

Elderberry Wine

Another of Mrs. Goodman's recipes

INGREDIENTS: Elderberries 1 quart; water 2 quarts; sugar, Lisbon coarse, but not the very coarsest Demerara or Barbados, ¾ lb. to every quart of juice. Jamaica pepper (allspice) ginger and a few cloves. Toast and yeast to 'work' it. Brandy 1 quart to 8 gallons of liquor.

TIME: 6 months to a year.

METHOD

1. Break the fruit in the water.
2. Run the liquor and rub the fruit through a hair sieve.
3. To every quart of juice put ¾ lb. sugar.
4. Boil the whole ½ of an hour with the Jamaica pepper, ginger and cloves.
5. Pour it into a tub, and when luke-warm, add toast and yeast to work it.
6. The liquor must be in a warm place to make it work, as it does not work so easily as other liquors.
7. When it ceases to hiss, strain it into the barrel, put 1 quart of brandy to 8 gallons of liquor and stop up the barrel.
8. Bottle in the spring or the following Christmas.

Mead

Recipe of Harriet Goodman, 1834–1918. Hepworth

'Drain the honey out of a honeycomb. Cover the comb with water in an earthen vessel. Let it stand a week or ten days. Strain. Add 1 oz. of 2 spices — ginger and cloves; or cinnamon and cloves to a gallon. Boil it till the flavour is obtained, let it get nearly cold and work (ferment) it with yeast on toast.'

N.B.—Mrs. Osmonde says: 'The drinks made by old Mrs. Goodman were all very good, especially the sugar beer: but the mead and ale were too strong for me.'

God's Kitchel

Suffolk

'God's Kichel, a cake given to godchildren at their asking a blessing.' This is the meaning given in Dunton's *Ladies' Dictionary* 1694.

In 1892 Lady Gomme (First President of the English Folk Cookery Association) collected and arranged an Exhibition of Local Feasten Cakes, in connection with the International Folk Lore Congress held in London in that year; and amongst a number of other cakes exhibited some God's Kitchels from Suffolk.

Cowell, in his *Law Dictionary* on the word 'Kichell,' says: 'It was a good old custom for godfathers and godmothers, every time their god-children asked them a blessing, to give them a cake, which was a God's-Kichell. It is a still proverbial saying in some countries: "ask me a blessing, and I will give you some plum-cake".'

[There appears to be a resemblance between the customs of God's Kitchels and Coventry Godcakes; though the cakes may be different I have not yet come across God's Kitchels.—ED.]

SURREY

Flead Cake

These two recipes are sent by Mrs. Oswell, Warren, Holmbury St. Mary, Dorking, who says it is a very nice nursery cake which can be made from the flead left over from the rendering of the lard.

INGREDIENTS: Flour 1 lb.; sugar, brown ½ lb.; ½ lb. currants; milk ½ pint; bicarbonate of soda 1 teaspoonful; mixed spice 2 teaspoonfuls; flead ½ lb.

TIME: to bake in good oven, 2 hours.

351

METHOD

1. Mix the flead left from the rendering of the lard (called in Shropshire 'scratchings'), and all the dry ingredients with the flour.

2. Melt the soda in a little milk, and add to milk. Mix well and bake as above.

Camp Treacle Pudding

'This recipe,' says Mrs. Oswell, 'is I *think* my own. I have never seen it in any cookery book. I used it at camp, and one of the Commissioners from the World Guide Camp, Hants, sent to me for it. It is an excellent way of using up left-over bread.'

INGREDIENTS: Butter (or margarine), golden syrup; sugar; bread, slices ½ inch thick, soaked in milk; milk sufficient for this purpose.

TIME: about 30 minutes.

METHOD

1. Soak the bread in milk.
2. Put the butter, syrup and sugar in a shallow pan.
3. Stir over heat till it browns.

4. Then put in the bread and cover with the mixture.
5. Leave for two minutes and serve quickly.

SUFFOLK

Suffolk Dumplins

1822

This recipe is given by Mrs. Mary Eaton, of Bungay

INGREDIENTS: Dough made with yeast and milk as for bread.

TIME: to boil 20 minutes.

METHOD

1. Let the dough rise one hour before the fire.
2. Make the dough into balls the size of a middling apple.
3. Throw them into boiling water, and let them boil 20 minutes.

4. To ascertain when they are done enough, stick a fork into one; and if it comes out clear, they are ready to take up.

N.B.—Do not cut, but tear them apart on the top with two forks, for they become heavy by their own steam. They should be eaten immediately, with gravy, or cold butter, or with meat.

Norfolk Dumplins

1822

This again is Mrs. Mary Eaton's receipt. [Will Norfolk people born and bred please tell me whether these or yeast dumplings are correctly called Norfolk Dumplins. There seems to be some difference of opinion—ED.] She says 'these are often called drop dumplins or spoon dumplins.'

INGREDIENTS: Milk ½ pint (8 fluid ounces); flour sufficient to make a thick batter; eggs 2; salt, a little.

TIME: only a few minutes.

METHOD

1. Make a thick batter with the flour and milk, eggs and salt.
2. Drop a little, a spoonful at a time, gently into boiling water; and if the water boil fast, they will be ready in a few minutes.
3. Take them out with a wooden spoon, and put them in a dish with a piece of butter.

In the book prepared by Mary L. Burgess and Phyllis B. Gates, and dedicated to the Norfolk Federation of Women's Institutes 1931, both the recipes given for Norfolk Dumplings are made with chemical raising agents, one with baking powder and the other with self-raising flour.

Hard Dumplins

1822

These may be made into dumplings or into one sausage-shaped pudding, which when cooked was cut into slices about 1 inch thick, and placed in the dripping pan under the meat, which was roasting in front of the fire, for about 20 to 30 minutes before it was dished up. It is said only a Sussex woman can make these hard dumplins or puddings successfully. [I remember my father, who was born at Worthing in 1822, telling me that 'a proper Sussex pudding was always made in this way.'—ED.]

INGREDIENTS: Flour; salt; water.

TIME: to boil nearly one hour.

METHOD

1. Make a paste or light dough of flour, salt and water.
2. Shape it into balls.
3. Dust them with flour, and boil them nearly an hour.

N.B.—Hard dumplins are best boiled with a good piece of meat, and (for variety) a few currants may be added.

Suet Dumplins

1822

INGREDIENTS: Suet 1 lb. (or the outside of a loin or neck of mutton) and shred it very fine; flour, ¼ lb.; salt a teaspoonful; eggs 2; milk, sufficient with the eggs to make it into a dough.

TIME: to boil ¾ to 1 hour according to size.

METHOD

1. Shred the suet or fat very fine.
2. Mix it well with the flour and salt.
3. And make into a moderately stiff dough with the eggs and milk.

4. Drop into boiling water (or boil in a cloth) as above.

N.B.—If made into one large pudding, put into a floured cloth and boil 4 hours. It eats well the next day, cut in slices and broiled. The outside fat of loin or neck of mutton finely shred makes a more delicate pudding than suet.

KENT

Kentish Sausage-meat

Miss Acton, 1845

INGREDIENTS: Lean of pork 3 lb.; fat 2 lb.; salt 2½ oz.; pepper 1 oz.; minced sage 3 large tablespoonfuls (a small nutmeg and a small dessertspoonful of pounded mace if liked).

METHOD

1. Chop the meat rather coarsely as sausages thus made are lighter, though not so delicate.
2. When the fat and lean are partially mixed strew over them 2½ oz. dry salt, beaten to a powder, and mixed with the 1 oz. ground black pepper, and three tablespoonfuls of sage, very finely minced.

3. Turn the meat with the chopping knife until all the ingredients are well-blended.
4. Test it by frying a small portion to see if it be properly seasoned, if not add more. (If liked nutmeg and mace as above may be added.)

N.B.—These sausages are not as a rule put into skins when made at home, but are simply formed into cakes, and, after being well floured, fried or grilled. They must be watched and often turned.

Delicious sausages in skins made from an old Kentish family recipe can be bought from Hornby and Maxted, butchers, 129 Earl's Court Road, London, S.W.5.

SUSSEX

Ifield Vicarage Hog's Pudding

An old Sussex dish

On September 14th, 1931, a letter was received from a gentleman who wrote: 'About 70 years ago when I was one of six private pupils at the Vicarage, Ifield, Sussex, when one of the Vicar's pigs was killed we used to have as a second course what we called "Hog's puddings"; they were generally served cold, done up like sausages in skins, in clusters of three or more, individually about the size of a golf ball but irregular in shape. They were more of a sweetmeat than a savoury, and broke apart with a snap and were dry rather than moist inside.'

By a curious coincidence the following recipe, of which I had never before heard, had reached me a few days previously on September 9th, at the office of the *Woman's Leader*.—Sent by Mrs. Humphreys, Dragon's Green, Shipley, Sussex.

INGREDIENTS: Fresh pork, flank 1 lb.; flour 1½ lb.; baking powder 1 teaspoonful; spice, a pinch; currants 1 lb.; some sausage skins.

TIME: to cook 45 minutes to boil the flank of pork, 1½ hours to boil the puddings.

METHOD

1. Cut the pork in slices, put into hot water and boil 45 minutes.
2. Mix the baking powder, spice and currants with the flour.
3. Mix well with 1 lb. of the lard.
4. Fill the sausage skins with the mixture.
5. Tie up in bunches.
6. Prick them with a fork.
7. Plunge them in boiling water.
8. Boil 1½ hours.
9. Take out and hang up to dry.
10. Break them asunder when eating them, and they will pop.

Grape Wine

Mrs. Wickens, Burford, Oxfordshire, 1928

Although grapes do not *always* ripen in the country out of doors, there are many vines which produce fruit that mature. Many may be glad of a simple way of using them to make wine.

METHOD

1. To every gallon of grapes when picked and bruised put 1 gallon of water.
2. Let it stand a day or two.
3. Then strain and well press it.
4. To every gallon of liquor put 3½ lb. of lump sugar.
5. Let it stand till dissolved, stirring occasionally.
6. Then put in cask.

N.B.—Small wooden casks holding five gallons can be bought for 12s. 6d. each, carriage paid, from George & Carter, 24–26 Alfred Street, Aston, Birmingham, and gallon jars with a tap for making herb beer can be obtained from Newball & Mason, Nottingham.

WARWICKSHIRE

Coventry Godcakes

These cakes in the form of an isosceles triangle are made at Coventry especially for New Year's Day, and are peculiar to that place. It was the custom from time immemorial for godchildren to visit their godparents on New Year's Day and receive from them a blessing; they were also given one of these cakes. For method of making *see* Eccles Cakes, Lancashire (p. 334) but puff pastry or flaky pastry is used.

[N.B.—At the first Exhibition of the English Folk Cookery Association held in January, 1931, Coventry godcakes were exhibited by Mr. R. H. Buckingham, 56 Earlsden Street, Coventry, Warwickshire, England, from whom they can always be obtained. Those photographed were bought from him on New Year's Day, 1932.—Ed.]

A Survival of Medieval Days

At Stratford-on-Avon once a year at the Statute Fair a whole ox is still roasted in the market-place. It is spitted at midnight, roasts all night on a revolving spit, is continually basted, and is ready to be eaten at mid-day twelve hours later.

WESTMORLAND

Whey Wig

Westmorland, 1814

During the hay-harvest the women drink a pleasant and sharp beverage made by infusing fresh mint or sage leaves in buttermilk whey, and hence called 'whey-wig.'

WILTSHIRE

Devizes Pie

1836

During the summer of 1928 a Wiltshire man who had made his home in New Zealand, wrote to the Town Clerk of Devizes to ask for the recipe of Devizes Pie. No one in the town had ever heard of it; then a recipe appeared in a small collection of county recipes, but no date was given nor its source. The Editor of this book, however, who was visiting Devizes discovered in her note-book (dated 1927) that it is given by Mrs. Dalgairns (1829), and the following year she found the following rather better recipe in *The Magazine of Domestic Economy*, of 1836. This is an example of the way in which direct research may be combined with research amongst printed and manuscript records. It is also an example of the way the name of a thing lingers on after other particulars are lost. In this book there are many recipes that have been rescued in similar fashion. A tiny scrap of information is noted; after a time (sometimes years) it is linked up with another, but not perhaps completely rescued till more time has elapsed. A great deal of collating has to be done as well as collecting.

RECIPE

1. Boil a calf's head, cut it into very thin slices, with some of the brains.
2. Add slices of pickled tongue, sweetbread, lamb, veal, a few slices of bacon, and some hard-boiled eggs.
3. Put them in layers in a piedish with plenty of seasoning between each of cayenne, white pepper, allspice and salt.
4. Fill up the dish with rich gravy that will jelly when cold.
5. Cover with a flour-and-water paste; make a hole in the middle.
6. Bake in a slow oven for about one hour.
7. And when perfectly cold, take off the crust, and
8. Turn the pie out upon a dish; and garnish with parsley and pickled eggs cut in slices.

WORCESTERSHIRE

Beastings Puddings

A Worcestershire Recipe

'This,' writes the lady who sends the information, 'was a baked custard made of beastings but without eggs; the beastings being the very rich milk (colostrum) given by a cow shortly after calving. There was a curious bit of folk lore connected with beastings. It could not be bought; the farmer's wife used to send a jugful to some of her oldest or best customers, "and will you please not wash out the jug." To return the jug *washed* was held to bring about the death of the new-born calf.'

YORKSHIRE

White Currant Wine

Ann Peckham, of Leeds, 1767

INGREDIENTS: White currants 1 quart, after being stringed, water 1 quart; to every gallon of liquor 2½ lb. lump sugar. A little isinglass; Mountain wine, 1 quart to every 4 gallons. To every gallon ⅛ lb. more sugar when barrelled.

TIME: 1 night and 1 month.

METHOD

1. Take your currants when they are full ripe.
2. Strip and break them with your hand till you break all the berries.
3. To every quart of pulp, put a quart of water.
4. Mix them well together and let them stand all night in your tub.
5. Then strain them through a hair sieve and to every gallon of liquor put 2½ lb. of double refined sugar.
6. When your sugar is dissolved, put it into your barrel.
7. Dissolve a little isinglass and put it in.
8. To every 4 gallons put in 1 quart Mountain or raisin wine.
9. Then bung up your barrel; and
10. When fine, draw it off.
11. Wash out your barrel with a little of the wine and strain the grounds through a bag, then put it through to the rest of your wine.
12. Put it all into your barrel again.
13. To every gallon put ⅛ lb. more sugar.
14. Let it stand a month, then bottle it.

White Currant and Ginger Cordial

This delicious cordial is very old indeed, and has been used in the family of Miss Elam, of Jedburgh, Yorkshire, for generations; huntsmen appreciated it and, says Miss Wright Smith who sends it, 'we always took a little on a day's tramp over the Fells. It is not exactly cheap but a little goes a long way.'

INGREDIENTS: White currants 1 lb.; brandy 1 quart; ground ginger ¼ oz.; lemon, the rind of one peeled very thin; ¾ lb. white sugar to 1 quart liquid.

TIME: to stand 24 hours.

METHOD

1. Crush the currants.
2. Pour the brandy over them.
3. Add the lemon peel and ground ginger.
4. Mix well and cover down closely.
5. Let it stand 24 hours, stirring from time to time.
6. Strain through flannel.
7. To each quart of liquid add ⅝ lb. white sugar.
8. Stir well and when quite dissolved bottle.

Gale Beer

Miss Dorothy Hartley, who is a leading authority on Medieval England, and is intensely interested in Folk Cookery sends the following note about 'Gale Beer,' and the name of Miss Hannah Buttery, Thornton-le-Dale, Pickering, Yorkshire, who can tell anyone how it is made. 'Gale,' Miss Hartley writes (from Johannesburg), 'is a sweet herb that grows in the moss and was in use in Caedmon's time; they probably made gale beer at St. Hilda's monastery up north.'

Fulford Biscuits

York

Miss Dorothy Hartley says she was told of these by a Yorkshire woman now living in South Africa, who also gave her the above information. Miss Hartley says 'they were made at Fulford, York, by an old woman who died about 10 years ago. They were round, about 6 inches across, and tasted like a mixture of Bath Oliver and plain water biscuit, but thicker, and they were delicious. The receipt may be lost, but Terry, of York, may have bought it.'

West Riding Oatcake or 'Riddle' Bread

[N.B.—It was Miss Dorothy Hartley also who gave me the name of Mr. James Leach, oatcake baker, 24 Hardcastle Yard, High Street, Skipton, and who was thus the means of West Riding Oatcake being featured daily at Simpson's, in the Strand. When this delicious West Riding Oatcake was mentioned in a letter to *The Times* on September 10th, 1931, over three hundred people wrote and asked for the maker's name and address. Other interesting information concerning these oatcakes will be found on page 78—ED.]

Gooseberry Wine

Ann Peckham, of Leeds, 1767

INGREDIENTS: Green Gooseberries 1 gallon; cold water 2 gallons; sugar 2 lb. to every gallon of liquor, ⅛ lb. more sugar to every gallon of liquor when barrelling.

TIME: 2 or 3 days, 1 month.

METHOD

1. Take your gooseberries before they be over-ripe.
2. Bruise them in a wooden bowl, but not too small lest you bruise the seeds.
3. Then measure them – to every gallon of bruised berries put 2 gallons of cold water.
4. Stir them well together and let them stay a day and a night close covered.
5. Then draw the liquor from the berries into a tub.
6. If it comes thick, you must strain it through a bag; to every gallon of liquor put 2 gallons of loaf sugar dissolved.
7. Stir it well together.
8. Put it into a barrel and let it work 2 days.
9. Then bung it up for a week.
10. Draw it out from the barrel through a bag.
11. Put the dregs out of the barrel and wash it out with a little of the liquor.
12. Add ½ lb. more sugar.
13. Stir it well together and put it into the same barrel again.
14. Bung it up for a month, then it will be fit for bottling.

N.B.—Rhubarb wine may be made in the same manner.

Mulberry Wine

Ann Peckham, Leeds, 1767

INGREDIENTS: Mulberries 1 quart; water 1 quart; sugar 3 lb. to every gallon of liquor. A little isinglass.

TIME: About 2 or 3 days; 6 months.

METHOD

1. Gather your mulberries when they are full ripe.
2. Beat them in a marble mortar.
3. To every quart of berries, put a quart of water.
4. When you put them into the tub mix them very well.
5. Let them stand all night.
6. Then strain them through a hair sieve; and
7. To every gallon of liquor put 3 lb. of sugar.
8. When your sugar is dissolved, put it into the barrel.
9. Take a little isinglass, pulled in pieces, dissolve it in a little of the wine, put it into your barrel and stir it about. You must not let it be overfull nor bung it up at first.

Raisin Wine

INGREDIENTS: Water 1 gallon; raisins 5 lb.; brandy 1 pint to every 2 gallons.

TIME: a fortnight, and 6 months in barrel.

METHOD

1. Pick the raisins from their stalks and pull in two.
2. Let them steep in water for a fortnight stirred every day.
3. Then pour off the liquor and squeeze the juice out of the raisins.
4. Put the liquor into a barrel which will just hold it, for it must be quite full.
5. Let it stand open till the wine has done hissing or making the least noise.
6. Then add a pint of brandy to every 2 gallons; and
7. Stop it up close.
8. Let it stand 6 months before you bottle it; and
9. Do not draw it out too near the bottom of your barrel.

N.B.—January, February or March are the best times to make it.

Wilfra Tarts

For Wilfra (or Wilfred) week, the first week in August, Mr. Herbert M. Bower says: 'On the first or second Saturday of August a mounted procession perambulates the streets of Ripon, impersonating St. Wilfred re-entering the town after absence abroad.'

Wilfra tarts are small jam tarts and cheesecakes baked in patty-pans lined with pastry.

YORKSHIRE, STAFFORDSHIRE, LINCOLNSHIRE, SUFFOLK, LEICESTERSHIRE, DERBYSHIRE, WILTSHIRE, HAMPSHIRE

Frumenty

Lady Robinson, of Whitby, writes (1931): 'Frumenty is still eaten on Christmas Eve with cheese and gingerbread in this neighbourhood.' Mr. Herbert M. Bower sends a Ripon recipe and informs us that, however it may be spelt, the name of this old dish is pronounced 'frummety.'

Mr. J. Wedgewood Myatt, writing from Stoke-on-Trent, says 'I can remember frumenty being brought in cans for sale and being ladled out. . . . I fancy it was called by many different names in different counties and the wheat was got in the gleaning principally.' He sends a recipe dated 1882.

Miss Cullen sends one from Boston, Lincolnshire; Mrs. Tanser, of Bath, gives me one from her childhood's home (a dairy farm) near Chipping Sodbury, Gloucestershire. Up to 1917 when it became difficult to get the wheat, bowls of frumenty were always prepared by Miss Pavitt (who died in 1928) for sale at her dairy in New Bond Street, Bath. Mrs. Osmonde tells me it was prepared and eaten in Suffolk until just before the war, and

Mr. Joseph Strong, of 7 The Brittox, Devizes, Wiltshire, still prepares the cree'd wheat for Mothering Sunday, or at any other time it is ordered, and sends with it a recipe for making Frumenty. This cree'd wheat when cold is a firm jelly in which the burst grains of wheat are embedded. It can be sent by post, and if desired it can when heated be sieved and the inner husk thus removed leaving only a thick white jellied mass, but most people like this inner husk left in, and consider it a healthy as well as agreeable form of 'roughage,' inestimable as a breakfast food, and a fine remedy for intestinal stasis.

It is still offered as a grateful and warming cup by cottagers to weary huntsmen during the hunting-season in Leicestershire. Not so very long ago it was sold in the streets of Leicester and Derby as it was in Boston, Lincolnshire, whilst in Yorkshire the bakers had special days for 'creeing' the wheat.

The difficulty in many places of late years has been to get the husked or 'pearled' wheat ready to cree, but a supply can now always be obtained from the Army and Navy Stores, London.

To Prepare the Husked or Pearled Wheat for Frumenty

1. Wash the wheat.
2. Put it in a pan or stoneware jar with a cover, and cover the wheat with cold water three times its own measure.
3. Put it in a hot oven early in the day and let it stay as the heat cools until next morning; or put it in a pan of hot water on the hob or stove for the same period or longer, or boil it up on the stove for 10 minutes and then plunge it quickly into a hay-box, or into a fireless cooker. The aim is the same—to stew or 'cree' the wheat in water for 24 hours, at the end of that time if the grains are not burst and set in a thick jelly they will be if the contents of the pot are boiled up for five minutes or perhaps a little longer: it depends on how far they are already cooked. Wheat thus prepared is known as Frumenty wheat, and is thus designated in recipes, which vary very much, from the plain frumenty wheat eaten as a breakfast food with milk and honey or treacle to the richness of the following recipes. There is one point that may interest many: frumenty wheat contains the whole grain with the exception of the extreme outer husk, and therefore is a good source of Vitamins B and A; with milk and honey it is a perfect food, and it was probably the food of the young man of the Iron Age whose skeleton was dug up during the excavations at Woodhenge, Salisbury Plain in 1927–28. Of this Sir Arthur Keith says: 'The unworn state of

the teeth, the reduced size of the ascending ramus of the lower jaw and the slight muscular impression show that the muscles of mastication were not used, and that the food was free from grit. There is not a trace of caries; all the teeth are sound.'

And of a second skeleton, a man over 40, belonging to the Early Bronze Age, he says: 'Considering the nature of the food in the Early Bronze period, we should expect to find the teeth deeply worn. His teeth are only slightly worn, indicating a prepared soft dietary.'

And in the Bible of 1551, the following appears (Leviticus xxiii, 14): 'And ye shall eat neither bread, nor parched corn, nor frumenty of new corne, untill the selfe same daye that ye have brought an offeringe unto your God.'

It does not seem as if there is any exaggerating in claiming frumenty as our oldest national dish. It can be made of pearl barley as well as of 'pearled' wheat.

Mr. Herbert Bower's Recipe

INGREDIENTS: Cree'd wheat 1 pint; milk 2 pints; allspice and a little flour.

TIME: About 10 to 15 minutes to boil up the cree'd wheat with the milk.

METHOD

1. Put the cree'd wheat and milk on together and boil up.
2. When it begins to thicken add some allspice, or (as some call it) sweet pepper, which can be bought at either the grocer's or chemist's.
3. Finally make a little flour into a thin cream with a little cold milk and stir it into the frumenty; boil up and serve.

Mrs. Millington also refers to sweet pepper as being a necessary ingredient to frumenty in the West Riding, of Yorkshire.

Lincolnshire Frumenty

Sent by Miss E. Cullen, of Dundee

INGREDIENTS: Frumenty wheat, 1 quart; milk 1 quart; stoned raisins 2 tablespoonfuls; sugar to sweeten, a little nutmeg.

TIME and METHOD as above.

Suffolk Frumenty

Mrs. Osmonde says it was made as above but sweetened with honey and flavoured with cinnamon. 'It was eaten during the twelve days at Christmas (December 25th to January 5th); some was placed in a plate outside the door at night for the "Pharisees" (fairies). This custom' she adds 'seems to me to show that frumenty was made and eaten before England became Christian.'

Staffordshire Frumenty

Sent by Mr. J. Wedgewood Myatt, September, 1882.

1. *To prepare the unhusked wheat.*

'This is the season when new wheat can be got, therefore take good white new wheat; just wet it a little; put it into a coarse bag and beat it with a stick until the external husk is loose enough to be rubbed off; wash well, change the water 5 or 6 times till free from bran; put it into a stew-pot with plenty of water; cover, and set it in oven (on a red tile) until the wheat is quite soft; when cold it will be a jelly with the burst cooked grains of wheat in it.' This is known as 'cree'd' wheat or 'frumenty wheat.'

2. *To prepare Cree'd or Frumenty Wheat for the Table.*

'When wanted put as much as is required into a pan with sufficient milk, stirring constantly with a wooden spoon. When nearly boiling add a small quantity of flour mixed smooth with milk, adding sugar, grated nutmeg, cinnamon, lemon peel, pimento (sweet pepper) or a bay leaf for flavouring, or you can thicken the frumenty with yolks of eggs mixed with a little milk (beaten well) or the whole of the eggs — this is used instead of flour for thickening. Currants or sultanas can be added, but the fruit must first be boiled separately to the point of bursting, and then be added to the frumenty and cooked with it for a short time.

Leicestershire and Derbyshire

Both these counties prepare frumenty in much the same way, and it was husked as above by Miss Pavitt, of Bath, and finished in similar fashion. Mrs. Tanser says her mother used to prepare it as above with eggs and fruit, but added also a little cream; she then put it into Bristol china bowls, and sent it to her best customers to be served as a cold dinner sweet for mid-Lent or Mothering Sunday. The bowl was returned.

Thomas Hardy's Frumenty

The frumenty sold at Weyhill Fair as described by Thomas Hardy in *The Mayor of Casterbridge* was evidently plain 'cree'd wheat,' 'laced' with rum—a very degenerate type.

Snowdon Pudding

1845

Miss Acton says: 'This pudding is constantly served to travellers at the hotel at the foot of the mountain from which it derives its name,' and states that the following is the 'genuine receipt.'

INGREDIENTS: Some fine raisins split open, stoned but not divided; butter; beef-kidney suet ½ lb.; bread-crumbs ½ lb.; rice-flour 1½ oz.; salt a pinch; lemon marmalade 6 oz.; (or oranges if lemon cannot be obtained; pale brown sugar 6 oz.; eggs 6 thoroughly whisked; lemons grated rinds of 2.

TIME: to boil 1½ hours. This quantity will fill a mould that will hold a quart. If half the quantity be made up and put into a pint mould it will only want boiling one hour, or even a little less.

METHOD

1. Butter a mould or basin rather thickly. and ornament it with the prepared raisins, pressing the cut sides well into the butter.
2. Mix all the dry ingredients well together.
3. And blend well with the well-whisked eggs till thoroughly mixed.
4. Then pour carefully into the decorated basin and boil as directed.
5. Serve with wine sauce (*see* p. 250).

ISLE OF MAN

Old Manx Dish

A good pot of boiling milk,
with a brave shake of meal on it,
with a cake of barley bread
with the thickness of your hand's
palm of butter on it.'

Translated by Miss E. Goodman, of Peel.

Sollaghan

This dish is served at breakfast on Christmas Day in the Isle of Man. The receipt has been very kindly given by Mrs. W. Cashen, of Peel.
1. Put some oatmeal in a pan on the fire, and
2. Keep stirring till it is dry and crisp.
3. Then skim the top of the broth pot on to it and stir well.
4. Eat with pepper and salt.

Good Friday Fritters (Limpets)

Mrs. Kermode says: 'We have an old custom on Good Friday of going to collect fritters (limpets) on the rocks to fry for supper,' and Mrs. Ampercy, of the Museum, Douglas, writes:
'On Good Friday, we collected sacks of fritters on the rocks and fried them for supper.'

Dumb Cake

'This cake,' says Mrs. Cashen, of Peel Castle, 'must be made of flour and water without any leaven, and is mixed and baked in the hot turf ashes. A piece must be eaten walking backwards to bed. A number may join in the performance and they will dream of their future husbands.'

N. IRELAND

Potato and Apple Cake

(*Another North of Ireland Recipe*)

Miss C. Clarke

INGREDIENTS: Potato Pastry 1 lb. (*see* Cornish Potato Cake p. 81) apples; sugar.

TIME: 1 hour in good oven.

METHOD

1. Grease a fireproof plate.
2. Line it with potato pastry.
3. Put on it a layer of peeled chopped and cored apples and sugar.
4. Cover with a layer of pastry.
5. Then another layer of apples and sugar.
6. Finally cover with pastry. Bake in a good oven.

N.B.—Often served hot for tea.

To Make Irish Butter

From Miss Wettin's Manuscript, 18th Century

INGREDIENTS: Cream (or evaporated milk) 1 pint; eggs 3 (whites only); isinglass 1 oz.; hot water enough to steep it; saffron to colour; orange flower water 1 spoonful; sugar to taste.

TIME: about 45 minutes.

METHOD

1. Steep the isinglass in hot water for 15 minutes.
2. Then add it to the cream.
3. And boil gently until it is half dissolved.
4. Colour it with saffron.
5. Add the orange flower water.
6. Sweeten it to taste.
7. Beat in the whites of eggs.
8. And heat it up again till all the isinglass is dissolved.
9. Strain it through a sieve into a dish.
10. When it is cold cut it into thin shreds.
11. This quantity makes a dish.
12. Lay it high as light as a feather.

N.B.—It must be crinkled round and round if it is cut in long pieces.

MIDLOTHIAN

Syrup of Clove July Flowers

Miss M. E. Cullen, Dundee

This is a Midlothian recipe; clove July Flowers are the old-fashioned strong-scented carnations.

INGREDIENTS: Flower petals 1 lb.; water 1 quart; cloves 1 dozen; loaf sugar 1 lb. to every pint of juice.

TIME: to boil 5 or 6 hours.

METHOD

1. Cut off the white ends of the petals.
2. Put them with the water and cloves into a stone jar.
3. Tie it up close with paper and place it in a pot of cold water.
4. Boil it up and let it boil 5 or 6 hours, taking care to add some more hot water from time to time, nor let the water boil into the jar.
5. Then drain through a sieve over a basin.
6. Take out the flowers, squeeze them in a clean cloth and to every pint of juice put in 1 lb. of loaf sugar.
7. When dissolved give it a boil.
8. When cold, bottle it and cork tightly.

A Basin of Buttermilk Curds

Miss James, J.P., London, another B.B.C. friend, writes:
'Do you know of a most delicious dish I had in Wales made of whey and buttermilk? It makes a most lovely curd like clotted cream; but as it only tastes like cream, and is not at all rich, you can eat a fair-sized basinful.'

Christmas Apple Pie

1770

At Potton, Bedfordshire, and the places adjacent, it was the custom at Christmas festivities to place on the table a large apple pie called an 'Apple Florentine.' This was made in a huge dish of pewter or Sheffield plate, or silver (or perhaps gold?) filled with 'good baking apples,' sugar and lemon, to the very brim; with a covering of rich pastry. When baked and before serving up, the crust was taken off, cut into triangular portions ready to be replaced on the apples, but before this was done a full quart of well-spiced ale was poured in quite hissing hot.

[I have seen, in 1928, at the King's Head, Aylesbury, Buckinghamshire, a huge dish that answers this description and was probably used for baking 'Florentines.' These were pies made in dishes without any undercrust and they were sometimes filled with veal and other meat. A new departure from the older English saucer pies made with a crust under and over and the old pudding-pies made in cup moulds, and left uncovered. I do not know whether apple pies are still called 'Florentines' in Bedfordshire, but I do know that an apple pie is considered as much an indispensable part of the Christmas feast in some places as orange jelly is in others.—Ed.]

VI

SOME SIMPLE ENGLISH DINNERS FOR EVERY MONTH IN THE YEAR

It is important to remember that the portions served should be small; it is much more attractive to offer a second helping than a single one that is too large.

JANUARY

POTTED LAMPERNS, WHOLEMEAL BREAD AND BUTTER
THE JUDGE'S CIRCUIT SOUP
SMALL MUTTON PIES
BOILED TURKEY AND CELERY HOT-POT
SALAD
BAKED APPLE PUDDING
ANCHOVY TOAST

FEBRUARY

CREAMED POTATO SOUP
BAKED PIKE
BOILED CALF'S HEAD AND GAMMON OF BACON
SERVED WITH MICHAEL KELLY'S SAUCE
ROAST TEAL
SERVED WITH ORANGE AND WATERCRESS SALAD
PANCAKES
DEVILLED BISCUITS

MARCH

SPRING SOUP
SALMON PIE
VEAL CUTLETS AND SEAKALE
SADDLE OF MUTTON
SALMAGUNDY
RICE FLUMMERY AND
STEWED PEACHES
TOASTED CHEESE

APRIL

HOP-TOP SOUP
GRILLED TROUT
ROAST LAMB, MINT SAUCE, MASHED POTATOES
HERB PUDDING
SWEDE TURNIP-TOPS
CREAMED FRUMENTY
CARLISLE GAOL TART. CURD CHEESECAKES
MARROW TOAST

MAY

DRESSED CRAB
POACHED EGGS ON STEWED CUCUMBER
SPITCHCOCKED SPRING CHICKEN AND CREAMED NETTLES
COWSLIP PUDDING-PIE
GOOSEBERRY FOOL
MRS. RAFFALD'S NICE WHET
18TH CENTURY

JUNE

CREAM CHEESE, RADISHES, SALAD AND TUNBRIDGE WAFERS
SHRIMP PIE
STEWED PIGEONS AND GREEN PEAS
ASPARAGUS
CAMBRIDGE CARAMEL CREAM PUDDING
STRAWBERRIES IN WINE
AND SOLID SILLABUB

JULY

CLEAR CARROT SOUP
LOBSTER SALAD
ROAST DUCK, MASHED TURNIPS AND NEW POTATOES
STEWED GREEN PEAS
STRAWBERRY AND RASPBERRY CREAM
GOOSEBERRY SAUCER PIE, CHERRY PIE
CORNISH CREAM
SCOTCH WOODCOCK

AUGUST

GREEN PEA SOUP
RED MULLET
ROAST GROUSE STUFFED WITH BANANAS
SWEET-CURED SUFFOLK HAM WITH LETTUCE AND PICKLED PEACHES
BILBERRY PIE
GRASSY CORNER PUDDING
POTTED CHEESE AND WEST RIDING OATCAKE

SEPTEMBER

VEGETABLE MARROW SOUP
GRILLED FRESH HERRING AND MUSTARD SAUCE
MUSHROOM LOAVES
ROAST RIBS BEEF
PARTRIDGE PUDDING
GREEN ARTICHOKES
MULBERRY TARTS
BLACKBERRY AND APPLE FOOL
HAM TOAST

OCTOBER

OYSTERS, HOME-MADE WHOLEMEAL BREAD AND BUTTER
ROAST HARE
RUNNER BEANS
BOILED FOWL, PARSLEY SAUCE, BACON AND CAULIFLOWER
SPEECH HOUSE PUDDING
STEWED PEARS
MUSHROOMS WITH ANCHOVY CREAM

ENGLISH DINNERS

NOVEMBER

CHESTERFIELD SOUP
SCOTTISH FISH CUSTARD
OXFORD SAUSAGES AND MASHED POTATOES
HINDLE WAKES
PUMPKIN PIE
PORT WINE JELLY
DEVILLED SARDINES

DECEMBER

GLOUCESTER CLEAR PHEASANT SOUP
BOILED COD AND OYSTER SAUCE
MOCK GOOSE
ROAST CYGNET
LORD JOHN RUSSELL'S PUDDING
APPLE FLORENTINE
ORANGE JELLY
CHEESE TOAST

VII

AUTHORITIES ON ENGLISH FOOD AND COOKERY

1. Manuscript and Printed Authorities

A.D. 1345 TO A.D. 1689. A collection of Ordinances and Regulations for the Government of the Royal Household, made in Divers Reigns from King Edward III to King William and Queen Mary. Also receipts in Ancient Cookery. Printed for the Society of Antiquaries and published in 1790.

ABOUT 1430 AND 1450. Two Fifteenth Century Cookery Books, from Harleian MSS. 279 and 4016, with extracts from Ashmole MS. 1429, Laud MS. 553, and Douce MS. 55. Edited by Thomas Austin (Early English Text Society).

1545. *A Proper Newe Booke of Cokerye*, in the Library of Corpus Christi College, Cambridge. Edited with valuable notes by Miss C. F. Frere, and published in 1913.

1615. *The English Hus-Wife*, by Gervase Markham, who was born in 1568. It contains a number of Elizabethan and earlier recipes, and was probably taken over to America in the *Mayflower*, September 6th, 1620.

1660. *The Accomplisht Cook*, by Robert May, born 1588.

1669 CHARLES II. *The Closet of Sir Kenelme Digby, Kt. Opened*. This book also has been well edited (by Anne Macdonell) and republished in 1910.

A.D. 1699. WILLIAM III. *Acetoria*, a discourse on Sallets, by John Evelyn. There is a modern reprint.

FIRST HALF OF 18TH CENTURY
The British Housewife, Mrs. Martha Bradley, of Bath.

MIDDLE OF 18TH CENTURY
The Experienced English Housekeeper, by Mrs. Raffald, of Doncaster, Cheshire, and Manchester.

LAST PERIOD OF 18TH CENTURY
A New System of Domestic Cookery, by Mrs. Rundell, born at Ludlow, Shropshire, 1745.

AUTHORITIES

FIRST PERIOD OF 19TH CENTURY

The Cook's Oracle, by Dr. William Kitchiner of The Strand, London. *See* article in *The Times*, Feb. 27th, 1927, and notes in this book.

SECOND PERIOD OF 19TH CENTURY

Modern Cookery, by Eliza Acton, born at Ipswich, 1799. Miss Acton's book is extremely good even after all these years. It was first published in 1845.

1846 *The Modern Cook.*
1861 *The Cook's Guide.*
1862 *The Royal English and French Confectioner.*
These three books are by Charles Elmé Francatelli, who was a pupil of the great French chef Carême, but prided himself on being born an Englishman. He was for a time head of the kitchen and Chief Cook to Her Majesty Queen Victoria, to the Earl of Chesterfield, to Lord Kinnaird, to Sir W. Massey Stanley, Bart., and to Rowland Errington, Esq., at Melton Mowbray.

1859–1861. *The Book of Household Management.* Edited by Mrs. Beeton.

Her husband, Mr. S. O. Beeton, was a publisher, and lived at 248 Strand, London, where the New Law Courts now stand, and this book was issued first in fortnightly parts as were most of his books. Its price was 3d., and it was the work of a young woman; a very talented young woman too, she must have been, because she was only twenty-nine years of age when she died in 1865. Therefore, when she began to edit this book she was not more than twenty-two or twenty-three. Her maiden name was Isabella Mary Mayson. In the edition of 1869, Mr. Beeton pays tribute to his late wife's clear writing, and practical directions. 'The arrangement of the first edition', he says, 'was so well conceived that it admitted of scarcely any reform.' Up to the new edition of 1880 only the slightest alterations and corrections were needed except such as time rendered necessary. Then Mr. Beeton died and the work was sold. In 1906 it was revised, and ceased to be representative of Mrs. Beeton's period.

[N.B.—I am particularly glad to be able to put on record the above facts (gathered in 1923 from a study of the earlier editions of Mrs. Beeton's work and in 1932, from documents in possession of her youngest son, Sir Mayson Beeton) because various articles and references have appeared in the Press during the last three years confusing Mrs. Beeton with Miss Acton. I may add these facts are printed with the approval of Sir Mayson Beeton. It was partly because of the way in which facts connected with

English food and cookery, and its literature, were distorted and falsified that the English Folk Cookery Association was founded for purposes of research. Obviously before we can claim a complete system of English Cookery, we must be able to show authentic records and have a central clearing house for them.

FLORENCE WHITE, Founder E.F.C.A.]

LAST PERIOD OF THE 19TH CENTURY

1894. In the January number of the *Quarterly Review* an article appeared on 'Old English Cookery'. It was by Miss M. M. Mallock, sister of W. H. Mallock, author of *The New Republic*, and niece of Anthony Froude, the historian. Miss Mallock was one of the first women to train in Domestic Economy and Cookery as preparation for social service. She trained at the Birmingham School, now closed. She wrote, and Macmillan's published in 1896 —

The Younger Son's Cookery Book. This is not a mere collection of recipes; it contains comparatively few. It is a book of instruction in the various processes of cookery, each illustrated by one recipe which is worked out only as an example of the directions given. As Miss Mallock's literary style is charming it is a delightful book, and I strongly recommend my readers to buy it and use it with this volume of *Good Things in England*, as it will teach many things for which space is lacking in the present volume. On the other hand *Good Things* contains much that Miss Mallock's book lacks. They should be used together. The name of the second and subsequent editions of *A Younger Son's Cookery Book* was altered to —

Economics of Modern Cookery, and it is still in request: new editions are frequently appearing. It is small and handy to use. As a woman remarked: 'I learnt to cook with Miss Mallock in one hand and a spoon in the other.'

1898. *Mrs. Roundell's Practical Cookery Book*.

Belonging to an old Yorkshire family, Mrs. Roundell gives us in this volume many family recipes hitherto unpublished. As mistress of Dorfold Hall, Nantwich, Cheshire, her book (which is now out of print) gives an extremely good idea of the catering required and the food enjoyed during the last half of the 19th century in an English country house. She knows her job from A to Z, and her advice is most valuable.

THE TWENTIETH CENTURY

1914. *Cookery for Every Household*, by Florence B. Jack.

This is an excellent book of instructions and recipes which can be thoroughly recommended as a reference book, but it is rather large and strictly practical; no attempt is made to deal with the origin or history of foods or with their food value, and it makes no pretence of being literary. The overbearing influence at this period of what has been amusingly called the *à la* school is, however, indicated by a number of the names of recipes being given in French as well as English, and this has some historical value as an indication of a predominant fashion lasting over a long period from which we are only just disengaging ourselves.

2. HERBS AND HERBALS

One of the chief characteristics of the twentieth century up to now (1932) has, however, been the revival of interest in the cultivation and use of herbs which culminated in the publication of:

A Modern Herbal, by Mrs. Grieve and Mrs. Leyel, an excellent, readable, and reliable work. (Jonathan Cape, 2 vols., 42s.)

3. DOMESTIC PRESERVATION OF FRUIT AND VEGETABLES

This is another indication of the times. The Royal Horticultural Society has done good national service by publishing Mr. and Mrs. Vincent Banks' well-tested instructions and recipes for *Fruit and Vegetables Bottling, Pulping, Drying and Canning (with and without sugar), Jams, Jellies, Pickles, Salad Vinegar and Bottled Foodstuffs*. It was edited by Mr. Wilks, Secretary to the R.H.S., who for many years (before the war of 1914–18) had been doing his best to revive in England popular interest in Fruit and Vegetable Preservation, and had received great encouragement from Mr. and Mrs. Banks. Excellent recipes are given, and the use of the bottling thermometer is explained.

1929. *Domestic Preservation of Fruit and Vegetables*. Ministry of Agriculture and Fisheries. Miscellaneous Publications No. 69.

This useful little publication takes the guesswork out of fruit and vegetable bottling as far as it goes, but it is not quite so comprehensive as Mr. and Mrs. Banks' pamphlet; the two should be used together.

Fruit-bottling, Jam-making, the Preparation of Jellies, Fruit syrups, Candied fruits, Chutneys, and Pickles, have been practised by housewives from earliest times. It is based on the work done at the Chipping Campden Research Station — under the auspices of Bristol University — by Mr. F. Hirst, Mr. W. B. Adam and Miss M. L. Adams. It gives scientific but simple instructions and recipes for the processes mentioned.

N.B.—These two pamphlets should be used together with *Good Things*, which contains recipes not included in either.

4. FOOD VALUES

Another striking feature of the first thirty years of the twentieth century has been the attention paid to food values. In —

1900 Edward Arnold published *Food and the Principles of Dietetics*, by Dr. Robert Hutchison, M.D. Edin., F.R.C.P., Physician to the London Hospital, and to the Hospital for Sick Children, Great Ormond Street. And this is still, in 1932, the standard work. It is based on the lectures he gave his students at the London Hospital, and is continually revised and brought up to date as each new edition is issued.

Food and Feeding (undated) by Sir Henry Thompson (1820–1904) treats of diet from the social standpoint, but of all sections of society. The dinners he gave in his own house at 35 Wimpole Street were served at eight o'clock, to eight persons, and consisted of eight courses. They were famous social functions, and were known as Octaves. King George V (then Prince of Wales) attended the 300th 'Octave' dinner.

5. VITAMINS

The discovery of vitamins called for a mass of scientific literature which was gradually conveyed to the public in scrappy forms by the popular Press, resulting frequently in a distortion of facts — sometimes in complete falsification of them. Correct information can be obtained at the Patent Office Library which has the finest collection of scientific books, papers, reports, etc., in the world.

In 1924 a *Report on the Present State of Knowledge of Accessory Food Factors*, compiled by a committee appointed jointly by the Lister Institute and Medical Research Council, was published by His Majesty's Stationery Office. It was reprinted in 1927 and additional knowledge is published as recorded and accepted. Anyone who wants information on food values cannot do better than write to H.M. Stationery Office for a list of its publications on Nutrition.

6. WOMEN'S PLACE IN ECONOMIC HISTORY

One of the most interesting results of research into English Folk Cookery is the revelation of the number of great commercial enterprises that have originated in the good cooking in the kitchen, still-room or dairy of some one woman.

The following are a few examples:

1. *Stilton Cheese*. Lady Beaumont's cheese, the receipt for which was taken by Elizabeth Scarbrow, the housekeeper, when she married from Quenby Hall, seven miles from Leicester, to Little Dalby. Quenby Hall, a fine Elizabethan mansion, is still in a good state of preservation.

AUTHORITIES

2. *Huntley and Palmer's Biscuits.* Mrs. Huntley was the wife of a Quaker schoolmaster, who had a boys' school at Burford, early in the nineteenth century. This house also is still standing.

3. *Everton Toffee.* This was made by Molly Bush, at Everton, a suburb of Liverpool. Molly's shop also is still standing.

4. *Romary's Wafer Biscuits.* Tunbridge Wells (*see* p. 330).

5. *Harvey's Sauce* (*see* Mrs. Combers' Sauce, p. 99).

October 14th, 1931 — January 15th, 1932.

> 1a Nevern Road,
>   Earl's Court,
>   London, S.W.5.

INDEX

INDEX

INDEX